Isaiah

THE CROSSWAY CLASSIC COMMENTARIES

Isaiah

by
John Calvin

Series Editors
Alister McGrath and J. I. Packer

CROSSWAY BOOKS
A DIVISION OF GOOD NEWS PUBLISHERS
WHEATON, ILLINOIS • NOTTINGHAM, ENGLAND

Isaiah

Copyright © 2000 by Watermark

Published by Crossway Books
 A division of Good News Publishers
 1300 Crescent Street
 Wheaton, Illinois 60187

First printing, 2000

Printed in the United States of America

ISBN 1-58134-156-3

Library of Congress Cataloging-in-Publication Data
Calvin, Jean, 1509-1564.
  Isaiah / John Calvin.
    p.   cm. — (The Crossway classic commentaries)
  ISBN 1-58134-156-3 (alk. paper)
    1. Bible. N.T. Isaiah—Commentaries.   I. Title.   II. Series.
BS1515.3.C35 2000
224'.1077—dc21   99-053547
                                                                         CIP

15	14	13	12	11	10	09	08	07	06	05	04	03	02	01	00
15	14	13	12	11	10	9	8	7	6	5	4	3	2	1	

First British edition 2000

Production and Printing in the United States of America for
CROSSWAY BOOKS
Norton Street, Nottingham, England NG7 3HR

ISBN 1-85684-195-2

Contents

Series Preface

The purpose of the Crossway Classic Commentaries is to make some of the most valuable commentaries on the books of the Bible, by some of the greatest Bible teachers and theologians in the last 500 years, available to a new generation. These books will help today's readers learn truth, wisdom, and devotion from such authors as J. C. Ryle, Martin Luther, John Calvin, J. B. Lightfoot, John Owen, Charles Spurgeon, Charles Hodge, and Matthew Henry.

We do not apologize for the age of some of the items chosen. In the realm of practical exposition promoting godliness, the old is often better than the new. Spiritual vision and authority, based on an accurate handling of the biblical text, are the qualities that have been primarily sought in deciding what to include.

So far as is possible, everything is tailored to the needs and enrichment of thoughtful readers—lay Christians, students, and those in the ministry. The originals, some of which were written at a high technical level, have been abridged as needed, simplified stylistically, and unburdened of foreign words. However, the intention of this series is never to change any thoughts of the original authors, but to faithfully convey them in an understandable fashion.

The publishers are grateful to Dr. Alister McGrath of Wycliffe Hall, Oxford, Dr. J. I. Packer of Regent College, Vancouver, and Watermark of Norfolk, England, for the work of selecting and editing that now brings this project to fruition.

THE PUBLISHERS
Crossway Books
Wheaton, Illinois

Introduction

Theologian, churchman, preacher, teacher, and educator extraordinaire, John Calvin was able to dictate his own terms when the Geneva authorities, who got rid of him in 1538, came cap in hand three years later begging him to return to the city because they could not get on without him. Among his conditions was that the Bible be lectured on and biblical languages be taught in the boys' school; and it was not long before he was giving regular Bible lectures there himself, in Latin, three times a week, with clergy and others in attendance alongside the budding teens. Out of these lectures, taken down and corrected for the press, came Calvin's commentaries on two prophets, of which this one on Isaiah was the first. It was printed in 1551, with a dedication to King Edward VI urging him to get on with the English Reformation, and again in 1559, carefully revised, dedicated this time to Queen Elizabeth, with however a similar message.

This is a great commentary on a great book. By common consent Isaiah, "the evangelical prophet," is foremost among prophetic writers for his range, grandeur, vividness, variety, and theological vitamin content. More weightily than any other, he fulfills the role distinctive to the prophetic ministry of the Old Testament as Calvin defines it. Prophets, said Calvin, were sent by God to reinforce the Mosaic law in people's minds and to amplify it as history wore on. They did this in three ways. First, they taught and underlined the "doctrine" of the law (*doctrina*, Latin for "teaching"; *religion* and *godliness* are English words that best catch the overtones of Calvin's usage). Second, the prophets reinforced the law's specific commands and threats, with applications to the present and visions of future judgment on sin and future mercy for saints. Third, they dwelt on the reality of the covenant of grace made known at Sinai and delineated Christ, who in due course would be manifested as the foundation, mediator, and guarantor of the covenant forever. "Whoever understands this will easily learn what we ought to seek in the prophets, and what is the purpose of their writings." Assuming that a single author is responsible for this long and complex book, and that the prophet's message was consistent and unified across the sixty-odd years of his public ministry, Calvin elucidates all these themes in Isaiah with elegance and skill.

Latter-day preachers, Calvin affirms, should take the prophets as models for much of their ministry. "Although we do not receive day by day a revelation of what we are to utter as a prediction, yet it is of high importance to us to compare the behavior of men of our own age with the behavior of that ancient people; and from their histories and examples we ought to make known the judgments of God; such as, what he formerly punished he will also punish with equal severity in our own day, for he is always like himself. Such wisdom let godly preachers acquire, should they wish to handle the doctrine of the prophets with a good result." To help preachers discern the unchanging truths about God and man that they are to teach and apply is one of Calvin's constant purposes as a commentator, and one that is very evident here.

"Calvin still towers above all interpreters, in large commending views of revelation in its whole connection, with extraordinary insight into the logical relations of a passage. . . . These qualities, together with his fixed belief of fundamental doctrines, his eminent soundness of judgment, and his freedom from all tendency to paradox, pedantic affectation, or fanciful conceit, place him . . . on a level with the very best interpreters of our day." So wrote Joseph Addison Alexander in 1846, and his words remain true in 2000. So enjoy!

J. I. PACKER

Preface
By John Calvin

A great number of statements are often made about the office of the prophets, but I think the shortest way of treating this subject is to trace the prophets back to the law, from which they derived their teaching, like rivers from their source. They took it as their rule, and those who speak only about the law may rightly be acknowledged as its interpreters.

The law is made up of three parts: first, the teaching about life; second, warnings and promises; third, the covenant of grace, which, being founded on Christ, contains within itself all the special promises.

As for the ceremonies, they were religious exercises that strengthened the attachment of the people to the worship of God and to godliness and consequently were added to the first tablet of the Ten Commandments. The prophets, therefore, explain more fully what is briefly stated in the Ten Commandments and lay down what the Lord most requires of us. Next, the warnings and promises, which Moses had proclaimed in general terms, are applied by them to their own time and are minutely described. Lastly, they express more clearly what Moses says more obscurely about Christ and his grace; they bring forward more abundant evidences of the free covenant.

To make this matter still clearer, we must go a little further back, to the law itself, which the Lord prescribed as a perpetual rule for the church, to be always in people's hands and to be observed by each succeeding generation. God forbids his people to consult magicians or soothsayers in case they are tempted to wander away from the teaching given by Moses. The Lord tells them to be satisfied with Moses' teaching alone. But at the same time he adds that he will ensure that Israel will never lack a prophet. He does this to meet any objection the people might raise, saying that their condition was worse than that of the pagans. To keep them from polluting themselves with the abominable practices of the Gentiles, God promises that he will raise up prophets through whom he will make his will known (see Deuteronomy 18:15). These prophets will faithfully convey the message that he has entrusted to them; so they will have no reason to complain in the future that they lack anything.

When the Lord promised to give them prophets, he commanded the people to rely on their interpretations and their teaching. He did not mean for them to add anything to the law, but to interpret it faithfully and to sanction its authority. So when Malachi exhorts the people to adhere to the purity of faith and to be steadfast in God's teaching, he says, "Remember the law of my servant Moses, the decrees and laws I gave him at Horeb for all Israel" (Malachi 4:4). He simply reminds them of God's law and orders them to be content with it. Does Malachi therefore mean that prophecies should be despised? Not at all. The prophecies were appendages of the law and are all summed up in the law; so that exhortation was sufficient. Those who understand the summary of the teaching and its main points and carefully observe them will certainly not neglect the prophecies. It would be absurd to boast of attending to the Word if we ignored its divine interpretations.

So when the prophets inculcate moral duties, they are not saying anything new but are only explaining those parts of the law that had been misunderstood. For example, the people thought they had carried out their duty when they had offered sacrifices and performed the outward services of religion, for the world measures God by its own standard and gives him worldly and false worship. The prophets strongly criticize this and show that ceremonies are of no avail when the heart is not sincere; God is worshiped by believing in him and by actually calling on his name. This had been clearly stated in the law, but it was necessary to remind the people of it frequently and to expose the hypocrisy of their ceremonies. As for the second tablet of the Ten Commandments, the prophets drew on it for their exhortations in order to show people that they should refrain from all injustice, violence, and deceit. Therefore, they do nothing but keep the people obeying the law.

The prophets gave distinctive warnings and promises; what Moses had stated in general terms, they described in great detail. They also had their own special visions, through which the Lord revealed future events in order to apply the promises and warnings for the benefit of the people.

As for the free covenant that God established with the patriarchs in ancient times, the prophets always reminded the people of it and told them about the coming of Christ, who was both the foundation of the covenant and the bond between God and the people. Whoever understands this will easily learn what we ought to seek in the prophets and what is the purpose of their writings. This is all that seems necessary to say on that subject.

So we may learn that we should imitate the prophets, who taught the doctrine of the law. Although we do not receive a daily revelation of what we are to predict, it is nevertheless most important that we should compare the behavior of people in our own age with the behavior of that ancient people. From their stories and examples we should make God's judgments known.

So much for the prophets in general. As far as the prophet Isaiah is concerned, the inscription clearly shows who he was and when he proclaimed his prophecies. It mentions the name of his father, **Amoz,** who is believed to have been the brother of Azariah, king of Judah. This shows that Isaiah came from a royal family, and on this point all the ancients are agreed. But neither his birth nor his close relationship to the king (the Jews assert that he was the father-in-law of Manasseh) could prevent him from being killed. He was treated no better than the lowest person in society.

The time when he prophesied is pointed out by means of the names of the kings who lived during his prophecies. It is clear that he prophesied for more than sixty-four years, for Jotham reigned for sixteen years (see 2 Kings 15:33), Ahaz as many (see 2 Kings 16:2), and Hezekiah for twenty-nine years (see 2 Kings 18:2). This adds up to sixty-one years. Add to this the number of years that he prophesied during Uzziah's reign and later during Manasseh's reign, through whom he was put to death, and there are at least sixty-four years of uninterrupted prophecies from Isaiah.

All God's servants should note this carefully, so they can see how patient they should be in their own situation, no matter how hard and difficult it may be. They should not think it is any disgrace to endure severe trials. They ought often to remember that Isaiah saw few successes despite his numerous labors. They should also remember that Jeremiah prophesied to the people for fifty years, which only resulted in their becoming more and more rebellious. However, no difficulties could turn Isaiah and Jeremiah away from their course. We, too, should carry out our duties and patiently endure every kind of persecution.

The following question may be in your mind: Did Isaiah himself or some other person write the inscription to his prophecy? None of the commentators I have read answers this question. I will tell you what I think, although I have not completely made up my mind on this matter. The prophets, after they had addressed the people in public, drew up a brief summary of their prophecy and put it on the gates of the temple so everyone could see it and become fully conversant with it. After a few days it was taken down by the ministers of the temple and placed in the Treasury, so that it might stand as a permanent record. The books of the prophets were probably compiled in this way. This may be inferred from Habakkuk 2:2 and Isaiah 8:1. People who have studied the prophets carefully and judiciously will agree with me that they are not always arranged in chronological order. It is a remarkable instance of God's providence that these prophecies have come down to us through the agency of the priests, whose duty it was to transmit the prophecies to posterity, even though they were often the bitterest enemies of the prophets.

Isaiah
Chapter 1

1. The vision concerning Judah and Jerusalem that Isaiah son of Amoz saw during the reigns of Uzziah, Jotham, Ahaz and Hezekiah, kings of Judah. The Hebrew word translated **vision** often signifies a prophecy. This word, as it stands in this verse, unquestionably means there is nothing in this book that was not made known to Isaiah himself. From this word we learn that the prophets did not speak of their own accord or draw on their own imaginations but were enlightened by God, who opened their eyes to see what they themselves would not have otherwise been able to understand. So the opening of Isaiah points to the teaching of the book, which does not contain human thoughts but rather the oracles of God; it convinces us that the book contains nothing but what was revealed by God's Spirit.

Concerning Judah. This tells us that the principal subject of the prophecy was **Judah.** Isaiah was sent to the Jews and to **Jerusalem.** Everything else in his prophecy may be said to be incidental to his main subject. However, it was not inconsistent with Isaiah's office to make known to other nations the calamities that would overtake them. In the same way Amos did not exceed the boundaries of his calling when he did not spare the Jews, although he had not been sent to them (Amos 2:4-5). See also the examples of this in the lives of Peter and Paul (Acts 10:17; 13:5; 14:1; 17:2, 10; 18:4, 19). We should view Isaiah in the same way. While he takes pains to instruct the Jews and directs his efforts particularly to them, he does not go beyond his set limits when he also takes a passing interest in other nations.

Judah and Jerusalem. Here **Judah** stands for the whole nation, and **Jerusalem** for the chief city in the kingdom.

2. Hear, O heavens! Listen, O earth! Here Isaiah is alluding to Moses and his famous song (Deuteronomy 32:1). This is unquestionably a very severe protestation. Both Moses and Isaiah turn to the elements, which are dumb and have no feeling, because people have no ears or are bereft of their senses. What could be more shocking than that the Israelites should revolt against God who had bestowed so many benefits on them?

For the LORD has spoken. This means: Listen to the charge that the Lord is about to level against the Israelites. The Lord is compelled to summon dead creatures as witnesses. At his bidding the elements observe the law they have been given, and heaven and earth perform their duty. The **earth** yields her fruits, and the **heavens** revolve at set periods. They do this with great accuracy even though they have no reason or understanding. But men and women, endued with reason and understanding and having God's voice frequently sounding in their ears and hearts, remain unmoved, as though they are bereft of their senses. They will not bend their necks and submit to God. Dumb and lifeless creatures witness against obstinate and rebellious people.

"I reared children and brought them up." Literally, this means: "I have made them great." But since Isaiah is speaking about children, the best translation is "I have nourished them" or "I have brought them up." The Lord had given the Israelites every sort of kindness. He had, as it were, exhausted himself. He elsewhere reproaches them, saying, **"What more could have been done for my vineyard than I have done for it?"** (5:4).

To apply this to our own times, we should realize that our condition is equal, or even superior, to the position the Jews had previously enjoyed. Their adoption into God's family bound them to keep the purity of his worship. We have a double obligation: Not only have we been redeemed by the blood of Christ, but he who once redeemed us is pleased to favor us with his Gospel, and in this way prefers us to all those whom he still allows to remain blinded by ignorance. If we do not acknowledge these things, we will deserve a more severe punishment than they do.

"But they have rebelled against me." God declares that the Israelites have turned their backs on him, like a son who leaves his father's house and shows there is no possibility of his return. It is indeed a terrible thing for a child to disobey his father, but even worse for the Israelites to reject such a kind Father. Isaiah uses the word **children** not in order to show them respect, but to highlight the dreadful nature of their rebellion.

3. "The ox knows his master, the donkey his owner's manger." This comparison emphasizes more strongly the nature of their rebellion. Isaiah now pronounces that the Israelites are worse than dumb animals that have no reason or understanding but who are at least capable of being taught. Isaiah sends them to the **ox** and to the **donkey,** so they can learn from them what their duty is. We should not be surprised at this, for animals often observe the order of nature better and show greater kindness than men themselves.

"But Israel does not know, my people do not understand." The name

Israel, which Isaiah contrasts with those animals, is emphatic. We know how much the descendants appreciated being known by this name, which God had bestowed on the holy patriarch because he had defeated the angel when he wrestled with him (see Genesis 32:28). So it was all the more dishonorable for the rebellious children to make a false boast about this honor now.

4. Ah, sinful nation. Isaiah had already rebuked Israel severely, but in order to expose their crime even more, he adds an exclamation, expressing even more strongly his abhorrence of such base ingratitude and wickedness.

A people loaded with guilt. The force of this metaphor should be noted. Not only does he mean that they had sunk into their iniquity as into a deep mire, but he also accuses them of being deliberately rebellious. It is like saying they were the slaves of sin or sold themselves to act wickedly.

When Isaiah adds, **a brood of evildoers,** he means that the Israelites are a wicked seed.

Children given to corruption! I think that the word translated **corruption** would be better translated "degeneracy." The prophet means they are so depraved that they are totally unlike their parents. The epithets which are now bestowed by Isaiah on his nation are dishonorable and are very different from the opinion that the Israelites held about themselves. This is the way in which we should wake up hypocrites. The more they flatter themselves and the further they are from being ruled by the fear of God, so much the more should we wield against them thunderbolts from our mouths. It is necessary to remove the false conviction of their holiness, righteousness, and wisdom that they often use as a disguise and as a basis for idle boasting.

They have forsaken the LORD. Isaiah states his reason for reproving the Israelites so sharply and severely. They had no reason to complain, as they often did, of being treated with excessive harshness and rigor. First he rebukes them for the source of all evils, their rebellion against God. Isaiah's purpose is not to convince the Jews that they are guilty of a single crime but to show that they are complete apostates.

The following words, **they have spurned the Holy One of Israel,** are added to highlight the enormity of their sin. They were showing contempt for the One who had chosen them alone from all the nations to be adopted into his family. God calls himself **the Holy One of Israel.** In admitting them into an alliance with him he had at the same time bestowed his holiness upon them. Wherever this name appears, it is ascribed to God on account of the effect it produces.

And turned their backs on him. This means that when the Lord gave them a way of living, they merely indulged their sinful passions. Their licentiousness was so unbridled that they completely rebelled against God.

5. Why should you be beaten anymore? The **why** here means "to what purpose?" or "For what end?" Isaiah is saying that the Jews have reached such a pitch of wickedness, it is not possible to believe that any punishments will do them any good. When desperate people become hardened, they prefer to be torn to shreds rather than submit to correction.

Why do you persist in rebellion? This confirms the previous statement. It is like saying, "You will still not stop your treachery. You even continue to add to your crimes. I see that you rush to commit more sins as if you had committed yourself to that purpose." God's aim here is to expose their incorrigible disposition, so that they are left without any excuse.

Your whole head is injured, your whole heart afflicted. Isaiah is making a comparison with the human body. If the body is too severely injured, there is no hope of recovery. He points to the two principal parts of the body on which it depends for its health—the **head** and the **heart.** The vital organs are so injured and corrupted that it is impossible to heal them.

6. From the sole of your foot to the top of your head there is no soundness. Isaiah continues the same comparison. The prophet is talking about the afflictions through which the nation has almost wasted away. He says that this constant weakness is evidence of their stubborn impenitence. They have **only wounds and welts and open sores,** from which diseased matter continually flows, as if some concealed fountain were supplying endless venom. By this metaphor he shows that their wound is incurable, since the supply of venom cannot be stopped. All this is greatly heightened by saying that no remedies have been applied. He uses three metaphors that he links together: They have **only wounds and welts . . . not cleansed or bandaged or soothed with oil.** Each metaphor has the same meaning: The nation, without any hope of relief, without comfort, without remedy, is reduced to a state of distress, in which the utmost severity of God is openly displayed.

7. Your country is desolate, your cities burned with fire. Literally, their country is "a desolation." Isaiah goes on to speak in more detail and more clearly about what he had already said in illustrations about their punishments. Their country has been reduced to a frightful state of devastation. I interpret all those statements to relate to past events. The prophet is not threatening God's vengeance but is describing dreadful calamities that have already taken place. He rebukes them for their indolence and stupidity in remaining unmoved by their afflictions.

Your fields are being stripped by foreigners right before you, laid waste as when overthrown by strangers. This is added to make the picture even more graphic. The calamity is made worse when it is brought about by men who are unknown—men who, coming from a distant country, are more cruel than the neighboring tribes. Such men destroy cities, burn houses and buildings, and spread destruction wherever they go.

From this we learn that when God starts to punish us, if we do not repent, he does not immediately desist but increases the punishments and constantly follows them up with more afflictions. So we should abstain from such obstinacy if we do not want to call down on our heads such destruction.

8. The Daughter of Zion is left like a shelter in a vineyard. He alludes to a custom that still exists in France, where the vine-keepers have a **shelter** for themselves when the grapes begin to ripen.

Like a hut in a field of melons. This next comparison, closely linked to the previous one, is taken from the custom of protecting **a field of melons** with men who keep watch during the night in **a hut.** Isaiah goes on to explain what he means by these two comparisons.

Like a city under siege. The prophet means that the evils he is speaking about will reach right to the very **city,** until it is broken and ruined and resembles a **shelter.**

9. Unless the LORD Almighty had left us some survivors, we would have become like Sodom, we would have been like Gomorrah. Here Isaiah concludes what he said before about God's punishments. The desolation that will take place, or rather that is present and that they now see, may be compared with the destruction of **Sodom,** were it not that the Lord snatched **some survivors,** a very small remnant, from the fire. The prophet is telling them that they should not be deceived by flattery. They would be in the same condition as **Sodom** and **Gomorrah** if God had not had compassion on them and preserved **some survivors.** This is in line with Jeremiah's words, "Because of the LORD's great love we are not consumed" (Lamentations 3:22).

There are two things to observe from this. First, the prophet describes utter destruction here. And yet, because God had to deal with his church and his beloved people, that judgment is mitigated by special grace, so that out of the general ruin of the whole nation God rescues his people, whom he rightly compares with a very small remnant. Since God punished the sins of the Jews in such a dreadful way, we must consider that we may share the same fate if we imitate their rebellion. God had set that nation apart for himself and had distinguished them from other people. So why should God spare us if we are hardened in our ungodliness and treachery?

The second thing to observe, as we see from Jeremiah's words in Lamentations, is that it is only because of the tender mercies of God that we are not utterly destroyed. If we consider the vast amount of wickedness among all sorts of people, we are amazed that even a single individual is left and that all have not been removed from the land of the living. "But I withheld my hand" (Ezekiel 20:22), says the Lord, so that some of the church was preserved in the world. This is the reason given by Paul, who is the best interpreter of this passage. He quotes it to show the haughtiness of the Jews, that they may not boast of their mere name, as if it had been enough that they were descended from the fathers of Israel. Paul reminds them that God could act toward them as he had toward their fathers, but that through his tender mercies "the remnant will be saved" (Romans 9:27). And why? So that the church may not utterly perish. For it is through the favor that the Lord shows toward the church that he still reserves some "descendants" (Romans 9:29). This statement should give us great comfort even during those heavy calamities that we tend to think are everywhere in the church.

If the church does not spread far and wide, people are prone to despise her. We also learn that we should not judge a church by the size of its congregation. We should be satisfied with knowing that although the number of the godly is small, God still acknowledges them as his chosen people. We should also recall Jesus' consoling words, "Do not be afraid, little flock, for your Father has been pleased to give you the kingdom" (Luke 12:32).

10. Hear the word of the LORD, you rulers of Sodom; listen to the law of our God, you people of Gomorrah! He confirms what he has already said: The Lord's vengeance is not cruel, for they deserved an even more severe punishment. While there was a difference between them and the inhabitants of Sodom concerning the punishment, their guilt was the same. So the same punishment would have been inflicted if the Lord had not spared them. If they received milder treatment, it was not because they sinned less heinously than the inhabitants of **Sodom** but because of the mercy of God.

When Isaiah gives to the **rulers** the name of **Sodom** and calls the **people** by the name of **Gomorrah,** he does not mean there is any difference between them, but that they are the same. The different names lend additional elegance, as if he said there is no greater difference between **rulers** and **people** than there is between **Sodom** and **Gomorrah.**

The prophet starts by stripping the Jews of their disguises, and he is right to do this. For while all hypocrites use strange coverings to conceal themselves from view, that nation was particularly addicted to this vice. They took great offense at the way in which Isaiah addressed them, but it was necessary to expose their wickedness and their haughty demeanor. All hypocrites should be dealt with like this.

By **the word** the prophet means **the law.** By quoting these words of Moses, he reminds them that he is not introducing anything new and is not adding anything to the law.

11. "The multitude of your sacrifices—what are they to me?" says the LORD. Isaiah now introduces God as the speaker, for a lawgiver not only issues commands but also gives a sound interpretation of the laws, so that they may not be abused. The previous reproof was unquestionably

20

unpalatable to the people. They gloried in the name of Abraham and boasted that they were his children. This is why the prophet arms himself with God's authority against them. It is as if he said, "You must realize that you do not have to deal with me but with God."

"**I have more than enough of burnt offerings, of rams and the fat of fattened animals; I have no pleasure in the blood of bulls and lambs and goats.**" He explains God's intention in demanding sacrifices: It is not because God places a high value on them, but so they may be aids to piety. The Jews were greatly mistaken when they thought their holiness consisted only in those services. They thought they had performed their duty admirably well when they offered sacrifices of slain beasts. And when the prophets demanded something more than this, the people complained that they were being treated harshly. Now the Lord says that he rejects and abhors these sacrifices. This may appear to be excessively severe, for he had appointed them, but all difficulties about this passage are easily removed by Jeremiah who says, "For when I brought your forefathers out of Egypt and spoke to them, I did not just give them commands about burnt offerings and sacrifices, but I gave them this command: Obey me, and I will be your God and you will be my people. Walk in all the ways I command you, that it may go well with you" (Jeremiah 7:22-23). He shows that the observance of ceremonies depends wholly on the word of God, and that it is as pointless to separate them from the word as it would be for the soul to be separated from the body. Jeremiah also says, "Do not trust in deceptive words and say, 'This is the temple of the LORD, the temple of the LORD, the temple of the LORD!'" (Jeremiah 7:4).

From these passages it is evident that the ceremonies are condemned because they have become separated from the word of God and from their souls. From this we see just how blind people are who cannot be convinced that all the trouble they take over worshiping God is pointless unless it flows from the heart.

12. "**When you come to appear before me, who has asked this of you, this trampling of my courts?**" What an admirable way to conclusively refute false worship! God declares that it is pointless for them to offer him anything that he does not require, for he does not want to be worshiped in any other way than he has commanded. How does it come about that people are so delighted with their ways of worship unless it is because they do not realize that all their services neither benefit themselves nor are acceptable to God? Otherwise they would at once remember that obedience is all that is required of them (see 1 Samuel 15:22).

13. "**Stop bringing meaningless offerings! Your incense is detestable to me. New Moons, Sabbaths and convocations—I cannot bear your evil assemblies.**" To drive the point home, Isaiah declares that such worship is not only unprofitable, but God detests and abhors it! Nothing is dearer to God than his own glory; so there is nothing that he detests so

much as being worshiped in a corrupt way. Some people have misunderstood this passage, thinking he is talking about repealing the law. That is not God's aim, for he tells the people through Isaiah that they should worship God in the right way and explains to them why these ceremonies were instituted. Since the beginning of the world the worship of God was spiritual. Isaiah now goes on to describe why these ceremonies were instituted and how they should be observed.

14. "Your New Moon festivals and your appointed feasts my soul hates. They have become a burden to me; I am weary of bearing them." The prophet, speaking for God, adds nothing new to his previous teaching. Concerning all ceremonies in which there is no spiritual truth but only the glare of a false pretense, he declares that they are not merely useless but wicked. God delights in truth, but especially in the worship due to his majesty. All superstitions are corruptions of the worship of God. It follows from this that they are wicked and unlawful.

I shall not comment in detail on the phrases used here, but they should not be passed over lightly, for the Lord sees how great is people's wantonness in contriving different ways of worship. So the prophet uses a variety of expressions to rebuke their evil ways.

15. "When you spread out your hands in prayer." The ancient custom of spreading out hands in prayer did not arise out of superstition. It comes from nature herself, which prompts people to declare, even through an outward sign, that they are going to God in prayer. As they are not able to fly to him, they raise themselves up by means of this sign. No instruction concerning this sign was given to the fathers, but they used it as men who had been inspired by God. So Isaiah is not condemning them for spreading out their hands in prayer but for their hypocrisy. They looked like people who were calling on God, but their hearts were set against him, as the prophet declares more fully in Isaiah 29:13: **"The Lord says: 'These people come near to me with their mouth and honor me with their lips, but their hearts are far from me. Their worship of me is made up only of rules taught by men.'"** (See also Psalm 145:18.) Where hypocrisy exists, there can be no true calling on God.

"I will hide my eyes from you; even if you offer many prayers, I will not listen." Isaiah expands on his previous statement by threatening that God will be deaf to their cries, no matter how many prayers they say. It is as if he said, "Though you are constant in prayer, that will not benefit you at all." Hypocrites think that the more they pray, the more holy they are.

"Your hands are full of blood." Isaiah starts to explain in more detail why God disapproves, and even disdainfully rejects, both their prayers and their sacrifices. It is because they are cruel and bloody, stained with every kind of sin, although they come before God with a hypocritical display.

16. "Wash and make yourselves clean." Isaiah exhorts the Jews to repent. From this we see that nothing can please God unless it comes from a pure conscience. God does not judge our deeds as we do, according to their outward appearance. It often happens that some particular action, although performed by a very wicked person, gains human applause. But in the sight of God, who sees the heart, a depraved conscience pollutes every virtue. Haggai taught that everything an unclean person touches is polluted. Isaiah has already declared that it is no good offering sacrifices to God or praying or calling on his name if we do not worship him in our hearts. Hence Isaiah demands that the Jews **make** themselves **clean,** in order that what they do may no longer be pointless. We should always deal in this way with people who are strangers to God.

God through Isaiah tells them to **wash.** He does not mean that people repent through the exercise of their free will, but he shows that the only remedy for them is to be pure in God's sight. We know that the sacred writers attribute to people what is done in them by God's Spirit (see Ezekiel 36:25).

"Take your evil deeds out of my sight!" The prophet now describes the fruits of repentance. He not only explains without a metaphor what it is to **wash** and to be **clean,** but he orders them to show through everything they do that they are being renewed by God. He tells them to show fruits of repentance in two ways. They are to **stop doing wrong,** and they are to **learn to do right** (verse 17). First, we must **stop** committing every act of injustice. We must not be like those idle people who think they have done enough just because they have not harmed anyone, and yet are never kind to anyone. Isaiah wants them not only to cease from evil but to do positive good.

17. "Learn to do right! Seek justice." Isaiah had told them to **stop doing wrong;** now he tells them to **learn to do right!** They must excel at doing good. Isaiah says they must **learn** to do this.

"Encourage the oppressed." Isaiah, as he often does, gives particular examples of the general principle he has just mentioned. Although he has already given a special exhortation to be kind and to **seek justice,** he wants to drive his point home even more and so gives some specific examples of what he means. People who want to be thought of as being good and righteous are rarely moved by a general instruction; but when we come to particular examples, they are forced, as it were, to apply it to their daily living.

"Defend the cause of the fatherless, plead the case of the widow." The prophet selects two groups of people who often suffer as a result of human wickedness. The **fatherless** and **the widow** are rarely supported by people because people derive no benefit from helping such despised and lowly people. Wealthy and influential men have many friends to help them, for they hope to be rewarded. But the Lord declares that he will take care of the **fatherless** and **the widow** and that he will avenge those who harm them. See Exodus 22:22-24.

18. "Come now, let us reason together," says the LORD. The Lord declares that the Jews will be speechless when they come before him. This is the way hypocrites should be dealt with, for they boldly enter into discussions with God, and there is no end to their arguments. So Isaiah tells them that if they choose to debate with God, God will be more than a match for them. In other words, Isaiah does not accuse innocent people and has no wish to enter into an argument. The prophet introduces the Lord, as if he said, "For my part, if it is necessary, I will debate with you. For the result will only show up your own obstinacy that prevents any reconciliation between us. The only way to end the controversy between us is if you bring a clean heart with you."

"Though your sins are like scarlet, they shall be as white as snow; though they are red as crimson, they shall be like wool." God declares that he is prepared to cleanse us and to make us **as white as snow.**

19. "If you are willing and obedient." Isaiah continues to plead God's cause against the people. He states in a few words that not only must the people take the blame for all the calamities they endured but that they have it in their own power to recover their prosperity and happiness. God is always ready to forgive them, provided that they do not harden their hearts.

"You will eat the best from the land." By this Isaiah means the fruits of the earth that supply the necessities of life. For in one sense the earth may be said to be unkind when it does not produce its fruits and keeps them, as it were, to itself. But I have no doubt that he is alluding to the promises of the law, in which God declares that those who fear him will be blessed by an abundant harvest (see Deuteronomy 28:11). Yet when he offers us the necessities for this earthly life, it is not because he wants our thoughts to be confined to our present happiness (which is the only thing hypocrites value and which entirely occupies their minds); it is in order that we may rise to the heavenly life. He wants to prepare us for the enjoyment of eternal happiness through tasting so much goodness on earth.

20. "But if you resist and rebel, you will be devoured by the sword." The wicked always think that the severity of the punishment is greater than their guilt, even when the Lord punishes them very gently. But the prophet warns them that there will be no end to their calamities until they are destroyed. Lest they imagine that they have nothing more to fear than the light punishment they had suffered so far, he declares that far heavier judgments from God await them.

For the mouth of the LORD has spoken. Since people are blinded by their lusts and are hardly moved by any warnings, the prophet awakes them from their deep sleep by reminding them that this declaration is not uttered by a mortal but comes from **the mouth of the LORD,** who does not change his mind as human beings do. Isaiah mentions **the mouth of the LORD** in order to shock them out of their sinful ways.

21. See how the faithful city has become a harlot! In order to add weight to this rebuke, and to expose the dreadfulness of the people's sin in having departed from God and from all uprightness, the prophet cries aloud as if he had seen some monstrous thing. He speaks of the city that had previously been a guardian of justice but is now a hideout for thieves. He speaks about her as one who had been a pure, chaste virgin but has now **become a harlot!**

By the word **faithful** Isaiah alludes, in my opinion, to the faithfulness in marriage that a wife should show toward her husband. I think **faithful** in this context means chaste, for immediately afterwards he uses another term to contrast with it, calling the city **a harlot.** Her immoral behavior does not bring a blush to her face. The Scriptures often call the church the wife of God (see Hosea 2:19-20). Jerusalem kept her honorable position so long as she kept her spiritual chastity and continued to worship God in purity. As soon as she stopped doing this she became **a harlot!**

She once was full of justice; righteousness used to dwell in her. Isaiah shows what fruits were produced through their previous allegiance to God. We may take **justice** as another name for uprightness.

But now murderers! Isaiah shows how Jerusalem had **become a harlot.** The city that had previously been renowned for its love of justice and righteousness was now full of **murderers.** This does not mean they were assassins or robbers but that by fraudulent methods, under the guise of justice, they had acquired other people's property. In short, he means that they did not act fairly and justly toward their fellowmen, even though they might be held in high esteem, as some wicked people are.

The state that Jerusalem was reduced to should make us reflect on how often Satan exercises what might be called unrestricted tyranny over God's church. For if ever there was a church, there was one at that time in Jerusalem. And yet Isaiah affirms that it was a den of robbers or a slaughterhouse where they cut people's throats. If Satan could cause such confusion in that church, let us not be surprised if the same thing takes place among us. We must work hard not to allow ourselves to be corrupted by such wicked examples.

22. Your silver has become dross, your choice wine is diluted with water. By making two comparisons Isaiah shows that the outward appearance of their affairs was not publicly overturned, even though their inner condition had changed and had been corrupted, so that they were very different from how they had previously been. For he says that **dross** now shines instead of **silver** and that their **wine,** though it retained its color, has lost its flavor. "Although you still make an empty show," says the prophet, "nothing pure will be found in you. The wine that used to be **choice wine**

is now corrupted; though its color may deceive the eye, its taste shows that it has been **diluted with water.**"

All this means that the Jews should put aside their hypocrisy and start to confess their sins. The comparisons made here are highly appropriate. **Dross** looks similar to **silver;** similarly, the color of **wine diluted with water** resembles that of pure wine. And yet both are far from having the purity that they claim. In the same way hypocrites, through their hypocrisy, may be said to assume the false color of **silver,** though they are no more valuable than **dross.**

23. Your rulers are rebels. There is a play on words here. Isaiah is not referring to rulers as though the ordinary people were holy and needed no reproof; rather, he points out the source of the evil. No disease is more harmful than one that spreads from the head to the whole body, and so no evil is more destructive among people than when a ruler is depraved.

Companions of thieves. Isaiah means they are so far from restraining theft that, on the contrary, they profit from it themselves. By receiving part of the booty, they give others permission to commit theft. And, indeed, when a judge is open to a bribe, some crimes will go unpunished.

They all love bribes and chase after gifts. Isaiah now points out why rulers have made themselves **companions of thieves.** It is out of avarice. When judges are devoted to the love of money, justice is utterly destroyed. This results, as one person has said, in judges' making laws and unmaking laws. See Exodus 23:8. No man is so upright, no man so sagacious, that his mind resists the blinding influence of **gifts.** Such judges are rightly called **companions of thieves.**

They do not defend the cause of the fatherless; the widow's case does not come before them. As the Lord especially commands us to care for the **fatherless** and **widows,** because they have no one to look after them, we are hardly surprised if he is displeased when they are abandoned by the rulers, who should have been their guardians and defenders. Since the **fatherless** and **widows** have neither foresight, nor industry, nor strength if no one comes forward to assist them, they are exposed to every kind of injustice. When no attention is paid to them, it follows that justice does not rule; rather, covetousness is the order of the day.

24. Therefore the Lord, the LORD Almighty, the Mighty One of Israel, declares . . . Isaiah first of all uses the word **Lord,** the word used to denote the relationship between a servant and his master. Then Isaiah uses the word for **the LORD Almighty** —that is, Jehovah, which denotes the eternal essence and majesty of God. Isaiah now wants to warn them of God's judgment and at the same time to remind them that the children of Abraham are God's special people. So he adds that God is **the Mighty One of Israel.**

"Ah, I will get relief from my foes and avenge myself on my enemies." By these words Isaiah intimates that God will not be pacified until he has satiated himself by inflicting punishment. This punishment will fall on his **enemies**. He is not speaking here about the Chaldeans or Assyrians, as some have thought, but of Jews, to whom, like a herald, the prophet proclaims war in the name of the Lord. This warning sounded harshly in their ears, for they thought that because they were linked with God, he was an enemy of their enemies. On the contrary, Isaiah declares that he is *their* enemy, because he had been so often provoked by their sins. This is how we must shake off the slothfulness of the hypocrites, who are constantly waging war against God and yet do not hesitate to allege that they enjoy his protection. We need not wonder, therefore, if the prophet sternly pronounces them God's **enemies**. They had broken God's covenant and so declared war on him.

And yet, to show that he does this unwillingly, as it were, God utters his warning with a kind of groan. Nothing is more in line with his nature than to do good; so whenever he is angry with us and treats us harshly, it is certain that our wickedness has compelled him to be like this, because we do not allow his goodness to take its free course. He is especially disposed to treat his own people with gentleness, and when he sees there is no longer any room for his forbearance, he takes measures, as it were in sorrow, to inflict punishment.

"And avenge myself on my enemies." In this second clause there is a repetition, a figure of speech often used by the Jews, who often expressed the same thought twice in one sentence. From this we also learn that God cannot rest until he has taken vengeance on a wicked and treacherous people.

25. "I will turn my hand against you; I will thoroughly purge ..." This brings a little relief from the previous warning. Although he still speaks of his severity, he also says that amidst those calamities the church will be preserved. The main aim here is to comfort the believers, so they will not think the church is utterly ruined. The Spirit of God, through the prophets, continually warns God's children, who tremble at his word, not to be overwhelmed and lose heart because of all the dire warnings.

Besides, the announcement **"I will turn my hand against you"** denotes God's presence, as if he said, "I will display my hand." He does this in two ways, either by warning the wicked or by delivering believers from their distresses. Since it is clear from the context that God wants to mitigate the severity of punishment, the phrase **"I will turn my hand"** must be viewed here as referring to the restoration of the church. Although he states in general terms that everyone is his enemy, he now modifies or limits that statement by addressing Jerusalem or Zion.

"I will thoroughly purge away your dross and remove your impurities." The purification of the church is God's own work. So he always lifts up his hand to punish transgressors, that he may bring back wanderers. He points out here a special favor that he bestows on his elect; so it follows that repentance is a true and particular work of the Holy Spirit. Otherwise the sinner, instead of benefiting at all, would become more and more hardened by the punishments.

The **dross** being **thoroughly** purged must not be understood to mean that God ever purifies his church completely from every stain in this world. Rather, it is like saying that his church's holiness will shine like pure silver. These words, therefore, indicate real purity, for the Jews had previously been content to wallow in their filth. This is a highly appropriate comparison, through which the prophet declares that though the church was then polluted by many defilements, some remnant would still remain, which, after the removal of the pollution, would regain its brightness. In this way he also links both clauses, for when he had previously spoken about their sins, he said, **your silver has become dross** (verse 22).

26. "I will restore your judges as in days of old, your counselors as at the beginning." He now speaks in plain language. Having said that the source of the evil was in the rulers, he shows that a divine hand will purify them when the Lord restores the church to perfect health. And, indeed, when those who rule are good and holy people, public order is maintained. But when wicked people have power, everything goes to ruin. By **judges** and **counselors** he clearly means magistrates. When he says they will be **as in days of old** and **as at the beginning,** he reminds them of God's extraordinary goodness, of which they had been deprived. God had graciously raised up the throne of David. Although the authority of the family of David had degenerated into a most terrible tyranny, they still boasted of being his true heirs. So the people are rightly reminded about the happiness from which they had fallen through their own fault, so that they might not be upset by the decline in numbers. For this was the means through which they would again possess that order that God had established.

"Afterward you will be called The City of Righteousness, The Faithful City." He describes the fruit of the reformation about which he has spoken, extending to the whole body. Before Jerusalem had rebelled against God, she had been a **Faithful City . . . called the City of Righteousness.** Now the prophet says that after she has been chastised, the same virtues will be illustriously displayed in her. Here, too, the essence of repentance is stated, for **Righteousness** means uprightness, when everyone obtains what belongs to them, and people live with each other without harming each other. The word **Faithful** has a wider meaning, for when a city is called **Faithful,** it means not only that justice and honesty between people are observed, but that the purity of God's worship is maintained. Therefore, it includes chastity and purity of mind. Isaiah is describing the fruit of true conversion. It is like saying, "When Jerusalem will be brought back to true godliness, people will be persuaded that she is renewed."

27. Zion will be redeemed with justice, her penitent ones with right-eousness. Isaiah confirms the same teaching. Because it was hard to believe the church would be restored, he shows that this does not depend on human will but is founded on the **justice** and **righteousness** of God. In other words, God will not allow his church to be completely destroyed, because he is righteous. Therefore the purpose of the prophet is to raise the minds of godly people from earthly thoughts and to think about the safety of the church, for which they will depend completely on God.

28. But rebels and sinners will both be broken together, and those who forsake the LORD will perish. In case hypocrites should imagine that any fruit of these promises belongs to them, he warns that they will **per-ish,** although God will redeem his church. Hypocrites have always been mixed with the church, and they apply God's promises to themselves. Here we should observe that great wisdom is needed by godly teachers. They must terrify the wicked with God's judgment, but at the same time they must support good people and strengthen them with some comfort, so that they will not be discouraged. See Psalm 91:7.

29. "You will be ashamed because of the sacred oaks in which you have delighted." It is as if the prophet said that no evil would be more destructive to them than their own superstition. "The idols," he says in effect, "that you call on for your protection and safety will bring destruction on you."

The image of both **oaks** and **gardens** is used to reprove every kind of false worship. Although there were many kinds of idolatry among the Jews, the practice mentioned here—choosing **oaks** and **gardens** for offering sacrifices—was the most common of all.

By the word **delighted** he reproves the mad, burning eagerness with which wicked people followed their superstitions. They should have earnestly devoted their whole heart to serve the one God, but they rushed to indulge in false worship, as if driven by animal lust. In nearly every human mind this disease exists naturally. Men have forsaken the true God and have run wild in following idols. Scripture often compares this mad-ness to the love of prostitutes, who shake off shame as well as reason.

"You will be disgraced because of the gardens that you have cho-sen." The prophet describes not only their excessive zeal but their pre-sumption in corrupting the worship of God. When he says they **have chosen . . . gardens,** he is contrasting this with submitting to God's law. Whatever may be the plausible appearances under which unbelievers endeavor to cloak their superstitions, it still remains true that "to obey is better than sacrifice, and to heed is better than the fat of rams" (1 Samuel 15:22). Similarly, Paul uses the words "self-imposed worship" to include all kinds of false worship that people contrive for themselves without God's command: "Such regulations indeed have an appearance of wisdom, with their self-imposed worship, their false humility and their harsh treatment of the body, but they lack any value in restraining sensual indulgence" (Colossians 2:23). Because of this God complains that the Jews have despised his word and have taken delight in their own inventions. It is as if he said, "It was your duty to obey, but you wanted to have an unfettered choice, or rather unbounded liberty." People cannot choose how God should be worshiped because this right is God's alone; and this single consideration is enough to condemn human inventions.

30. **"You will be like an oak with fading leaves, like a garden without water."** The prophet appears to be alluding to gardens to which they had improperly restricted the worship of God. In other words, "You take pleasure in your gardens and trees, but you will be like withered trees that have lost their foliage." God therefore mocks the vain boasting of idolaters who flatter themselves with such contrivances and think that heaven is open to them when they engage in such ceremonies.

31. **"The mighty man will become tinder and his work a spark; both will burn together, with no one to quench the fire."** As a fire is made up of dry fuel like **tinder,** "in the same way," says the prophet in essence, "you and your idols will be gathered into one heap, as when a pile of wood is built up, so that you may be consumed together, so that the idols may be like **tinder** and the mind like a spark, so that one conflagration may consume them all." Images and idols arouse God's wrath, kindling it into a flame that cannot be quenched.

Isaiah
Chapter 2

1. This is what Isaiah son of Amoz saw concerning Judah and Jerusalem. This prophecy confirms the teaching he has just given about the restoration of the church. It is difficult to cherish the hope of safety when we are, so to speak, in the midst of destruction, while God's wrath burns and consumes everything far and wide. At such times the bare promises are hardly enough to support us and allay our fears. That is why the Lord determined that in addition to the consolation that had already been proclaimed there should be added this special vision. I have no doubt, therefore, that this vision agrees with what is stated in 1:26-27.

Here we learn the purpose of visions. Teaching sometimes does not have enough weight for us; so God adds visions, that through them he may seal his teaching to us. This vision is linked to the previous promise; so we learn from it the useful teaching that all visions of every kind that God gave to his prophets must be linked to the promises, to confirm them. And thus we perceive God's astonishing goodness more and more. Not satisfied with giving us his bare word, he gives us pictures of the events, so to speak.

2. In the last days. When Isaiah mentions the end or completion of days, let us remember that he is speaking about the kingdom of Christ. We must also understand why he speaks about Christ's kingdom in this way. It was because until that time everything might be said to be in a state of suspense, so that the people might not concentrate on the present condition of things, which were only a shadow, but on the Redeemer, by whom the reality would be declared. Since Christ came, therefore, if that time is compared with ours, we have actually arrived **in the last days.** It was the duty of the fathers who lived at that time to go, as it were, with outstretched arms to Christ. The restoration of everything depended on his coming; so they had good reason to look forward with hope to that time. It was indeed always useful for them to know that under Christ the condition of the church would be more perfect—especially because there were limits to imagery, for the Lord chose to arouse them in various ways expressly to keep them in suspense.

But there was a special importance attached to this prediction. For 400 years or thereabouts there were innumerable occasions on which they might have given up, if they had not remembered **the last days** in which the church was to be perfectly restored. During the various storms, therefore, by which the church was nearly overwhelmed, every believer, when shipwrecked, seized on this word as a plank on which to float into the harbor. But notice that while **the last days** began at the coming of Christ, they flow on in uninterrupted progress until he appears the second time for our salvation (see Hebrews 9:28).

The mountain of the LORD's temple will be established as chief among the mountains; it will be raised above the hills, and all nations will stream to it. This vision might be thought absurd, because not only was Zion a hill of no special height when compared with the huge mountains on earth, but also the prophet had just predicted its destruction. How, then, could it be believed that Mount Zion, after losing all its greatness, would again shine with such luster as to draw the eyes of **all nations** to her? And yet she is extolled as if she were higher than Olympus. "Let the Gentiles boast as much as they please about their high mountains," says Isaiah in effect. "They will be nothing in comparison with that hill, even though it is low and small." In the natural course of events, this was most unlikely. Would Zion be raised up to the clouds? Wicked people doubtless scoffed at this prediction, for the ungodly have always been ready to attack God.

Isaiah used this prophecy to bring comfort to the people during their captivity. So although there was no temple and no sacrifices, and although everything was in ruins, this hope would still be cherished in the hearts of godly people. This is how they would reason: "The mountain of the Lord is indeed forsaken, but there he will live, and this mountain will be the greatest one in the world." To stop them from doubting this, the prophet sketches a picture of the glory of God here.

3. Many peoples will come and say . . . In the previous verse he gave one reason why Mount Zion would be elevated to such a high position— because all nations would flow to it, as if the rivers were overflowing from a great abundance of water. He now gives his reason. People might ask why various nations flocked to it in crowds from distant lands; he says their motive was the desire to serve God.

"Come, let us go up to the mountain of the LORD, to the house of the God of Jacob." Through these words he first declares that the godly will be filled with such an ardent desire to spread the doctrines of true religion that everyone will not be satisfied with his own salvation; his personal knowledge will make him want to draw other people along with him. This shows us that the normal way to gather a church is through the human voice. God could bring each person to himself by a secret influence, but he uses human agents so he may awaken our anxiety for each others' salvation. Isaiah then shows that those who teach and exhort should not sit down and command other people but should walk along with them as companions.

"**He will teach us his ways.**" Isaiah shows that God cannot be worshiped rightly until we have been enlightened by doctrine. He also shows that God is the church's only teacher, and so we should hang on his every word. The office of teaching is committed to pastors solely in order that God may be heard through them. Those who want to be thought of as ministers of Christ must conform to that.

"**So that we may walk in his paths.**" Now Isaiah says they must be obedient. The instruction that comes to us from the mouth of the Lord is not mere speculation but directs the course of our life and leads us to obey him. We should note that God's commands are called **ways** and **paths** in order to teach us that those who deviate from God's commands in the slightest go completely astray. Thus every kind of unlawful freedom is restrained. Everyone, from the least to the greatest, must observe this rule of obedience, so that they keep themselves within the limits of God's word.

The law will go out from Zion, the word of the LORD from Jerusalem. This explains the previous verse, in which Isaiah said that Mount Zion would be placed above all mountains; that is, that she will be raised to the highest honor when she becomes the source of saving doctrine, which will flow from her to the whole world.

Since we know this prediction was fulfilled when the preaching of the Gospel began at that very place, we must not take the word **law** in a limited sense. For at that time its figures and bondage were abolished. (See Mark 16:15; Luke 24:47.) Hence we conclude that the term is applied, without limitation, to the Word of God. When the prophets say that the waters will spring out of the temple to water the whole world (see Ezekiel 47:1), they are expressing metaphorically what Isaiah lays down here in plain language. The source of saving doctrine will come from that place, for from it the apostles and other teachers spread the Gospel throughout the whole world.

Note why the prophet said this—so that he might fortify the godly against various changes that otherwise, on many occasions, might have crushed their spirits. It is as if he said, "Whatever your situation may be, and although you may be oppressed by afflictions on all sides, continue to cherish this assured hope, that **the law will go out from Zion, the word of the LORD from Jerusalem.** For this is an infallible decree of God that no event will make void."

4. He will judge between the nations and will settle disputes for

many people. He means that the doctrine will be like a king's scepter, that God may rule among all nations. In this figure of speech the Hebrew word *shaphat,* **judge,** means "to govern" or "to reign."

They will beat their swords into plowshares and their spears into pruning hooks. Isaiah shows the benefit that will result after Christ has brought the Gentiles and the nations under his dominion. Nothing is more desirable than peace, but pride, ambition, and covetousness lead men to fight each other. Men are naturally drawn by their evil passions to disturb society, but Isaiah promises that this evil will be corrected. The Gospel is the doctrine of reconciliation (see 2 Corinthians 5:18), removing the enmity between us and God; so it also brings peace and harmony between men.

He does not merely say, **they will beat their swords into plowshares** but **and their spears into pruning hooks.** Thus he shows there will be a great change among people. Instead of attacking each other, they will cultivate peace and friendship between each other, for **plowshares** and **pruning hooks** are useful and necessary in farming. He therefore shows that when Christ reigns, those who had previously been motivated by mischief will be full of acts of kindness.

Nation will not take up sword against nation, nor will they train for war anymore. The prophet means they will not train themselves in destructive arts and will not strive with each other in acts of cruelty and injustice, as they had done previously. But the complete fulfillment of this prophecy should not be looked for on earth. It is enough if we experience the beginning and if, being reconciled to God through Christ, we cultivate mutual friendships and abstain from doing harm to anyone.

5. Come, O house of Jacob. It is as if he said, "Look, the Gentiles come together to Mount Zion, and neighbors exhort each other. They submit to receiving instruction from God and to being reproved by him. So why do you Israelites, who are heirs of God's promises, draw back? Will the Gentiles submit to God, but you will refuse to acknowledge his authority? Has so great a light been kindled in every part of the world, but you will refuse to be enlightened by it? Will so many waters flow, and you will not drink? What madness is this, that when the Gentiles run so eagerly, you sit still in idleness?"

Let us walk in the light of the LORD. He means that **the light** is ready to guide their feet, but they disregard it by closing their eyes, and even try to put it out. Yet its brightness draws people from distant lands.

6. You have abandoned your people, the house of Jacob. Isaiah now accuses the people of having a perverse disposition. It is as if he bursts out in astonishment before God saying, "Why should I waste words on a nation that you, Lord, have rightly rejected because it has given itself up to idolatry and has departed from your Word?"

This may also be a prediction of future punishment that Isaiah foresaw through the Spirit. It is as if he said, "It is hardly surprising if ruin and desolation are about to overtake Mount Zion because of their evil deeds." He may have wanted to stop such a terrible spectacle, which would lead to despair, so that those who were capable of being cured might be moved to repent and turn back to God before the calamity arrived. God's servants should always try to do good, even to the reprobate if possible (see 2 Timothy 2:25).

They are full of superstitions from the East. They were full of vices they had learned from the people of the East. It is easy to imitate evil, and nothing is more natural than for corruptions to spread from one place to another.

They practice divination like the Philistines and clasp hands with pagans. The prophet accuses them of trying to please the Gentiles and thus becoming entangled in their vices. They preferred not just mortals, but wicked mortals, to God.

7. Their land is full of silver and gold; there is no end to their treasures. Their land is full of horses; there is no end to their chariots. We must look at the order in which the prophet mentions things here as he lists the reasons why the Lord rejected his people. In the previous verse he started with divinations and pagans. Now he comes to **silver and gold.** Then he mentions **horses** and **chariots.** There can be no doubt that, having first condemned idolatry, he reproves them, second, for covetousness and, third, for sinful trust, when people leave God and seek their own grounds of confidence. This nation is not condemned for possessing **silver and gold** but for burning with insatiable covetousness and for trusting in **horses** and **chariots.**

8. Their land is full of idols; they bow down to the work of their hands, to what their fingers have made. He repeats what he has already said about their idolatry but in more detail. He starts by mentioning, **they bow down to the work of their hands, to what their fingers have made.** How stupid they were to worship wood and stone instead of God. To **bow down** to an idol was to give it divine worship.

9. So men will be brought low and mankind humbled. Being **brought low** and **humbled** are two allusions to the bowing down before idols that he has just mentioned. In other words, "They have bowed themselves down before idols; therefore God will bring them low under a great weight of calamities."

But do not forgive them. The prophets, ablaze with zeal for God, pour out prayers under the direct control of the Spirit and threaten to justly punish the ungodly. But at the same time it must be understood that Isaiah here makes an unspoken reference to the remnant. So the meaning of this sentence amounts to this: The restoration of a new church must not be expected until God has executed judgment by destroying the temple.

10. Go into the rocks, hide in the ground. Isaiah means that God's judgment is more to be dreaded than a thousand deaths, and that for the sake of escaping that judgment they will wish they could go down into the grave.

. . . from the dread of the LORD and the splendor of his majesty! In other words, "It is according to the measure of his own glory that God ought to be dreaded by the ungodly, in whose destruction he displays his boundless power." Pastors should learn from this how to deal with drowsy consciences. They must awaken such persons through God's judgment, that they may view that judgment with real dread.

11. The eyes of the arrogant man will be humbled and the pride of men brought low; the LORD alone will be exalted in that day. Wicked people, relying on their present wealth, treat the warnings of the prophet with disdain. Isaiah is determined to stamp out their arrogance. It is like saying, "The time will come when your pride, through which you vainly contend against God, will be brought down."

When Isaiah speaks of **the eyes of the arrogant man,** he is using an outward sign to denote an inner, mental pride. Sinful confidence almost always betrays, in its very looks, contempt for God and man. See Psalm 101:5.

12. The LORD Almighty has a day in store for all the proud and lofty, for all that is exalted (and they will be humbled). In this verse the prophet confirms in more details what he has just been speaking about. From the vehement way in which he heaps up words, we may easily infer how bold the wickedness of that time was. We learn from these words that God avows himself to be the enemy of all the proud. The appointment of **a day** is therefore the same as God saying that the wicked will not be able to escape being crushed by his hand. If we were convinced of this ourselves, would we not abhor pride, which provokes God's anger against it?

13-14. . . . for all the cedars of Lebanon, tall and lofty, and all the oaks of Bashan, for all the towering mountains and all the high hills. The metaphor introduced here of **the trees of Lebanon, tall and lofty** does not obscure light but sheds light on the subject. No matter how high the endeavors of mortals may be, they will never be able to reach the tops of **the cedars of Lebanon** or **the towering mountains.** Thus Isaiah shows proud men how idle and foolish they are to believe that their elevation will be their defense.

15. . . . for every lofty tower and every fortified wall. What Isaiah now says about towers and walls is not figurative. We know how men who think they are well defended congratulate themselves on no longer needing God's assistance. So Isaiah uses lofty towers and fortified walls as objects of false security.

16. . . . for every trading ship and every stately vessel. Trade between nations is not being condemned here, but, as so frequently happens, abundance leads to pride and cruelty, and that is what Isaiah is condemning.

17. The arrogance of man will be brought low and the pride of men humbled; the LORD alone will be exalted in that day. The prophet declares that he had his eyes on **the arrogance of man.** God is not displeased with the steep mountains or tall cedars, for he created them. But Isaiah tells us that evil lies in men who vainly trust in what is high and lofty. The Lord will easily subdue them, and they will have to acknowledge that they gain nothing from their insolence and presumption.

18. And the idols will totally disappear. In his rebuke God through Isaiah has already linked idolatry with luxury and covetousness and other vices; now he links them with the warning of punishment.

19. Men will flee to caves in the rocks and to holes in the ground from dread of the LORD and the splendor of his majesty, when he rises to shake the earth. These words must refer to the terror that people experienced at the hands of the Chaldeans and Assyrians. God used them to chastise his people; although they were wicked, they promoted God's glory. Isaiah speaks like this about the Assyrians and Chaldeans because we see **the splendor of his majesty** in the punishments that the Lord will inflict on the Jews through them. The same thing is confirmed by the words **he rises,** referring to God's judgment seat.

20. In that day men will throw away to the rodents and bats their idols of silver and idols of gold, which they made to worship. Idolaters are amazingly delighted with their own superstitions and ungodly worship. They commit endless sins, but they still take refuge in imagining that their worship appeases God. So the prophet deprives idolaters of this cloak, warning them that they will no longer be able to conceal their pollution. The Lord will compel them to throw away their idols, and they will acknowledge that they had no good reason for placing their hope and confidence in them.

21. They will flee to caverns in the rocks and to the overhanging crags from dread of the LORD and the splendor of his majesty, when he rises to shake the earth. This repetition is not superfluous, although Isaiah uses the same words as a few verses earlier—for what is as difficult as impressing on people's minds the sincere fear of God? God's judgment had to be placed before these hypocrites, and yet they were hardly moved. The ungodly preferred to be swallowed up rather than come before God's eye.

22. Stop trusting in man, who has but a breath in his nostrils. Isaiah urges the ungodly to stop deluding themselves. In other words: "I see that you are blinded and intoxicated by false hope, so that no argument can prevail with you. You do this because you claim too much for yourselves. But man is nothing, and you have to deal with God, who can reduce the world to nothing at a stroke."

The words **a breath in his nostrils** denote human weakness, the fact that human life is like a **breath** that disappears in a moment (see Psalm

104:29; 146:4, KJV; see also 78:29). We ought to **stop trusting in man.** We are forbidden to place any confidence in men. We should not even trust our own wisdom or energy. "This is what the LORD says: 'Cursed is the one who trusts in man, who depends on flesh for his strength and whose heart turns away from the LORD" (Jeremiah 17:5).

Of what account is he? Man has nothing left for which to congratulate himself. This expression exposes man's love of self, which intoxicates him and opposes God's grace.

Isaiah
Chapter 3

1. See now, the Lord, the LORD Almighty, is about to take from Jerusalem and Judah both supply and support: all supplies of food and all supplies of water. The prophet continues with the same subject he was dealing with at the close of the previous chapter. He warns the Jews that their wealth, no matter how great it may be, will not prevent God's wrath from burning up all their defenses. It follows from this that they are behaving like madmen when they put their trust in weapons of war and in armor.

See now indicates that time is running out. It is as if Isaiah makes the wicked the eyewitnesses of this event. It often happens that those who do not openly ridicule God's judgments ignore them. "What has that got to do with us?" they ask.

The Lord, the LORD Almighty, is about to take from Jerusalem and Judah . . . The prophet emphasizes that God's hand is no great distance away. He calls God **the Lord, the LORD Almighty,** so that God's majesty may jolt them out of their stupor. The prophet warns the Jews that **both supply and support** will be removed. This means, "God will take away every assistance that you think supports you, so that nothing is left for you to put your trust in."

All supplies of food and all supplies of water. The prophet warns them that their harvest will be taken from them, so that they will die as a result of famine (see Leviticus 26:26; Ezekiel 4:16). The people will have no food to strengthen them, either because they will not have bread and water or, if they have them, will derive no nourishment from them.

2. The hero and warrior, the judge and prophet, the soothsayer and elder. Isaiah mentions people who contribute to the safety and good order of nations and cities. He warns that the Jews will be completely deprived of these, so that they will have neither wisdom nor bravery at home, nor military forces abroad.

The **hero** and **warrior** were the men of war. The **judge** stood for every kind of governor and the **prophet** for every kind of teacher. The **soothsayer** was probably someone who penetrated dark matters not by using omens and superstitious arts but by extraordinary acuteness and skill.

3. The captain of fifty and man of rank, the counselor, skilled craftsman and clever enchanter. As the Romans had centurions (captains of hundreds), so the Jews had captains (rulers of fifties). **Man of rank** may apply to men in private life who were noted for their prudence. The **skilled craftsman** was needed to maintain the prosperity of a nation, and Isaiah says that through lack of them the destruction of the Jews was at hand. **Clever enchanter** literally means "skilled in muttering or in a subdued tone of speech." They may have been wise men who gave advice in private.

4. I will make boys their officials; mere children will govern them. Isaiah now describes how sad and wretched the change will be when competent and faithful rulers will be taken from among them, whom God will replace with cowardly and worthless people. This will make God's vengeance even more plain.

By **boys** and **children** are meant not only those who are young in age, but those who have weak minds and feeble constitutions.

This passage may be summed up as follows: "When God takes away those gifts and alters the condition of a people, however this may happen, either by changing the form of government or by taking away the rulers, the anger of God should be acknowledged."

5. People will oppress each other—man against man, neighbor against neighbor. The young will rise up against the old, the base against the honorable. Isaiah describes the utmost confusion that is about to overtake the Jews. This happens to any nation as soon as government is removed. But the confusion described by the prophet is most disgraceful. A child will dare insult an old man, and the dregs of society will rise up against the **honorable.**

6. A man will seize one of his brothers at his father's home, and say, "You have a cloak, you be our leader; take charge of this heap of ruins!" In other words, "Not only the common people but also the nobles and the wealthy will decline the task of government."

7. But in that day he will cry out, "I have no remedy. I have no food or clothing in my house; do not make me the leader of the people." The words **cry out** express absolute and vehement refusal. **"I have no remedy."** It is as if you sought healing from someone and he said he had no skill in the art of healing or that the disease was incurable.

8. Jerusalem staggers, Judah is falling; their words and deeds are against the LORD, defying his glorious presence. In case it was thought that God is excessively cruel when he punishes people with such severity, the prophet gives a brief explanation of this calamity. The destruction of that ungodly people was righteous because in so many ways they persisted in provoking God.

He speaks about their destruction as if it had already taken place. It appears that the past may be taken for the future here, as is the case in many other passages.

Defying his glorious presence [KJV, **to provoke the eyes of his glory**]. This expression denotes that they had intentionally resolved to insult God, for those things that are done before our eyes, if they are displeasing to us, are the more offensive. The word **glorious** also deserves our attention, for it is evidence of extraordinary madness if we have no feeling of reverence when God's majesty is presented to us.

9. The look on their faces testifies against them. The prophet had to deal with impudent hypocrites who boasted that they were good men, and he says that their countenance testifies what kind of people they are. It will not be necessary to bring witnesses from distant lands to prove their wickedness.

They parade their sin like Sodom; they do not hide it. They had devoted themselves to iniquity in such a way that they boasted shamelessly of their transgressions. They did this as if it had been honorable to trample on all distinctions between right and wrong. See Genesis 18:20; 19:5.

Woe to them! They have brought disaster upon themselves. In other words, "You cannot accuse God, as though he is punishing you unjustly. Acknowledge that it has been done by yourselves. Give glory to a righteous judge, and lay the whole blame on yourselves."

10. Tell the righteous it will be well with them, for they will enjoy the fruit of their deeds. As such severe punishments often upset pious minds, the prophet reminds them of God's providence. Even when there is apparent confusion, God never ceases to distinguish between good people and bad.

Tell the righteous it will be well with them. This means, "Let every ground of doubt be removed, and let us be fully convinced that the righteous man will excel and prosper." Since it is difficult to believe this, he adds, **for they will enjoy the fruit of their deeds.** That is, they will not lose their reward for their good behavior.

11. Woe to the wicked! Disaster is upon them! They will be paid back for what their hands have done. This clause contrasts with the previous one. From this we infer the prophet's purpose—namely, to comfort the godly and to frighten the wicked with God's judgment. When a severe calamity occurs, affecting everyone indiscriminately, we doubt that it comes from God's providence. Or we may say that the world is governed by blind chance. From this comes the wicked idea that there is no difference between the rewards for the good and for the bad, and as a result of these gloomy thoughts worldly appetites lead many people to despair.

The prophet shows that God's judgment is right, so that people will continue to fear God. He therefore invites people to praise God for his justice. It is as if he said, "Do not think that blind chance rules the world, or that God punishes with blind violence and with no regard for justice. You must hold on to the settled principle in your mind that it will be well with the righteous. God will repay them as he has promised and will not disappoint them."

12. Youths oppress my people, women rule over them. O my people, your guides lead you astray; they turn you from the path. The reproach that Isaiah brings against the Jews is that while they obstinately shake off the yoke of God, they are ready to give abject submission to others and will perform any services, no matter how shameful and degrading they are. Isaiah says that their rulers are the cause of evil and that they corrupt everything, since their duty was to correct men and to point out the right way through their own example.

13. The LORD takes his place in court; he rises to judge the people. When wickedness reigns, we ask, "Where is God? Isn't his glory being trampled on?" Isaiah meets this difficulty by saying, "Though the nation is wicked, yet because the rulers themselves are corrupt and even pollute the whole nation with their vices, God sits as judge in heaven and will at length call them to account and give everyone what he deserves."

14. The LORD enters into judgment against the elders and leaders of his people. The rulers think that no one will judge their actions and do not submit to God himself. Since, therefore, they are so unbridled that they never heed any warnings, the prophet summons them to God's judgment seat. **The elders and leaders** thought they were free from the restraints of the law because of their position as **leaders of his people.** But they will be called to account by God.

"It is you who have ruined my vineyard." The metaphor of a vine is very common where a nation, and particularly the nation of Israel, is the subject. "I had planted you like a choice vine of sound and reliable stock. How then did you turn against me into a corrupt, wild vine?" (Jeremiah 2:21). The prophet shows them the extent of their sin. They paid no more attention to the people whom God had loved with special affection than if they had ruled over a pagan nation.

The word **you** is emphatic. Isaiah was addressing the vinedressers themselves who, instead of devoting themselves, as they should have done, to the cultivation of the vine, devoured it like animals. How treacherous they were when they **ruined [the] vineyard** they should have been protecting! In contrast to this, the Lord shows what great care he takes of his own people, and how warmly he loves them. He not only calls the church his vine, but he says he will not stand for the wickedness of those who rule over it tyrannically.

"The plunder from the poor is in your houses." It is the most wicked act of cruelty to plunder the poor and needy person who cannot defend himself and who should rather have been protected.

15. "What do you mean by crushing my people and grinding the faces of the poor?" declares the Lord, the LORD Almighty. Isaiah gives further details of the haughty, cruel, and oppressive way in which the rulers governed. In order to give his reproof the maximum weight, he reminds them that God is speaking through him.

16. The LORD says, "The women of Zion are haughty." This is a warning against the ambition, luxury, and pride of some women.

"Walking along with outstretched necks." Isaiah rightly says that pride is the source of evil. He says this is evident from the way in which these women walked. As it is a sign of modesty to look down, so to have excessively high looks is a sign of insolence.

"Flirting with their eyes." This denotes shameless lust, which is often expressed through the eyes. The eyes of chaste women are sedate, not wandering or unsteady.

"Tripping along with mincing steps, with ornaments jingling on their ankles." This is all part of the indecent way in which they expressed their unrestrained immorality.

17-23. "Therefore the Lord will bring sores on the heads of the women of Zion; the LORD will make their scalps bald." In that day the Lord will snatch away their finery: the bangles and headbands and crescent necklaces, the earrings and bracelets and veils, the headdresses and ankle chains and sashes, the perfume bottles and charms, the signet rings and nose rings, the fine robes and the capes and cloaks, the purses and mirrors, and the linen garments and tiaras and shawls. Since neither gentle advice nor any words can reform them, the Lord will deal with them in a different way. He will not use severe language but will take vengeance, like an army. Since they had shown their obstinacy from head to foot, the Lord will show marks of his vengeance on every part of their body. He begins with the head and then moves on to other parts.

I will not explain the meaning of each of their ornaments, since even the best Hebrew scholars cannot identify all of them. It is enough to understand the general purpose of the prophet. He heaps up and enumerates these trifles so that their wide variety will reveal the indulgence and evil intentions of these women.

24. Instead of fragrance there will be a stench; instead of a sash, a rope; instead of well-dressed hair, baldness; instead of fine clothing, sackcloth; instead of beauty, branding. It is clear that the country described here abounds in aromatic herbs. Isaiah means that ointments and fragrance were abused by them in many ways, for people's sinful desires are ingenious and can never be satisfied. Isaiah introduces a series of contrasts. The women who had previously walked around well-dressed will in the future go around naked and wounded. **A sash** is contrasted with **a rope**; instead of having **well-dressed hair,** they will be bald. In sum, both men and women are instructed to use God's gifts in a self-disciplined way. This applies to food and clothes and to all their behavior.

25. Your men will fall by the sword, your warriors in battle. Isaiah describes the punishment that God will bring upon them through wars. It will affect all of the people.

26. The gates of Zion will lament and mourn; destitute, she will sit on the ground. We know public meetings took place at the gates. Just as the gates sometimes rejoiced with the citizens of a town, so they are said here to **lament and mourn** because of the terrible desolation.

Isaiah compares Jerusalem to a woman (**she**) who is sad as she mourns because she is a widow. It was normal for mourners to **sit on the ground.** That nation was in the habit of using ceremonies and outward signs much more than we do. This can all be summed up by saying that the city will have lost her inhabitants.

Isaiah
Chapter 4

1. In that day seven women will take hold of one man and say ... Isaiah continues with the same subject; unquestionably this discourse is linked to the last chapter. He describes in more detail the nature of the desolation that he had previously warned them about. If the warnings are not expressed in the strongest possible terms, hypocrites will disregard them, so that God's severity never produces its proper effect on them. It is as if he said, "Do not think that anything other than total destruction awaits you, so that hardly **one man** will be found for **seven women.**"

Regarding the phrase **take hold of,** it is, no doubt, inconsistent with modesty for a woman to offer herself to a man. But the prophet says that not only will they do this, but **seven women** will, as it were, lay hands on a man and keep hold of him since there are so few men.

The extent of the calamity is further expressed by the next sentence: **"We will eat our own food and provide our own clothes."** A husband has a duty to support his wife and family; so there must indeed be very few men around if women will lower themselves to agree that a husband does not have to provide for her.

"Only let us be called by your name." When a woman marries, she becomes part of her husband's family and takes his name.

"Take away our disgrace!" This is said because women are sometimes treated with disdain when they are unable to obtain a husband. Also, among ancient people offspring were thought to be an important blessing.

2. In that day the Branch of the LORD will be beautiful and glorious. The announcement of a dreadful calamity might have upset the godly and led them to doubt the firmness of God's covenant. There is a great deal of difference between saying, "I will make the descendants of David my servant ... as measureless as the sand on the seashore" (Jeremiah 33:22) and saying they would be destroyed in some dreadful massacre. As Isaiah spoke about the restoration of the church in chapter 2, so he now promises that a new church will arise, just as a bud or shoot springs up in an uncultivated field.

This passage is usually expounded as referring to Christ. This supported by Zechariah's words, "Here is a man whose name is the Branch" (Zechariah 6:12). **The fruit of the land** is taken by some to refer to Christ's human nature, and **the Branch** to his divinity. After careful examination of this, I do not hesitate to regard **the Branch of the LORD** and **the fruit of the land** as denoting an unusual and abundant supply of grace that will relieve the hungry.

And the fruit of the land will be the pride and glory of the survivors in Israel. It might have been deemed cold comfort if the prophet had only said that few would be saved. But he speaks about **the pride and glory of the survivors in Israel,** leading the believers to hope that this judgment will not overwhelm them. The excellence of the church does not stem from its great numbers, but from the purity that God bestows on it and from the glorious ministry of the Spirit of God among his elect.

3. Those who are left in Zion, who remain in Jerusalem, will be called holy. Isaiah repeats the idea that when the pollution of the people has been washed away, what remains is pure and **holy.**

All who are recorded among the living in Jerusalem. Those who have their names written in the book of life are God's elect. The profane multitude, who only have their name written on earth, will be cut off. See Ezekiel 32:32; 13:19; cf. Luke 10:20.

4. The Lord will wash away the filth of the women of Zion; he will cleanse the bloodstains from Jerusalem by a spirit of judgment and a spirit of fire. The prophet refutes the idea that the church will be diminished by the calamities that fall on her. For he states that God **will wash away the filth** and remove the corruptions in his church. I think that **the bloodstains from Jerusalem** do not just refer to murders and other atrocious crimes but to defilements and stains of every description.

By a spirit of judgment and a spirit of fire. Here **judgment** stands for uprightness. It refers to those who had deeply fallen but who are now restored to their previous condition. He then mentions **a spirit of fire,** by which the **filth** must be burned and consumed. There are two things to be noted by this expression. First, the purification of the church is accomplished by the Spirit; and, second, the effects that this produces sometimes cause the Spirit to be called **a spirit of judgment** and sometimes **a spirit of fire.** Whenever expressions of this sort occur in Scripture—"The Lord will do these things by the Spirit of truth, of power, or righteousness"—we may change the expression thus: "by the truth, by the power, by the righteousness of the Spirit." The word **judgment** explains what is of greatest importance in the restoration of the church—that is, when those things that were confused or decayed are restored to good order. **Fire** points to the method by which the Lord restores the church to her purity.

5. Then the LORD will create over all of Mount Zion . . . In other words, "There will be no corner of Mount Zion on which the grace of God does not shine."

And over those who assemble there a cloud of smoke by day and a glow of flaming fire by night. When he wants to speak of a full blessing, Isaiah alludes to what Moses related when the Lord delivered the people from Egyptian slavery and sent pillars of cloud by day and pillars of fire by night (see Exodus 13:21). What this amounts to is: When God brings back the church from its Babylonian captivity, the deliverance will be no less striking and magnificent than when the nation went out of Egypt. This does not mean that during their journey from Babylon to Judea they would be accompanied, as in the wilderness, by **cloud** and **fire**; but God would display his grace and kindness by other methods that are no less remarkable.

Over all the glory will be a canopy. In other words, "Everyone will bear the evidence and marks of their deliverance." We are reminded that we will share in God's grace only by bearing his image and through his glory shining in us.

6. It will be a shelter and shade from the heat of the day, and a refuge and hiding place from the storm and rain. The prophet underlines what we have already noticed: God will be our constant guide until he brings us to the end of our journey. Yet we are reminded that believers will always be exposed to numerous calamities. The great consolation is that the Lord will be our **shelter and shade** in the most terrible calamities. See Psalm 121:6-7.

Isaiah
Chapter 5

1. I will sing for the one I love a song about his vineyard. In the previous chapter Isaiah's aim was to describe the condition of the people of Israel, so that everyone might see their faults and thus be led to shame and to sincere repentance. In this present chapter he, as it were, holds up a mirror so the people can see their miserable condition. If it had not been for this, they would have flattered themselves too much in their sins and would not have patiently listened to any instructions. A striking and lively picture of their wickedness had to be presented. To lend this added weight, Isaiah uses this preface. Great and memorable events were usually described in verse, so that they could be repeated by everyone, and so they would be remembered forever (see Exodus 15:1 and Deuteronomy 31:30—32:1). Isaiah composed this song so that he might make the wickedness of the people crystal-clear to them.

There is no doubt that by **the one I love** he means God. It is as if he said, "I am going to compose a poem on behalf of God, so that he may earnestly reason with the people about their ingratitude." Saying that God was speaking (verse 3 on) gave additional force to his meaning. Some may ask, Why does Isaiah call God his friend? The answer is given by John, when he says that the church is made up of the friends of the bridegroom (see John 3:29). Prophets belonged to that group of people. From this we learn that not only Paul but all the prophets and teachers who served God were jealous for God's bride (see 2 Corinthians 11:2). All God's servants should be greatly moved by this, for what does a man think is more valuable than his wife? The one to whom anyone will entrust his dearly loved wife must be thought to be faithful.

My loved one had a vineyard. The metaphor of a vineyard is often used by the prophets, and it would be impossible to find a more appropriate comparison. "I had planted you like a choice vine of sound and reliable stock. How then did you turn against me into a corrupt, wild vine?"

(Jeremiah 2:21). This shows in two ways how highly the Lord values his church, for no possession is dearer to a man than a vineyard, and nothing demands so much constant work. Not only, therefore, is the Lord declaring that we are his beloved inheritance—he is also pointing out how much care he lavishes on us.

On a fertile hillside. Isaiah begins by saying that God had placed his people in a favorable situation, like a person who plants a vine on a pleasant and fertile hill. The word **hillside** is said by some to refer to the site of Jerusalem, but I think this is a forced reading. It rather belongs to the construction of the prophet's allegory. God was pleased to take this people under his care and protection, just as a vineyard is carefully planted on **a fertile hillside**. It is better to plant vines on hills and high places than low down in the plains. As the poet Virgil said, "The vine loves the open hills; the yews prefer the north wind and the cold."

2. He dug it up and cleared it of stones and planted it with the choicest vines. He built a watchtower in it and cut out a winepress as well. Then he looked for a crop of good grapes, but it yielded only bad fruit. Isaiah complains that the nation that had enjoyed such privileges now undervalues God's kindness. For instead of yielding **a crop of good grapes . . . it** yielded only bad fruit.

3. "Now you dwellers in Jerusalem and men of Judah, judge between me and my vineyard." God through Isaiah now makes these people the judges of their own cause, as is often done when the accused party has no way to escape the accusation.

4. "What more could have been done for my vineyard than I have done for it?" First the Lord inquires what could have been expected from the best farmer or steward that he had not done for his vineyard. From this he concludes that they had no excuse for withholding from him the fruit of his labor.

"When I looked for good grapes, why did it yield only bad?" In other words, "Since I carried out every part of my duty and did more than anyone could have expected in tending my vineyard, why does it yield me such a poor return? Instead of the fruit I expected, it yields what is absolutely bitter."

5. "Now I will tell you what I am going to do to my vineyard: I will take away its hedge, and it will be destroyed; I will break down its wall, and it will be trampled." Having condemned the Jews, as it were, by their own words, God now says he will take vengeance for their contempt of his grace, so that they will not escape being punished.

6. "I will make it a wasteland, neither pruned nor cultivated, and briers and thorns will grow there. I will command the clouds not to rain on it." God constantly bestows on us innumerable benefits; so we should be earnestly on our guard lest, by withdrawing first one and then another, he punishes us for despising them.

7. The vineyard of the LORD Almighty is the house of Israel, and the men of Judah are the garden of his delight. So far the prophet has been speaking figuratively; now he reveals the purpose of his song. Previously he warned the Jews about judgment; now he shows that they are not only guilty but have been convicted. Their ingratitude was plain for all to see. Isaiah does not explain every part of the metaphor. It was enough to point out its main idea. The whole nation was **the vineyard**; the individual people were the plants.

And he looked for justice, but saw bloodshed; for righteousness, but heard cries of distress. He begins without metaphor to show how wickedly the Jews had degenerated. Every kind of injustice and violence abounded among them. It was right to accuse them of despising God on the grounds of acting cruelly toward human beings, for where cruelty reigns, religion is extinguished.

8. Woe to you who add house to house and join field to field till no space is left and you live alone in the land. He now reproves their insatiable avarice and covetousness, from which cheating, injustice, and violence arise. It is not wrong in itself to **add house to house and join field to field**; but it is wrong when this is done with a greedy heart. Thus the prophet describes those who never have enough and whom no wealth can satisfy. Covetous people are so keen to possess everything themselves that they think everything other people possess is something they desire. Hence Chrysostom made this observation: "Covetous people, if they could, would willingly take the sun from the poor."

9. The LORD Almighty has declared in my hearing: "Surely the great houses will become desolate, the fine mansions left without occupants." God through his prophet warns them that vengeance is close at hand. **"Surely the great houses will become desolate."** This is a just punishment, through which the Lord punishes covetous people. In the same way the Roman satirical poet Juvenal ridicules the insatiable ambition of Alexander the Great. That leader learned from the philosophy of Anacharsis that there were many planets, and he sighed to think that he had worn himself out with many toils and yet had still not made himself master of even one world. "One globe does not satisfy the Macedonian youth. He writhes in misery on account of the narrow limits of the world, as if he were confined to the rocks of Gyaros, or to the puny Seriphos. But when he enters the city framed by potters, he will be content with a tomb. Death alone acknowledges how small are the dimensions of the bodies of men" (*Satire X*, 168-173).

Similar instances occur every day, but we do not notice them. The Lord shows us, as in a mirror, the absurd vanity of men who spend a vast amount of money in building palaces that later become the homes of owls and bats. But nothing will persuade man to lay aside his covetousness (see Amos 5:11; 6:11).

10. "A ten-acre vineyard will produce only a bath of wine, a homer of seed only an ephah of grain." He predicts that the same thing will happen to their fields and vineyards. Covetous people will not obtain the returns they want, because their greed is insatiable. The fields are so barren that they scarcely yield one tenth of the seed planted in them.

11. Woe to those who rise early in the morning to run after their drinks, who stay up late at night till they are inflamed with wine. The prophet does not intend to enumerate all of the prevailing vices but only points out the ones they were especially addicted to. Having reproved covetousness, he now attacks drunkenness, which undoubtedly was also a prevailing vice.

To **rise early** means to be earnestly employed in doing anything (see Ecclesiastes 10:16). **Who stay up late at night** means that from dawn to dusk they engage in drunken carousing and never tire of drinking. Abundance and luxury are closely linked, for when people enjoy abundance, they abuse it by intemperance.

12. They have harps and lyres at their banquets, tambourines and flutes and wine. He mentions the instruments of pleasure by which people addicted to intemperance feed their appetites. Isaiah is not speaking against music, but he describes a nation wallowing in every kind of luxury and too much disposed to indulge in pleasures. This is clear from what follows.

But they have no regard for the deeds of the LORD, no respect for the work of his hands. In other words, "They are as constant in luxurious indulgence, and as devoted to it, as if this had been why they had been born. They do not consider why the Lord supplies them with everything they need." People were not born to eat and drink and wallow in luxury, but to obey God, to worship him devoutly, to acknowledge his goodness, and to endeavor to do what is pleasing in his sight.

13. Therefore my people will go into exile for lack of understanding. The people perished because they despised instruction. He calls them **my people,** the nation that enjoyed the exceptional privilege of being singled out from other peoples so they could rely on God's guidance and live by his rule of life. (See Deuteronomy 4:6-7.)

Their men of rank will die of hunger and their masses will be parched with thirst. He now adds another punishment; namely, they will suffer severe famine. This will not be confined to ordinary people but will afflict **men of rank,** on whom God's vengeance will come. We conclude from this that the source of all our calamities is that we do not allow ourselves to be taught by God's Word.

14. Therefore the grave enlarges its appetite and opens its mouth without limit; into it will descend their nobles and masses with all their brawlers and revelers. In this verse the prophet heightens the alarm of people who were at their ease and not yet sufficiently affected by the warnings they had been given. The prophet warns them that something even more terrible will happen to them—they will be swallowed up by death. In other words, "Death will carry you away, and all that you possess also—your delicacies, wealth, pleasures, and everything else you put confidence in."

15. Both low and high will be humbled, and the eyes of the arrogant brought low. This verse summarizes the prophet's teaching, pointing out that their punishments will result in their being brought low, and the Lord alone exalted (see 2:11, 17). Adversity is so distasteful to us that we see nothing good in it. When God speaks about punishments, we detest and abhor them because we do not perceive his justice. But the prophets remind us that as long as people carry on in their sins, God's justice is in some degree denied or unseen. In other words, "Do you imagine that when God has endured you so long, you will in the end be able to tread him under your feet? He is certain to arise, and he will be exalted in your destruction."

16. But the LORD Almighty will be exalted by his justice. In other words, "The God of hosts, whom ungodly people insolently tread under their feet, will be raised on high when he reveals himself as the judge of the world." In this way he ridicules the foolish confidence of the ungodly.

And the holy God will show himself holy by his righteousness. The language now becomes more vehement, so that wicked people may not make wrong assumptions and assure themselves of uninterrupted happiness that they cannot have if they set aside God's holiness. But since God is **holy** by nature, he must **show himself holy by his righteousness.**

17. Then sheep will graze as in their own pasture; lambs will feed among the ruins of the rich. The prophet wishes to bring comfort to the godly, who trembled at hearing the dreadful judgments of God. The more a person is under the influence of religion, the more he feels the hand of God's presence, and the more he is aware of God's judgment. In short, fear and reverence for God cause us to be deeply moved by everything that is presented to us in his name. "Therefore," says Isaiah in effect, "although it may seem that God is about to destroy the whole nation, he will show himself to be a faithful shepherd to his **lambs** and will **feed** them in the normal way."

But the prophet also wants to repress the haughtiness of the rulers, who oppressed the poor and godly and yet boasted that they were the church of God. He reminds them, therefore, that it is an idle boast for them to assume they are part of God's flock. They are goats, not **lambs.** The **lambs** will never be happy until they are separated from the goats.

18. Woe to those who draw sin along with cords of deceit, and wickedness as with cart ropes. The prophet inserted a short consolation to allay the fears of the godly. Now he returns to his warnings. By **cords** he means the temptations by which men allow themselves to be deceived and harden their hearts against God. When anyone is tempted to sin, his conscience secretly asks him, "What are you doing?" Sin never makes so much progress as when no checks are put on it; God gave people consciences for their own good. But these people obstinately bind themselves to sin, and so they are without any excuse.

19. . . . to those who say, "Let God hurry, let him hasten his work so we may see it. Let it approach, let the plan of the Holy One of Israel come, so we may know it." He now specifies one class of sins. Nothing can be worse than when people not only lay aside all thought of divine judgment but despise everything that is said about it. This is denoted by words that are full of contempt and wicked confidence: **"Let God hurry, let him hasten his work."**

Work here stands for judgment, for God appears to be doing nothing when he does not punish the sins of the ungodly. But when he rises up to execute judgment and inflict punishment, then his **work** is seen.

The ungodly think that God does nothing and does not care about the affairs of men. They imagine there is some God, but they do not acknowledge his judgment at all. In the meantime they resolve to be of good cheer. The ungodly say to themselves, "Let these prophets and ministers cry out and bawl and hold out terrors and warnings. We will wait without any concern about what they tell us, and in the meantime we will enjoy ourselves." Here the prophet shows how the ungodly ridicule and show contempt for God's Word. Peter depicts the ungodly as saying, "Where is this 'coming' he promised? Ever since our fathers died, everything goes on as it has since the beginning of creation" (2 Peter 3:4).

20. Woe to those who call evil good and good evil. He now particularly reproves the insolence of those who endeavor to overthrow all distinctions between **good** and **evil**. They conceal, excuse, and disguise wicked actions, as if they could change the nature of everything through their sophistry; but they deface good actions by their false accusations. Such people, the prophet tells us, are those **who put darkness for light and light for darkness, who put bitter for sweet and sweet for bitter.** By this he means that their folly is monstrous, for it would tend to confound and destroy all the principles of nature.

21. Woe to those who are wise in their own eyes and clever in their own sight. He pronounces a curse on obstinate scorners who oppose God's instructions and warnings. Nothing is more destructive than a deceitful show of wisdom. Piety starts with a willingness to be taught, renouncing our own judgment and then following wherever God calls. We must become fools according to worldly wisdom if we desire to be God's disciples. **In their own eyes** means "in their own conceit."

22. Woe to those who are heroes at drinking wine and champions at mixing drinks. By calling them **heroes** and **champions** he is deliberately accusing them of wasting their strength in bacchanalian rivalries. It is disgraceful to see a healthy man display his strength through drinking.

23. . . . who acquit the guilty for a bribe, but deny justice to the innocent. He censures their corrupt judgment seats. He points out why there is no room for justice in these places—namely, they are under the influence of bribes. See Exodus 23:8 and Deuteronomy 16:19.

24. Therefore, as tongues of fire lick up straw and as dry grass sinks down in the flames, so their roots will decay and their flowers blow away like dust. The prophet again shows what dreadful punishment awaits the nation and warns that the stubborn will be completely destroyed because they will not allow themselves to be brought back onto the right path.

For they have rejected the law of the LORD Almighty. He accuses them of showing contempt for God's law. He accuses them of open rebellion, as if he said that because it was not only in a few instances that they were rebellious, they could be regarded as treacherous apostates who had totally forsaken God.

And spurned the word of the Holy One of Israel. He complains that they not only despised the Word of God but—what is far more shocking—turned away from it or threw it away in wicked disdain. If contempt for the law of God is the source and sum of all that is evil, there is nothing against which we ought more carefully to guard than that Satan should take away our reverence for it.

25. Therefore the LORD's anger burns against his people; his hand is raised and he strikes them down. The great majority of people, as soon as they have escaped any calamity, forget their punishments and no longer regard them as God's judgments. Isaiah sharply rebukes this insensitivity. It is as if he said, "Have you so quickly forgotten the calamities under which you recently groaned? Where did this distressful casting out of dead bodies come from, except that God had raised his arm against you? And if God has discharged the office of a judge, why do not those recent punishments induce you to fear him and make you refrain from drawing down a succession of chastisements by new sins?"

The mountains shake. By this comparison the dreadful nature of those punishments of which they were insensible is described in such a way that the stupidity of the people is seen more clearly.

And the dead bodies are like refuse in the streets. Yet for all this, his anger is not turned away, his hand is still upraised. Isaiah refers back to what he had previously said. He tells them that God's **hand** is not yet drawn back and that it may yet pursue them and inflict plagues of the same kind, or ones of even greater severity. We should diligently meditate on these statements in order to shake off that drowsiness to which most men are frequently liable, even after they have been punished.

26. He lifts up a banner for the distant nations. In this verse and in the following ones, he describes the nature of the punishment that the Lord would inflict on his people. They were about to suffer from the Assyrians a similar or even a heavier calamity than that which their brethren the Israelites had recently endured. Many distresses had indeed been suffered by themselves from the Assyrians, though the kingdom of Judah was not yet overturned. Besides, what had overtaken the kingdom of Israel might be viewed as a mirror in which they could behold God's wrath and righteous punishment.

He whistles for those at the ends of the earth. This means that when God wishes to assemble various nations and weld them into one fighting force, it will not be a confused collection of people but will resemble a body that has a visible head that rules and guides. He uses the word **whistles** rather than a stronger word such as "sound a trumpet" or anything like that to show that God does not need to sound a trumpet in order to call the enemies to battle, and that he has no difficulty in inflicting punishment when the time for taking vengeance is fully at hand, for by a mere nod he can accomplish everything.

The metaphor **he whistles** is taken from beekeeping. Beekeepers draw the bees out of their hives into the fields and lead them back again by a whistle. "In that day the LORD will whistle for flies from the distant streams of Egypt and for bees from the land of Assyria" (Isaiah 7:18).

Here they come, swiftly and speedily! This confirms what I observed above: We ought not to judge the Lord's anger by present appearances. Although everything appears to give assurances of peace, war will suddenly break out from the most unlikely quarter.

We ought to observe here that wars are not started accidentally or through human plans but by God's command, as if he assembled the soldiers by the sound of a trumpet. So whether we are afflicted by battle or by famine or by pestilence, let us know that all this comes from the hand of God, for all things obey him and follow his direction.

27. Not one of them grows tired or stumbles, not one slumbers or sleeps; not a belt is loosened at the waist, not a sandal thong is broken. Everything will be prepared and arranged in such a way that there will be no delay or obstruction on their march. They will not even slumber. There is an example of this expression in the Psalms: "He who watches over Israel will neither slumber nor sleep" (121:4). This Hebrew phrase has no equivalent in either Greek or Latin.

28. Their arrows are sharp, all their bows are strung. He means they will be provided with all the necessary weapons. In this example he includes all the weapons of war.

Their horses' hoofs seem like flint, their chariot wheels like a whirlwind. By this he means that they will not be molested on their journey and that they will arrive in Judea without being tired out. Similarly, he compares **their chariot wheels** to **a whirlwind.** The ancients used chariots for war, and so he mentions not only **horses** but **wheels.** He is saying that no length of journey would prevent the Lord from carrying the enemies forward without delay, for the destruction of the Jews.

29. Their roar is like that of the lion, they roar like young lions; they growl as they seize their prey and carry it off with no one to rescue. This denotes fierceness and cruelty. He compares the Chaldeans to **lions,** which we know are savage by nature. This is like saying they would not be moved by any feeling of compassion or tenderness, but rather they would be savage beasts.

30. In that day they will roar over it like the roaring of the sea. And if one looks at the land, he will see darkness and distress; even the light will be darkened by the clouds. The prophet adds this so that the Jews might understand that the Chaldeans' fierce attack is not accidental; they have been appointed by God and are guided by his hand. **The roaring of the sea** means the attack will be so violent that it will be like a flood in which the whole of Judea will suffer ruin. "The Jews," he says in effect, "will do what is usually done at a time of perplexity. They will cast their eyes up and down to discover a way of escape. But wherever they look, whether to heaven or to earth, they will find no relief; on every side calamity will overwhelm them." We may sometimes escape the hand of men, but how can we escape the hand of God?

Isaiah
Chapter 6

1. In the year that King Uzziah died. This is usually the beginning of the sixth chapter, but some think that it is the beginning of the book itself, and that when the prophecies of Isaiah were collected together an error was made. The reasons they give for this are: The prophet here declines the office of a teacher, which he would not have refused if he had already discharged it; he appears to be a mere novice as yet unacquainted with his calling; and he declares that he has now seen the Lord and that he has not seen him before.

But such arguments I consider to be too feeble and unsatisfactory. I reply that it should not be thought strange that he was so completely overwhelmed by this extraordinary vision that he forgot he was a prophet. There was no feeling in him that was not overpowered by God's presence. Like one who had lost his senses, he willingly plunged himself into darkness; or rather, like one who despaired of life, he of his own accord chose to die. Godly people are brought low and utterly confounded when the Lord manifests his presence. And in the person of his servant, God intended to strike his rebellious people with alarm. Therefore, we need not be surprised if Isaiah offers an apology for himself under the overwhelming influence of fear and because he had not felt the weight of his office as he now felt it, having seen an illustrious display of God's majesty.

So I think Isaiah uttered the former predictions during the reign of Uzziah, even after that king had been struck with leprosy. When he died and Jotham succeeded him, this vision was presented to Isaiah. We know what upset is caused by a change of kings; so we need not be surprised that Isaiah had his calling sealed again. But the prophecy that follows will show clearly enough that he had been a public teacher for some time before he **saw** the Lord. For it relates to the blinding of the people, whose obstinacy he had experienced to such an extent that he might have been induced to cease from his undertaking, seeing that he was doing no good. The Lord, therefore, confirms him by this vision, so that the opposition would not prevent him from discharging his office boldly and performing what he undertook at God's command.

I saw the Lord seated on a throne, high and exalted, and the train of his robe filled the temple. People ask how Isaiah could see God, who is spirit (see John 4:24) and therefore cannot be seen with physical eyes. But we should be aware that when God showed himself to the fathers, he never appeared as he actually is, but in such a way that human understanding could receive it. Isaiah, therefore, was shown such a form as enabled him to perceive God's inconceivable majesty, according to his capacity. Thus he attributes to God a **throne,** a **robe,** and a bodily appearance.

From this we learn a useful doctrine. Whenever God grants any token of his presence, he is unquestionably present with us, for he does not entertain us by meaningless shapes. Since, therefore, it was no deceitful representation of God's presence, Isaiah rightly declares that he **saw the Lord.** Similarly, when Scripture says John saw the Holy Spirit in the shape of a dove (John 1:32), the name of the Holy Spirit is applied to the outward sign, because in the representation there was no deception. He did not see the essence of the Spirit but had a clear and undoubted proof, so that he had no doubt that the Spirit of God rested on Christ.

Second, it may be asked who this **Lord** was. John tells us that it was Christ (John 12:41), and rightly so, for God only ever revealed himself to the fathers in his eternal Word and in his only begotten Son. In this passage God is also mentioned, and it is correct to say that Isaiah saw the glory of Christ, for "he is the image of the invisible God" (see Colossians 1:15).

He could not have given a better description of God, in regard to place, than in the person of a judge **seated on a throne,** that his majesty might strike terror into the Jews. We will see later the dreadful judgment that the Lord pronounced from his judgment seat, but in case we should suppose that the prophet contrived the way in which he would portray God, we ought to know that he faithfully describes the actual form in which God was represented and shown to him.

Almost all commentators understand **the train** to mean the fringes of **his robe.** He means that God looked venerable and far beyond any human form. There is great weight in the detail that he appeared in **the temple,** for he had promised he would meet his people there, and the people expected answers from that place, as Solomon had expressly stated at its dedication (see 1 Kings 8:30). Therefore, in order that the people might understand that these things came from God, on whom they called every day, and on whom they relied with a vain confidence that puffed them up, this vision was shown to the prophet in **the temple.** It was also not uncommon for the prophets to say that the Lord spoke to them from his temple or from his sanctuary.

2. Above him were seraphs. Having declared that God appeared to him full of majesty and glory, he adds that God was accompanied by angels, whom the prophet calls **seraphs**. This description holds out to us, as in sunlight, the brightness of God's infinite majesty, that we may learn from it to behold and adore his wonderful and overwhelming glory.

Each with six wings. This representation is instructive. Those wings arranged in this way contained some mystery that it was the Lord's will not to remain wholly unknown.

With two wings they covered their faces, with two they covered their feet, and with two they were flying. The **two wings** with which the angels **were flying** mean nothing other than their ready and cheerful performance of God's commands. The **two wings** with which **they covered their faces** clearly show that even angels cannot endure God's brightness, and that they are dazzled by it in the same way as we are when we attempt to gaze on the radiance of the sun. If angels are overwhelmed by God's majesty, how rash people are if they intrude into such heights! Let us, therefore, learn that our inquiries about God ought never to go beyond what is proper and lawful, that our knowledge may soberly and modestly taste what is otherwise far above our capacity.

3. And they were calling to one another. It was necessary that all these things should be presented to the prophet in a vision, in order to produce a stronger impression on the people and on Isaiah himself. The vision was just as necessary for him as for the whole nation because painful struggles awaited him, and he could not have announced those events boldly if he had not previously been strengthened.

When we are told that the angels were employed in uttering the glory of God, let us realize that we are to imitate this. The most holy service we can give to God is to be employed in praising his name.

"Holy, holy, holy is the LORD Almighty." The ancients quoted this passage when they wanted to prove there are three persons in the one essence of the Godhead. I do not disagree with their opinion, but if I had to argue with heretics I would choose stronger evidence. The repetition of **Holy, holy, holy** points to unwearied perseverance, as if the prophet said that the angels never cease from singing the praises of God since God's holiness supplies inexhaustible reasons for them.

"The whole earth is full of his glory." Isaiah shows that God's praises are not to be confined to narrow limits, for they are to fill **the whole earth**. This ties in with the following prophecy about the blinding of the Jews (verse 10), which opened the way for the Gentiles to enter the church of God. They occupied the place the Jews had abandoned and left empty.

4. At the sound of their voices the doorposts and thresholds shook. This noise indicated that it was not a human voice that the prophet had heard, for no mortal has a voice powerful enough to make **doorposts and thresholds** shake. The Lord did not intend merely to establish the authority of his voice over the prophet but to confirm it to posterity in all ages, that it might never be forgotten. Today may we tremble whenever he speaks.

And the temple was filled with smoke. This was the common and ordinary sign that the Lord used with his people in olden times. We read that whenever Moses entered the Tent of Meeting, smoke diffused through it so that the people could not see either Moses or the Tent of Meeting (Exodus 33:9). The **smoke,** therefore, that Isaiah describes was not an unusual occurrence. It was God's usual way of demonstrating that he would display his power in executing judgment on the people.

But one might ask why God manifested his presence by this sign rather than by any other. The question may be answered in two ways. First, it was always the will of God to repress people's insolence in pushing their inquiries about his majesty beyond what is proper. For on this point almost everyone is too rash and daring. They want to rise above the clouds and penetrate God's secrets, while they do not see what lies at their feet. God had good reason to use **smoke**—to remind people of their weakness. He forbids us to inquire or search beyond what he has revealed to us in his Word. As Augustine says, "That is a learned ignorance." So whenever **smoke** of this kind is mentioned, we know that it lays a restraint on us from indulging curiosity in our researches into God's purpose.

Second, this **smoke** ought to strike fear into us, as it did to David when he described an angry and terrible God as being surrounded by "clouds and thick darkness" (Psalm 97:2).

5. "Woe to me!" I cried. "I am ruined!" The prophet now relates how powerfully he was affected by the vision. He was so terrified by seeing God that he expected his own immediate destruction. He gives us the reason for thinking this: **"For I am a man of unclean lips."** He was so terrified that he resembled a dead man. There is no need for us to be surprised at this; the whole man, so far as his body is concerned, must be reduced to nothing, that it may be renewed according to God's wishes.

"And I live among a people of unclean lips." This is added by way of explanation; he includes himself as an individual along with the ordinary people. He was tainted with the pollution that extends to the whole body, and he forgets the purity he had received from God. We should learn from this universal teaching that everyone's **lips** are impure and **unclean** until the Lord cleanses them.

"And my eyes have seen the King, the LORD Almighty." Does the sight of God bring death to human beings? It seems strange that the sight of God, or our approach to him, should take away life, of which he is the source and giver. The answer is that this is an accidental result. It takes place because of us and not because of God's nature. Death is within us, but we do not perceive death unless it is compared with God's life. This is unquestionably what the prophet means, for he does not merely say that he is dead, but he gives us the reason—because he has **unclean lips.**

6. Then one of the seraphs flew to me. The prophet shows what kind of relief was brought to him when he was so terrified that he thought he was dead. The Lord had already cleansed him, but this additional cleansing is greater. We must not merely conclude that Isaiah's lips were impure because they are now cleansed; rather we should ask why it is done. It is because the Lord intended to enlarge and extend his favor toward him and to elevate him to a higher position, so that he might have greater influence over the people.

With a live coal in his hand, which he had taken with tongs from the altar. This **live coal** or fire was divine or heavenly. By this image Isaiah was taught that all purity flows from God alone.

7. With it he touched my mouth and said, "See, this has touched your lips; your guilt is taken away and your sin atoned for." We see how God alone condescends to meet human weakness. He puts the tongs in the hand of a seraph, so he can take a live coal from the altar and apply it to the prophet's mouth. This was, no doubt, done in a vision. But through the help of this outward sign God assisted the prophet's understanding. There is no reason to believe that the live coal possessed any virtue, for it is God alone who can cleanse our pollution, wherever it exists.

The confirmation brought by the sign was not without effect: The blessing that it signified was bestowed on Isaiah at the same time, so that he knew he had not been deceived. From this we may infer that in the sacraments the reality is given to us along with the sign. When the Lord holds out a sacrament, he does not feed our eyes with an empty and meaningless symbol but joins the truth with it, in order to testify that by means of it he acts on us efficaciously.

First of all, we ought to believe that the truth must never be separated from the signs, though it ought to be distinguished from them. We perceive and feel a sign, such as the bread that is put into our hands by the minister at the Lord's Supper. But because we ought to seek Christ in heaven, our thoughts ought to be carried there. By the hand of the minister he presents to us Christ's body, that it may be enjoyed by the godly, who rise by faith to have fellowship with him. He bestows it, therefore, on the godly, who raise their thoughts to him by faith; for he cannot deceive.

Unbelievers indeed receive the sign. But because they linger in the world and do not arrive at Christ's heavenly kingdom, they have no experience of the truth. Anyone who does not have faith cannot raise his thoughts to God and therefore cannot partake of Christ. Faith alone opens for us the gate of the kingdom of God. And, therefore, whoever wishes to eat the body of Christ must be carried by faith to heaven beyond human conception. In short, the Spirit of God alone can make us share in that fellowship. And yet it does not follow that people's unbelief detracts at all from the truth of the sacrament, since God always presents to us a spiritual matter. But wicked people treat it with scorn, just as the grace of God is offered by the Gospel, but all do not receive it, though they actually hear it and are compelled to yield assent to the truth.

Also, we learn from this passage that the sacraments are never separated from the Word. The angel does not here act the part of a mute but gives the signs and then immediately adds the teaching, to show what was intended by it. It would have been no sacrament if teaching had not been added, from which Isaiah could learn for what purpose the coal was applied to his mouth. Let us therefore learn that the main part of the sacraments consists in the Word, and that without it the sacraments are turned into stage plays. This shows that there is nothing to prevent Isaiah, who has been perfectly cleansed and is free from all pollution, from appearing as God's representative.

8. Then I heard the voice of the Lord. The prophet now starts to speak about the purpose of his vision. God appeared to him with such glorious majesty in order to ordain him anew as a prophet. It was because he was called to deliver an incredible message about the Jews being made blind. He also knew that God had cleansed him, and this prepared him for any task, no matter how difficult.

Saying, "Whom shall I send?" The prophet presents the Lord as if he were speaking and as if he could not find a man qualified for such a message.

"And who will go for us?" I incline to the opinion that this passage points to the three persons of the Godhead, just as we read elsewhere, "Let us make man in our image" (Genesis 1:26). God talks with himself in the plural. And here unquestionably he holds a consultation with his eternal Wisdom and his eternal Power—that is, with the Son and the Holy Spirit.

And I said, "Here am I. Send me!" So ready a reply shows how great is that cheerfulness that springs from faith, for he who only recently lay like a dead man now dreads no difficulty. From this we observe that we cannot undertake anything in the right way without the evidence of our calling. Otherwise we will pause and hesitate at every step.

When the prophet says, **"Here am I,"** he means he is ready to obey God's commands. This expression is often used in Scripture to denote obedience.

9. He said, "Go and tell this people: 'Be ever hearing, but never understanding; be ever seeing, but never perceiving.'" This shows still more clearly how necessary the vision was if Isaiah was not to fail in his ministry. It was a grievous stumbling block that he must endure such obstinacy and rebellion in God's people, and that not for a year or two, but for more than sixty years. For this reason he needed to be fortified, that he might be like a bronze wall against such stubbornness. In other words, "You will indeed teach without any good effect; but do not regret your teaching, for I enjoin it upon you. And do not refrain from teaching because it yields no advantage; only obey me and leave to my disposal all the consequences of your labors. I give you all this information, so that the event may not frighten you as something strange and unexpected." (See 2 Corinthians 2:15-16.)

10. **"Make the heart of this people calloused; make their ears dull and close their eyes. Otherwise they might see with their eyes, hear with their ears, understand with their hearts, and turn and be healed."** Here the previous statement is expanded. God forewarns Isaiah not only that his labor in teaching will be fruitless, but also that by his instruction he will blind the people. It will occasion greater dullness and stubbornness and will end in their destruction. He declares that the people, bereft of reason and understanding, will perish, and they will have no escape. At the same time the Lord affirms that the prophet's labors, although they bring death and ruin on the Jews, will be an acceptable sacrifice as far as he is concerned.

This is truly a remarkable declaration. Not only does Isaiah foretell what was later fulfilled under the reign of Christ, but his words contain a most useful doctrine, which will be of perpetual use in the church of God. All who want to work faithfully in the ministry of the Word will be laid under the necessity of meeting with the same result.

It is unquestionably harsh to say that God sends a prophet to **"Make the heart of this people calloused; make their ears dull and close their eyes."** It appears as if these things are inconsistent with God's nature and therefore contradict his Word. But we should not think it strange if God punishes people's wickedness by blinding them in the highest degree. The prophet shows that this blindness is caused by the people themselves. The whole blame of the evil is laid on the people for rejecting the amazing kindness of God.

11. **Then I said, "For how long, O Lord?"** Although the prophets are severe in announcing the wrath of God against men, they do not lay aside human feelings. It is therefore necessary for them to maintain a twofold character. They must proclaim God's judgment with great and unshaken courage, so that they would rather choose that the world should be destroyed and utterly ruined than that any part of God's glory should be taken away. And yet they are not devoid of feeling or unmoved by compassion for their brothers, whose destruction they are obliged to foretell. These two feelings, although they appear to be inconsistent, are in full harmony, as appears from the example of Jeremiah, who at first complains of the hard task assigned to him of proclaiming destruction to the people, but afterwards regains his courage and proceeds boldly to discharge the duties of his office. "'Ah, Sovereign LORD,' I said, 'I do not know how to speak; I am only a child.' . . . 'Get yourself ready! Stand up and say to them whatever I command you. Do not be terrified by them, or I will terrify you before them'" (Jeremiah 1:6, 17).

How did God answer Isaiah's question? **"Until the cities lie ruined and without inhabitant, until the houses are left deserted and the fields ruined and ravaged."** This is an additional aggravation. It is possible that countries might be laid waste, and yet that one city remain; even that cities might be stormed and laid desolate, and yet very many houses left standing. But here the slaughter, he tells us, will be so great that not only the cities but even the houses will be destroyed; the whole land will be reduced to frightful and lamentable desolation. However, even in the middle of the heaviest calamities some remnant is still left. Although Isaiah said this only once, we must understand that it is also spoken to us. This punishment has been pronounced against all who obstinately disobey God or who with a stiff neck struggle against his yoke. The more violent their opposition, the more resolutely will the Lord pursue them until they are utterly destroyed.

12. **"Until the LORD has sent everyone far away and the land is utterly forsaken."** These words contain nothing new but are merely an explanation of the previous verse and a description, in different words, of the ruin that will overtake Judea—namely, that God will send the inhabitants **far away.** God says that those who survive the war will not be exempt from punishment, for they will be carried off into captivity. And then he adds a general clause about the desolation of the land. In effect he says that it would be desolate and bereft of inhabitants because some would flee, others would be driven into exile, and others would be killed by the sword. Such is the reward prepared for obstinate and rebellious people, who add crime to crime until God's indignation rises to such a height that it cannot be appeased.

13. **"And though a tenth remains in the land, it will again be laid waste. But as the terebinth and oak leave stumps when they are cut down, so the holy seed will be the stump in the land."** This refers to a small number of godly people. By **holy seed** he means the elect, who would be preserved by the free mercy of God and thus would survive the captivity. That banishment might be thought of as a cleansing of the church, by which the Lord took away the ungodly. After they had been cut off, he collected a people, small in number but truly consecrated to himself.

Isaiah
Chapter 7

1. When Ahaz son of Jotham, son of Uzziah, was king of Judah, King Rezin of Aram and Pekah son of Remaliah king of Israel marched up to fight against Jerusalem, but they could not overpower it. Here is related a remarkable prophecy about the wonderful deliverance of Jerusalem when it appeared to have been utterly ruined. The prophet explains all the circumstances, so that by means of them the miracle may be more fully displayed.

That the prophet speaks of the second war that was fought by **Rezin** and **Pekah** may easily be inferred from the sacred history, for in the previous war Ahaz was vanquished, and a vast number of people were carried into captivity, who were later restored by the Israelites when the prophet, in the name of God, commanded that it should be done. Having collected an army again (see 2 Kings 16:5), the kings of Israel and Syria attacked Ahaz because they thought he had been worn out by the previous war and had no power to resist. The second war is mentioned to show how great the miracle was. Ahaz had no strength left to resist such great armies, the flower of the whole nation having been swept away in the previous war; and such people as remained were quite disheartened and had not yet recovered from the terror arising out of their recent defeat. God's goodness and power are therefore displayed even more clearly as he had pity on such a great distress and helped his people and rescued them from the jaws of death when everyone thought their condition was hopeless.

2. Now the house of David was told, "Aram has allied itself with Ephraim"; so the hearts of Ahaz and his people were shaken, as the trees of the forest are shaken by the wind. The **house of David** means the king's palace and court. The prophet is saying that Ahaz and his counselors had been told of the conspiracy against Judea.

From the king's palace terror spread to the whole nation. When they heard of the alarm of the king and the princes, the body of the people were bound to become frightened in the same way. As soon as the news was received, all were struck with such fear that no one could control himself. He expresses their trembling by an appropriate metaphor, often used by us today when we say someone "trembles like a leaf." They would therefore have been utterly ruined if the Lord had not intervened.

We learn from this that if we have any spark of faith, we ought not to distrust God when we are in danger. There is always a difference between the fear of the godly and of the ungodly. The ungodly find no way to calm their minds. The godly immediately turn to God, in whom they know they have a safe harbor. So even though they are harassed, they stay calm.

3. Then the LORD said to Isaiah, "Go out, you and your son Shear-Jashub, to meet Ahaz at the end of the aqueduct of the Upper Pool, on the road to the Washerman's Field." We see how God, remembering his covenant, anticipates this wicked king by sending the prophet to meet him. He does not wait for his prayers but of his own accord promises that he will grant deliverance. The place is named in order to give authenticity to the story.

4. "Say to him, 'Be careful, keep calm and don't be afraid. Do not lose heart because of these two smoldering stubs of firewood—because of the fierce anger of Rezin and Aram and of the son of Remaliah.'"
This means that Ahaz should be composed and should not be agitated, for people become unsteady when they are frightened. He tells them not to be **afraid,** for faith, which places our salvation in the hand of God, is the opposite of fear. In other words, "Do not allow yourselves to be discouraged. If you are assailed by fierce and severe attacks, maintain unshaken resolution, that you may not be overpowered by dangers. If you live for God, you will be able to overcome all your distresses."

For the same reason he adds, **"Do not lose heart."** To **lose heart** means "to melt away." The apostle later had good reason to exhort us to strengthen our hearts by faith (see Hebrews 11:27; 13:9). From this we infer that the prophet meant nothing except that Ahaz should undauntingly await the fulfillment of what the Lord had promised him.

Because of these two smoldering stubs of firewood. Isaiah employs a neat metaphor to reduce the fear the Jews had about those two very powerful kings who had filled their minds with terror. Their rage and cruelty seemed like a devouring fire that was enough to consume the whole of Judea and could not be quenched. Isaiah, on the other hand, does not call them "firebrands" (for that might have been thought to be something great) but only **two smoldering stubs of firewood.** This metaphor is full of consolation, for it tells us to form a very different opinion of the violence of the ungodly from what it appears to be. One would think they are endued with such great power that they could burn and destroy the whole world. To reduce their terror, the Lord declares that what we thought was burning, a perpetual burning, is only a little smoke that will not last long.

5. "'Aram, Ephraim and Remaliah's son have plotted your ruin, saying. . . .'" Although God foretold that their threats were empty, he does not try to conceal that their devices are cruel and hurtful if they are not restrained by him. By **have plotted** he means destructive counsel, for these two kings had formed an alliance to destroy Judea. To express this more forcibly, and to place it, as it were, before their eyes, he relates their actual words.

6. "'"Let us invade Judah; let us tear it apart and divide it among ourselves, and make the son of Tabeel king over it."'" These kings hoped that as soon as they came into Judea, they would immediately terrify the whole nation by the extent and power of their army, and so the people would have no ability or inclination to resist. When they brought together such an enormous army, it is unlikely that they would rely on a long siege (for Jerusalem was strongly fortified); they would have expected the inhabitants of Jerusalem to be terrified and alarmed at the size of their forces and to make an immediate surrender.

Who **Tabeel** was cannot easily be ascertained from history. Probably he was some Israelite, an enemy of the house of David, whom those kings wanted to set up as one of their own dependents.

7. "'Yet this is what the Sovereign LORD says: It will not take place, it will not happen.'" What he had already stated was intended to show more fully how great and unusual the deliverance was. When the Lord intends to help us in our trials, he shows the greatness of the danger, that we may not think he promises less than is necessary. He does not usually give a mitigated view of the evils that press upon us but rather holds out their full extent and afterwards makes a promise and shows that he is able to deliver us, though we may appear to be ruined. Such was the method adopted by the prophet, for he might have told them in plain terms what would happen and might have encouraged the king and the nation not to be terrified or discouraged at the sight of those armies. But he opened up the scheme and design of those kings and then contrasts with them the promise and decree of God, that his wonderful assistance may be displayed more strikingly.

This is the sacred anchor that alone upholds us amidst the storms of temptation; in adversity we will never be able to stand if God takes his Word away from us. So although the king was almost overwhelmed with despair, Isaiah shows that there is nothing so dreadful that it may not be despised, provided that one fortifies himself by God's promise and patiently looks for that which is not yet seen and that even appears to be incredible. This expression deserves notice, the bare Word of God was contrasted with the vast army and scheme of the kings.

8. "'For the head of Aram is Damascus, and the head of Damascus is only Rezin.'" In other words, "Those two kings have their limits. They aspire to your kingdom; but I have set bounds on them that they cannot go beyond." Damascus was the capital of Syria. He is saying, then, that those kings ought to be satisfied with their possessions and that their future condition would be the same as it then was.

"'Within sixty-five years Ephraim will be too shattered to be a people.'" Having said that it is now useless to attempt to extend their boundaries, he foretells the calamity of the kingdom of Israel; for by the word **shattered** he means that the kingdom of Israel will be annihilated, so that it will no longer exist. The Israelites were carried into captivity and incorporated with another nation. The Israelites were led into captivity in the sixth year of King Hezekiah, and Ahaz reigned not more than sixteen years; therefore it is certain that this calculation of **sixty-five years** ought not to be made from the day on which Isaiah was sent to deliver this message, for it was only twenty years later that the ten tribes were carried into captivity.

9. "'The head of Ephraim is Samaria, and the head of Samaria is only Remaliah's son.'" This is a repetition by which he confirms what he has already said: God had set bounds to the kingdom of Israel for an appointed time. The meaning therefore is, "In the meantime, until the sixty-five years are up, Israel enjoys a kind of truce. His head will be Samaria. Let him be satisfied with his boundaries and not aim at anything beyond them, for he will remain in this condition until he is utterly destroyed and is no longer reckoned to be a people."

"'If you do not stand firm in your faith, you will not stand at all.'" In other words, "This is the only support on which you can rely. Wait calmly for what the Lord has promised—deliverance. If you do not wait for it, what is left for you but destruction?" From this we should draw a universal doctrine: When we have departed from the Word of God, although we may think we are firmly established, in reality ruin is at hand. Our salvation is bound up with the Word of God. Either we must believe the promises of God, or it is in vain for us to expect salvation.

10. Again the LORD spoke to Ahaz. The Lord knew that King Ahaz was so wicked that he would not believe the promise; so he orders Isaiah to support him by adding a sign. We need to be careful to understand the use of signs—that is, the reason God performs miracles: It is to confirm us in our belief in his Word. When we see his power, if we have any hesitation about what he says to us, our doubt is removed by seeing the thing itself; miracles added to the Word are seals.

11. "Ask the LORD your God for a sign, whether in the deepest depths or in the highest heights." God allows Ahaz an unrestricted choice of a miracle—to demand either what belongs to earth or what belongs to heaven. But perhaps in the word **depths** there is something still more emphatic, as if he said, "It is up to you to choose. I will immediately show that my dominion is higher than this world, and that it likewise extends to all depths, so that at my pleasure I can raise the dead from their graves." Whatever may be our doubts, he not only pardons us, he even helps us in our doubts, not only by his Word, but by adding miracles; and he exhibits these not only to believers but also to the ungodly, as seen in the example of this king.

12. But Ahaz said, "I will not ask; I will not put the LORD to the test." With a plausible excuse he refuses the sign that the Lord offered to him. That excuse is, he alleges he is unwilling to tempt the Lord. If a person relies on God's Word alone and disregards everything else, it might be thought that he deserves the highest praise, for there can be no greater perfection than to yield full submission and obedience to God. But a question arises: Do we tempt God when we accept what he offers to us? Certainly not. Ahaz is therefore speaking falsely when he pretends that he is refusing the sign because he is unwilling to tempt God, for there can be nothing better than to obey God. Indeed it is the highest virtue to ask nothing beyond the Word of God. And yet if God chooses to add anything to his Word, we ought not to think it a virtue to reject that addition as superfluous. It is no small insult offered to God when his goodness is despised in such a way. While we do right to believe the Word of God, we should not despise the assistance he has chosen to add to strengthen our faith.

For instance, the Lord offers to us in the Gospel everything necessary for salvation, for when he brings us into a state of fellowship with Christ, the source of all blessings is truly contained in him. What then is the purpose of baptism and the Lord's Supper? Must they be regarded as superfluous? Not at all, for anyone who actually and without flattery acknowledges his weakness, of which all from the least to the greatest are conscious, will gladly avail himself of those aids. Let us therefore learn to embrace the signs along with the Word, since it is not for human beings to separate them.

When Ahaz refuses the sign offered to him, he displays both his obstinacy and his ingratitude, for he despises what God offered for his good. Hence it is evident how far we ought to ask for signs—namely, when God offers them to us; and therefore anyone who rejects them when they are offered is also rejecting the grace of God. Similarly, fanatics today disregard baptism and the Lord's Supper and consider them childish elements. They cannot do this without at the same time rejecting the whole Gospel, for we must not separate those things that the Lord has commanded us to hold together.

But it may be asked whether it is not sometimes right to ask the Lord for signs. We have an instance of this in Gideon, who wished to have his calling confirmed by some sign (Judges 6:17). The Lord granted his prayer and did not disapprove of such a desire. I answer, though Gideon was not commanded by God to ask a sign, yet he did so, not at his own suggestion, but by an operation of the Holy Spirit. We must not abuse his example, therefore, so that each of us may freely allow himself that liberty; for people are so forward that they do not hesitate to ask for innumerable signs from God without any good reason. Such effrontery ought to be restrained, that we may be satisfied with those signs that the Lord offers us.

There are two kinds of signs. Some are extraordinary and may be called supernatural, such as that which the prophet will immediately add and also that which was offered to Hezekiah (Isaiah 38:7). Some are ordinary and in daily use among believers, such as baptism and the Lord's Supper, which contain no miracle or at least none that may be perceived by the eye or by some of the senses. What the Lord miraculously performs by his Spirit is unseen, but in those that are extraordinary the miracle itself is seen. Such is also the purpose of all signs, for as Gideon was strengthened by an astonishing miracle, so we are strengthened by baptism and the Lord's Supper, though our eyes behold no miracle.

13. Then Isaiah said, "Hear now, you house of David!" It looked honorable but was actually intolerable wickedness to exclude the power of God; and therefore the prophet is full of indignation and sharply rebukes wicked hypocrisy. It would have been honorable for them to be reckoned the descendants of David, provided they imitated his piety; but it is to their reproach that he calls them the posterity or family or **house** of **David.** It was indeed no small matter that the grace of God was rejected by the family from which would come the salvation of the whole world.

"Is it not enough to try the patience of men? Will you try the patience of my God also?" He makes a comparison between God and men; not that it is possible to make an actual separation between God and the prophets and holy teachers of whom he speaks, who are nothing other than God's instruments. The prophet therefore adapts what he says to the impiety of Ahaz and of those who were like him. They thought they had to deal with men. Undoubtedly in ancient times people spoke the very words that we hear today from the mouths of the ungodly: "Aren't these mere men who speak to us?" In this way they try to disparage the doctrine that comes from God.

14. "Therefore the Lord himself will give you a sign." Ahaz had already refused the sign that the Lord offered to him, given when the prophet remonstrated against his rebellion and ingratitude. Yet the prophet declares that this will not prevent God from giving the **sign** he had promised and appointed for the Jews. But what **sign?**

"The virgin will be with child and will give birth to a son, and will call him Immanuel." This passage is obscure, and the Jews have tried to pervert its true exposition. They are hard-pressed by this passage, for it contains a famous prediction concerning the Messiah. Some allege that the person here mentioned is Hezekiah, and others that it is the son of Isaiah. Those who apply this passage to Hezekiah are very impudent, for he

72

must have been a full-grown man when Jerusalem was besieged. Thus they show that they are grossly ignorant of history.

As to those who think it was Isaiah's son, that is an utterly frivolous conjecture, for we do not read that a deliverer would be raised up from the descendants of Isaiah.

Immanuel is far too illustrious a title to be applied to any man. There can be no doubt that the prophet is referring to Christ.

All writers, both Greek and Latin, handle this passage as if there were no difficulty in it. They merely assert that Christ is here promised from the Virgin Mary. But there is no small difficulty in the objection that the Jews bring against us, that Christ is here mentioned without any sufficient reason. That is what they argue, and they demand that the context of the passage be examined: "Jerusalem was besieged. The prophet was about to give them a sign of deliverance. Why should he promise the Messiah, who was to be born 500 years later?" By this argument they think they have gained the victory because the promise concerning Christ had nothing to do with assuring Ahaz of the deliverance of Jerusalem.

King Ahaz had rejected the sign that God had offered him, and the prophet now reminds him of the basis of the covenant, which even the ungodly did not venture to reject openly. The Messiah must be born, and this was expected by everyone because the salvation of the whole nation depended on it. The prophet, therefore, argues thus: "By rejecting the promise, you are trying to overturn God's decree; but it remains inviolable, and your treachery and ingratitude will not hinder God from always being the Deliverer of his people; he will raise up his Messiah."

The word **virgin** is derived from a word meaning "to hide" (because the shame and modesty of virgins does not allow them to appear in public), but there is no point troubling about this since the Jews dispute much about that word, saying that it does not signify "virgin" because Solomon used it to denote a young woman who was betrothed. We agree with them when they say the word does sometimes denote a young woman; yet it is frequently used in Scripture when the subject relates to a virgin. What wonderful thing would the prophet be promising if he spoke merely of a young woman who conceived through intercourse with a man? It would certainly have been absurd to offer this as a sign or a miracle.

It is, therefore, plain enough that he is speaking about a virgin who was to conceive not by the ordinary course of nature, but by the gracious influence of the Holy Spirit. And this is the mystery that Paul extols in lofty terms—that God appeared in the body (see 1 Timothy 3:16).

"And will call him." The Hebrew verb here is feminine: "She will call him." We know that the father always has the right to name a child, for this is a sign of the power and authority of fathers over children; generally that authority does not belong to women. But here it is given to the mother. Therefore it follows that this child is conceived by the mother in such a way that he does not have a father on earth; otherwise the prophet would misuse the ordinary custom of Scripture, which ascribes this office to men. Yet, it also ought to be observed that the name was not given to Christ at the suggestion of his mother, for in such a case it would have had no weight. The prophet means that in proclaiming the name, the virgin will be like a herald because there will be no earthly father to perform that office.

"**Immanuel.**" This name was unquestionably bestowed on Christ. The only-begotten Son of God clothed himself with our flesh and united himself with us by taking our nature. He is therefore called "God with us" (or "united to us"), which cannot apply to a man who is not God.

15. "He will eat curds and honey when he knows enough to reject the wrong and choose the right." Here the prophet proves the true human nature of Christ, for it was altogether incredible that he who was God should be born of a virgin. To stop us from thinking that we are presented with some apparition, he describes the marks of human nature, showing through them that Christ will actually appear in flesh or in the nature of man; that is, he will be reared in the same way that children usually are.

16. "But before the boy knows enough to reject the wrong and choose the right, the land of the two kings you dread will be laid waste." I interpret the word **boy** here as referring not to Christ but to children in general. Here I differ from many other commentators. It is unlikely that this promise of the overturn of the kingdoms of Syria and Samaria, which immediately followed, would be deferred for 500 years—that is, until the coming of Christ; indeed, that would have been altogether absurd. The meaning therefore is, "Before the children who are to be born can distinguish between good and evil, the land will be laid waste."

By **the land** I understand Israel and Syria; though they were two lands, they are counted as one because of the alliance between the two kings.

17. "The LORD will bring on you and on your people and on the house of your father a time unlike any since Ephraim broke away from Judah—he will bring the king of Assyria." Here the prophet, on the other hand, threatens the wicked hypocrite who pretended that he was unwilling to tempt God and yet called for those whom the Lord had forbidden him to call for help (see Exodus 23.32). This is in agreement with what goes before, for the prophet cites more urgently the treachery and ingratitude of the king, who had rejected both the Word of God and the sign and had made himself unworthy of every promise.

A time unlike any since Ephraim broke away from Judah. Scripture speaks like this when it describes any serious calamity, for the Jews could not have received a severer chastisement than when, by the withdrawing of the ten tribes, not only was the kingdom divided but the body of the nation was torn.

Hence, as I have already said, we see how God, while he punishes hypocrites, at the same time remembers believers and opens the way for his mercy. We ought to observe this wonderful arrangement, that amidst the most dreadful persecutions the church remains safe. Who would ever have thought that Jerusalem would be delivered from the vast army of the two kings? Or that the kingdom of Syria, which was then in a flourishing condition, would quickly be overturned? Or that Samaria was not far from destruction? And in the meantime that the Assyrians, on whom the Jews relied, would do them more harm than the Israelites and Syrians had ever done? All these things the Lord did for the sake of preserving his church, but at the same time in such a way that he took vengeance on the wickedness of King Ahaz.

18. In that day the LORD will whistle for flies from the distant streams of Egypt and for bees from the land of Assyria. The Jews thought the Assyrians were bound by their alliance with them; but the prophet ridicules this folly and declares that nation will be ready at God's bidding to drive them in any direction he thinks fit. In other words, "There will be no need for great exertion, for as soon as God gives the sign, they will instantly run." Thus the Lord shows what belongs to his secret design—by a whistle he compels the most powerful nations to be obedient.

19. They will all come and settle in the steep ravines and in the crevices in the rocks, on all the thornbushes and at all the water holes. He continues the same metaphor, for bees often seek nests for themselves in caverns, valleys, bushes, and similar places, as if he had said there would not be a corner in which the enemy would not settle down and dwell. It is unnecessary to trouble ourselves about explaining why he speaks of thornbushes rather than of other things, for the language is figurative. And yet I have no doubt that he intended to state that whether the Jews hide themselves in caverns or seek concealment in valleys, there will be no escape, for the enemy will take possession of the whole country.

Hence we again infer what we noticed above: Nothing takes place by chance; everything is governed by God's hand. Again, although wicked people may become angry and blindly attack people, God puts a bridle on them, that they may promote his glory. From this we ought to derive wonderful consolation in the middle of those disturbances by which the Christian world is so deeply afflicted.

20. In that day the Lord will use a razor hired from beyond the River—the king of Assyria—to shave your head and the hair of your legs, and to take off your beards also. Isaiah now uses a different metaphor and says that the enemies by whom the Lord had determined to afflict Judea at the appointed time are like a **razor,** with which the beard and **hair** are shaved. What he means he immediately explains: The

Assyrians will serve as a **razor** in the hand of God, and they will come from a distant country.

From beyond the River. This means that the River Euphrates will not hinder the Assyrians from carrying out God's command. Isaiah likewise adds that it will not be some part of that nation rushing forward of its own accord into foreign territories or wandering without a settled leader; the king himself will lead them, so that the nation and the king at the same time will overwhelm Judea, and it will sink under such a burden.

It is not without reason that he says this **razor** is **hired**; he expresses by this the dreadful nature of the calamity that would fall on them by the hands of the Assyrians. If a person uses a hired horse or a hired sword, he will use it the more freely and will not spare or take care of it in the same way he would if it were his own. Thus the Lord threatens that he will not spare the **razor,** even if he blunts it, which means that he will send the Assyrians with great violence. If the Lord took such dreadful vengeance on the Jews for the reasons that the prophet has already spelled out, we ought to fear lest we are punished in the same way; or rather, we ought to dread the razor with which he has already begun to shave us.

21. In that day, a man will keep alive a young cow and two goats. In these verses, down to the end of the chapter, the prophet describes the state of a country torn and wasted. He wants to present a striking and lively picture of such overwhelming distress that wherever you turn your eyes, nothing is to be seen but traces of frightful desolation. Those who had previously been used to rearing large numbers of oxen and sheep will be satisfied with having a few. He means, therefore, that all will be reduced to very deep poverty.

22. And because of the abundance of the milk they give, he will have curds to eat. All who remain in the land will eat curds and honey. It appears as if the prophet intended to show that the men will be so few in number that a small quantity of milk will be sufficient for them all. It is a far heavier affliction that a country should lack inhabitants than that it should have a small supply of herds and flocks. In verse 21 Isaiah said that Judea would be so impoverished that very few herds and flocks would be left. Now he adds that the men will be still fewer, for a very little milk will be sufficient for the inhabitants of the land.

23. In that day, in every place where there were a thousand vines worth a thousand silver shekels, there will be only briers and thorns. This is reminiscent of the common expression, "to sell for a trifle," used when something is sold at a very low price. Any field, however barren or uncultivated, might be sold at a higher price if due attention were paid to the cultivation of the land, as is usually done where there is a crowded population.

Isaiah gives a reason for the price fall, which makes it evident that he speaks of desolation: **There will be only briers and thorns.** That is, there will be no one to cultivate the land, which is what usually happens when a heavy calamity has been sustained.

24. Men will go there with bow and arrow, for the land will be covered with briers and thorns. By **bow and arrow** here I understand hunting. "The land will be approached not by husbandmen but by hunters, and they will not plant or dress vines but will chase wild beasts." In short, frightful desolation will change the aspect of the land.

25. And on all hills that shall be digged with the mattock [NIV, hoe], there shall not come thither the fear of briers and thorns: but it shall be for the sending forth of oxen, and for the treading of lesser cattle (KJV). Here the prophet appears to contradict himself. Having previously spoken of the desolation of the land, he now describes what may be called a new condition: Where **briers and thorns** were, there **cattle** will feed. Some people have applied these words to the consolation of the people. But the prophet means something quite different. He means that hills, which were far away from a crowded population and could not be approached without much difficulty, will be suitable for cattle because of the great number of people who go there. That is, because men will go to desert mountains, which formerly were inaccessible, there will be no need to be afraid of briers, because of the many inhabitants. Men will seek to live in hills formerly desolate and uncultivated because the whole country is unsafe.

Isaiah
Chapter 8

1. The LORD said to me, "Take a large scroll and write on it with an ordinary pen: Maher-Shalal-Hash-Baz." This prophecy contains nothing new but is a confirmation of the preceding one, in which Isaiah predicted the approaching desolation of the kingdom of Israel and Syria. He had foretold that both countries would be deprived of their kings before the children who were soon to be born could distinguish between good and evil—that is, before they were grown up (see Isaiah 7:16.) But no threats frighten wicked people; so this prediction had to be repeated and demonstrated by some outward sign.

First, in order to arouse the nation more effectually, God commands that this prophecy be made known publicly in writing, that everyone may understand it. We said earlier that it was usual for prophets with a message for the people to sum it up in a few words and to fix it to the gates of the temple (see Habakkuk 2:2). But here something peculiar is expressed, for God does not merely command Isaiah to write the prophecy but demands **a large scroll,** so that it may be read at a distance.

Maher-Shalal-Hash-Baz. God determined not to waste words because there was no time for controversy; so he represents the matter by an outward sign. The prophets had frequently threatened vengeance, and no good had come of it. So Isaiah shows it now by a striking example, that it might make a deeper impression on their minds and be etched on their memory. Whenever the words **Maher-Shalal-Hash-Baz** were mentioned, they would recall the destruction of Israel and Syria.

2. "And I will call in Uriah the priest and Zechariah son of Jeberekiah as reliable witnesses for me." As this was a matter of great importance, God calls **witnesses,** as is usually done on important occasions. By **reliable** he means true and worthy of credit; and yet one of them was an ungodly and worthless apostate who, wishing to flatter his king, erected an altar resembling the altar at Damascus and openly defended

79

ungodliness and unlawful modes of worship. God's words through Isaiah do not mean that man was a good and excellent person, but that his office gave him such influence that nobody could reject him, and that his testimony would be, as they say, free from every objection.

I think this prophecy was attached to the gates of the temple, **Uriah the priest and Zechariah son of Jeberekiah** acting as **witnesses**; for Isaiah does not speak of a vision but of a command of God, which he obeyed in order that these words, like a common proverb, might be repeated by every person.

3. Then I went to the prophetess, and she conceived and gave birth to a son. And the LORD said to me, "Name him Maher-Shalal-Hash-Baz." What follows happened to the prophet, I have no doubt, in a vision, for the purpose of sealing the former prediction. The vision given to Isaiah was that he had a child by his wife and was told to give him this name. There would, of course, be nothing absurd in saying that the prophet actually had a son by his wife. But as it is unlikely that this name was given to any man, and as there is no evidence to prove it, I am inclined to think this was a vision given to the prophet in order to confirm the former prediction. He calls his wife a **prophetess** not in the same sense in which the wife of a king is given the honorary title of queen, but because in this vision she is in public view.

4. "Before the boy knows how to say 'My father' or 'My mother,' the wealth of Damascus and the plunder of Samaria will be carried off by the king of Assyria." This makes it still more evident that the prophet intended to predict the desolation of the kingdoms of Israel and of Syria. He does this to comfort the godly and to expose the foolish fear of the wicked king, who would not allow the Lord to help him. For Ahaz rejected not only the promises but also the sign that was offered. As a result of this, the prophet goes further and further in reproving his wickedness and that of the whole nation. "You do indeed believe nothing, but the Lord will assist his own; and you will quickly see sudden and unexpected changes by which the Lord will deliver his people." The prophet's purpose, therefore, is to reprove the ungodly for their rebelliousness and at the same time to show that God is always true to his character.

5-6. The LORD spoke to me again: "Because this people has rejected the gently flowing waters of Shiloah and rejoices over Rezin and the son of Remaliah ..." To make sure Ahaz does not rest on false hopes, the prophet suddenly interrupts his discourse about the general safety of the godly and threatens unbelievers with punishment. He says that they **rejected the ... waters of Shiloah** because the Jews despised and disdained their condition. This means they saw that they had no strong fortresses and looked in another direction, to the wealth of the kingdom of Israel. Seeing how few and poor they were, they trembled and placed no confidence in God but only in outward assistance. Thus they rejoiced in the riches of others.

7. **"Therefore the Lord is about to bring against them the mighty flood waters of the River—the king of Assyria with all his pomp. It will overflow all its channels, run over all its banks."** Notice the metaphors that the prophet uses. It is as if he said, "Because the people are not satisfied with their condition and desire the riches of others, I will show them what it is to have a powerful king." For instance, think of a small nation, whose king is held in low esteem, having powerful neighbors over whom an illustrious king reigns. Suppose they said, "How delightful it would be to serve that prosperous king or the kings of France; their power is irresistible!" Would not God be right to punish such an unlawful desire? The more powerful kings are, the more they oppress their people. The Lord reproves the mad desire of the Jews who were not satisfied with their condition and looked not to the Lord but to the resources of powerful kings. This reproof is far more graceful in these metaphors than if he had spoken in plain and direct language.

He compares **the River** (the Euphrates), the most celebrated river in all the East, to **Shiloah.** By the rapid **waters of the River** he means the Assyrians, who would destroy the whole of Judea and waste it like a deluge.

From this destruction of the Jews let us consider our own interests. The church is almost always devoid of human aid. If we were too well provided for, we would be dazzled by our wealth and resources and forget our God. We ought rather to so recognize our weakness that we depend wholly on God. The small and gentle waters should be more highly valued by us than the large and rapid rivers of the nations, and we ought not to envy the great power of the ungodly. See Psalm 94:4-7.

8. **"And sweep on into Judah, swirling over it, passing through it and reaching up to the neck. Its outspread wings will cover the breadth of your land, O Immanuel!"** The verb here translated **sweep on** sometimes signifies "pass through" but here means "attack and cut off"; that is, this river will not only water Judea but will overflow it, so as utterly to drown it, for it will spread far and wide on every part. He adds, **reaching up to the neck.** The comparison is with someone who enters a river, dipping into it gradually, until the water reaches to the neck. Judea will be flooded by that rapid river—that is, by the Assyrians—until it is plunged **up to the neck.** He means Jerusalem, which was the capital of the country.

The breadth of your land. That is, in all directions. He pursues his metaphor in his prophecy and shows how violent the Assyrians will be. He continues in his discourse against the Jews, as he had begun to do in the two previous verses. Having foretold the destruction of the Israelites and Syrians, he now warns that the Jews, in their turn, will be punished for their unbelief.

To understand this better, Isaiah's most beautiful and closely connected discourse must be examined. First, he turns aside to address others, for Ahaz was unworthy of being addressed. In the previous chapter he had said that the Lord would give a sign. Next, he added the way in which Jerusalem would be preserved—by the sudden changes that were to take place in Syria and Samaria. This was confirmed at the beginning of this chapter, both by a commandment and by a vision. He now comes to the Jews themselves, that they might not hope to escape without being punished or be too highly elated by the destruction of their enemies; he declares that for them also a reward is prepared, and that they too will be punished for their wickedness and treachery because they despised the Lord and would not trust his promises, signs, and acts of kindness.

"O Immanuel!" Why does the prophet address Christ instead of simply the land? (There can be no doubt that the name **Immanuel** means Christ.) I think the prophet added this name in order to hold out to good people some promise of hope and to comfort them in such a great calamity. It is as if he said, "Nevertheless, the land will be yours, O Immanuel; in it you will live." This was, therefore, added to intimate that the land, though torn and wasted, belongs to God and not to human beings.

9. **Raise the war cry, you nations, and be shattered! Listen, all you distant lands. Prepare for battle, and be shattered! Prepare for battle, and be shattered!** The prophet becomes confident after mentioning **Immanuel**—that is, God, who would assist his people. At the same time he cherishes increased hope in a context of opposition to enemies. Although it might be thought those enemies had accomplished their objective when they depopulated the country, nevertheless the Lord would be victorious and would preserve his people against the cruelty of their enemies. Turning his attention, therefore, away from the sight of that calamity, the prophet turns to Christ and by contemplating him acquires such courage that he ventures to taunt his enemies as if he had vanquished them. We must imagine the prophet on a watchtower, from which he sees the distressed condition of the people and the victorious Assyrians proudly exulting over them. Refreshed by the name and the sight of Christ, he forgets all his distress as if he had not suffered and, freed from all his wretchedness, rises against the enemies whom the Lord would immediately destroy. Note carefully that we contend against the same temptations amidst the afflictions that the church endures and by which it is almost overwhelmed; and yet we may direct our eyes to Christ, by whom we shall be able to triumph over Satan and over enemies of every description.

10. **Devise your strategy, but it will be thwarted; propose your plan, but it will not stand.** Having spoken of the forces of the enemies, he now comes to their counsels, as if saying, "Although the enemies may abound

not only in armor and in strength but in counsel and wisdom, still they will accomplish nothing." He forewarns them that the craftiness of the enemies and all the plans by which they endeavor to gain advantage over the people of God will in the end be unsuccessful; they will accomplish nothing, though they lack nothing and though they may have a great abundance of forces, counsels, and crafty designs.

For God is with us. Literally, "For Immanuel." For my own part, I have no doubt that he is alluding to the name he gave to Christ; although he means that God assists his people, yet as the majesty of God is not of itself sufficient to support us, he contemplates God himself in the person of the Mediator, in whom alone he has promised to assist us.

11. The LORD spoke to me with his strong hand upon me, warning me not to follow the way of this people. He said . . . Here the prophet contends against another kind of temptation—that is, against the unbelief of the people. In order to make that more clear, it ought to be observed that there were two remarkable temptations, one external and the other internal. The external temptation came from professed enemies, such as the Assyrians; when the people saw their plundering and cruelty, they thought all was over for them because that nation had almost brought them to utter ruin. The other temptation was internal, for that sacred people, who boasted that they had been chosen by God, relied on the assistance of human beings rather than of God. This was a most dangerous temptation; for it appeared as if that nation, by its unbelief, was refusing the promises of God that were offered to them every day and that continually rang in their ears. The Lord, therefore, determined that both the prophet and his disciples should be armed against a temptation of this kind.

The beautiful metaphor of **his strong hand upon me** has not been understood, I think, by many commentators. He is alluding to fathers or teachers who, when their words do not have sufficient effect, seize the hand of their children or scholars and hold them close to compel them to obey. This is well understood to be very necessary and is actually experienced by all who faithfully serve the Lord; no temptation is more severe than when people in whom faith ought to dwell revolt—in a word, when faith appears to be banished from the world.

12. "Do not call conspiracy everything that these people call conspiracy; do not fear what they fear, and do not dread it." First, we must consider the condition of **these people,** for they saw that they had few capable warriors against such powerful enemies. They longed for outward assistance. They thought they would be utterly ruined if they received no help from others. I understand the word **conspiracy** to mean that they thought it necessary to have the help of allies. It is as if he said, "Do not be distressed if your countrymen make unlawful alliances, and do not consent to them."

From this verse we see why they were upset. They were terrified, but instead of seeking help from the Lord they turned to the Assyrians. This was the only way they thought they could survive.

13. "The LORD Almighty is the one you are to regard as holy." We have said that the reason dangers lead to panic is that wretched men do not raise their eyes and minds to heaven. The prophet now, therefore, proposes a suitable remedy to allay their fears, that those who dread the evils that threaten them may learn to give God the honor due to him. **To regard as holy** the God of armies means to exalt his power, remembering that he governs the world and that the beginning and the end of good and evil actions are at his disposal. Hence it follows that in some respects God is robbed of his holiness when we do not immediately go to him when we are perplexed.

"He is the one you are to fear, he is the one you are to dread." He is right when he adds that God himself should be feared by the people, for this tells them that a just and lawful punishment awaits them for their contempt of God, and so they tremble at danger in this way. Although he mentions not only **fear** but also **dread,** he does not mean that the Jews should be filled with horror at the name of God but that they should show reverence for him.

14. "And he will be a sanctuary; but for both houses of Israel he will be a stone that causes men to stumble and a rock that makes them fall. And for the people of Jerusalem he will be a trap and a snare." He promises that the true worshipers of God will enjoy tranquillity of mind because the Lord, covering them, as it were, under his wings, will quickly dispel all their fears. The prophet meant, "The Lord will be your best and most faithful guardian. Though others stumble against him, you do not need to be terrified; remain steadfast in your calling."

Both houses of Israel. The nation was divided into two kingdoms, Ephraim and Judah; and therefore he mentioned both. There were indeed individual exceptions, but he speaks here of both countries.

Wherever we look, very great temptations meet us from every direction. So we ought to remember the useful instruction that it is nothing new if a great number of people, and almost all who claim to belong to the church, stumble against God.

15. "Many of them will stumble; they will fall and be broken, they will be snared and captured." He goes on threatening the ungodly, as he began to do earlier; he says that those who refuse to trust in God will not escape punishment.

"They will be snared and captured." This agrees with the latter metaphor, in which he compared God to **a snare** (verse 14). The ungodly, therefore, should not imagine that they are stronger or wiser than God; for they will find that he excels them in strength and wisdom, which will be to their destruction.

16. Bind up the testimony and seal up the law among my disciples. The Lord now addresses the prophet, who must contend with apostates and rebels; he encourages him to do his duty with boldness and perseverance. This was very necessary, for Isaiah had met with great obstinacy in the people. If he had only considered their present condition of unbelief and his fruitless and unsuccessful exertions, he would have given up. Because of this, the Lord determined to confirm and seal his calling, not only on his account but for the sake of all who obeyed his teaching.

God compares this teaching to a sealed letter: It may be felt and handled by many people, but it is only read and understood by a few—that is, by those to whom it is sent and addressed. The Word of God is received by few—that is, by the elect—though it is offered indiscriminately to all. The Word is therefore sealed to those who derive no advantage from it; but it is sealed in such a way that the Lord unseals and opens it to his own people by the Spirit.

From this very useful doctrine we conclude that teachers and ministers of the Word should constantly persevere in discharging their office, although it may seem as if everyone rejects it. The Lord will reserve for himself some disciples by whom his letter will be read with advantage, though it is closed to others. The prophet uses the same metaphor later, when he says the Word is like a closed book (Isaiah 29:11).

17. I will wait for the LORD, who is hiding his face from the house of Jacob. I will put my trust in him. In other words, "Seeing that the Lord chooses disciples to whom his doctrine is sealed, I will wait for him, even though he hides his face from Jacob—that is, even though he has rejected and cast off his people." This is a remarkable passage, and by meditating continually on it we will certainly be greatly encouraged. Although it may seem as if the whole world has rebelled, we should still persevere boldly; even though God has hidden his face from his people, and those who professed his name have been cast off, still we ought to wait for him with unshaken hope. This is the only remedy that is left to us.

The word **wait** is very emphatic; it is like saying, "Still I will not turn aside from God; I will persevere in faith."

18. Here am I, and the children the LORD has given me. We are signs and symbols in Israel from the LORD Almighty, who dwells on Mount Zion. Here the prophet not only testifies that he will wait patiently but also shows his courage by appearing in public along with the remaining disciples he had won for God. It is as if he said, "Others may withdraw, but I am ready to obey you; and I bring along with me those whom you have been pleased to preserve in a wonderful way through my ministry." He therefore declares by these words his unshaken courage and promises that he will persevere in faith and obedience to the Lord, even if everyone else rebels.

By **children** are meant the various classes of servants, as is usually referred to in Hebrew. He is speaking about the disciples whom he had mentioned earlier. Hence we see what is demanded from those who want to be reckoned among the true disciples of the Lord—namely, to declare with Isaiah that they are submissive and ready to hear and that, as soon as the Lord has spoken, they will obey. Teachers ought to bring disciples with them, and not merely send them. The apostle to the Hebrews applies this passage to Christ (Hebrews 2:13), saying that we should consider ourselves to be followers not only of Isaiah but of Christ himself, our leader and instructor. In this way we should press forward with greater alacrity.

By saying **the LORD has given me,** the prophet shows to whom our faith ought to be ascribed. It is to God, thanks to his undeserved election. Isaiah taught publicly, admonished everyone, and invited all without exception to come to God; but his doctrine is of advantage only to those who have been given to him by God. By **given** he means those whom God drew by an inward and secret work of his Spirit. In a similar way Christ declared that the elect were given to him by the Father (John 17:6). Thus we see that readiness to believe does not depend on human will; rather, some of the multitude believe because, as Luke tells us, they had been foreordained (see Acts 13:48.) "Those he predestined, he also called" (Romans 8:30), and he efficaciously seals in them the proof of their adoption, so that they may become obedient and submissive.

The addition of the words **who dwells on Mount Zion** carries great weight, for although the people abounded in every kind of crime and enormity, they still boasted that they were devoted to God and, abusing his promises, condemned the true servants of God who reproved them. On the other hand the prophets, in order to shake off the people's false confidence and pride, declared they were the servants of the one true God, whom the people falsely boasted of worshiping on Mount Zion. God had not chosen to live there as if, being bound to the spot, he would accept false and spurious worship; he wished to be sought and worshiped according to his Word. So when Isaiah claims for his master God **who dwells on Mount Zion,** he is sharply criticizing hypocrites because by their false boasting they indulge in foolish pride whenever they say "The temple of the Lord" (see Jeremiah 7:4), which was in actuality an idol in which they boasted contrary to the Word.

19. When men tell you to consult mediums and spiritists, who whisper and mutter, should not a people inquire of their God? Isaiah continues the previous subject: All godly people should not only use the authority of God as a shield but should defend themselves with it, like a bronze wall, against all ungodliness. He therefore entreats them to resist courageously if anyone tempts them to engage in superstition and unlawful ways of worship. The plural nouns are used by him to indicate that this was a vice that pervaded all ranks and that abounded everywhere, as if he said, "I see what will happen. You will be placed in great danger, for your countrymen will endeavor to draw you away from the true God; being themselves ungodly, they will wish you to be like them." At the same time he shows how wickedly the people had departed from God's law and covenant by shamelessly promoting **mediums and spiritists.**

While some ponder and hesitate whether or not it is right to consult mediums, let us be ready with our answer: God alone ought to be consulted. The prophet is alluding to Deuteronomy 18:10-15, where the Lord forbade them to go to mediums and spiritists. It was therefore the will of the Lord that they should depend entirely on his Word and should learn from it alone whatever they needed to know.

Why consult the dead on behalf of the living? In other words, "The Lord desires to be our teacher and so has appointed prophets, that we may learn from them his will, for a prophet is the mouth of the Lord. It is therefore unlawful to go to the dead, who have not been appointed for that purpose. God did not intend to use the dead to instruct us."

20. To the law and to the testimony! The **testimony** is here linked with **the law,** not as if it were different but by way of explanation. In short, we ought to take the word **testimony** as describing a quality of the law, to inform us what advantage we derive from it; namely, God reveals himself to us in the law and lays down what he demands from us and everything that we need to know. In other words, "Forsake all the superstitions on which they are so madly bent; for they are not satisfied with having God alone and call on innumerable inventions." Christ also spoke in this way: "They have Moses and the prophets; let them listen to them" (Luke 16:29).

From this we learn that everything that is added to the Word must be condemned and rejected. It is the will of the Lord that we depend wholly on his Word. Everything that is introduced by people on their own authority will be nothing but a corruption of the Word; and consequently, if we wish to obey God, we must reject all other instructors. He likewise warns us that if we abide by the law of the Lord, we will be protected against superstitions and wicked forms of worship. Paul calls the Word of God the sword of the Spirit (see Ephesians 6:17), and thus Satan and all his schemes are put to flight by the Word.

If they do not speak according to this word, they have no light of dawn. This passage is usually explained to mean that wicked people trifle with their inventions and expose their impostures because there is no light in them. For my own part, I consider this a reason for encouraging believers to persevere: If wicked men depart from true doctrine, they will see nothing but their own blindness and darkness. We ought to despise their folly, that it may not be an obstacle to us. Christ also teaches us that we should boldly ignore such people, so that we are not at all affected by their blindness or obstinacy. "Leave them," he says; "they are blind guides. If a blind man leads a blind man, both will fall into a pit" (Matthew 15:14).

21. Distressed and hungry, they will roam through the land; when

they are famished, they will become enraged and, looking upward, will curse their king and their God. To prevent believers from being caught by common errors, he adds how dreadful the punishment is that awaits the ungodly when they have rebelled against God and have worked to induce others to join in the same revolt.

By **king** some suppose that he means God. But I draw a distinction between **king** and **God.** Wicked men are first blinded by a false confidence in idols, and afterwards they place their defense in earthly things. When the Jews had a king, they were proud of his glory and power; and when Isaiah preached, wicked men enraged the king against him and even aroused the whole of the nation to follow the king as their standard-bearer. Since, therefore, their false boasting had been partly in the idols and partly in the king, he threatens that they will be afflicted with so many calamities that they will be constrained to abhor both their gods and the king. It is the beginning of repentance when we loathe and drive far from us everything that kept us back or led us away from God.

22. Then they will look toward the earth and see only distress and darkness and fearful gloom, and they will be thrust into utter darkness. This means that the Jews will be converted to God because they will be deprived of every assistance on earth and will see nothing but frightful calamities wherever they look. These words are partly figurative and partly literal, for **gloom** and **darkness** simply mean adversity, according to the custom of Scripture. But he adds, **thrust into utter darkness.** This aggravates the calamity to an amazing degree, for if someone who is in darkness is pushed, he is in far more danger of stumbling than before. Thus the prophet intimates that to a heavy calamity another still heavier will be added, that they may be more completely ruined. He means that God's judgments will be so dreadful, and his punishments so severe, that they will be constrained to look up to heaven.

Isaiah
Chapter 9

1. Nevertheless, there will be no more gloom for those who were in distress. In the past he humbled the land of Zebulun and the land of Naphtali, but in the future he will honor Galilee of the Gentiles, by the way of the sea, along the Jordan. The prophet Isaiah begins to comfort the wretched with the hope that things will get better, so that they may not be swallowed up by their distress. He therefore addresses them in case they should think they were ruined, for he says that the chastisements that are now to be inflicted will be lighter than those that came before.

But why does the prophet say that this calamity, which was far more dreadful, would be more mild and gentle? Jerusalem, after all, would be defeated, the temple thrown down, and the sacrifices abolished, though they had remained untouched during the previous calamities. It might be thought that these were the most severe of all trials, and that the previous ones, in comparison, were light. But it ought to be observed that while in the former instances there was no promise, an explicit promise was added to this warning. By this alone can temptations be overcome and punishments made light. If the Lord strengthens us by offering his assistance, there is no affliction so heavy that we shall not reckon it to be light.

This can be made clear by the following comparison. A man may happen to be drowned in a small stream; and yet, if he had fallen into the open sea but got hold of a plank, he might have been rescued and brought to shore. In a similar way the slightest calamities will overwhelm us if we are deprived of God's favor; but if we rely on the Word of God, we can come out of the heaviest calamity uninjured.

He calls it **the way of the sea** because Galilee was next to the coast of the Mediterranean Sea, and on one side it was bounded by the river **Jordan.** It is called **Galilee of the Gentiles** not only because it was next to Tyre and Sidon, but because it contained a great number of Gentiles, who were mixed in with the Jews. From the time that Solomon granted this country to King Hiram (1 Kings 9:11), it could never be subdued in such a way that some part of it was not possessed by the Gentiles.

2. The people walking in darkness have seen a great light; on those living in the land of the shadow of death a light has dawned. He speaks of future events in the past tense and thus brings them into the immediate view of the people, so that in the destruction of the city, in their captivity, and in what appeared to be their utter destruction they might see the **light** of God. It may therefore be summed up in this manner: "Even in darkness—indeed, in death itself—there is good ground for hope, for the power of God is sufficient to restore life to his people when they appear to be already dead." If we want to ascertain the true meaning of this passage, we must remember what has been stated already: The prophet, when he speaks of bringing the people back from Babylon, is not looking at a single age but includes all the rest, until Christ came and brought the most complete deliverance to his people. The deliverance from Babylon was but a prelude to the restoration of the church and was intended to last not just for a few years but until Christ would come and bring true salvation, not only to their bodies but to their souls.

Having spoken of the captivity in Babylon, which held out the prospect of a very great calamity, the prophet shows that this affliction will be less severe than that which Israel had endured previously, because the Lord had fixed a term and limit to it—namely, seventy years (see Jeremiah 25:11-12 and 29:10), after the expiration of which the **light** of the Lord would shine on them. By this confident hope of deliverance, therefore, he encourages their hearts when overpowered by fear, that they might not be distressed beyond measure. And thus he made a distinction between the Jews and the Israelites, who were not promised deliverance so soon. The prophets had given the elect remnant some taste of the mercy of God; but since Israel's redemption was a sort of addition to that of Judah, and was dependent on it, the prophet is right to declare that a new **light** has been revealed, because God has determined to redeem his people.

He compares the captivity in Babylon to **darkness** and **death,** for those who were kept there were wretched and miserable and like dead men, as Ezekiel says (see Ezekiel 37:11-12). They looked as if no ray of light had ever shone on them. Yet he shows that this will not prevent them from enjoying light and recovering their former liberty; and that liberty he extends not to a short period but, as we have already said, to the time of Christ.

3. You have enlarged the nation and increased their joy. At the beginning of the chapter, the prophet had made a preliminary statement, saying that this blessing of redemption was greater than all other blessings, though it might appear to be unworthy of being so highly extolled on account of the small number of those who were redeemed. Now he repeats the same comparison, or one not very different from it—namely, that this favor of God would be more remarkable than when he had previously multiplied his people. This might at first sight be thought to be highly inappropriate; for if we compare the condition of the Jewish kingdom before the Babylonian captivity with its condition after the return from it, we may be led to think that the period when its original possession was unimpaired was a season of greater prosperity. It was only a small remnant who returned, compared to the multitude who had been carried away. Besides, they did not have free possession of their land but might be said to be tenants; they had to pay tribute to the Persians and retained hardly any semblance of their former rank. Who, therefore, would not have preferred the prosperous reign enjoyed by David's family to the present condition?

But the prophet declares that this latter condition, though it might appear greatly inferior and even more wretched, ought to be preferred to that which was prosperous and splendid, and he shows that it will yield greater joy than when they had an abundant share of wealth and all kinds of possessions. Haggai similarly testified that the glory of the new temple would be greater than the glory of the former one (see Haggai 2:9), though at first sight it might appear to be otherwise. It is as if Isaiah said, "There never was greater joy, though the number of people was greater. Though we are few and contemptible in number, yet by the light with which you, Lord, shine on us, you have cheered us to such a degree that no joy of our former condition can be compared with the present." This is so because that redemption might be regarded as a prelude to the full and perfect salvation that was at length obtained through Christ.

They rejoice before you as people rejoice at the harvest, as men rejoice when dividing the plunder. He means that their joy was true and complete, not slight or temporary. People often rejoice, but with a deceitful and transitory joy followed by mourning and tears. He affirms that this joy is so deeply rooted that it can never perish or be destroyed. Such is the meaning of the phrase **before you**; nothing cheers the godly so much as when the face of God shines sweetly on them.

4. For as in the day of Midian's defeat, you have shattered the yoke that burdens them, the bar across their shoulders, the rod of their oppressor. He explains the reason for their joy: Believers, when they have been delivered from a frightful and cruel tyranny, will feel as if they have been rescued from death. To illustrate God's grace, he reminds them how shameful and burdensome was the slavery by which the Jews had been oppressed and afflicted; and this is his object in heaping up the expressions **the yoke that burdens them, the bar across their shoulders, the rod of their oppressor.** That the redeemed may not think lightly of God's favor, the prophet tells them to consider how bitter their slavery was; thus they appreciated their deliverance all the more.

Next, he extols the excellence of this favor on another ground: God has openly displayed his hand from heaven. For this purpose the prophet adduces an ancient and memorable instance. As God had overthrown the Midianites without human help, in a wonderful and amazing way (see Judges 7:19-21), so now there will be a similar and illustrious display of power. God will deliver his people from a cruel tyranny, when not one of the wretched Jews will venture to lift a finger. Notice that God sometimes assists his people by using ordinary means; but when he sees that this hinders people from beholding his hand, which may be said to be concealed, he sometimes works alone and by evident miracles, so that nothing may prevent or obscure the manifestation of his power. Thus in this victory of Gideon, when the enemies were routed without any human agency, God's arm appeared openly. To this deliverance, therefore, Isaiah compares the future deliverance of the people, in which the hand of God will be displayed no less openly and illustriously.

5. Every warrior's boot used in battle and every garment rolled in blood will be destined for burning, will be fuel for the fire. Isaiah contrasts the victory that God was about to give to his people with other victories. Others conquer by slaughtering their enemies, but the Lord will conquer by his own hand alone. When the Lord acts by himself, we perceive more clearly that he is the Author of our life and salvation. It is evident that the present subject is not merely the deliverance the people obtained from Cyrus, permitting them to return to their native country; these words must be viewed as extending to the kingdom of Christ.

6. For to us a child is born, to us a son is given, and the government will be on his shoulders. And he will be called Wonderful Counselor, Mighty God, Everlasting Father, Prince of Peace. Isaiah now argues why this deliverance ought to be preferred to the rest of God's benefits: Not only will God bring the people back from captivity, but he will place Christ on his royal throne, so that under him supreme and everlasting happiness may be enjoyed. Thus Isaiah teaches that they should not confine their attention to the present benefit but should consider the end and refer everything to it. "This is your highest happiness, that you have been rescued from death, not only so you may live in the land of Canaan, but so you may arrive at the kingdom of God."

Hence we learn that we ought not to quickly forget the benefits we receive from God but should raise our minds to Christ. Otherwise, the benefit will be small and the joy will be transitory, because they will not lead us to taste the sweetness of a Father's love if we do not keep in mind God's free election, which is ratified in Christ. In short, the prophet does not want the people to be wholly occupied with the joy occasioned by the outward and short-lived freedom they had obtained; he wants them to look at the end—that is, at the preservation of the church until Christ, the only Redeemer, appears; he ought to be the ground and perfection of all our joy.

A child is born. The Jews twist this passage and interpret it as relating to Hezekiah, though he had been born before this prediction was uttered. But Isaiah speaks of it as something new and unexpected; further, it is a promise, intended to arouse believers to the expectation of a future event. Therefore, there can be no hesitation in concluding that he is describing a child who was yet to be born.

Wonderful Counselor. Notice that these titles are not alien to the subject but are adapted to the case in hand, for the prophet describes what Christ will show himself to be toward believers. The redemption he has brought surpasses the creation of the world. It amounts to this: The grace of God, which will be exhibited in Christ, exceeds all miracles.

The Redeemer will come endowed with absolute wisdom. Let us remember that the prophet does not here reason about the hidden essence of Christ but about the power he displays toward us. It is not, therefore, because he knows all his Father's secrets that the prophet calls him **Counselor,** but rather because he is in every respect the highest and most perfect teacher. All that is necessary for salvation is opened up by Christ in such a way and explained with such familiarity that he addresses the disciples no longer as servants but as friends.

He is called **Mighty God** for the same reason that in Isaiah 7:14 he was called "**Immanuel.** If in Christ we find nothing but human flesh and nature, our glorying will be foolish and vain, and our hope will rest on an uncertain and insecure foundation. But if he shows himself to be to us God, even the **Mighty God,** we may rely on him with safety. It is good for us that he is called strong or **Mighty** because our contest is with the devil, death, and sin (see Ephesians 6:12), enemies too powerful and strong, by whom we would be vanquished immediately if Christ's strength had not made us invincible. Thus we learn from this title that there is in Christ abundance of protection for defending our salvation, so that we desire nothing beyond him; he is God, who is pleased to show himself strong on our behalf. This application may be regarded as the key to this and similar passages, leading us to distinguish between Christ's mysterious essence and the power by which he has revealed himself to us.

The name **Father** is used to mean author because Christ preserves the existence of his church through all ages and bestows immortality on the body and on the individual members. We ought, therefore, to elevate our minds to that blessed and everlasting life that as yet we do not see but that we possess by hope and faith (see Romans 8:2).

Prince of Peace. This is the last title, and by it the prophet declares that the coming of Christ will be the cause of full and perfect happiness, or at least of calm and blessed safety. The Hebrew word for *peace* often signifies prosperity, for of all blessings none is better or more desirable than peace. The general meaning is that all who submit to Christ's dominion will lead a quiet and blessed life in obedience to him. Hence it follows that life without this King is restless and miserable.

But we must also take into consideration the nature of this peace. It is the same as that of the kingdom, for it resides chiefly in the conscience; otherwise we must be engaged in incessant conflict and liable to daily attacks. Not only, therefore, does he promise outward peace but that peace by which we who were God's enemies return to a state of favor with him. Justified by faith, says Paul, we have peace with God (see Romans 5:1).

7. Of the increase of his government and peace there will be no end. Isaiah begins to explain and confirm what he said before (Christ is the **Prince of Peace**) by saying that his **government** extends to every age and is perpetual; **there will be no end** to the **government** or to **peace.** This was also repeated by Daniel, who prophesies that Christ's kingdom is an everlasting kingdom (see Daniel 7:27). Gabriel also alluded to this when he carried the message to the virgin Mary; and he gave the true exposition of this passage, for it cannot be understood to refer to anyone but Christ. He shall reign, says the angel, over the house of Jacob forever, and of his kingdom there shall be no end (see Luke 1:33). We see that the mightiest governments of this world are unexpectedly overturned and suddenly fall, as if they had been built on a slippery foundation.

To **government** he adds the eternity of **peace,** for one cannot be separated from the other. It is impossible for Christ to be King without also keeping his people in calm and blessed **peace** and enriching them with every blessing. But since they are exposed to innumerable attacks every day and are tossed and perplexed by fears and anxieties, they ought to cultivate that peace of Christ (see Philippians 4:7), so that they might retain their composure amid the destruction of the whole world.

He will reign on David's throne and over his kingdom. David was promised that the Redeemer would spring from his seed (2 Samuel 7:12-13); his kingdom was nothing but an image or faint shadow of that more perfect and truly blessed state that God had determined to establish by the hand of his Son. The prophets remind the people of that remarkable miracle by calling Christ the Branch of David (Jeremiah 33:15).

Establishing and upholding it with justice and righteousness from that time on and forever. The words **justice and righteousness** do not here refer to outward affairs of state. We must observe the analogy between the kingdom of Christ and its qualities; being spiritual, it is established by the power of the Holy Spirit. In a word, all these things must be viewed as referring to the inner person—that is, when we are regenerated by God to true righteousness. It is true that outward righteousness follows, but it must be preceded by that renewal of mind and heart. We are not Christ's, therefore, unless we follow what is good and just and bear on our hearts the stamp of that righteousness that has been sealed by the Holy Spirit.

The zeal of the LORD Almighty will accomplish this. By zeal I understand that ardent desire that God will display in preserving his church by removing all difficulties and obstructions that might otherwise have hindered its redemption.

8. The Lord has sent a message against Jacob; it will fall on Israel. Here he relates a new prediction; I think this discourse is separated from the previous one because the prophet is now going back to speak of the future condition of the kingdom of Israel, which was at that time hostile to the Jews. We know that the Jews had good reason for being alarmed at the forces and power of that kingdom, especially when it had made a league with the Syrians, because they saw they were not strong enough to oppose them. In order, therefore, to yield comfort to the godly, Isaiah shows what will be the future condition of the kingdom of Israel.

By **Jacob** and **Israel** he means the same thing; but the diversity of expression is elegant and is intended to show that the wicked gain nothing by their opposition when they endeavor either to turn away from them or to alter God's judgment.

9. All the people will know it—Ephraim and the inhabitants of Samaria—who say with pride and arrogance of heart . . . Here the prophet attacks the obstinacy of the people because, though they had been repeatedly chastised by God's scourges, they were so far from repentance that they reckoned their losses to be gain and became more hardened.

10. "The bricks have fallen down, but we will rebuild with dressed stone; the fig trees have been felled, but we will replace them with cedars." These are the words of men who were obstinate and who despised the calamity they had sustained, as if it had been an advantage to them. They say, "The brick houses have been thrown down so that we may dwell in splendid palaces; and since the trees have been cut down, we shall plant more fruitful ones."

11. But the LORD has strengthened Rezin's foes against them and has spurred their enemies on. The Israelites had been proud of their alliance with the king of Syria. Isaiah warns of a change that will take away all their hope and utterly frustrate their designs, for the Assyrians later fought against the Syrians. Accordingly, when Rezin had been killed (2 Kings 16:9), that country was entirely ruined.

12. Arameans from the east and Philistines from the west have devoured Israel with open mouth. Yet for all this, his anger is not turned away, his hand is still upraised. The prophet shows what will happen after the death of Rezin. Namely, the Syrians, after the death of their king, rather than being allies will suddenly become enemies and will make war against Israel; and this is in fact what took place. From this example we ought to learn what it is to rely on human power and the alliances of kings, especially when, in consequence of being entangled by unlawful covenants, we become careless and fall asleep.

Have devoured Israel with open mouth. In other words, "Israel will be exposed as a prey to her enemies, so that on every hand she will be devoured both by the Syrians and by the Philistines."

His anger is not turned away. The ungodly ought to have been frightened that though they had suffered much, they had more to endure. New punishments continually await such persons because they inflame God's wrath even more.

13. But the people have not returned to him who struck them, nor have they sought the LORD Almighty. It is a very severe rebuke that although the Lord not only warns us verbally but actually pushes us forward and constrains us by various chastisements, we still become hardened and do not allow ourselves to be drawn away from our crimes and our lusts. This rebuke applies not only to the Israelites but to us also.

14. So the LORD will cut off from Israel both head and tail, both palm branch and reed in a single day. By **branch** he means the stronger and more powerful; by **reed** he means the feebler people—that is, those of lowest rank. He therefore means that God's vengeance hangs over them and spares neither the strong nor the weak, neither the highest nor the lowest, because no part is sound or uninfected by the general disease.

15-16. The elders and prominent men are the head, the prophets who teach lies are the tail. Those who guide this people mislead them, and those who are guided are led astray. Because of our sins, which are evident in all kinds of people, God's wrath is kindled against the highest and the lowest. We ought, especially at the present day, in the middle of every kind of evil, to fear lest when the wrath of God has begun to burn, it may consume everything, high and low.

Those who guide this people mislead them. No excuse is given to anyone for seeking to make bad rulers a cloak for their own transgressions. This is often done, but if the blind lead the blind, as Christ says, both will fall into the ditch. It is certain that the only people who are ruined by wicked and treacherous leaders are those who of their own accord wish to be led astray.

17. Therefore the Lord will take no pleasure in the young men, nor will he pity the fatherless and widows. The Lord warns that he will pay no regard either to gender or to age.

For everyone is ungodly and wicked, every mouth speaks vileness. By this he does not mean slight dissimulation but inward contempt in the heart, by which consciences are stupefied, so that no instructions produce any effect on them. It is as if he said they were deeply sunk in their depravity.

Yet for all this, his anger is not turned away, his hand is still upraised. Since the prophet repeats this warning (see verses 12, 21), let us always recall that the indignation of God is not yet appeased, though we may think he has already punished us severely for our sins.

18. Surely wickedness burns like a fire; it consumes briers and thorns, it sets the forest thickets ablaze, so that it rolls upward in a column of smoke. This flame will seize every part of Judea. Two things are here expressed: The punishment of sin proceeds from the judgment of God, and yet the blame lies with the sinners themselves, that they may not remonstrate with God as if he had dealt cruelly with them.

19. By the wrath of the LORD Almighty the land will be scorched and the people will be fuel for the fire; no one will spare his brother. In the last clause and in the following verse, the prophet describes the methods and means by which the Lord will execute his vengeance. When we see no enemies whom we have cause to dread, we will arm ourselves for our destruction. In other words, "The Lord will find no difficulty in executing the vengeance he threatens; for even if there is no one to attack us from outside, he will ruin us by civil wars."

20. On the right they will devour, but still be hungry; on the left they will eat, but not be satisfied. Each will feed on the flesh of his own offspring. The first clause denotes either insatiable covetousness or insatiable cruelty. Let us therefore remember that it is a dreadful proof of heavenly punishment when brothers inflict mutual wounds.

21. Manasseh will feed on Ephraim, and Ephraim on Manasseh; together they will turn against Judah. Yet for all this, his anger is not turned away, his hand is still upraised. After Manasseh and Ephraim have worn themselves out by mutual wounds, both will unite against Judah, in order to destroy it.

Isaiah
Chapter 10

1. Woe to those who make unjust laws, to those who issue oppressive decrees. Isaiah now attacks the people more closely, as he did in chapters 1 and 2, to make them feel that they are justly afflicted; for people never acknowledge that their punishment is fair until they have been manifestly convicted and constrained.

2. To deprive the poor of their rights and rob my oppressed people of justice, making widows their prey and robbing the fatherless. The poor are deprived of their rights, are robbed for the sake of the rich, and go away mocked from the judgment seats of men while everything is laid open to plunder. Meanwhile, the powerful and wealthy are warned not to think they have not been punished; although no avenger is seen now, the Lord will avenge.

3. What will you do on the day of reckoning, when disaster comes from afar? This refers to judgment, for God visits us in two ways—in mercy and in judgment.

To whom will you run for help? Where will you leave your riches? He declares that it is in vain for them to rely on their allies, for, compared with God's hand, those allies will be fruitless and of no help at all. No one has any reason to flatter himself; we shall all be like stubble when the Lord's wrath has been kindled against us (Psalm 83:13).

4. Nothing will remain but to cringe among the captives or fall among the slain. Yet for all this, his anger is not turned away, his hand is still upraised. From what immediately follows, we learn that a dreadful and alarming destruction is threatened; for he repeats what he had already said frequently, that the wrath of the Lord is not yet apparent, but he will exercise more frightful punishments for avenging himself. This teaches us that nothing is more truly desirable than to be moved by a sincere feeling of repentance and to acknowledge our fault, that we may obtain pardon from the Lord.

5. "Woe to the Assyrian, the rod of my anger." What now follows relates to the threatening of punishment but at the same time mingles some consolation in order to alleviate the distress of the godly. Indeed, the greater part of the discourse is occupied with the teaching that all the afflictions that will be brought on them by the Assyrians are a temporary scourge inflicted by God, but that unbelievers, after having indulged themselves too freely, will at length be brought to submission.

"In whose hand is the club of my wrath!" This may be viewed as referring to the Assyrians and may be explained as a repetition of the previous statement, with a slight change of words. The general meaning is: "All the strength that the enemy possesses comes from the wrath of God, and they are moved by his secret impulse to destroy the people, for otherwise he would not move a finger."

6. "I send him against a godless nation, I dispatch him against a people who anger me, to seize loot and snatch plunder, and to trample them down like mud in the streets." God calls Israel a **godless** nation because it has no uprightness or sincerity. He says he has given free rein to the enemies' ferocity, that they may indulge in every kind of violence and injustice without control. We must not understand this to mean that the Assyrians were excused because they had been commanded by God. There are two ways in which God commands—by his secret decree, of which people are not conscious, and by his law, in which he demands from us voluntary obedience.

7. "But this is not what he intends, this is not what he has in mind; his purpose is to destroy, to put an end to many nations." God through the prophet threatens that the Assyrians also will have their turn and in due time will receive just punishment; and yet it is not unreasonable that they should distress, plunder, devour, and slay other nations, because their own punishment is reserved for them.

8. "'Are not my commanders all kings?'" he says. The prophet here gives a lifelike picture of the presumption of a heathen king boasting that he has everything in his power.

9. "'Has not Calno fared like Carchemish? Is not Hamath like Arpad, and Samaria like Damascus?'" Here he mentions by name certain cities or fortified places. When we read this story, let us learn that we ought not to be proud of being strong, for he who has exalted us will be able to cast us down. And if he reproves the Assyrian for that haughtiness, how much more should people be reproved when they boast that they are righteous and holy?

10-11. "'As my hand seized the kingdoms of the idols, kingdoms whose images excelled those of Jerusalem and Samaria—shall I not deal with Jerusalem and her images as I dealt with Samaria and her idols?'" Wicked men are so proud that they attribute their victories to their own strength and do not hesitate to exalt themselves against God and all that is worshiped. Indeed, they claim that they pay homage to the objects of their own worship—that is, to the idols they have contrived for themselves—and bow before them and offer sacrifices to them, thus indicating that they ascribe their victories to the gods.

12. When the Lord has finished all his work against Mount Zion and Jerusalem, he will say, "I will punish the king of Assyria for the willful pride of his heart and the haughty look in his eyes." Until now the prophet had explained what would happen to the pride of the king of Assyria after his victory over Israel; but now he foretells what will happen to the king himself and what will be God's purpose against him. Wicked men do everything as if God were not in heaven and cannot frustrate their designs. God promises, in a word, that after allowing the Assyrian ruler to display himself beyond measure, he will in his turn be an avenger, for it belongs to him to repress the pride of the flesh.

Mount Zion here means the church, and **Jerusalem** is used in the same sense. The prophet uses the temple and the royal city, as the head, to describe the whole body, describing the whole kingdom by means of the most important parts.

13. "For he says: 'By the strength of my hand I have done this, and by my wisdom, because I have understanding. I removed the boundaries of nations, I plundered their treasures; like a mighty one I subdued their kings.'" The prophet again repeats the highly blasphemous words that the Assyrian king uttered, for he ascribes to his power and wisdom all the victories that he obtained. **The strength of my hand** means vast armies collected out of various nations.

14. "'As one reaches into a nest, so my hand reached for the wealth of the nations; as men gather abandoned eggs, so I gathered all the countries; not one flapped a wing, or opened its mouth to chirp.'" That king adds that it is no trouble for him to vanquish other kings and amass their wealth; and he illustrates this by a comparison. It is as if one were looking for a nest that had been deserted by the birds, and so one takes the eggs without difficulty. If the parent birds were sitting on the eggs, having an instinctive desire to protect their nest, they would attack the robber. But this tyrant boasts that no one ventured so much as to open their mouth against him, and therefore he had no difficulty in bringing all the kingdoms under his dominion. Accordingly he lays claim to all these things and attributes them to his wisdom and makes no acknowledgment of God's providence.

15. Does the ax raise itself above him who swings it, or the saw boast against him who uses it? As if a rod were to wield him who lifts it up, or a club brandish him who is not wood! Isaiah now ridicules the Assyrians even more for their mad effrontery. He says this is like an **ax** or **rod** or **club** despising the hand that sets them in motion and being proud of their activity, although it is clear that they have no power of their own to move.

In this passage Isaiah chiefly shows that all human efforts are fruitless if God does not grant success; and therefore the Assyrians, even if they had attempted everything, would not have succeeded, if the Lord had not given victory.

16. Therefore, the Lord, the LORD Almighty, will send a wasting disease upon his sturdy warriors. The Assyrian monarch trusted in his wealth and his forces, but Isaiah says that the Lord will take them away.

Under his pomp a fire will be kindled like a blazing flame. This means that the greater the splendor of his prosperity, the more abundant will be the fuel for the conflagration.

17. The Light of Israel will become a fire. In fire are two things—light and heat. As the Lord consumes the enemies by his heat, so he enlightens the godly by his light. When he shines on the godly, he imparts life and nourishment to them; but he consumes and destroys the ungodly.

Their Holy One a flame. This means that God determines to protect the people whom he has chosen and whom he has separated from the rest of the nations to be a special people for himself.

In a single day it will burn and consume his thorns and his briers. This means that God will burn them with a sudden and unexpected conflagration. The language here denotes an uncommon and dreadful burning that usually overtakes the wicked suddenly, when they think all is well with them.

18. The splendor of his forests and fertile fields it will completely destroy, as when a sick man wastes away. He continues the same metaphor of burning and declares that the fire will consume both the highest and the lowest and will leave nothing uninjured.

19. And the remaining trees of his forests will be so few that a child could write them down. When he adds that the remnant **will be so few,** he confirms what he has just said: The devastation, after the calamity God brings on the Assyrians, will be so great that there will be no difficulty in counting the survivors.

20. In that day the remnant of Israel, the survivors of the house of Jacob, will no longer rely on him who struck them down but will truly rely on the LORD, the Holy One of Israel. The prophet now returns to the elect people, and he describes the result of the chastisement that was at hand.

21. A remnant will return, a remnant of Jacob will return to the Mighty God. This is a confirmation of the previous statement.

22. Though your people, O Israel, be like the sand by the sea, only a remnant will return. Destruction has been decreed, overwhelming and righteous. God destroys the foolish confidence of the hypocrites. They thought it was enough to be the physical descendants of holy Abraham, and therefore, on the sole ground of their birth, they wished to be accounted holy. Yet he exhorts the godly to have patience, that they may learn to wait calmly for that calamity and diminution of their number, lest when it took place it should be unexpected and upset them.

23. The Lord, the LORD Almighty, will carry out the destruction decreed upon the whole land. This repetition again wounds the self-complacency of those who proudly despised God. It was almost incredible that the Jews, to whom so many promises had been given, should perish, as it were, in an instant; and this appeared to be inconsistent with the unchangeable nature of God. The prophet therefore declares that the Lord is the author of this **destruction** in order to stamp out the pride of wicked people who rely on their present prosperity.

24. Therefore, this is what the Lord, the LORD Almighty, says: "O my people who live in Zion, do not be afraid of the Assyrians, who beat you with a rod and lift up a club against you, as Egypt did." He continues with the same consolation, which belongs to the godly alone, who at that time were undoubtedly few in number. He adds a ground of consolation: Namely, that calamity will be nothing but the lifting up of a **rod** to chastise but not to destroy them.

25. "Very soon my anger against you will end and my wrath will be directed to their destruction." He means not only the siege of Jerusalem, when Sennacherib surrounded it with a large army (2 Kings 18:17), but also the rest of the calamities, when Jerusalem was overthrown (2 Kings 25:4), the temple razed, and the inhabitants taken prisoner.

26. The LORD Almighty will lash them with a whip, as when he struck down Midian at the rock of Oreb; and he will raise his rod over the waters, as he did in Egypt. Here Isaiah uses the word **whip,** not rod, meaning that the Lord will treat the enemies much more harshly and severely than they had treated the Jews. He threatens them with extermination and makes it more plain with two examples. First, that of the Midianites (Judges 7:25), who were cut off by a dreadful slaughter in the valley of Oreb, which was so named from their leader. Second, that of the Egyptians, whom the Lord sank in the Red Sea when they were pursuing his people (Exodus 14:27-28).

27. In that day their burden will be lifted from your shoulders, their yoke from your neck; the yoke will be broken because you have grown so fat. Isaiah wants to comfort the godly who were involved in the present distress. It might be thought that the promise failed and that the calamities that immediately followed were utterly at variance with it. Yet he confirms the promise that God will not only rescue them from Babylon but will also help them against the besieging army of the tyrant, whom he will not allow to go beyond what has been threatened.

28. They enter Aiath; they pass through Migron; they store supplies at Micmash. With the siege of the holy city at hand, Isaiah sets before their eyes the whole of Sennacherib's march, that the hearts of the godly, by long and careful study of it, may remain steadfast. This delineation was powerfully calculated to allay their fears when godly men saw that the Assyrians did not move a step but by the appointment of God.

29. They go over the pass, and say, "We will camp overnight at Geba." Ramah trembles; Gibeah of Saul flees. He mentions **Ramah** in preference to the rest because it was the nearest town; and he describes the flight of the inhabitants of some towns as if the mere report had so frightened them that they gave up their country into the enemy's hand.

30. Cry out, O Daughter of Gallim! Listen, O Laishah! Poor Anathoth! By the words **Cry out** he denotes the howling and cries that will be heard at a distance. It is very common, in the Hebrew language, to call cities daughters. He says that the howling will be so great that it will be heard even by the neighboring cities; the groans uttered in **Anathoth** will even be heard at **Laishah**.

31. Madmenah is in flight; the people of Gebim take cover. In exaggerated language the prophet says the city was shaken as if it had been removed to another place. This relates to the disorderly movements of a people in flight; it is like saying the inhabitants of that city were thrown into as great a commotion as if the city had been razed to its foundations.

32-33. This day they will halt at Nob; they will shake their fist at the mount of the Daughter of Zion, at the hill of Jerusalem. See, the Lord, the LORD Almighty, will lop off the boughs with great power. The lofty trees will be felled, the tall ones will be brought low. This helps show their fear even more, for Sennacherib, having conquered the whole country, will threaten Jerusalem as if he could storm it with great ease.

In saying **the mount of the Daughter of Zion** he includes the whole city, because that part was higher and commanded a view of the other quarters of the city. From this confidence of the tyrant, he shows that Jerusalem was not far from utter destruction, for the whole country, and even the city, was struck with such terror that no one ventured to oppose him. So the prophet is using these details to give a more impressive view of the kindness of God. Jerusalem's preservation, like a sheep rescued from the jaws of a lion, must be ascribed to God's extraordinary favor and goodness, and not to human aid, of which there was none.

34. He will cut down the forest thickets with an ax; Lebanon will fall before the Mighty One. There is no difficulty in explaining this metaphor, for it is plain enough that the trees denote all that is powerful, excellent, or lofty. Thus Isaiah foretells the destruction and ruin of Judea, which he compares to cutting down the **forest thickets.** By this he means there is nothing so valuable that the enemies will not destroy it, until they have stripped the whole land of its ornaments.

He mentions **Lebanon** because it was greatly celebrated for fruitful and highly valuable trees. If he had been speaking of the Assyrians, it would not have been appropriate to introduce the destruction of Lebanon. Hence we infer that the prophet, in this passage, is again threatening the Jews.

Isaiah
Chapter 11

1-2. A shoot will come up from the stump of Jesse; from his roots a Branch will bear fruit. The Spirit of the LORD will rest on him—the Spirit of wisdom and of understanding, the Spirit of counsel and of power, the Spirit of knowledge and of the fear of the Lord. As the description of such dreadful calamities might terrify the godly and give them reason for despair, it was necessary to hold out consolation. When the kingdom was destroyed, cities thrown down, and desolation spread over the whole country, there might have been nothing left but grief and lamentation; and therefore they might have tottered and fallen or been greatly discouraged if the Lord had not provided this consolation for them. Isaiah therefore declares what the Lord will do afterwards and how he will restore that kingdom. He pursues the metaphor that he employed toward the conclusion of the previous chapter. He had said that Jerusalem would be destroyed like a forest consumed by a single conflagration (Isaiah 10:17-19; cf. 10:33-34). Its future desolation would be like that of a country formerly covered with forests, when the trees had been cut down, and nothing could be seen but ashes.

This prediction in chapter 11 applies solely to the person of Christ, for until he came no such branch arose. It certainly cannot be applied to Hezekiah or Josiah, who from their very infancy were brought up in the expectation of occupying a throne.

The Spirit of the LORD will rest on him. He now begins to speak of Christ plainly and directly. Before, it was sufficient to represent the consolation by a simile in order to make clear the full contrast between the burning of the wood and its springing up anew.

The Spirit of the LORD refers to Christ's human nature; he could only be enriched with the gift and grace of the Father if he became man. Besides, in coming down to us, he received the gifts of the Spirit, so that he could bestow them upon us.

The Spirit of wisdom and of understanding. It is unnecessary to give great attention to single words, but if anyone wants to draw a slight distinction between **wisdom** and **understanding,** I consider it to be that the word **wisdom** includes all that relates to the regulation of life, and **understanding** is added to explain it. If we are endowed with this **wisdom,** we will have great discernment.

The Spirit of counsel and of power, the Spirit of knowledge and of the fear of the LORD. Here **counsel** means judgment by which we can thread our way through intricate affairs. **Understanding** would not be sufficient without **counsel,** but with it we can act with caution in doubtful matters. The word **power** is easily understood. **Knowledge** differs little from **understanding,** except that it relates more to the act of knowing and thus declares what has taken place. **The fear of the LORD** means a sincere desire to worship God.

The prophet is not here enumerating all the gifts of the Holy Spirit, as some have thought.

3. And he will delight in the fear of the LORD. Here **the fear of the LORD** denotes a fixed rule of judging. The prophet specifically distinguishes between the heavenly judgment of Christ and earthly judgments, in order to inform us that the outward mask of holiness or uprightness is of no use in his presence.

He will not judge by what he sees with his eyes, or decide by what he hears with his ears. This means, "When we come to the judgment seat of Christ, not only will outward actions be on trial as before human government, but people's lives will be examined by the standard of true godliness. Humankind cannot penetrate into the heart—those we suppose to be excellent people often have nothing but a hollow mask. But Christ does not judge by outward appearance" (see Luke 11:37 and following; John 2:23-25).

4. But with righteousness he will judge the needy, with justice he will give decisions for the poor of the earth. Here he shows that Christ will be the guardian of the poor, or he points out the people to whom the grace of Christ strictly belongs—namely, to the poor or meek—that is, to those who, humbled by a conviction of their poverty, have laid aside the proud and lofty attitudes that often swell people's minds until they have learned to be meek through the subduing influence of God's Word. So he says that Christ will be the protector and guardian, not of all people, but of those who know they are poor and destitute of everything good. Christ also said this to John's disciples when he said that the Gospel is preached to the poor (Matthew 11:5).

He will strike the earth with the rod of his mouth; with the breath of his lips he will slay the wicked. The prophet here extols the efficacy of the Word, which is Christ's royal scepter. By **the rod of his mouth** is meant a scepter that consists of words, and in the second clause he repeats the same idea in the phrase, **the breath of his lips.** In other words, Christ will have no need to seek help from others to defeat his enemies and to strike down everything that opposes his government, for a mere **breath** or a word will be enough.

5. Righteousness will be his belt and faithfulness the sash around his waist. The prophet describes two ornaments belonging to the belt—**righteousness** and **faithfulness.** This is like saying, "He will not appear like other kings, clothed with purple and a crown or girded with a belt; rather, **righteousness** and **faithfulness** will shine from him."

6-7. The wolf will live with the lamb, the leopard will lie down with the goat, the calf and the lion and the yearling together; and a little child will lead them. The cow will feed with the bear, their young will lie down together, and the lion will eat straw like the ox. The prophet goes back to describing the character and habits of those who have submitted to Christ. It is as if he said that the golden age will return in which perfect happiness existed, before the fall of mankind and the shock and ruin of the world that followed it. (See Hebrews 2:8.)

Although Isaiah says wild and tame beasts will live in harmony, so God's blessing may be seen clearly and fully, his chief meaning is that the people of Christ will have no inclination to inflict injury or be fierce or cruel. They were previously like lions or leopards but will now be like sheep or lambs, for they will have laid aside every cruel and brutish disposition. By these expressions he simply means that those who formerly were like savage beasts will be mild and gentle.

And a little child will lead them. This means that beasts that formerly were cruel and untamed will be ready to yield cheerful obedience, so that there will be no need for violence to restrain their fierceness. Yet we must attend to the spiritual meaning noticed above, that all who become Christ's followers will obey Christ, though they may formerly have been savage wild beasts, and will obey him in such a way that as soon as he lifts his finger they will follow his footsteps (Psalm 110:3).

8. The infant will play near the hole of the cobra, and the young child put his hand into the viper's nest. Isaiah continues to illustrate the same sentiment that when people have been brought into a state of favor with God and have been cleansed from their depravity by the Spirit of regeneration, they will likewise be free from every hurtful disposition.

9. They will neither harm nor destroy on all my holy mountain, for the earth will be full of the knowledge of the LORD as the waters cover the sea. He now says plainly that men themselves, having laid aside the depravity that is in them by nature, will be inclined, of their own accord, to do what is right. He is talking about believers who have been truly regenerated to "a new life" (Romans 6:4); for although in the church many hypocrites full of wickedness are mixed with the elect of God, yet they are like the Ishmaelites, whom God will cast out at the proper time.

ISAIAH

The prophet has good reason to add that this invaluable blessing flows from the knowledge of God. It abases all flesh and teaches people to commit themselves to his trust and guardianship and brings them into a state of brotherly harmony when they learn that they have the same Father (Malachi 2:10).

As the waters cover the sea. There is an implied comparison between the abundance of knowledge and the first taste that God gave to the ancient people under the law. The Jews were kept in the rudiments of childhood, but the perfect light of wisdom has shone on us fully in the Gospel, as was also foretold by Jeremiah (see Jeremiah 31:34).

10. In that day the Root of Jesse will stand as a banner for the peoples; the nations will rally to him. Again the prophet returns to the person of Christ and repeats the same comparison he introduced at the beginning of the chapter, that of a root or branch springing from a decayed trunk, of which no trace appeared; and he predicts that the Gentiles, who used to abhor the Jews, will from that time bow before their King with lowly homage.

He compares Christ to a **banner** stretched aloft. We know this was fulfilled by the preaching of the Gospel and indeed was more illustrious than if Christ had soared above the clouds.

And his place of rest will be glorious. These words are commonly explained as referring to the burial of Christ, for afterwards they apply also to his death. Indeed the burial of Christ was nothing but an appendage to his death. But when I take a closer view of the whole, by **place of rest** the prophet means in this passage the church (see Psalm 132:14). He bestows an honorable name on the assembly of the godly because he chooses to live among them always.

11. In that day the Lord will reach out his hand a second time. The prediction about the future glory of the church was incredible. So Isaiah explains how he will restore it: God will display the power of his hand, as if to do something memorable and uncommon.

To reclaim the remnant that is left of his people. He confirms what he has said by another argument. Although it appeared as if God had disregarded his people, he would not allow himself to be deprived of his inheritance. We may sum this up by saying that God will take care of the salvation of his church, so as not to be robbed of his right. He expressly calls them a **remnant** because this deliverance belonged only to a small seed (compare Isaiah 1:9; 10:22). In short, he repeats what he said before: "Although God disperses his church, yet it is impossible that he can ever cast it away altogether, for it is as dear to him as our inheritance is to any of us."

From Assyria, from Lower Egypt, from Upper Egypt, from Cush, from Elam, from Babylonia, from Hamath and from the islands of the sea. He speaks not only of the Assyrians, who had led the people captive, but also of other nations among whom the Jews were scattered. Although

108

most of the people were carried off to Babylon, some fled into Egypt, some into Ethiopia, and some into other countries.

12. He will raise a banner for the nations and gather the exiles of Israel; he will assemble the scattered people of Judah from the four quarters of the earth. This verse explains verse 11.

13. Ephraim's jealousy will vanish, and Judah's enemies will be cut off; Ephraim will not be jealous of Judah, nor Judah hostile toward Ephraim. Here he promises that the church will be in such a peaceful state that the Israelites and the Jews will not engage in civil disputes or suffer from their enemies, and they will not be liable to hatred or envy, as they were before.

14. They will swoop down on the slopes of Philistia to the west; together they will plunder the people to the east. They will lay hands on Edom and Moab, and the Ammonites will be subject to them. He means there is also another way in which the Lord will assist his people: He will conquer their enemies and subdue them under his dominion. Having spoken of the safety of the church, Isaiah now declares that she will be victorious over her enemies. He mentions those nations with which the Jews incessantly carried on wars, for on the one hand the Philistines and on the other the **Ammonites** and Moabites were continually attacking them. On one side also were the Edomites. The Lord, therefore, promises that although the church is not absolutely without enemies, she will gain advantage over them by suffering and will in the end be victorious.

15. The Lord will dry up the gulf of the Egyptian sea; with a scorching wind he will sweep his hand over the Euphrates River. The Lord, by his amazing power, will open for his people a way that previously appeared closed.

He will break it up into seven streams so that men can cross over in sandals. The river being deep, he says he will dry it up, so that it will not be necessary to take off their shoes in crossing it, though this would have been necessary if even a small amount of water had remained.

By these metaphors the prophet simply means that nothing will stand in God's way when he chooses to rescue his people from captivity; it will be the same as the deliverance they experienced before. He wanted to set this before their eyes, so to speak, because the means of this deliverance was not seen. If this promise had been stated in plain terms, it might not have produced such a deep impression on their minds as by offering them this remarkable example.

16. There will be a highway for the remnant of his people that is left from Assyria, as there was for Israel when they came up from Egypt. This verse contains nothing new but explains the previous verse. The people would perceive the same power of God in the deliverance from Babylon as they had perceived in the deliverance from Egypt.

Isaiah
Chapter 12

1. In that day you will say: "I will praise you, O LORD. Although you were angry with me, your anger has turned away and you have comforted me." Isaiah now urges all godly people to give thanks. Yet the exhortation has also this object—that the promise may be more fully believed. He seals it with this indirect exhortation so as to make them convinced that it is certain.

The leading thought of the song is that although God was right to be offended at his people, he was satisfied with inflicting a moderate chastisement and showed that he was willing to be pacified. When we have been relieved from distresses, let us call to mind that our punishment is ended because in his fatherly love God spares us in our weakness.

2. "Surely God is my salvation; I will trust and not be afraid. The LORD, the LORD, is my strength and my song; he has become my salvation." In the midst of our afflictions it is right to see by faith the salvation of God. Yet here Isaiah is speaking about knowledge derived from experience. He gives us an example of a joyful song in which God shows by outward signs that he is pacified toward his church.

When we are fully convinced that salvation is laid up for us in God, this is a solid foundation of full confidence and the best remedy for allaying fears. But for this we must have previously trembled and have been uneasy and distressed and tortured by painful emotions. Hence we conclude that faith generates confidence, as cause and effect. By faith we perceive that salvation is laid up for us in God, and a calm and peaceful state of mind arises from that; but when faith is lacking, there can be no peace of conscience.

The reason the Lord is called the **song** of the godly is that he bestows on them abundant kindness in order to encourage them to perform the duty of thankfulness.

3. With joy you will draw water from the wells of salvation. In this verse he confirms that this chapter may be regarded as a seal to confirm the promise that God gave of his people's redemption. In other words, "The salvation of God has been set before you, as if it were a constant running fountain from which you can draw water in abundance."

This is a very beautiful metaphor, for in this life nothing is more necessary than water. No kind of scarcity gives us more uneasiness or more distress than a lack of water. Thus he declares that everything necessary for supporting life flows to us from the undeserved goodness of God.

4. In that day you will say: "Give thanks to the LORD, call on his name." He exhorts them not only to sing praise and give thanks to God individually, but to encourage others to do the same.

"Make known among the nations what he has done, and proclaim that his name is exalted." He means that the work of this deliverance will be so excellent that it ought to be proclaimed not in one corner only but throughout the whole world. He wished, indeed, that it should be made known to the Jews first of all, but then that it should be spread abroad to all people.

5. "Sing to the LORD." He continues his exhortation, showing where this thanksgiving should come from. He shows that it is our duty to proclaim God's goodness to every nation.

"For he has done glorious things." He means there are abundant grounds for singing. If we consider the work of our deliverance as we ought to, we will have abundant grounds for praising God.

"Let this be known to all the world." He glances at the calling of the Gentiles and confirms that the work is such that it ought not to be concealed in a corner but ought to be proclaimed everywhere.

6. "Shout aloud and sing for joy, people of Zion, for great is the Holy One of Israel among you." Again he urges the godly to rejoice in the Lord, at the same time reminding them of the nature of true joy and what it is founded on. We have no other happiness than to have God dwelling among us. Except for this, our life would be wretched and unhappy, even if we had abundance of other blessings and of every other kind of riches.

Isaiah
Chapter 13

1. An oracle concerning Babylon that Isaiah son of Amoz saw. From this chapter to chapter 24, the prophet foretells what dreadful and shocking calamities awaited the Gentiles and those countries that were best known to the Jews, either on account of their being contiguous to them or through commerce and alliances; and he has weighty reasons for doing this.

There is nothing harder to convince people of than the fact that God's providence governs this world. It is true that many people acknowledge it in words, but very few have it actually engraved on their heart. We tremble and shudder at the very smallest change, and we inquire into the causes as if it depended on human decisions. What will happen, then, when the whole world is thrown into commotion and the face of affairs is so completely changed in various places that it appears as if everything is going toward ruin?

It was therefore very useful that Isaiah and other prophets should teach about calamities of this nature, so everyone might understand that those calamities took place only by God's secret and wonderful purpose.

The word **oracle** was generally used by God's prophets whenever they warned about any event that would bring affliction, in order to inform the people that no such event happened that the Lord himself did not lay as a burden on people's shoulders.

Isaiah specifically states that what he is about to utter was revealed to him by a heavenly vision, so the weight thus given to it might render it victorious over all human judgments.

2. Raise a banner on a bare hilltop, shout to them; beckon to them to enter the gates of the nobles. He means that the Persians and Medes will no sooner begin to advance into Babylon at the command of God than their road will be plain and easy in spite of every obstruction. The prophet warns that nothing will hinder God from opening up a way and entrance to the enemies.

3. I have commanded my holy ones; I have summoned my warriors to carry out my wrath—those who rejoice in my triumph. Here the prophet introduces the Lord as speaking and issuing his commands. He calls the Medes and Persians **holy ones**—that is, those whom he has prepared. He warns that Babylon will be destroyed by the Medes and Persians just as if they obeyed God's call. Although they were prompted into battle by their own ambition, pride, and cruelty, yet God directed them, without their knowing it, to execute his judgment.

4. Listen, a noise on the mountains, like that of a great multitude! Listen, an uproar among the kingdoms, like nations massing together! The LORD Almighty is mustering an army for war. He adds an even more vivid description. The prophets are not satisfied with speaking unless they also give a bold picture of the events themselves. It is as if he said, "Now, indeed, you hear a man speaking, but know that this voice will be so powerful that at the sound of it nations will be roused, peoples will make a noise, and vast crowds will shout and roar to bring destruction on the inhabitants of Babylon. This proclamation, therefore, will be as efficacious, even after I am dead, as if you now saw what I foretell."

5. They come from faraway lands. He repeats more fully that the operations of war do not spring up at random from the earth. Isaiah justly ascribes sovereignty to God, adding that armed men are nothing but the weapons of his indignation (verse 5b). He says they will come **from faraway lands** to overturn the monarchy of Babylon. We are not afraid of dangers unless they are at hand.

From the ends of the heavens. There being no trouble around them to threaten them, he gives warning that the calamity will come from a distance. Although everything appears to be calm and peaceful, and although we are not at variance with our neighbors, God can bring enemies from **the ends of the heavens.** There is no reason, therefore, why we should promise ourselves a lasting and prosperous condition, even if we are not threatened with any immediate danger. If this prediction had reached the inhabitants of Babylon, they would undoubtedly have laughed at it as a fable.

The LORD and the weapons of his wrath. Isaiah means that the Medes and Persians may be regarded as darts in the hand of God, so that he may execute his vengeance by means of them.

To destroy the whole country. When he says **the whole country** to represent Babylon, he is looking at the extent of the kingdom, so they will not think that the great number of provinces, by which they were surrounded on all sides, could ward off enemy attacks.

6. Wail, for the day of the LORD is near; it will come like destruction from the Almighty. He continues the same argument, telling the inhabitants of Babylon to howl. When the Lord delays his judgment, he appears to stop discharging his office, like judges when they do not ascend the judgment seat. We would gladly make God immediately pass sentence against the wicked. But he has his own appointed time and knows when it is proper both to punish the bad and to assist the good.

7. Because of this, all hands will go limp, every man's heart will melt. He shows that the Lord's power to destroy the inhabitants of Babylon will be so great that they will have no means of withstanding his anger.

8. Terror will seize them, pain and anguish will grip them. Where does this **terror** come from? From God. This kind of terror, for which there was no apparent cause, classical authors called panic.

They will writhe like a woman in labor. They will look aghast at each other, their faces aflame. So far as the inhabitants of Babylon were concerned, there was, indeed, good reason to be afraid when they saw they were being attacked by valiant and warlike nations. But the prophet warns that though they were able to resist, they would still be like half-dead people because God was working secretly to make them faint and fall down. For the same reason he adds that **they will look aghast at each other.** Everyone will be amazed at his neighbor. The final clause, in which he attributes to them faces of flame, expresses still more strongly the intensity of the terror.

9. See, the day of the LORD is coming—a cruel day, with wrath and fierce anger—to make the land desolate and destroy the sinners within it. He repeats that although the inhabitants of Babylon are now at ease and rely on their wealth, the day of the Lord is at hand, and it will terrify those who are at ease. The godly, on the other hand, whenever the name of God is mentioned, derive the greatest delight and joy from hearing it; nothing can please them more.

10. The stars of heaven and their constellations will not show their light. The rising sun will be darkened and the moon will not give its light. To highlight the fear of God's judgment, the prophets often added to their warnings exaggerated ways of speaking, to set God's anger, so to speak, before their eyes and to affect all their senses, as if all the elements were arising to execute his vengeance.

The **sun,** the **moon,** and the **stars** are mentioned because they are striking proofs of God's fatherly kindness toward us. Accordingly, when the sun, moon, and stars shine in heaven, God may be said to cheer us by his bright and gracious countenance. Their not showing light indicates the opposite.

11. I will punish the world for its evil, the wicked for their sins. Here the prophet is not speaking about the whole world. The city of Babylon was the seat of the most powerful of all monarchies; so he applies to it the word *world,* and he does so emphatically.

I will put an end to the arrogance of the haughty and will humble the pride of the ruthless. The prophet brings consolation to the godly by assuring them that although God spares the inhabitants of Babylon for a time, he will at length punish them for their injustice and cruelty. He expresses this still more clearly by taking notice of a particular vice—namely, **pride**. For this reason also he reproves their tyranny. But we ought also to draw from this the useful doctrine that it is impossible for us to escape the Lord's punishment if we are puffed up with vain confidence and flatter ourselves.

12. I will make man scarcer than pure gold, more rare than the gold of Ophir. Here he describes in a particular manner how cruel and savage will be the war that is waged against Babylon. The general meaning is that Babylon will not only be destroyed but will be utterly exterminated.

13. Therefore I will make the heavens tremble; and the earth will shake from its place at the wrath of the LORD Almighty, in the day of his burning anger. This is another dramatic figure of speech. God cannot too earnestly urge this doctrine, not only to terrify the wicked, but to bring consolation to the godly, who are often distressed when all is well with the wicked.

14. Like a hunted antelope, like sheep without a shepherd. He says they will all be like **a hunted antelope,** a timorous creature, and like scattered **sheep.** They will not return to their homes or posts.

Each will return to his own people, each will flee to his native land. The prophet speaks here of foreigners who had been brought to help protect the city.

15. Whoever is captured will be thrust through; all who are caught will fall by the sword. Here he says that no one will escape from Babylon and that all who are there will perish.

16. Their infants will be dashed to pieces before their eyes. He draws a picture of extreme cruelty. The invading army does not spare even defenseless children.

Their houses will be looted and their wives ravished. These things happen when the enemy has forgotten all humanity.

17. See, I will stir up against them the Medes. The prophet has predicted the destruction of the Babylonians, and now he says that God will accomplish this.

Who do not care for silver and have no delight in gold. He does not mean that the Medes were not guilty of plundering and covetousness. On the contrary, he means that the battle will be cruel and bloody, that they will aim at nothing but a general slaughter.

18. Their bows will strike down the young men; they will have no mercy on infants nor will they look with compassion on children. The cruelty of the Medes will be so great that they will not spare even infant children; no allowance will be made for age.

19. Babylon, the jewel of kingdoms, the glory of the Babylonians' pride, will be overthrown by God like Sodom and Gomorrah. Here the prophet intended to give a brief summary of his prophecy about the

Babylonians, but he enlarges it by some additions to show more fully that it will be completely destroyed. In this way the prophets referred to the punishment of the wicked.

The example of **Sodom and Gomorrah** is frequently used by the prophets to tell us that although the method of punishment is not the same, yet, since the judgment of God is impartial, that memorable display that he gave in Sodom (see Genesis 19:24) refers to all the reprobate. No less dreadful a punishment awaits those who are hardened in their sins by similar obstinacy.

20. She will never be inhabited or lived in through all generations; no Arab will pitch his tent there, no shepherd will rest his flocks there. The Babylonians will be destroyed in such a way that their ruin will be perpetual. The picture is further heightened by adding that the desolation will be so great that **no Arab will pitch his tent there,** nor will the **shepherd . . . rest his flocks there.**

21. But desert creatures will lie there, jackals will fill her houses; there the owls will dwell, and there the wild goats will leap about. He continues the description of a desert place and says that Babylon will be destitute of inhabitants.

22. Hyenas will howl in her strongholds, jackals in her luxurious palaces. Her time is at hand, and her days will not be prolonged. He expresses the same thing again and shows how dreadful that change will be, to show that it proceeds from the judgment of God, and not from chance.

Isaiah
Chapter 14

1. The LORD will have compassion on Jacob; once again he will choose Israel and will settle them in their own land. God's election is eternal. He does not **choose** us as if this had never before come into his mind; we were chosen before the foundation of the world (Ephesians 1:4), and he never repents of his choice (Romans 11:29). But when the Lord chastises his people, it seems as if he is rejecting them. So when the Lord calls us, that is, confirms his election, he is said to **choose** us; and when he gives evidence that he is displeased, he is said to reject us. The meaning, therefore, is, "The Lord has treated his people as severely as if he had rejected them; yet by the actual event he will at length show and prove that he has adopted them, by giving abundant evidence of his election and by having compassion on them forever."

Aliens will join them and unite with the house of Jacob. The prophet foretells the calling of the Gentiles. In other words, "The Lord will not only restore them to the possession of the land of Canaan but will increase their numbers; for he will link the Gentiles with them, that the two peoples may become one and the same body."

2. Nations will take them and bring them to their own place. He means that the foreign nations will be willing to become their companions. An instance of this is given in Ezra 1:6, when the people were brought back from Babylon. But that was only a slight foretaste of those things that were accomplished by Christ, to whom all these statements must be referred.

And the house of Israel will possess the nations as menservants and maidservants in the LORD's land. They will make captives of their captors and rule over their oppressors. The Jews being in some sense the firstborn (Exodus 4:22) in the house of God, we who are linked to them appear as if we had assembled under their roof, for they go before us and hold the highest rank above all the nations.

3. On the day the LORD gives you relief from suffering and turmoil and cruel bondage. Isaiah adds a confirmation of the former promises. The Lord provides for our weakness, for we find it difficult to fully believe in his Word when our circumstances appear to contradict it. But it is our Lord's way of putting our faith to the test when he still promises the salvation of which all hope has been taken away.

4. You will take up this taunt against the king of Babylon: How the oppressor has come to an end! How his fury has ended! The ruin of Babylon will be so great that it will become a proverb, which usually happens in great and amazing events.

5-6. The LORD has broken the rod of the wicked, the scepter of the rulers, which in anger struck down peoples with unceasing blows, and in fury subdued nations with relentless aggression. By repeating **the rod of the wicked, the scepter of the rulers,** he means that no imperial power can maintain unjust tyranny indefinitely. And immediately afterward he states more clearly that the monarchy of the Babylonians will be destroyed because it is unjust and tyrannical.

7-8. All the lands are at rest and at peace; they break into singing. Even the pine trees and the cedars of Lebanon exult over you and say, "Now that you have been laid low, no woodsman comes to cut us down." He shows how greatly tyrants are hated by the whole world: **They break into singing.**

To liven up what he is saying, he adds a personification, introducing the trees as speaking and congratulating themselves that since the tyrant is dead, they will now gladly stand at ease. The prophet sets out to show that the Heavenly Judge cannot endure tyrants, who are abhorred by the whole world.

9. The grave below is all astir to meet you at your coming; it rouses the spirits of the departed to greet you—all those who were leaders in the world; it makes them rise from their thrones—all those who were kings over the nations. He has already attributed joy to the trees, and now he uses similar imagery, attributing speech to the dead. The whole passage is ironical and full of keen sarcasm. It is as if he said, "Not only the living, but also the dead will rejoice at his death. The departed also will treat him as he deserves."

10. They will all respond, they will say to you, "You also have become weak, as we are; you have become like us." These are taunts with which the dead jeer the tyrant who has joined them, as if they asked him why he too is dead like other men. Tyrants are blinded by their greatness and do not think they are mortal; they make themselves demigods and adore themselves.

11. All your pomp has been brought down to the grave, along with the noise of your harps; maggots are spread out beneath you and worms cover you. The bodies of princes, like those of the common people, must at length become corrupted and be devoured by worms, even though costly and splendid sepulchers are built for them.

12. How you have fallen from heaven, O morning star, son of the dawn! You have been cast down to the earth, you who once laid low the nations! Isaiah resumes what he was saying earlier on, personifying the dead, and concludes that the tyrant differs in no respect from other men, though his object was to lead men to believe that he was a god.

13. You said in your heart, "I will ascend to heaven; I will raise my throne above the stars of God; I will sit enthroned on the mount of assembly, on the utmost heights of the sacred mountain." The prophet ridicules the pride of the Babylonian monarch who, relying on his greatness, ventured to promise to himself uninterrupted success, as if he had the power of determining the events of his life. Such men do not consider that they are in the hands of God but believe they will do everything by their own ability.

14. "I will ascend above the tops of the clouds; I will make myself like the Most High." As there is a seed of religion implanted in us by nature, we are constrained, even against our will, to entertain belief in some superior being who excels in all things; no one is so mad as to wish to cast down God from his throne, for nature teaches us that we ought to worship and adore God. Hence also the Gentiles, though they were ignorant of God, rendered worship to their idols. Therefore it may be thought improbable that the king of Babylon wished to drive out God and to reign in heaven. Yet the prophet does not accuse him falsely. The ungodly do not believe they ought to reign instead of God; yet, when they exalt themselves more than is proper, they take away a portion of what belongs to him and claim it for themselves, which is the same as if they wished to pull him down from his throne.

15. But you are brought down to the grave, to the depths of the pit. The Lord from on high laughs at the pride of the ungodly; when they have swallowed everything up by their covetousness and want to burst through the clouds and heaven itself by their effrontery, he will at length expose them to the mockery of all, after having, in the twinkling of an eye, overturned their schemes.

16. Those who see you stare at you, they ponder your fate: "Is this the man who shook the earth and made kingdoms tremble . . . ?" The prophet again, personifying the dead, mocks that wicked king.

17. ". . . the man who made the world a desert, who overthrew its cities and would not let his captives go home?" The prophet expresses the cruel and savage disposition of the tyrant by saying that he **made the world a desert.** He shows how wretched tyrants are, for they have God for their enemy and are hated by other people.

18. All the kings of the nations lie in state, each in his own tomb. He contrasts the king of Babylon with other kings in order to show in the next verse that after his death he will be more wretched than all the rest.

19. But you are cast out of your tomb like a rejected branch; you are covered with the slain, with those pierced by the sword, those who descend to the stones of the pit. Like a corpse trampled underfoot . . . Isaiah shows that the king of Babylon will be covered with such disgrace that he and other Babylonian kings will even be cast out of the sepulcher that they possessed by inheritance, a disgraceful spectacle.

20. You will not join them in burial, for you have destroyed your land and killed your people. The offspring of the wicked will never be mentioned again. The Lord punishes the pride of wicked people who wish to spread their name and to leave a perpetual remembrance of themselves, for all irreligious people have this purpose in their labors and exertions. In contrast, the Lord blots out their name and remembrance, which appeared to be inscribed on lasting records; and the result is that they are abhorred by everyone. It happens to all tyrants that though they are universally applauded and flattered while they are alive, after their death they and their posterity are universally despised. It is therefore evident that they are detested by God, by angels, and by human beings.

21. Prepare a place to slaughter his sons for the sins of their forefathers; they are not to rise to inherit the land and cover the earth with their cities. Here Isaiah prophesies more plainly than before against the king of Babylon. He speaks of all of his descendants, saying that this destruction extends to them also.

22. "I will rise up against them," declares the LORD Almighty. The Lord now declares that he will do what he had already (through the prophet) commanded others to do. It is God's work when the wicked are ruined, though he may employ human agents in executing his judgments.

"I will cut off from Babylon her name and survivors, her offspring and descendants," declares the LORD. It has been mentioned often enough before that this destruction did not overtake Babylon until after the death of Alexander the Great. By the phrase **her offspring and descendants** God through Isaiah means not only the posterity but the remembrance, which wicked men are so keen to obtain in order that they may be applauded for many ages after their death. This also the Lord took away from Babylon, so that the only memory of it that was left would be accompanied by dishonor and reproach.

23. "I will turn her into a place for owls and into swampland; I will sweep her with the broom of destruction," declares the LORD Almighty. It will not be a place where people live but will be like a hideous cavern in which wild beasts lurk.

24. The LORD Almighty has sworn, "Surely, as I have planned, so it will be, and as I have purposed, so it will stand." For a fuller confirmation, an oath was necessary. There is nothing more difficult to convince us of than that wicked people will be ruined, for we see them flourishing and having all means of defense and seemingly placed out of danger and free from all fear. We are dazzled by their brightness, so that we can scarcely believe God when he foretells their ruin and destruction. So he uses an oath in order to leave no room for doubt.

25. "I will crush the Assyrian in my land; on my mountains I will trample him down. His yoke will be taken from my people, and his burden removed from their shoulders." Though Isaiah is speaking of Babylon, the image of **the Assyrian** describes the whole of that nation's forces.

Jerusalem was situated among the **mountains,** and the whole country was despised for that reason. The prophet is speaking contemptuously; the land was regarded by its enemies as of little value because it was mountainous. But this very contempt serves to magnify the power of God, for from his **mountains** he shakes off the dominion of this powerful monarchy.

26. This is the plan determined for the whole world; this is the hand stretched out over all nations. The Lord is not satisfied with one or two confirmations and can scarcely refrain from proclaiming his judgment more and more abundantly, because he well knows that our minds are naturally prone to distrust. No confirmation suffices for us, even though his promises are frequent and sweeping and solemn. God therefore wishes to remedy this disease, and that is the point of the repetition; we must not think it is superfluous.

27. For the LORD Almighty has purposed, and who can thwart him? His hand is stretched out, and who can turn it back? Isaiah here employs what may be regarded as a concluding exclamation, to confirm the preceding statement more fully. In short, he intimates that there can be no repentance or change in God (Numbers 23:19); whatever happens, even in the midst of an endless diversity of events, he always remains like himself, and no occurrence can thwart his purpose.

28. This oracle came in the year King Ahaz died. Chapter 15 ought to have begun at this point, for the prophet begins a new subject. This shows how absurdly the chapters are divided, or rather torn asunder. Having spoken of the Babylonians, he passes now to the Philistines, who, being near neighbors of the Jews, cherished deadly hostility against them.

29. Do not rejoice, all you Philistines, that the rod that struck you is broken; from the root of that snake will spring up a viper, its fruit will be a darting, venomous serpent. He begins by checking the vain and groundless confidence with which the Philistines were puffed up, and by adding **all you** he intimates that all of them would suffer this calamity.

We ought to draw from this a general principle that when we are weighed down by adversity, and when the ungodly rejoice as if we were ruined and as if they alone were prosperous, God declares that their joy is without foundation. The church will always rise again and be restored to her former prosperous condition, even if everyone decides that she is ruined.

30. **The poorest of the poor will find pasture, and the needy will lie down in safety. But your root I will destroy by famine; it will slay your survivors.** Now he promises that the Lord will deliver **the poorest of the poor** from their misery and will again feed and nourish them. Hence we perceive that the Philistines were cut down and destroyed for the benefit of the people of God. In like manner, the Lord promised Abraham and his posterity, "I will bless those who bless you, and whoever curses you I will curse" (Genesis 12:3). Those who are hostile to the children of God will certainly find that God is hostile to them.

The needy will lie down in safety. The prophet compares his people to sheep, whom we must resemble if we want to have God for our keeper. No metaphor is more frequently employed in Scripture than this. When the Lord chastises us, we are like sheep that are scattered and exposed to wolves and robbers. But when he punishes our enemies, he wants to gather us together again, that we may dwell in a safe and quiet place. This is what Isaiah means when he says, **in safety.**

But your root I will destroy by famine. He now turns to the Philistines, whom he compares to a tree that strikes its roots so deep that we would think it cannot in any way be rooted out. But if the root dries up, the tree, however deeply laid, must decay. Hence we ought to infer that the condition of the wicked is never so firmly established that the Lord cannot easily overturn it; not only will he cut off branches, but he will also dry up and destroy the **root** that is hidden underground.

31. **Wail, O gate! Howl, O city! Melt away, all you Philistines! A cloud of smoke comes from the north, and there is not a straggler in its ranks.** He threatens that there will be mourning in each of the cities, and mourning of no ordinary kind, for it will be spread through every one of the most crowded assemblies.

32. **What answer shall be given to the envoys of that nation? "The LORD has established Zion, and in her his afflicted people will find refuge."** By this he means that the destruction of the land of the Philistines will be a marked proof of God's compassion toward his people, that all may understand that the Lord is the guardian and protector of Judea, which he had chosen to be his own.

Isaiah
Chapter 15

1. An oracle concerning Moab: Ar in Moab is ruined, destroyed in a night! Kir in Moab is ruined, destroyed in a night! Here the prophet prophesies against the Moabites, who were neighbors to the Jews and were related to them. The Moabites were descended from Lot, who was Abraham's nephew (Genesis 11:31; 19:37). Those nations being so closely related, humanity at least demanded that they should maintain friendly intercourse with each other. But no relationship prevented the Moabites from cherishing hostility toward the Jews or even from harassing them whenever it was in their power, which is evidence of a savage and barbarous disposition.

In a night! This means a sudden and unexpected occurrence that the Moabites did not fear.

2. Dibon goes up to its temple, to its high places to weep; Moab wails over Nebo and Medeba. The prophet has already named two of the cities of the Moabites, **Ar** and **Kir.** He now adds a third, **Nebo,** and lastly he mentions a fourth, **Medeba.** This destruction will not only seize the extremities of that country but will reach its inmost recesses, so that no corner will be exempt.

Moab wails over Nebo and Medeba. Every head is shaved and every beard cut off. Every nation has its peculiar ceremonies to denote mourning or joy. The Italians and other western nations allowed the hair and beard to grow when they were in mourning; eastern nations, on the other hand, shaved the head and beard because they regarded them as ornamental, and when they reversed their ordinary custom it was a sign of mourning.

3. In the streets they wear sackcloth; on the roofs and in the public squares they all wail, prostrate with weeping. He carries on with the same subject, describing more fully the signs of mourning, in which eastern nations abound more than others.

4. Heshbon and Elealeh cry out, their voices are heard all the way to Jahaz. Therefore the armed men of Moab cry out, and their hearts are faint. Here he names other cities, **Heshbon and Elealeh,** for his aim is to bundle up all the cities of that country, so to speak, that they may be involved in the general destruction. In other words, none of them will be exempt.

5. My heart cries out over Moab; her fugitives flee as far as Zoar, as far as Eglath Shelishiyah. They go up the way to Luhith, weeping as they go; on the road to Horonaim they lament their destruction. At length Isaiah assumes the character of a mourner. Some may think it strange and inconsistent for him to bewail the calamity of the Moabites, feeling he ought rather to have lamented the destruction of the church and to have rejoiced at the ruin of her enemies. It is customary with the prophets, however, to assume in this manner the character of those whose calamities they foretell and thus to exhibit their condition, as though they were on stage, by which means they produce a stronger impression than if they delivered their instruction in a direct form.

6. The waters of Nimrim are dried up and the grass is withered; the vegetation is gone and nothing green is left. By an exaggerated form of expression he gives a greater view of this desolation. He says **the grass is withered,** which happens when God leaves any soil destitute of all nourishment. The prophet informs them that a land that is deprived of God's blessing will be like a desert without any beauty.

7. So the wealth they have acquired and stored up they carry away over the Ravine of the Poplars. He describes what usually happens when countries are invaded by an enemy. All the inhabitants convey their riches elsewhere and lay them up in some safe place, so they can bring them back later when peace has been restored.

8. Their outcry echoes along the border of Moab; their wailing reaches as far as Eglaim, their lamentation as far as Beer Elim. He means that every part of that country all around will be full of crying and **howling** (KJV), because that destruction reaches from one extremity to another. Besides the crying he twice mentions **howling** (KJV), to denote excessive grief, for men who are in despair surrender themselves entirely to lamentation.

9. Dimon's waters are full of blood, but I will bring still more upon Dimon. Here the prophet describes not only grief and howling, flight and trembling, or the covetousness of enemies in plundering their wealth, but the slaughter of men. How great this must have been when a large and magnificent river such as the **Dimon** was **full of blood!**

A lion upon the fugitives of Moab and upon those who remain in the land. He tries to give depth to the picture of that distressing calamity, adding that even the small remnant that is rescued from the slaughter will fall into the jaws of lions. The hand of the Lord pursues the wicked in such a manner that there is no way they can escape; if they avoid one danger, they immediately meet with another. Let us remember that these things are spoken by the prophet for the consolation of the godly, that they may fortify their minds by some promise against the cruelty of their enemies, who will at length be destroyed and will find no refuge either in their gods or in fortresses or in hiding-places or in flight.

Isaiah
Chapter 16

1. Send lambs as tribute to the ruler of the land, from Sela, across the desert. Here the prophet scoffs at the Moabites for not acknowledging God at the proper time but rather recklessly waiting for the stroke of his hand, until they were completely destroyed. This is, therefore, a condemnation of late repentance, when people cannot be brought to obedience by any warnings but continue opposing God obstinately.

To the mount of the Daughter of Zion. That is, to God's authorized temple, in which sacrifices were offered according to the injunction of the law (Deuteronomy 12:5-7; 2 Chronicles 7:12). This is a remarkable passage against obstinate people who set aside all instruction and fearlessly despise God, until they are visited by his judgments.

2. Like fluttering birds pushed from the nest, so are the women of Moab at the fords of the Arnon. The prophet now shows what he meant by the former mockery, saying that the Moabites ought not at that time to think of sending sacrifices because they would not be able to provide for their safety in any way except by leaving their native country. By the metaphor of **birds** he describes the terror with which they will be struck, so that they will flee even at the rustling of a leaf. He threatens that the Moabites, who had abused their tranquillity, will have a trembling and wearisome flight.

3. "Give us counsel, render a decision. Make your shadow like night—at high noon. Hide the fugitives, do not betray the refugees." He continues the same subject. If we want to understand this passage aright, we must set before our minds the dreadful ruin of the Moabites. We are reminded of their crimes so that we may all see more clearly how deservedly they are punished. When everything was in their power, they freely indulged in licentiousness and would not listen to any reproof; but now, when they are deprived of everything, they groan and seek remedies that are nowhere to be found.

"**Make your shadow like night.**" The Moabites might have given some relief to the wretched Jews when they were harassed by the Assyrians; or at least, if they had had a spark of humanity, they ought to have protected the fugitives. But on the contrary, they persecuted them and added to their afflictions, which were already oppressive. It was quite right that the Moabites should be subjected to the same cruelty they had exercised toward others; that, when they had been driven from their dwellings and were exiles and wanderers, they should find no solace, no **shadow** to shelter them from the heat. Why should they enjoy the consolations they had barbarously refused to others?

At high noon. This refers to the most scorching heat. This metaphor is frequently used in Scripture.

4. "Let the Moabite fugitives stay with you; be their shelter from the destroyer." The oppressor will come to an end, and destruction will cease; the aggressor will vanish from the land. The prophet addresses the Moabites as if he were humbly beseeching them in the name of the people at large. "You are neighbors, related to us by blood. So receive and assist those who are in distress: and if you do not choose to assist, at least do them no harm." God, who usually supports his people, is represented by the prophet as being like a supplicant. It is certain that the Moabites did not at all act in this manner toward the Jews but, on the contrary, joined their efforts with the Jews' enemies to harm them. But as I said a little earlier, the prophet sets before our eyes the justice that even nature demands, that the cruel violation of it may be all the more abhorred.

This passage ought to be carefully observed, for God shows here how great is the care that he takes of his people, since the injuries done to them affect him in the same manner as if they had been done to himself. He declares by Zechariah that whenever they are touched, "the apple of his eye" is touched (Zechariah 2:8). He hears the groaning (Psalm 102:20) and observes the tears of wretched men who call upon him (Psalm 12:5; 38:9); and although this may not always be visible to us, he shows in due season that he has heard.

5. In love a throne will be established; in faithfulness a man will sit on it—one from the house of David—one who in judging seeks justice and speeds the cause of righteousness. All consolations are transitory and fading if we do not refer them to Christ. Let our eyes therefore be fixed on him if we wish to be happy and prosperous, for he has promised that we will be happy even when bearing a cross (Matthew 5:10-11), that agony and torments will open up the way to a blessed life (2 Corinthians 4:17), and that all the afflictions that we suffer will add to our happiness (Romans 8:28).

The **justice** and the **righteousness** that are ascribed to him are nothing but the protection under which he receives us, which he will not allow to be infringed; he will not allow wicked people who injure us to pass unpunished, as long as we patiently and calmly commit ourselves to his protection.

6. We have heard of Moab's pride—her overweening pride and conceit, her pride and her insolence—but her boasts are empty. The prophet added this statement by way of anticipation. Men might find unbelievable his promises about restoring the throne of the king and destroying the Moabites, who at that time were in a flourishing state of riches and were defended by strong fortresses and who, puffed up with the prosperity they then enjoyed, were exceedingly proud. Besides, the haughtiness with which they scorned the unhappy Jews was a disagreeable and powerful weapon for discouraging them or forcing doubt into their minds. To provide against this temptation, Isaiah relates that their boasting was well known, but that their pride would not prevent God from overthrowing them. This reminds us that pride is highly displeasing to God, and that the more men are puffed up with their riches, the nearer they are to destruction.

7. Therefore the Moabites wail, they wail together for Moab. Lament and grieve for the raisin cakes [foundations, KJV] of Kir Hareseth. He declares more plainly what has already been said: This pride, and the cruelty that springs from it, will be the cause of their destruction. Since the Lord resists the proud (James 4:6; 1 Peter 5:5), it is impossible that he will *not* lay low this haughtiness by which the church is basely and shamefully trampled underfoot. According to this example, the end of all proud men must be mournful.

Kir Hareseth was obviously a chief and royal city.

8. The fields of Heshbon wither, the vines of Sibmah also. The rulers of the nations have trampled down the choicest vines, which once reached Jazer and spread toward the desert. Their shoots spread out and went as far as the sea. Here the prophet describes allegorically the desolation of the whole country. There is reason to believe that it abounded in the choicest vines, as may readily be inferred from this and the parallel passage (Jeremiah 48:32). When prophets threaten destruction to countries, they usually delineate their more remarkable features. The cities mentioned by the prophet were the chief cities of Moab.

9. So I weep, as Jazer weeps, for the vines of Sibmah. O Heshbon, O Elealeh, I drench you with tears! The prophet here takes upon him the character of another person, lamenting and groaning in the name of the Moabites. It is undoubtedly true that believers always shudder at the judgments of God and cannot lay aside the feelings of human nature, so as not to commiserate the destruction of the wicked. Yet he does not describe his own feelings; his intention is to give additional weight to his instruction, so that no one may have any doubt that it will happen. That is why he adopts the person of a Moabite, as on a stage, showing the mourning and

131

grief that will be felt by everyone after that calamity. Thus he confirms the promise that the Jews might otherwise have thought incredible.

The shouts of joy over your ripened fruit and over your harvests have been stilled. In other words, "When you prepare to gather in your harvest and your vintage, the enemies will rush in, so that instead of joy and cheerful song, you will hear their shouting, which will drive you far away."

10. Joy and gladness are taken away from the orchards; no one sings or shouts in the vineyards; no one treads out wine at the presses, for I have put an end to the shouting. He confirms in different words what he has just said: The whole country will be desolate and forsaken, so that it will never again enjoy a harvest or a vintage.

11. My heart [bowels, KJV] laments for Moab like a harp, my inmost being for Kir Hareseth. Assuming the character of a Moabite, the prophet again describes excessive lamentation, proceeding from grief so intense that even the **bowels** make a distressing noise. By this imagery he wanted to point out the reality. By again naming **Kir Hareseth,** the chief city, he describes the destruction of the whole country.

12. When Moab appears at her high place, she only wears herself out; when she goes to her shrine to pray, it is to no avail. Idolaters in their affliction hope to obtain some relief from their idols.

13. This is the word the LORD has already spoken concerning Moab. This concluding sentence is the ratification of the prophecy. It means that he has pronounced the decree of God himself, and that he has brought nothing forward that did not proceed from the Lord. He lays aside the person of a man and introduces God as speaking in this manner.

14. But now the LORD says: "Within three years, as a servant bound by contract would count them, Moab's splendor and all her many people will be despised, and her survivors will be very few and feeble." The time is fixed, not only for the sake of certainty, but also in order that believers may not become faint through longer delay.

God particularly mentions **her many people** because their number was great, and because they boasted of it and thought they were invincible. When he adds that **her survivors will be very few and feeble,** he means there will be such a great change that they will be nothing like their previous condition—nothing will be left but a sad and shocking sight.

Isaiah
Chapter 17

1. An oracle concerning Damascus: "See, Damascus will no longer be a city but will become a heap of ruins." Here Isaiah prophesies against the kingdom of Syria, naming its capital city. It was right that this calamity, like others that came before it, should be described, so that the righteous might confidently believe that God would one day assist them and would not always allow them to be oppressed by wicked people. The king of Syria had formed an alliance with Israel against Judah, as we saw in chapter 7. Because the Jews were not able to contend with him and were deprived of other aids, they might also entertain doubts about God's assistance, as if he had utterly abandoned them. So he frees them from these doubts by threatening the destruction of that kingdom, from which they would readily conclude that God fought in defense of his people.

The prophet expressly mentions **Damascus,** but it does not follow that the other parts of the kingdom are exempt. The prophets made a habit of including the fate of the whole nation when they referred to its metropolis.

2. The cities of Aroer will be deserted and left to flocks, which will lie down, with no one to make them afraid. He draws a picture of a country that has been ruined, showing that the places where cities had been built will be devoted to pasture, and that the only dwellings left there will be huts and shepherds' tents.

3. "The fortified city will disappear from Ephraim, and royal power from Damascus; the remnant of Aram will be like the glory of the Israelites," declares the LORD Almighty. He points out why the Lord determined to cut off the kingdom of Syria. They had drawn the kingdom of Israel to their side for the purpose of making war against Judah. The Israelites were undoubtedly attracted by the allurements of the Syrians to form an alliance with them against their brethren.

4. "In that day the glory of Jacob will fade; the fat of his body will

waste away." When the Lord through Isaiah next threatens them with leanness, his object is to reprove their indolence. Similarly, the prophets frequently reprove the people for their fatness (see, for example, Jeremiah 5:28). On account of their prosperity and the fertility of the country, they became proud, just as horses that are fat and excessively pampered stubbornly resist control. But however fierce and stubborn they might be, God threatens that he will take away their fatness.

5. "It will be as when a reaper gathers the standing grain and harvests the grain with his arm—as when a man gleans heads of grain in the Valley of Rephaim." He uses a simile to show how great the desolation will be. "As the reapers," he says, "gather the corn in armfuls, so this multitude, though large and extended, will be mowed down by the enemy."

6. "Yet some gleanings will remain, as when an olive tree is beaten, leaving two or three olives on the topmost branches, four or five on the fruitful boughs," declares the LORD, the God of Israel. This metaphor has a different meaning from the previous one. As if the name of the nation were to be entirely blotted out, he had expressly foretold that nothing would be left after the slaughter. He now adds a consolation, lessening the severity of the destruction; for he declares that although the enemy had resolved to consume and destroy everything, still some remnant would be left. Similarly, when we pick grapes it is never so complete as not to allow some grapes or even clusters to remain concealed under the leaves; and the olive tree is never so thoroughly shaken as not to leave at least some olives on the tops of the trees. Consequently, to whatever extent the enemy may rage, and the vengeance of God be kindled, still he foretells that the Judge, notwithstanding his severity, will reserve a small number for himself and will not allow the enemy attacks to fall upon his own elect. Hence it follows that even in the heaviest vengeance there will still be room for mercy.

7. In that day men will look to their Maker. The prophet now shows the result of this chastisement. Although they perceive nothing but the wrath of God, yet they ought to reflect that the Lord, who never forgets himself, will continually preserve his church, and their punishment will help them.

And turn their eyes to the Holy One of Israel. This simply means that after turning away, we return to a state of favor with him.

8. They will not look to the altars, the work of their hands, and they will have no regard for the Asherah poles and the incense altars their fingers have made. This contrast shows more clearly that the looking that he spoke of in verse 7 relates to hope and confidence, for he says that every kind of sinful confidence will vanish when people have learned to hope in God. And indeed no one can obtain a clear view of God except by driving superstition far away. We are thus taught that obstacles of this kind ought to be removed if we wish to approach God.

9. In that day their strong cities, which they left because of the Israelites, will be like places abandoned to thickets and undergrowth. And all will be desolation. He follows up on what he had begun to say about driving out the inhabitants of the country. As the Israelites thought they were safe when they trusted in their fortified cities, he warns them that their cities will be of no more use than if enemies were marching unhindered through desert places.

10. You have forgotten God your Savior; you have not remembered the Rock, your fortress. Therefore, though you set out the finest plants and plant imported vines . . . He shows why the Lord exercises such severity against the ten tribes: It is so that they may not complain of being unjustly afflicted or too harshly treated. The sum of what is stated is: All those evils came to them because they had wickedly despised God. It was the most base and inexcusable ingratitude, having received so many favors, to prostitute their hopes to heathen nations and to idols, as if they had never in any respect experienced the love of God. Accordingly, the prophet expressly calls the Lord **the Rock, your fortress.**

11. . . . though on the day you set them out, you make them grow, and on the morning when you plant them, you bring them to bud, yet the harvest will be as nothing in the day of disease and incurable pain. This denotes the incessant labor that is bestowed on plants and seeds. In other words, "Although you labor hard in dressing the vines, and though you begin your toil at the crack of dawn, you will gain nothing; for by the mere shaking of the branches, the fruit will fall off of its own accord, or perhaps your vines will be plundered." Thus the word **plant** denotes the unwearied toil that husbandmen and vinedressers bestow on plants and vines. This is a very severe punishment and undoubtedly proceeds from the curse of God; for if someone who owns nothing is driven out and banished from a country, he will not suffer as much as someone who has well cultivated fields, particularly if he has worked them for a long time. In this manner the Lord determined to punish the Israelites, because they abused the fertility of the country in the middle of their abundance.

12. Oh, the raging of many nations—they rage like the raging sea! Oh, the uproar of the peoples—they roar like the roaring of great waters! The word **nations** is here used because the army had been collected from the many nations of which the Assyrian monarchy was composed. The metaphors the prophet adds are intended merely to exhibit more forcibly what has been stated already: He compares them to a sea or a flood that overflows a whole country.

13. Although the peoples roar like the roar of surging waters, when he rebukes them they flee far away, driven before the wind like chaff on the hills, like tumbleweed before a gale. In other words, "Those who were unmindful of God must be punished for their wicked revolt and must be, as it were, overwhelmed by a flood. But the Lord will restrain

135

this savage disposition of the enemies, for when they have exercised their cruelty, he will find a way of casting them out and driving them away." This is a remarkable consolation, by which he intended to support the remnant of the godly.

14. In the evening, sudden terror! Before the morning, they are gone! This is the portion of those who loot us, the lot of those who plunder us. The meaning is, "When a storm arises in the evening and dies down soon afterward, no trace of it is found in the morning. Similarly, cheerful prosperity will suddenly arise, contrary to expectation." The prophet wants to say two things—first, that the attack of the enemy will be sudden; and second, that the ravages they commit will not last long.

Isaiah
Chapter 18

1. Woe to the land of whirring wings along the rivers of Cush ... I cannot determine with certainty which nation Isaiah refers to, although he shows plainly that it bordered on Ethiopia. **The land of whirring wings** probably means that its sea was well supplied with harbors, so that it had many vessels sailing to it, making it wealthy; small and poor states could not maintain such trade with foreign countries.

2.... which sends envoys by sea in papyrus boats over the water. Go, swift messengers, to a people tall and smooth-skinned, to a people feared far and wide, an aggressive nation of strange speech, whose land is divided by rivers. It would appear that this nation solicited the Egyptians or Syrians to harass the Jews, or that the Assyrians employed them for the purpose of harassing the Jews, or that they had formed an alliance with the Egyptians in order that by their united force they might prevent the power of the Assyrians from increasing beyond bounds. Nothing more than conjectures can be offered because we have no histories that give any account of this, and where historical evidence is wanting, we must resort to probable conjectures.

Papyrus boats were commonly used by the Egyptians.

3. All you people of the world, you who live on the earth, when a banner is raised on the mountains, you will see it, and when a trumpet sounds, you will hear it. Isaiah shows that this work of God will be so manifestly excellent that it will draw the attention not only of the Jews but of all nations. It is as if he said that the most distant nations will be witnesses of this destruction, because not only will the **banner** be seen by all, but the sound of the trumpets will be heard throughout the whole world. This will plainly show that the war did not originate with men but with God himself, who will prove himself to be the author of it by remarkable tokens. When wars are carried on, everyone sees clearly what is done; but most people ascribe the beginning and end of them to chance. On the other hand, Isaiah shows that all these things ought to be ascribed to God because he will display his power in a new and extraordinary manner. Sometimes he works so as to conceal his hand and to keep people from perceiving his work, but sometimes he displays his hand in such a way that everyone has to acknowledge it. That is what the prophet meant.

4. This is what the LORD says to me: "I will remain quiet and will look on from my dwelling place." Having threatened a slaughter of the Ethiopians or their neighbors, and at the same time having shown that this will bring comfort to the Jews or ironically reprove the foolish confidence with which the Jews had been deceived, God through Isaiah now adds that he will in time regulate these confused changes in such a way as to gather his chosen people to him.

"Like shimmering heat in the sunshine." By this beautiful metaphor the prophet expresses more fully what he had said before. Isaiah appears to mean that although God does not act in a bustling way like men or proceed with undue eagerness and haste, he has in his power concealed methods of executing his judgments without moving a finger.

"Like a cloud of dew in the heat of harvest." We know that rain is well suited to ripen the fruits, and likewise the heat that follows the rain penetrates the fruits with its force and drives the moisture more inward, by which it hastens their maturity and renders them more productive. The prophet meant that though calamities and distresses await the reprobate, still everything proceeds so much to their wish that they appear to be supremely happy, as if the Lord intended to load them with every kind of blessing; but they are being fattened like oxen destined for slaughter, for when they appear to have reached the highest happiness, they suddenly perish.

Hence it follows that we ought not to form an estimate of God's judgments according to outward appearances; for when people imagine themselves to be quite safe, they are not far from destruction and from utter ruin. Thus God through his prophet speedily comforts believers, so that they will not suppose that it fares better with reprobates as long as God forbears to strike; though he appears to cherish in his bosom those whom he sustains, he will quickly reduce them to nothing. These statements ought to be applied to those wretched and disastrous times when the tyrants who oppress the church are the only persons who are prosperous and abound in all kinds of wealth and contrive in such a manner as if everything were under their control because they surpass other men in power, skill, and cunning. But let us recognize that all these things are done by the appointment of God, who promotes their endeavors and renders them successful, that he may at length slay and destroy them in a moment.

5. For, before the harvest, when the blossom is gone and the flower becomes a ripening grape, he will cut off the shoots with pruning

knives, and cut down and take away the spreading branches. When the harvest is close at hand, and when the grapes are nearly ripe, the whole produce, in the expectation of which wicked men had rejoiced, will suddenly be snatched from them. The prophet continues the same subject and confirms by these metaphors what he has said before: The wicked are not immediately cut off but flourish for a time, and the Lord spares them; but when the harvest is at hand, when the vines put forth their buds and blossoms, so that the sour grapes make their appearance, the branches themselves will be cut down. Thus when the wicked are nearly ripe, not only will they be deprived of their fruit, but they and their offspring will be rooted out.

Hence we have the great consolation that when God conceals himself, he is trying our faith and is not allowing everything to be carried along by the blind violence of fortune, as heathens imagine. God is in heaven, and also in his tabernacle, dwelling in his church as in a lowly house; but at the right time he will come forth. Let us thus examine our consciences and ponder everything, that we may sustain our minds by such a promise as this, which alone will enable us to overcome and subdue temptations. Let us also consider that the Lord declares that he advances and promotes the happiness of wicked people in order to exhibit and display his mercy more illustriously. If he instantly cut them down and took them away like a sprouting blade of wheat, his power would not be so manifest, nor would his goodness be so fully ascertained as when he permits them to grow to a vast height, to swell and blossom, that they may afterwards fall by their own weight or, like large and fat ears of wheat, cuts them down with pruning-knives.

6. They will all be left to the mountain birds of prey and to the wild animals; the birds will feed on them all summer, the wild animals all winter. He means that they will be cast aside as a thing of no value.

7. At that time gifts will be brought to the LORD Almighty from a people tall and smooth-skinned, from a people feared far and wide, an aggressive nation of strange speech, whose land is divided by rivers—the gifts will be brought to Mount Zion, the place of the Name of the LORD Almighty. This mode of expression is customary with the prophets. When they speak of the worship of God, they describe it by outward acts such as altars, sacrifices, washings, and the like. And indeed the worship of God is within the soul, and so there is no way in which it can be described but by outward signs, by which people declare that they worship and adore God. But he calls the place **Mount Zion** because it was consecrated to God, and God commanded that sacrifices should be offered there.

Isaiah
Chapter 19

1. An oracle concerning Egypt: See, the LORD rides on a swift cloud and is coming to Egypt. The prophet here prophesies against **Egypt** because it was a kind of refuge to the Jews whenever they saw any danger approaching them. When they had forsaken God, to whom they ought to have had recourse, they thought the only help they had left was from the Egyptians. It was therefore necessary for that kingdom to be overthrown, so that its wealth or its forces might no longer deceive the Jews.

The expression **the LORD rides on a swift cloud** is found in other passages of Scripture as well, but in a general form (see Psalm 104:3). The prophet applies it to this prediction because the Egyptians thought they were so well fortified on all sides that there was no way God could approach them. He therefore ridicules their foolish confidence and exhibits his exalted power when he **rides on a swift cloud,** by which he will easily make a descent upon them, and neither walls nor bulwarks will hinder his progress.

The idols of Egypt tremble before him. Isaiah declares that the **idols** will be of no avail to the Egyptians, although they rely on their assistance and think they are under their protection. No nation ever was so much addicted to superstitions, for they worshiped cats, oxen, crocodiles, plants of every sort, and even onions; there was nothing to which they did not ascribe some kind of divinity. But the power of all the false gods that the Egyptians had taken for their protectors would be overthrown.

And the hearts of the Egyptians melt within them. By the word **hearts** Isaiah means the courage that sometimes fails even the bravest men, so that they do not attempt any action, even when their strength and forces are abundant. Thus he declares that they will be at war with God, who will **melt** their hearts within them before they are called to contend with their enemies.

2. "I will stir up Egyptian against Egyptian—brother will fight

against brother, neighbor against neighbor, city against city, kingdom against kingdom." Here he describes more particularly the calamity that the Lord had determined to bring upon Egypt. By the expression "I will stir up" he means the internal struggles in which those who ought to defend each other cut one another down. No evil can be more destructive than this to a state or a people. It was important also to convince the Jews that God, in whose hands are human hearts (Proverbs 21:1), could by his unseen influence inflame the Egyptians to mutual animosity so that they would slay each other, though they were victorious over foreign enemies.

3. "The Egyptians will lose heart, and I will bring their plans to nothing; they will consult the idols and the spirits of the dead, the mediums and the spiritists." Isaiah's enumeration probably proceeds by gradual advancement. Superstitious people are so restless that nothing can satisfy them. They are fickle and unsteady and sometimes resort to one remedy and sometimes to another. And indeed Satan deceives them in such a manner that at first he offers them the appearance of peace and quietness, and they think they have fully obtained it; but then he shows them that they have not reached it and distresses and harasses them more and more and compels them to seek new grounds of confidence. Our minds can obtain rest and peace in God alone. Undoubtedly the prophet also condemns certain arts as contrary to reason; for God has revealed all that is necessary to be known by means of the arts and sciences, which he intended to be used and which he approves. If anyone wants to be wise in any other manner, he must have Satan for his teacher.

4. "I will hand the Egyptians over to the power of a cruel master, and a fierce king will rule over them," declares the Lord, the LORD Almighty. Isaiah now shows what will happen to the Egyptians when they have lost courage and have been deprived of understanding. All that will be left for them will be to be reduced to slavery; for a nation destitute of these things must fall of its own accord, even if it is not violently attacked by any enemy.

5. The waters of the river will dry up, and the riverbed will be parched and dry. He follows up the subject he had already begun: The fortifications by which the Egyptians thought they were admirably defended would be of no avail to them. They reckoned themselves to be invincible because they were surrounded by the sea, by the Nile, and by fortifications;. Historians tell us that it was difficult to gain entrance to them because the Nile had no mouth; so they could easily prevent ships from landing. They therefore boasted that their situation was excellent; but fortresses are useless when God has decided to punish us.

6. The canals will stink; the streams of Egypt will dwindle and dry up. The reeds and rushes will wither. What he now adds about fortifications has the same purpose as the previous verse.

7. . . . also the plants along the Nile, at the mouth of the river. Every

sown field along the Nile will become parched, will blow away and be no more. When the prophet warns that the fields will dry up, he means that the whole country will be barren. For the same reason he says that even at its very **mouth,** from which the water springs, there will be a lack of water, so that in that place the vegetation will be withered.

8. The fishermen will groan and lament, all who cast hooks into the Nile; those who throw nets on the water will pine away. Isaiah is still keeping the condition of Egypt in view. The prophets used figures of speech by which, when any country is mentioned, they chiefly name those things that abound in that country and for which it is celebrated. Thus, when they are speaking about a vine-bearing country, they mention vines; if it abounds in gold, they speak of gold; if it abounds in silver, they speak of silver. Accordingly, when he speaks of Egypt, which was well watered and contained plenty of streams, he mentions fishing. Egypt's wealth consisted chiefly in its vast numbers of fishermen, and if they were taken away the country would be weakened. If the nation is deprived of its ordinary food, great poverty will follow. He therefore describes an astonishing change that will affect the whole country.

9-10. Those who work with combed flax will despair, the weavers of fine linen will lose hope. The workers in cloth will be dejected, and all the wage earners will be sick at heart. The prophet indirectly taunts them with their unbecoming luxury, alleging that the Egyptians cover themselves with linen garments in the same manner as if they clothed themselves with a net. If this meaning is adopted, it will agree with the following verse; and indeed I do not see how such exquisite skill in weaving can be applied to fishing. But if it is thought better to understand the whole as relating to fishing, the meaning will be that those who had been much employed in fishing and had found it to be a profitable occupation will be overwhelmed with sorrow.

11. The officials of Zoan are nothing but fools; the wise counselors of Pharaoh give senseless advice. How can you say to Pharaoh, "I am one of the wise men, a disciple of the ancient kings"? When he says, **The officials of Zoan are nothing but fools** he contrasts wisdom with folly—and with good reason, for it is impossible to stop people from being convinced of their own wisdom, which leads them to believe, in opposition to God himself, that they are wise.

He scoffs at **the wise counselors of Pharaoh** for wanting to be regarded and believing themselves to be very wise, although they are the most foolish of all men.

I have heard an amusing anecdote about the Emperor Maximilian, who was very eager to inquire into his descent and was induced by a silly trifler to believe that he had traced his lineage to Noah's ark. This subject made so powerful an impression on him that he left off all business, applied himself earnestly to this single investigation, and would allow no one to draw him away from it, not even the ambassadors who came to talk with him about important matters. Everyone was astonished at this folly and silently blamed him for it, but no one had the power or courage to suggest a remedy. At length his cook, who was also his jester and often entertained him with his sayings, asked leave to speak and, as one who was desirous to uphold the Emperor's dignity, told him that this eagerness to trace his descent would neither be useful nor honorable. He said, "At present I revere your majesty and worship you as a god; but if we have to go back to Noah's ark, we shall all be cousins, for we are all descended from it." Maximilian was so deeply affected by this that he became ashamed of his undertaking, though formerly neither friends nor counselors could dissuade him from it. He realized that his name, which he wanted to make more illustrious by inquiring into his remote ancestors, would be altogether degraded if they came to its earliest source, from which princes and peasants, nobles and workers are descended.

What is seen even by jesters and fools must be great madness; it is not a recent vice but is deeply rooted in the minds of almost everyone. In order to avoid it, let us learn to depend on God alone, and let us prefer the blessedness of adoption to all riches and lineage and nobility. So far as relates to the kings of Egypt being descended from very ancient kings who had kept possession of the throne for many ages, they were as proud as if wisdom had been born with them. They too are **fools.**

12. Where are your wise men now? Let them show you and make known what the LORD Almighty has planned against Egypt. The Egyptians had their diviners from whom they thought that nothing, however secret, was concealed. They consulted them about the smallest and greatest affairs and held their replies to be oracles. The prophet mocks that vanity, saying in effect, "How can they tell what they do not know? Have they been admitted to the counsel of God?"

13. The officials of Zoan have become fools, the leaders of Memphis are deceived; the cornerstones of her peoples have led Egypt astray. Zoan was one of the chief cities of Egypt. **The cornerstones of her peoples** refers to the wise men; the Egyptians thought themselves so powerfully defended by them that no evil could befall them. But Isaiah says that this is too feeble a support because, having been deceived in their counsels, they were ruining Egypt. Therefore he holds up to mockery pretended wisdom that, when it is not accompanied by the fear of God, ought to be called vanity and folly, and not wisdom.

14. The LORD has poured into them a spirit of dizziness; they make Egypt stagger in all that she does, as a drunkard staggers around in his vomit. It was unexpected and incredible that the leaders of a wise and prudent nation would destroy the country by their stupidity. The prophet therefore ascribes it to God's judgment, so that the Jews might not shut their eyes against such a striking and remarkable example. Irreligious men usually attribute the judgments of God to chance when anything new or unexpected has happened. The expression here is metaphorical, as if one were to mix wine in a cup—the Lord intoxicates the wise men of this world so that they are stunned and amazed and can neither think nor act aright.

15. There is nothing Egypt can do—head or tail, palm branch or reed. This is the conclusion of the previous statement. All the Egyptians will be stupefied to such a degree that whatever they undertake will be fruitless. This must certainly happen where there is no counsel, and it is the righteous punishment of our pride and rashness. The prophet intended to describe the result and effect, in order to show that it will be unhappy and miserable.

Head or tail means that all ranks, from the highest to the lowest, without exception, will be deprived of counsel, so that they will not succeed in anything.

16. In that day the Egyptians will be like women. He repeats what he said before: The Egyptians will not respond to the crisis in a way that is manly.

They will shudder with fear at the uplifted hand that the LORD Almighty raises against them. Isaiah shows that this war will be entirely carried on by the Lord, and therefore the Egyptians cannot stand against it because they are not dealing with human beings.

17. And the land of Judah will bring terror to the Egyptians; everyone to whom Judah is mentioned will be terrified, because of what the LORD Almighty is planning against them. I think the prophet intended to point out the reason why the Lord would make such a display against the Egyptians. It was because they had brought destruction on the Jews, for they had turned them aside from the confidence that they ought to have placed in God.

18. In that day five cities in Egypt will speak the language of Canaan and swear allegiance to the LORD Almighty. One of them will be called the City of Destruction. After threatening the Egyptians, and at the same time explaining the reason for the divine judgment, the prophet comforts them and promises the mercy of God. He declares that they will be partly restored and will regain a prosperous and flourishing condition; he says that out of six cities five will be saved, and only one will perish. He expresses their agreement with the people of God and also the faith by which they will make profession of the name of God; for **speak the language** stands for confession. He shows that their behavior will be holy, for when they **swear allegiance to the LORD Almighty** they will make profession that they worship the true God.

19. In that day there will be an altar to the LORD in the heart of Egypt, and a monument to the LORD at its border. Isaiah continues what he was saying in verse 18, stating more clearly that the appearance of Egypt will be renewed because true religion will flourish there, the pure worship of God will be set up, and all superstition will collapse. He uses the word **altar** as a sign of the worship of God, for sacrifices and oblations were the outward acts of piety. By **the heart of Egypt** he means the chief part of the whole kingdom, as if he said "in the very metropolis" or "in the very heart of the kingdom."

20. It will be a sign and witness to the LORD Almighty in the land of Egypt. When they cry out to the LORD because of their oppressors, he will send them a savior and defender. We cannot serve God unless he first bestows his grace upon us, for no one will dedicate himself to God until he is drawn by his goodness and so embraces him with all his heart. God must call us to him before we call upon him; we can have no access until he first invites us.

And he will rescue them. We learn from these words the useful lesson that God assists us through Christ, by whose agency he gave deliverance to his own people from the beginning. Christ has always been the Mediator by whose intercession all blessings were obtained from God the Father; and now that he has been revealed, let us learn that nothing can be obtained from God but through him.

21. So the LORD will make himself known to the Egyptians, and in that day they will acknowledge the LORD. They will worship with sacrifices and grain offerings; they will make vows to the Lord and keep them. Isaiah now adds the most important thing, for we cannot worship the Lord or call upon him until we have first acknowledged him to be our Father. What he adds about **vows** is likewise a part of the worship of God. The Jews used to express their gratitude to God with vows, and they gave special thanks by a solemn vow when they had received any extraordinary blessing from God.

22. The LORD will strike Egypt with a plague; he will strike them and heal them. They will turn to the LORD, and he will respond to their pleas and heal them. From what has already been said the prophet draws the conclusion that the punishment he has mentioned will be advantageous to the Egyptians because it will prepare them for their conversion. He says in effect that it will be for Egypt's good that the Lord will punish her.

In a word, let us remember the order that the prophet points out to us. First, wounds prepare people for repentance; second, they are healed because they are delivered from eternal destruction; third, when they have been brought to the knowledge of their guilt, they obtain pardon; fourth, God is gracious and reconciled to them; fifth, chastisements cease after they have obtained pardon from God. There is no one who ought not to acknowledge personally what Isaiah here says about the Egyptians, in whom the Lord holds out an example to the whole world.

23. In that day there will be a highway from Egypt to Assyria. The Assyrians will go to Egypt and the Egyptians to Assyria. The Egyptians and Assyrians will worship together. The prophet now foretells that the Lord will spread his goodness throughout the whole world. He says in effect, "It will not be shut up in a corner or exclusively known, as it used to be, by a single nation." Here he speaks of two nations that were the most inveterate enemies of the church and that appeared to be farther removed than any other from the kingdom of God. Since the nations named here made war with God openly and persecuted his church, much more might have been expected of more distant nations.

24-25. In that day Israel will be the third, along with Egypt and Assyria, a blessing on the earth. The LORD **Almighty will bless them, saying, "Blessed be Egypt my people, Assyria my handiwork, and Israel my inheritance."** Isaiah concludes the promise he had briefly glanced at: The Egyptians and Assyrians, as well as the Israelites, will be **blessed.** Formerly the grace of God was to some extent confined to **Israel,** because it was only with that nation that the Lord had entered into covenant.

Isaiah
Chapter 20

1. In the year that the supreme commander, sent by Sargon king of Assyria, came to Ashdod and attacked and captured it—In chapter 19 Isaiah prophesied about the calamity that threatened Egypt and at the same time promised her God's mercy. Now he introduces the same subject, showing that Israel will be put to shame by this punishment of the Egyptians, because they placed their confidence in Egypt. He now adds Ethiopia (**Cush**, verse 3), which makes it probable that the Ethiopians were in league with the Egyptians, as we shall see again in chapter 37.

In order to teach the Jews to rely on God alone, the prophet here predicts what awaits their useless helpers. The warning is very timely, for the Ethiopians had begun to repel the Assyrians and had forced them to draw back, and nothing could have pleased the Jews more. So these successful beginnings would not make them forget God, the prophet predicts that this help will only last for a short time because both the Ethiopians and the Egyptians will be disgracefully vanquished.

2. At that time the LORD spoke through Isaiah son of Amoz. He said to him, "Take off the sackcloth from your body and the sandals from your feet." And he did so, going around stripped and barefoot. The Lord confirms this prophecy by using a symbol, commanding Isaiah to walk naked. However, it must not be thought that the prophet went about entirely naked.

3. Then the LORD said, "Just as my servant Isaiah has gone stripped and barefoot for three years, as a sign and portent against Egypt and Cush . . ." Why should Isaiah go around **stripped and barefoot for three years**? Because that was the time given to the Egyptians and Ethiopians to repent.

4. "So the king of Assyria will lead away stripped and barefoot the Egyptian captives and Cushite exiles, young and old, with buttocks bared—to Egypt's shame." The words **captives** and **exiles** are taken collectively to show the great crowds of emigrants. God says there will be no distinction made on account of age, for both **young and old** will be led into captivity.

5. "Those who trusted in Cush and boasted in Egypt will be afraid and put to shame." The Lord through Isaiah now shows for whose benefit he had foretold these things about the Egyptians and Ethiopians. It was to teach the Jews that in the middle of their afflictions they were to hope in God, and not to run after any foreign aid, which the Lord had forbidden.

6. "In that day the people who live on this coast will say, 'See what has happened to those we relied on, those we fled to for help and deliverance from the king of Assyria! How then can we escape?'" He censures them for wandering off heedlessly. The same will happen to us if God invites us and we refuse the sure refuge that he offers to us. We will lie destitute in shame and disgrace.

Isaiah
Chapter 21

1. An oracle concerning the Desert by the Sea: Like whirlwinds sweeping through the southland, an invader comes from the desert, from a land of terror. The prophet had taught that their hope should be placed not in the Egyptians, but in the mercy of God alone. He had also predicted that calamities would come on the nations upon whose favor they relied. Now he adds a consolation to encourage the godly. He declares that a recompense has been prepared for the Chaldeans, to whom they will be captives. From this we see that God takes account of the injuries his people endure. Although Babylon was taken and plundered by the Persians and Medes, Isaiah declares that its destruction will come because of Judea. In this way God will avenge the injuries done to the nation for whom he had promised to be a guardian.

2. A dire vision has been shown to me: The traitor betrays, the looter takes loot. Elam, attack! Media, lay siege! I will bring to an end all the groaning she caused. The object was to soothe the people's grief, and it may be thought inappropriate to call a vision that is the occasion of joy **a dire vision.** But this refers to the Babylonians who, puffed up with their prosperity, dreaded no danger. Wealth often produces pride and indifference. It is as if he said, "It is useless to hold out the riches and power of the Babylonians, for even if a stone is hard, a hard hammer will break it."

3. At this my body is racked with pain, pangs seize me, like those of a woman in labor; I am staggered by what I hear, I am bewildered by what I see. Here the prophet represents the people as actually present, for it would not have been enough simply to foretell the destruction of Babylon if he had not confirmed the belief of the godly so that they felt as if the actual event was set before their eyes. Such a representation was necessary. Here the prophet is not describing the feelings of his own heart, as if he had compassion on the Babylonians; on the contrary, he assumes, for the time, the character of a Babylonian. "Vivacity is here imparted to the description by the prophet speaking of himself as of a Babylonian present at Belshazzar's feast, on the night when the town was surprised by Cyrus" (Stock).

4. My heart falters, fear makes me tremble; the twilight I longed for has become a horror to me. Excessive terror makes the heart falter. He tells how Babylon's destruction will be sudden and unlooked for, for a sudden calamity makes us tremble more than one that has been long foreseen and expected.

5. They set the tables, they spread the rugs, they eat, they drink! Get up, you officers, oil the shields! The king of Babylon was thus feasting and indulging in mirth with all his courtiers when he was overtaken by a sudden and unexpected calamity because he had disregarded and scorned the enemy. The day before it happened, it might have been thought incredible, for the conspiracy of the party that betrayed the king had not yet been discovered. At the time when Isaiah spoke, no one would have thought an event so extraordinary would ever take place.

6. This is what the Lord says to me: "Go, post a lookout and have him report what he sees." To the objection that he talks about incredible things as if they had actually happened, Isaiah replies that he does not declare them at random. The person whom the ruler appointed to be **lookout** sees from a distance what others do not know. Thus Isaiah saw by the revelation of the Spirit what was unknown to others.

7. "When he sees chariots with teams of horses, riders on donkeys or riders on camels, let him be alert, fully alert." What he adds in this verse and the following ones contains a vivid description of that defeat.

8. And the lookout shouted, "Day after day, my lord, I stand on the watchtower; every night I stay at my post." The watchman's saying he is in his **watchtower** continually, day and night, tends to confirm the prediction, as if he said that nothing can be more certain than this vision, for those whom God has appointed to keep watch are neither drowsy nor shortsighted.

9. "Look, here comes a man in a chariot with a team of horses. And he gives back the answer: 'Babylon has fallen, has fallen! All the images of its gods lie shattered on the ground!'" The prophet makes known, by God's command, what will happen. The speaker here may be either God or Darius or the watchman. It makes little difference to the meaning, for Darius, being God's servant in this matter, is not inappropriately represented as the herald of that judgment.

10. O my people, crushed on the threshing floor, I tell you what I have heard from the LORD Almighty, from the God of Israel. The prophet has good reason for giving God these two names. The first title, **the LORD Almighty** (the Lord of hosts) always applies to God. But here, undoubtedly, the prophet had his eye on the matter in hand, contrasting God's power with all the troops of the Babylonians. For God has not a single army but innumerable armies with which to subdue his enemies. Then he calls him **the God of Israel** because by destroying Babylon God showed himself to be the defender and guardian of his people. The overthrow of that monarch procured freedom for the Jews. In short, all these things were done for the sake of the church, which is what the prophet is considering here. This is not addressed to the Babylonians, who undoubtedly laughed at these predictions, but to believers, whom he exhorts to rest assured that though they were oppressed by the Babylonians and scattered and tossed about, still God would take care of them.

11. An oracle concerning Dumah. It is evident from Genesis 25:14 that this nation was descended from a son of Ishmael. The cause of its destruction, predicted here, cannot be known with certainty, and this prophecy is obscure on account of its brevity.

Someone calls to me from Seir, "Watchman, what is left of the night? Watchman, what is left of the night?" It is probable that the Edomites, who asked the question, were not far from them and were apprehensive about the danger as one in which they were themselves involved. Isaiah introduces them as inquiring of the **watchman,** not merely through curiosity but with a view to their own advantage, what he had observed in **the night.** When one person asks a question, a second and a third person follow him, asking the same thing, and this is what the repetition means; the inquiry was made not by one individual only but by many people, as often happens in cases of doubt and perplexity, when every man is afraid on his own account and does not believe what is said by others.

12. The watchman replies, "Morning is coming, but also the night. If you would ask, then ask; and come back yet again." This means that the anxiety will not last merely for a single day or for a short time. It is like **the watchman** replying, "What I tell you today, I will tell you again tomorrow. If you are afraid now, you will also be afraid tomorrow." It is a most wretched condition when people are so tortured with anxiety that they hang in a state of doubt between life and death.

13. An oracle concerning Arabia: You caravans of Dedanites, who camp in the thickets of Arabia. He now passes on to the Arabians and predicts that they too, in their own turn, will be dragged to God's judgment seat. Isaiah does not ignore any of the nations that were known to the Jews.

14. Bring water for the thirsty; you who live in Tema, bring food for the fugitives. Isaiah emphasizes how the Lord struck the Arabians so that they trembled, thinking of nothing but escape, not even having time to collect what they needed for the journey. He is therefore saying that the Arabians will come into the country of the Dedanites empty and destitute of everything. They will have no food, and so he urges the inhabitants to go out and meet them with bread and water or else they will faint.

15. They flee from the sword, from the drawn sword, from the bent bow and from the heat of battle. He means that the calamity will be dreadful and that the Arabians will have good reason for fleeing, because their enemies will pursue them with arms and with swords; so the only way they can be safe is to take flight. The reason he predicts their defeat is clear enough. The Jews had to obtain early information about what would take place much later, so as to learn that the world is governed by God's providence and not by chance, and also (from the example of others) to see that God is the judge of all nations.

16. This is what the Lord says to me: "Within one year, as a servant bound by contract would count it, all the pomp of Kedar will come to an end." He adds that the defeat of the Arabians, which he has prophesied, is at hand. This greatly comforted the Jews.

17. "The survivors of the bowmen, the warriors of Kedar, will be few." The LORD, the God of Israel, has spoken. The prophet warns that this slaughter will not be the end of their evils, because if any escape in Arabia, they will gradually decrease. In other words, "The Lord will not merely impoverish the Arabians in a single battle but will pursue them to the end, until all hope of relief is taken away and they are utterly exterminated."

Isaiah
Chapter 22

1. **An oracle concerning the Valley of Vision: What troubles you now, that you have all gone up on the housetops . . . [?]** Isaiah again prophesies against Judea (Judah), which he calls **the Valley of Vision.** He gives this name to the whole of Judea rather than to Jerusalem, about which he speaks later.

2. **. . . . O town full of commotion, O city of tumult and revelry?** He means that it was full of people. Whenever great crowds of people are brought together, there is a lot of noise. In the middle of such a great crowd of people, there was less reason to fear anything.

Your slain were not killed by the sword, nor did they die in battle. To show God's vengeance still more clearly, he says that those who were killed there did not die bravely in battle. Thus he shows that they lacked manly courage, and their timid and cowardly hearts were sure proof that they had all been forsaken by the Lord, with whose help they would have resisted bravely. Isaiah therefore does not mean that the defeat would be accompanied by shame and disgrace but rather that they had no courage to resist, because of God's wrath. Unquestionably he uses this fact to beat down their foolish pride.

3. **All your leaders have fled together; they have been captured without using the bow. All you who were caught were taken prisoner together, having fled while the enemy was still far away.** Specifically mentioning their **leaders** shows more strongly how shameful the situation was, for the **leaders** ought to have been the first to put themselves at risk for the safety of the people. They were the shields that ought to have guarded the common people. So long as Jerusalem kept its ground and prospered, these statements might be thought incredible, for it was a very strong and fortified city; but they boasted about God's protection, thinking that in some way God was bound to his temple. In their pride they thought that no power or armies could defeat it. "Do not trust in deceptive

155

words and say, 'This is the temple of the LORD, the temple of the LORD, the temple of the LORD!'"(Jeremiah 7:4). It might be thought a most remarkable prophecy that they would have no courage, that they would flee, and that even so they would not be able to escape.

4. Therefore I said, "Turn away from me; let me weep bitterly. Do not try to console me over the destruction of my people." Here the prophet assumes the character of a mourner in order to affect the hearts of the Jews more deeply. In doing so, he bitterly bewails the condition of God's church. This passage must not be explained in the same way as some of the previous passages, in which he described the grief and sorrow of foreign nations. He speaks here of the fallen condition of the church, of which he is a member, and therefore he sincerely bewails it and invites others by his example to join in the lamentation. What has happened to the church ought to affect us in the same way as if it had happened to each of us individually. (See Psalm 69:9.)

5. The Lord, the LORD Almighty, has a day of tumult and trampling and terror in the Valley of Vision, a day of battering down walls and of crying out to the mountains. God's prophet again declares that the Lord is the author of this calamity. To stop the Jews from gazing around in all directions, wondering why their enemies prevail against them, he pronounces that they are fighting against God. Although this doctrine is frequently taught in Scripture, it is not superfluous. Too often we are not humbled in the presence of our Judge; we direct our eyes to outward remedies rather than to God, who alone can cure our distresses. Isaiah uses the word **day,** as is usual in Scripture, to signify an appointed time. When God overlooks people's transgressions, he appears to give up some of the claims of his rank, which, however, he may be said to receive back again at the proper and appointed time.

6. Elam takes up the quiver, with her charioteers and horses; Kir uncovers the shield. I think the prophet is reproaching the Jews for being obstinate and rebellious, because they did not repent even though the Lord had punished them, and because he tells the story of something that happened in the past, in order to remind them how utterly they had failed to benefit from the Lord's punishments. This is how this verse should be separated from the previous statements. To begin with he foretold things that would happen to the Jews; now he shows how justly they are punished, and how richly they deserve those sharp punishments that the Lord inflicts on them. For the Lord had previously called them to repentance not only by words but by deeds, and yet no reformation of life followed, though their riches were exhausted and the kingdom weakened; they obstinately persisted in their wickedness. All that was left was for the Lord to destroy them wretchedly, for they were stubborn and resistant to the Lord's urgings.

7. Your choicest valleys are full of chariots, and horsemen are posted

at the city gates. At that time they used two kinds of chariots, one for carrying luggage, and the other for warfare. Here he means those chariots in which the horsemen rode into battle.

8. The defenses of Judah are stripped away. He shows how distressed the Jews were when they were so hard-pressed by the siege.

And you looked in that day to the weapons in the Palace of the Forest. Sacred history informs us that this **Palace of the Forest** was built by Solomon to contain the armory of the whole kingdom (see 1 Kings 7:2). "The name of 'the house of the forest' was given to it, because it was made out of cedars from the forest of Lebanon, and because it rested on four rows of fifteen large pillars of cedar. When the inhabitants of Jerusalem heard of the invasion by the Assyrian army, they went to this armory to draw from it arms for defending the city" (Rosenmuller).

9. You saw that the City of David had many breaches in its defenses. So long as they thought they were far from danger, they disregarded the **breaches** in their walls. But when news of war arose, they began to be anxious about them and made plans to rebuild them to stop the enemy from entering through them.

You stored up water in the Lower Pool. This pool provided water for the cisterns, so the besieged would not be in lack.

10. You counted the buildings in Jerusalem and tore down houses to strengthen the wall. He means that the city was closely examined on all sides, so that there might not be a house or building that was not defended.

11. You built a reservoir between the two walls for the water of the Old Pool, but you did not look to the One who made it, or have regard for the One who planned it long ago. Instead of resorting first of all to God, as they ought to have done, they forgot and despised him and directed their attention to ramparts, ditches, walls, and other preparations for war.

12. The Lord, the LORD Almighty, called you on that day to weep and to wail, to tear out your hair and put on sackcloth. The prophet cites the wicked obstinacy of the people along with additional aggravations. What left them altogether without excuse was the fact that while they were exposed to such great dangers, they despised the godly remonstrances of the prophets and rejected God's grace when he wanted to heal and restore them. It is proof of consummate depravity when people completely lay aside all feeling and fearlessly despise both instruction and punishments and obstinately kick against the goads (see Acts 9:5, KJV). This makes it evident that they have been given over to a reprobate mind (see Romans 1:28).

13. But see, there is joy and revelry, slaughtering of cattle and killing of sheep, eating of meat and drinking of wine! "Let us eat and drink," you say, "for tomorrow we die!" The clause **for tomorrow we die!** shows clearly why the prophet complained so loudly about eating meat and drinking wine. It was because they turned all the prophets' warnings into a subject of jesting and laughter. I wish there were no examples of this kind with us today! Most people sneer and ridicule every warning that comes from God's holy mouth.

14. The LORD Almighty has revealed this in my hearing: "Till your dying day this sin will not be atoned for," says the Lord, the LORD Almighty. God adds a dreadful warning: This wickedness will never be forgiven. The meaning of the Hebrew here is as if the Lord said, "Do not think that I am true or that I have any divine perfections if I do not take vengeance on such great wickedness."

Here Isaiah states generally that nothing so displeases God as impenitence, by which, as Paul said, we heap upon ourselves God's wrath (see Romans 2:5) and shut out all hope of pardon.

15. This is what the Lord, the LORD Almighty, says: "Go, say to this steward, to Shebna, who is in charge of the palace . . ." This is a special prediction against a single individual. Having spoken about the whole nation, he here turns to **Shebna,** whom he mentions later on: **He sent Eliakim the palace administrator, Shebna the secretary, and the leading priests, all wearing sackcloth, to the prophet Isaiah son of Amoz** (37:2).

16. "What are you doing here and who gave you permission to cut out a grave for yourself here, hewing your grave on the height and chiseling your resting place in the rock?" Shebna had built a sepulcher at Jerusalem, as if he were to live there continually and to die there. The prophet therefore asks why he built a splendid and costly sepulcher in such a conspicuous place.

17. "Beware, the LORD is about to take firm hold of you and hurl you away, O you mighty man." In other words, "You will be cast out of that place into a distant country, where you will die ignominiously."

18. "He will roll you up tightly like a ball and throw you into a large country. There you will die and there your splendid chariots will remain—you disgrace to your master's house!" By this comparison Isaiah means that nothing will prevent the Lord from throwing Shebna out into a distant country, although he thinks his power is firmly established. He has been extremely careful about his sepulcher and has given orders about it as if he were certain where he would die, but Isaiah declares that he will not die in Jerusalem but in a foreign country, to which he will be banished.

19. "I will depose you from your office, and you will be ousted from your position." Isaiah says nothing new here but concludes the previous prediction. The change of person shows that the prophet sometimes speaks in his own name and sometimes in the name of God.

20. "In that day I will summon my servant, Eliakim son of Hilkiah." This means, "I will give a sign to my servant, that he may know that it is I who have raised him to that honorable rank." There is a special relationship here between the master and the servant that does not apply to ungodly men when they obey their own inclinations and wicked passions. But this man, **Eliakim,** acknowledged the Lord and sincerely obeyed him.

21. "I will clothe him with your robe and fasten your sash around him and hand your authority over to him." He now explains that it was only because of God's intention that Shebna was deposed and that Eliakim replaced him. The **robe** and the **sash** were emblems of a magistrate's office.

"He will be a father to those who live in Jerusalem and to the house of Judah." The prophet means that Eliakim will act like a father because he has been endued with the Spirit of God. Those who wish to be regarded as lawful rulers and prove that they are God's servants must show that they are fathers to their people.

22. "I will place on his shoulder the key to the house of David; what he opens no one can shut, and what he shuts no one can open." The keys of the house were given to the stewards, so that they had the power to open and close the doors of the house when they needed to. This means that the whole organization of the house was handed over to them.

23. "I will drive him like a peg into a firm place; he will be a seat of honor for the house of his father." Isaiah uses an apt metaphor, from which godly magistrates—and there are not many of them—ought to draw much consolation. They may conclude that not only has God raised them to that honorable rank, but they are established as if they had been fixed there by God's hand. And indeed, where the fear of the Lord dwells, there the stability and power and authority of kings, as Solomon says, are established by justice and judgment (see Proverbs 16:12; 25:5; 29:14).

24. "All the glory of his family will hang on him: its offspring and offshoots—all its lesser vessels, from the bowls to all the jars." It is as if he said that Eliakim would be fully qualified for discharging his duties and would not be indolent in his office. Metaphorically, the phrase **lesser vessels** denotes that there will be uniform justice or equal laws. In other words, "He will not only support nobles but will also attend to the interests of the lowest ranks."

25. "In that day," declares the LORD Almighty, **"the peg driven into the firm place will give way; it will be sheared off and will fall, and the load hanging on it will be cut down."** The LORD has spoken. This appears to be inconsistent with what he said in verse 23, but he is no longer speaking about Eliakim but is returning to Shebna, who was about to be cast down from his rank, as Isaiah had said.

Isaiah
Chapter 23

1. An oracle concerning Tyre: Wail, O ships of Tarshish! For Tyre is destroyed and left without house or harbor. From the land of Cyprus word has come to them. Tyre was very wealthy on account of all her trade with other nations. Carthage, Utica, Leptis, Cadiz, and other towns sent presents to Tyre every year, acknowledging her as their mother.

Isaiah warns about the destruction of Tyre because it had been hostile to the people of God, as we may infer from what Ezekiel said. We should always carefully note the reason for their destruction because it was the prophet's intention to show that God reveals his fatherly care toward his people by opposing all her enemies (see Ezekiel 26:2).

Isaiah tells the **ships of Tarshish** to **wail** because when Tyre has been destroyed they will have nothing to do.

2. Be silent, you people of the island and you merchants of Sidon, whom the seafarers have enriched. This is intended to highlight the ruin of Tyre. Although he uses the word **island** in the singular, he means all the islands in the Mediterranean Sea and the countries beyond the sea, especially the neighbors who frequently traveled by sea to Tyre to trade there. He tells them to **be silent,** like people who are stunned, for they will make no more voyages to Tyre.

3. On the great waters came the grain of the Shihor; the harvest of the Nile was the revenue of Tyre, and she became the marketplace of the nations. He intimates that the riches of Tyre will not prevent it from being destroyed. Therefore he extols its wealth so that God's judgment may be seen more clearly, and so everyone may know that no ordinary calamity befell it. The more unexpected it was, the more clearly would it appear as God's work.

4. Be ashamed, O Sidon, and you, O fortress of the sea, for the sea has spoken: "I have neither been in labor nor given birth; I have neither reared sons nor brought up daughters." This verse is added to heighten the picture. The prophet gives Tyre an eminent title—**fortress of the sea**—as if she reigned alone in the middle of the sea.

Be ashamed, O Sidon. Here and in verse 2 he especially mentions the merchants of **Sidon.** That city was highly celebrated but greatly inferior to Tyre. It was a port about twenty-four miles from Tyre, and so it greatly benefited from the trade in which Tyre engaged; the wealth of Tyre overflowed to them. The result was that they suffered more severely than others from the destruction of Tyre, which is why the prophet says, **Be ashamed, O Sidon.**

5. When word comes to Egypt, they will be in anguish at the report from Tyre. In this verse Isaiah declares that the impending destruction will affect the people of Tyre as much as the people of Egypt.

6. Cross over to Tarshish; wail, you people of the island. In other words, "The shore that used to be well supplied with harbors will be forsaken, so that ships will sail in a very different direction." When a harbor has been ruined, merchants usually search for another one.

7. Is this your city of revelry, the old, old city, whose feet have taken her to settle in far-off lands? The prophet mocks Tyre and ridicules her pride because she boasted about her ancient name.

8. Who planned this against Tyre, the bestower of crowns, whose merchants are princes, whose traders are renowned in the earth? He calls Tyre **the bestower of crowns,** for this city enriched many. The general meaning is that she enriches her citizens as if she made them kings and princes.

9. The LORD Almighty planned it, to bring low the pride of all glory and to humble all who are renowned on the earth. God strips such people of their rank, degrades them, and treats them as vile and worthless people. God rebukes haughtiness and declares war on it.

10. Go through your land; the Daughter of Tarshish, like the Nile, will no longer be a haven for you. I think Isaiah is alluding to the situation of the city, which was protected on all sides by ditches, mounds, ramparts, and the sea.

11. The LORD has stretched out his hand over the sea and made its kingdoms tremble. He has given an order concerning Phoenicia that her fortresses be destroyed. Tyre's riches covered the whole sea. She would not perish alone but would involve many **kingdoms** in her ruin.

12. He said, "No more of your reveling, O Virgin Daughter of Sidon, now crushed! Up, cross over to Cyprus; even there you will find no rest." It was hard to believe that a city so celebrated and powerful, so well defended and fortified and linked with many allies, would be destroyed and overturned.

He calls Tyre **O Virgin** metaphorically, because before that time her riches had been untouched and had suffered no injury. This is like saying,

"Previously you skipped lightly, like heifers in the bloom of youth; but when you suffer violence, there will be an end of your joy."

13. Look at the land of the Babylonians, this people that is now of no account! The Assyrians have made it a place for desert creatures; they raised up their siege towers, they stripped its fortresses bare and turned it into a ruin. He uses an example to confirm what he had predicted about the taking of Tyre. Those things could hardly be believed, especially by the people of Tyre, who thought they were far from ruin.

14. Wail, you ships of Tarshish; your fortress is destroyed! He repeats what he has already said. The Cilicians constantly traded with the people of Tyre because they were close by.

15. At that time Tyre will be forgotten for seventy years, the span of a king's life. But at the end of these seventy years, it will happen to Tyre as in the song of the prostitute. Having spoken about the capture of Tyre, Isaiah next declares how long her calamity will last. The prophet predicts that this city will be desolate for **seventy years.**

16. "Take up a harp, walk through the city, O prostitute forgotten; play the harp well, sing many a song, so that you will be remembered." He compares Tyre to a prostitute who after spending her whole youth in debauchery has at last grown old and is therefore forsaken and despised by everyone.

17. At the end of seventy years, the LORD will deal with Tyre. She will return to her hire as a prostitute and will ply her trade with all the kingdoms on the face of the earth. Although the Lord will afflict Tyre in such a way that she will appear to be ruined, he says that she will obtain mercy because, rising at length out of her ruins, she will be restored to her former vigor.

18. Yet her profit and her earnings will be set apart for the LORD; they will not be stored up or hoarded. Her profits will go to those who live before the LORD, for abundant food and fine clothes. This was another instance of divine compassion toward Tyre. This verse should be contrasted with the previous one, as if he said, "And yet the merchandise of Tyre will be consecrated to God." Here we have an astonishing proof of God's goodness, which penetrated not only into this abominable brothel but almost into hell itself.

Isaiah
Chapter 24

1. See, the LORD is going to lay waste the earth and devastate it; he will ruin its face and scatter its inhabitants. This prophecy, so far as I can judge, is the conclusion of all the descriptions that have been given since chapter 13, in which Isaiah predicted destruction not only for the Jews and Israel, but for the Moabites, Assyrians, Egyptians, and other nations.

2. It will be the same for priest as for people, for master as for servant, for mistress as for maid, for seller as for buyer, for borrower as for lender, for debtor as for creditor. By these words he means the utmost desolation, in which there will no longer be any distinction between the different classes and professions of people. He means that all civil government will break down, because in such calamities those who are richest are reduced to the greatest poverty. In short, he describes the most appalling desolation.

3. The earth will be completely laid waste and totally plundered. The LORD has spoken this word. He is saying that these changes will not be accidental but are the work of God.

4. The earth dries up and withers, the world languishes and withers, the exalted of the earth languish. All this helps to explain the desolation of the whole **world**—that is, of **the world** that was known to the Jews.

5. The earth is defiled by its people; they have disobeyed the laws, violated the statutes and broken the everlasting covenant. When he says they have **broken the everlasting covenant,** he is referring to the covenants in which the Lord, who adopted his people, promised that he would be their God (see Exodus 19:6; 29:45; Leviticus 26:12). He accuses them of ingratitude because when the Lord revealed himself in this way, he was showing his love, and yet they **violated,** disobeyed, and had **broken** his **statutes,** his **laws,** and his **everlasting covenant.**

6. Therefore a curse consumes the earth; its people must bear their guilt. Therefore earth's inhabitants are burned up, and very few are

left. When the prophet says, **and very few are left,** we see that this prediction cannot be explained as relating to the last day of judgment. Rather, the prophet is predicting those desolations that threatened various nations, so that the godly might fear, repent, and be ready to endure everything.

7-8. The new wine dries up and the vine withers; all the merrymakers groan. The gaiety of the tambourines is stilled, the noise of the revelers has stopped, the joyful harp is silent. In other words, "Until now you have had many luxuries and pleasures, but the Lord will make you lead a very different kind of life." Isaiah speaks about the future as if it were present, so that they could see it more clearly.

9. No longer do they drink wine with a song; the beer is bitter to its drinkers. To **drink wine** is not in itself evil, because God has given it for people to enjoy. But here the prophet describes the banquets of drunkards, which were full of licentiousness, songs, and insolence. Again, because they abused their enjoyment of plenty, he warns them that they will be in need. People who wallow in luxury abuse the goodness of God.

10. The ruined city lies desolate; the entrance to every house is barred. This is evidence of solitude and expresses the desolation of the city.

11. In the streets they cry out for wine; all joy turns to gloom, all gaiety is banished from the earth. He means that **wine** is scarce. For where hunger is, it is accompanied by unending complaints, not just in private but **in the streets.**

12. The city is left in ruins, its gate is battered to pieces. The prophet describes the desolation of Jerusalem and of many other cities.

13. So will it be on the earth and among the nations, as when an olive tree is beaten, or as when gleanings are left after the grape harvest. As this statement is inserted between the warnings and the consolation, the prophet seems to be addressing the chosen people, and not all nations indiscriminately.

14. They raise their voices, they shout for joy; from the west they acclaim the LORD's majesty. He gives more details about the consolations that he has previously briefly mentioned in Isaiah 10:19-22. He now says that the small number of the godly who will be left will nevertheless rejoice and utter a cry so loud that it will be heard in the most distant countries.

15. Therefore in the east give glory to the LORD; exalt the name of the LORD, the God of Israel, in the islands of the sea. He uses the expression **the name of the LORD** to intimate that all nations will call on the true God. All nations have a knowledge of God that is natural to them, and they also all easily turn aside to superstition and false worship (see Romans 1:21-23). But here he is speaking about spreading true religion throughout the world. This shows even more clearly that the prophecy relates to the kingdom of Christ, under which true religion has penetrated into foreign and ungodly nations.

16. From the ends of the earth we hear singing: "Glory to the Righteous One." But I said, "I waste away, I waste away! Woe to me! The treacherous betray! With treachery the treacherous betray!" This verse contains two statements that appear to contradict each other. It starts with a joyful description of the praises of God and then passes on to complaints and lamentations, in which Isaiah bewails the treachery of transgressors who overturn religion and godliness. So far as the praises are concerned, as we have said, we can neither praise God nor call on him until he reveals himself to us and gives us a taste of his goodness, that we may entertain hope and confident expectation of life. When we feel nothing but the wrath of God, we are dumb to his praises. And therefore when he says that the praises of God will be heard, he means that the Gospel will spread through the whole world so that people may acknowledge God to be their Father and may thus praise him.

17. Terror and pit and snare await you, O people of the earth. The prophet now speaks against the sins of the people. Previously he declared that not just one nation but very many and very distant nations would have abundant grounds for thanksgiving. He now moves on to other teaching. I think these words are separate from the previous verses because Isaiah again warns the wicked, so that they may know that in the midst of the church's prosperity they will be miserable.

18. Whoever flees at the sound of terror will fall into a pit; whoever climbs out of the pit will be caught in a snare. The floodgates of the heavens are opened, the foundations of the earth shake. This argument confirms what had already been said: It was impossible for them to escape God's vengeance. God's judgment will reach to the highest heaven and to the depths of the earth.

19. The earth is broken up, the earth is split asunder, the earth is thoroughly shaken. He highlights his descriptions of punishments by using a variety of expressions. He explains the same thing in various ways and thus arouses sluggish minds.

20. The earth reels like a drunkard, it sways like a hut in the wind; so heavy upon it is the guilt of its rebellion that it falls—never to rise again. He states that there will be no remedy for their evils. The distresses of the world will be so severe that it cannot be restored to its original condition.

21. In that day the LORD will punish the powers in the heavens above and the kings on the earth below. No power is too lofty to be exempt from these divine retributions.

22. They will be herded together like prisoners bound in a dungeon; they will be shut up in prison and be punished after many days. This is a metaphorical expression, for they were not all captives; but he speaks of them as reduced to servitude as if a man held in his hand the enemies whom he subdued. He therefore depicts God as a conqueror who shuts up enemies in prison.

23. The moon will be abashed, the sun ashamed; for the LORD Almighty will reign on Mount Zion and in Jerusalem, and before its elders, gloriously. He continues to give consolation. It is as if he said, "When the Lord visits his people and cleanses his church from defilement, he will establish a church so illustrious that it will darken the sun and stars by its brightness."

Isaiah
Chapter 25

1. O LORD, you are my God; I will exalt you and praise your name, for in perfect faithfulness you have done marvelous things, things planned long ago. This thanksgiving is connected with the previous prophecies. Isaiah considers not only what he predicted, but why the Lord afflicted so many nations with various calamities. It was in order that the Lord might subdue those who had previously been incorrigible and who had no fear of God.

2. You have made the city a heap of rubble, the fortified town a ruin, the stronghold of the foreigners to be a city no more; it will never be rebuilt. Some commentators think this refers to Jerusalem. But I think the prophet does not speak of a single city but of many cities, which he says will be reduced to heaps.

3. Therefore strong peoples will honor you; cities of ruthless nations will revere you. In other words, "You will not only strike and afflict, O Lord, but you will make the punishments effective. For through them you will reduce people's ferocity, so that those who were previously estranged from you will bend their neck to you."

4. You have been a refuge for the poor, a refuge for the needy in his distress, a shelter from the storm and a shade from the heat. For the breath of the ruthless is like a storm driving against a wall. Here we see the fruit of conversion—namely, that the Lord raises us from the dead and brings us, as it were, out of the grave, stretching out his hand to us from heaven, to rescue us from hell.

5. . . . and like the heat of the desert. You silence the uproar of foreigners; as heat is reduced by the shadow of a cloud, so the song of the ruthless is stilled. If the Lord did not come to our aid when violent men threatened our lives, we would be in danger of being killed. We sometimes see the great rage of wicked men. If the Lord did not overturn them, what could a feeble man do against them?

6. On this mountain the LORD Almighty will prepare a feast of rich food for all peoples, a banquet of aged wine—the best of meats and the finest of wines. The prophet makes known the grace of God, which was to be revealed by the coming of Christ. He uses the same metaphor that David used when he described the kingdom of Christ, saying that the poor and rich will sit down at this feast and will eat and be satisfied (see Psalm 22:26, 29). By this metaphorical language Isaiah means that no class of people will be excluded from sharing in this generous provision.

7. On this mountain he will destroy the shroud that enfolds all peoples, the sheet that covers all nations. The Lord promises that he will take away the veil by which they were kept in blindness and ignorance. It was by the light of the Gospel that this darkness was dispelled.

8. He will swallow up death forever. The Sovereign LORD will wipe away the tears from all faces; he will remove the disgrace of his people from all the earth. The LORD has spoken. The prophet links two things that make for complete happiness. The first is that life is perpetual, for to those who in other respects are happy for a time, it is a wretched thing to die. The second is that this life is accompanied by joy; otherwise it might be thought that death would be preferable to a sorrowful and afflicted life.

9. In that day they will say, "Surely this is our God; we trusted in him, and he saved us. This is the LORD, we trusted in him; let us rejoice and be glad in his salvation." This passage warns believers that their salvation rests on hope and expectation. For the promises of God were, so to speak, suspended until the coming of Christ. Besides, we ought to notice the condition of those times. It appeared as if either God's promise had come to nothing or he had rejected the posterity of Abraham. Certainly, though they looked far and wide, God was not to be seen by them at that time. They must have been endued with astonishing patience to endure such heavy and sharp temptations. Accordingly, he tells them to wait quietly for the coming of Christ, for then they will clearly perceive how near God is to those who worship him.

10. The hand of the LORD will rest on this mountain. The prophet's purpose here is to comfort the godly, who but for this would have thought that God had forsaken and abandoned them.

But Moab will be trampled under him as straw is trampled down in the manure. In other words, "As straw is trodden down in their fields, so will the Lord tread down the Moabites."

11. They will spread out their hands in it, as a swimmer spreads out his hands to swim. God will bring down their pride despite the cleverness of their hands. A **swimmer** does not rush forward but gently spreads out and quickly draws back his arms as he cuts through and subdues the waters. Similarly, the Lord does not always exert great strength to cut down the wicked; but without any effort, without using armies, without any noise or uproar, he destroys them and puts them to flight, no matter how well prepared for the battle they appear to be.

12. He will bring down your high fortified walls and lay them low; he will bring them down to the ground, to the very dust. The prophet now addresses the country of Moab. It was well **fortified** and was proud of its **walls** and fortifications. But he affirms that the lofty towers and other defenses, no matter how strong and seemingly impregnable, will be of no avail.

Isaiah
Chapter 26

1. In that day this song will be sung in the land of Judah: We have a strong city; God makes salvation its walls and ramparts. Here the prophet shows that after the people's return from captivity they will be defended by God's power; under his protection, Jerusalem will be as safe as if she had been surrounded by ramparts, a moat, and a double wall.

2. Open the gates that the righteous nation may enter, the nation that keeps faith. In other words, "The inhabitants of the restored city will be different from before: They will maintain righteousness and truth." At the time this promise might have looked as if it had failed. When they were driven out of the country and taken into captivity, no consolation remained. So when the temple was destroyed and the city sacked, they might have objected, "Where are those **gates** that he tells us to **open?** Where are the people who are to **enter?**" Yet we see that these things were fulfilled, and that nothing was ever divinely predicted that the Lord did not accomplish. We ought, therefore, to remember these old stories, so that we may always be strengthened by their example.

3. You will keep in perfect peace him whose mind is steadfast, because he trusts in you. The peace of the church is founded on God's eternal and unchangeable purpose. In order to stop godly minds from wavering, it is most important to look to the heavenly decree. It is a fixed decree of God that all who hope in him will enjoy eternal peace.

By the word **peace** I understand not only serenity of mind but every kind of happiness—as if he said that God's grace alone can enable us to live happily.

4. Trust in the LORD forever, for the LORD, the LORD, is the Rock eternal. The power of God, which is the object of faith, is perpetual. When the prophet speaks of the strength and power of God, he does not mean power that is idle, but active power that is actually exerted on us. This teaching has a wider application, for it tells us that we ought to contemplate the nature of God. As soon as we turn aside from beholding it, we only see what is fleeting, and then we immediately faint. Faith ought to rise above the world, for neither truth nor God's justice or goodness is temporary and fading—God always remains like himself.

5. He humbles those who dwell on high, he lays the lofty city low; he levels it to the ground and casts it down to the dust. The prophet comforts the Jews because the seemingly invincible power of Babylon might have terrified them if the Lord had not supported them by this promise. "You have no reason to be afraid of Babylon's strength; she will fall quickly and will not stand before the Lord's power."

6-7. Feet trample it down—the feet of the oppressed, the footsteps of the poor. The path of the righteous is level; O upright One, you make the way of the righteous smooth. The prophet is not praising the righteousness of the godly, as some have supposed, but is showing that, through God's blessing, they prosper throughout their lives.

8. Yes, LORD, walking in the way of your laws, we wait for you; your name and renown are the desire of our hearts. This verse contains a very beautiful doctrine, without which it might have been thought that the earlier statements were without foundation. Isaiah had said that God will be our guide during our whole lives, so that we will not fall despite much opposition. We might therefore conclude that these promises have not been kept, since we are so hard-pressed. Accordingly, when God tries our patience, we ought to strive and yet trust in him. Here the prophet tells us that though we see no easy and delightful path, and though the road is not made smooth under our feet but rather we must struggle through many hard places, there is still room for hope and patience.

9. My soul yearns for you in the night; in the morning my spirit longs for you. When your judgments come upon the earth, the people of the world learn righteousness. The prophet confesses that he and others were trained by God's punishments. No one obeys God if the Lord does not raise his hand and claim his right to rule.

10. Though grace is shown to the wicked, they do not learn righteousness; even in a land of uprightness they go on doing evil and regard not the majesty of the LORD. Isaiah contrasts this statement with the previous one. He had said that the godly, even when they are afflicted, or see others afflicted, still rely on God's love and trust him. But now he declares that there is no way the wicked can be brought to love God.

11. O LORD, your hand is lifted high, but they do not see it. Let them see your zeal for your people and be put to shame; let the fire reserved for your enemies consume them. This explains the previous statement. The prophet had said that the wicked pay no attention to the majesty of the LORD, and now he explains that majesty is what is visible in the deeds of God. Some might plead ignorance and say they have not seen God's deeds, but the prophet says that God's **hand is lifted high,** so that it is not just visible to a few people but shines conspicuously.

12. LORD, you establish peace for us; all that we have accomplished you have done for us. This statement helps comfort the godly. It is as if he said, "We will see what the end of the wicked will be. You will prevent them from sharing with your children and will take them away as enemies by fire; but we will be happy."

13. O LORD, our God, other lords besides you have ruled over us, but your name alone do we honor. This song was composed to refresh the believers who were to be banished from the land that was a picture of eternal happiness. They were to be deprived of sacrifices and holy assemblies and almost every consolation, crushed by the heavy yoke of the Babylonians, banished from their country, that they might direct their groans to God in order to seek relief. Isaiah therefore speaks in the name of believers who to outward appearance had been rejected by God and yet did not stop testifying that they were the people of God and put their trust in him.

14. They are now dead, they live no more; those departed spirits do not rise. You punished them and brought them to ruin; you wiped out all memory of them. The prophet again speaks of the unhappy end of the wicked, whose prosperity often upsets us, just as we read in the Psalms (see 37:1; 73:3, 17).

15. You have enlarged the nation, O LORD; you have enlarged the nation. You have gained glory for yourself; you have extended all the borders of the land. In other words, "We were previously a small people, but we have multiplied and increased." The Gentiles were joined with the Jews on the condition that they should be united into one people. Thus the Lord added a vast multitude, for the children of Abraham were called out of all nations.

16. LORD, they came to you in their distress; when you disciplined them, they could barely whisper a prayer. The Hebrew word used for **whisper** here means "mutter." This word therefore must not be thought to mean an articulated prayer, but something that indicates that the heart is wrung with intense pains, for those who are tortured by extreme anguish can hardly speak or express their feelings. In prosperity people speak with open mouths, but when they are cast down in adversity, they hardly venture to mutter.

17. As a woman with child and about to give birth writhes and cries out in her pain, so were we in your presence, O LORD. He compares believers to a woman in labor who, we know, endures terrible pain. So the prophet says that their anguish breaks out into loud cries. He is describing that dreadful anguish by which the hearts of the godly are sorely and dreadfully tormented when they see that God is angry with them and when their consciences reprove them.

18. We were with child, we writhed in pain, but we gave birth to wind. We have not brought salvation to the earth; we have not given birth to people of the world. As long as the wicked flourish, the children of God must be unhappy and become like women in labor. And this condition must be quietly endured by us if we want to have a place in the church of God.

19. But your dead will live; their bodies will rise. You who dwell in the dust, wake up and shout for joy. Your dew is like the dew of the morning; the earth will give birth to her dead. Isaiah continues the same consolation, addressing his words to God. This shows that nothing is better for us than to bring our thoughts to God whenever we struggle with temptations. The general meaning here is that as God guards believers, although they are like **dead** people, yet they **will live** amidst death itself or will rise again after their death.

20. Go, my people, enter your rooms and shut the doors behind you; hide yourselves for a little while until his wrath has passed by. In this verse Isaiah urges the children of God to exercise patience, to shut themselves up in solitude, to bear their troubles and afflictions with moderation, and to stand unmoved in opposition to the fierce storms that seem likely to overwhelm them.

21. See, the LORD is coming out of his dwelling to punish the people of the earth for their sins. The earth will disclose the blood shed upon her; she will conceal her slain no longer. It is grievous to the godly to see wicked people raging without being punished or restrained by God. They feel as if he has forsaken them. Isaiah therefore meets this temptation and shows that although the Lord keeps himself out of sight for a time, at the right time he will avenge the injuries that his people have received.

176

Isaiah
Chapter 27

1. In that day, the LORD will punish with his sword, his fierce, great and powerful sword, Leviathan the gliding serpent, Leviathan the coiling serpent; he will slay the monster of the sea. Here the prophet speaks in general about God's judgment and thus includes all of Satan's kingdom. Having previously spoken about God's vengeance being displayed against tyrants and wicked people who have shed innocent blood, he now announces this vengeance.

2. In that day—"Sing about a fruitful vineyard." He says that this song may be sung in the church and predicts that though it would be reduced to fearful ruin meanwhile, it will later be restored so that it yields much fruit, and this will give good reason for singing.

3. "I, the LORD, watch over it; I water it continually. I guard it day and night so that no one may harm it." Here the Lord asserts his care and diligence in dressing and guarding the vine; he says in effect that he left nothing undone that an industrious farmer should have attended to.

4. "I am not angry. If only there were briers and thorns confronting me! I would march against them in battle; I would set them all on fire." This verse is full of wonderful comfort, for it expresses the incredible warmth of love that the Lord has toward his people, even though they rebel and are wicked. He shows that he cannot hate his elect but has to show his fatherly kindness toward them, even while he brings severe punishments upon them.

5. "Or else let them come to me for refuge; let them make peace with me, yes, let them make peace with me." How earnestly God desires to be reconciled to us is clearly seen in the repetition of the words, **make peace.** He might have said in a word that he is merciful and ready to bestow pardon. When he repeats the words, **let them make peace with me, yes, let them make peace with me,** he is declaring that he hastens most willingly and earnestly to blot out all our offenses.

6. In days to come Jacob will take root. In other words, "Although I will reduce the number of people in my church, it will still be restored to its earlier flourishing condition, so it may fill the whole world. After I reconcile it, it will grow and grow."

Israel will bud and blossom and fill all the world with fruit. This happened when Christ came, collecting and multiplying God's people through the Gospel.

7. Has the LORD struck her as he struck down those who struck her? Has she been killed as those were killed who killed her? Isaiah confirms the previous statement and shows that even in punishment there is definite proof of God's goodness and mercy. Though the Lord chastises his people, he moderates the severity so as always to leave room for compassion.

I think this verse is talking about a difference between believers and reprobates. God punishes both indiscriminately, but not in the same way. When he takes vengeance on the reprobates, he gives free rein to his anger because his only object is to destroy them. They are "objects of his wrath—prepared for destruction" (Romans 9:22) and have no experience of the goodness of God. But when he punishes the godly, he restrains his wrath and has another and totally different object in view. He wishes to bring them back to the right path and to draw them to himself, that provision may be made for their future happiness.

8. By warfare and exile you contend with her—with his fierce blast he drives her out, as on a day the east wind blows. This is the second example of divine compassion toward all the elect, whom he punishes so that they may not perish.

When the prophet speaks about the **day the east wind blows** he has in mind a situation in Judea when the easterly wind blows and has an adverse effect. This wind is thought to be the equinoctial wind that in many countries is very destructive.

9. By this, then, will Jacob's guilt be atoned for, and this will be the full fruitage of the removal of his sin: When he makes all the altar stones to be like chalk stones crushed to pieces, no Asherah poles or incense altars will be left standing. The prophet shows that the godly have no good reason to grumble about God's punishments. On the contrary, they ought to acknowledge that their salvation is promoted in this way, because otherwise they would not acknowledge the grace of God. Punishments expiate our offenses indirectly but not directly, because they lead us to repentance, which again, in its turn, brings us to obtain forgiveness of sins.

10. The fortified city stands desolate, an abandoned settlement, forsaken like the desert; there the calves graze, there they lie down; they strip its branches bare. The prophet means that Jerusalem and the other cities of Judea must be destroyed and that, although the Lord wants to spare his chosen people, it is impossible for them to be preserved. Godly people would have become disheartened when they saw that holy city overthrown and the temple demolished. But from these predictions they learned that God would have many ways of preserving his church.

11. When its twigs are dry, they are broken off and women come and make fires with them. For this is a people without understanding; so their Maker has no compassion on them, and their Creator shows them no favor. The purpose of this verse is to heighten their terror still further. In the end he removes all hope of pardon, for even if a remnant was preserved, that did not mean the wrath of God would stop raging against the multitude at large. Isaiah made this statement in order to show more clearly how ungrateful the people were and to show how justly they deserved to be punished. Having been formed and preserved by God, they treated him with dishonor and contempt.

12. In that day the LORD will thresh from the flowing Euphrates to the Wadi of Egypt, and you, O Israelites, will be gathered up one by one. He softens the harshness of the previous statement.

It was a dreadful judgment of God to remove all hope of mercy and favor from the people. The prophet speaks metaphorically, comparing the gathering of the church to the threshing of wheat, by which the grain is separated from the chaff. This means that the people were so completely overwhelmed by their captivity that they seemed like grain concealed or scattered here and there under the chaff. It was necessary for the Lord to thresh them so they could be gathered in.

13. And in that day a great trumpet will sound. Those who were perishing in Assyria and those who were exiled in Egypt will come and worship the LORD on the holy mountain in Jerusalem. This explains the previous verse. The prophet speaks metaphorically, showing that God's power will be so great that he will easily bring his people back. Kings assemble large armies by the sound of a trumpet, and Isaiah shows that it will be easy for the Lord to gather his people, on whom prophecy had just as much effect as the trumpet by which soldiers are mustered.

Isaiah
Chapter 28

1. Woe to that wreath, the pride of Ephraim's drunkards, to the fading flower, his glorious beauty, set on the head of a fertile valley—to that city, the pride of those laid low by wine! Isaiah now starts on a new subject (for this discourse must be separated from the previous one). He shows that the anger of the Lord will quickly overtake first Israel and then the Jews (Judah). The kingdom of Israel was probably still intact when the prophet made these predictions. This cannot be stated for certain, but there are good reasons for thinking that the ten tribes had not at that time been led into captivity.

2-3. See, the Lord has one who is powerful and strong. Like a hailstorm and a destructive wind, like a driving rain and a flooding downpour, he will throw it forcefully to the ground. That wreath, the pride of Ephraim's drunkards, will be trampled underfoot. The glory and splendor of the Israelites will be laid low, thrown **forcefully to the ground.**

4. That fading flower, his glorious beauty, set on the head of a fertile valley, will be like a fig ripe before harvest—as soon as someone sees it and takes it in his hand, he swallows it. The prophet repeats some of the words of verse 1. We know how difficult it is to terrify and humble those who have been blinded by prosperity, those whose eyes are covered by success in the same way as by fatness. They will be like Dionysius II who became temporarily blind as a result of gorging himself at banquets. Justin, in a brief sketch of that tyrant, informs us that "after defeating his rivals, he abandoned himself to indolence and gluttony, which brought on such weakness of sight that he could not bear daylight. The consciousness of being despised for his blindness made him even more cruel than before, and led him to fill the city with murders as much as his father had filled the jails with prisoners, so that he became universally hated and despised." In a similar way pleasure and luxury blind people's minds, so that they know neither God nor themselves. The prophet frequently presses the same truth home on people who were stupid, that they might understand what would otherwise have seemed incredible to them.

5. In that day the LORD Almighty will be a glorious crown, a beautiful wreath for the remnant of his people. Having spoken about the kingdom of Israel, he passes on to the tribe of Judah and shows that, amidst God's vengeance, there will soon be room for compassion. Although the ten tribes will perish, the Lord will preserve a **remnant** that he will consecrate to himself, so there **will be a glorious crown.** The church is never disfigured in such a way that the Lord does not adorn it with beauty and splendor.

6. He will be a spirit of justice to him who sits in judgment, a source of strength to those who turn back the battle at the gate. The prophet explains how the Lord will adorn the remnant with additional splendor. He mentions the true art of civil government, which consists mainly of two things—**judgment** and **strength.** Since it is by these two defenses that kingdoms rule themselves, he promises his people **a spirit of justice** and **a source of strength.** At the same time he shows that God gives both of these gifts and that they should not be expected from anyone else.

7. And these also stagger from wine and reel from beer: Priests and prophets stagger from beer and are befuddled with wine; they reel from beer, they stagger when seeing visions, they stumble when rendering decisions. He returns now to the ungodly people who despised God, those who were Jews in name only. Their ingratitude was displayed in that although they had striking evidence of God's anger when they saw their brothers severely punished, they would not return to the right path. Isaiah speaks of **beer** and **wine** metaphorically (I do not think this refers to ordinary drunkenness). He says they were like drunkards because they lacked knowledge and sound understanding.

8. All the tables are covered with vomit and there is not a spot without filth. He pursues the same metaphor, drawing a picture of what usually happens to men who are given over to drunkenness. It is certainly an ugly sight to see **tables covered with vomit.** There can be no doubt that the prophet wanted to sum up the idea that no sincerity or uprightness was left among the Jews.

9. "Who is it he is trying to teach? To whom is he explaining his message?" Here the prophet shows by an expression of amazement that the disease of the people is incurable and that God has no other remedies to cure them, for he had tried them all without any effect.

"To children weaned from their milk, to those just taken from the breast?" The prophet complains that the stupidity of the people may be said to hinder God from attempting to cure them of their vices. Therefore he compares the Jews to very young infants who are only just beginning to speak, and whom it would be a waste of time to attempt to teach.

10. "For it is: Do and do, do and do, rule on rule, rule on rule; a little here, a little there." This shows clearly that the Lord is complaining about laboring fruitlessly when he instructs this unteachable people, just as if one were to teach children who must have elementary instructions repeated to them over and over again. They quickly forget what they have been taught, and so their teacher has to spend a whole day teaching them a single letter.

11. Very well then, with foreign lips and strange tongues God will speak to this people. God became like a barbarian to a people without understanding. "God will thunder in their ears, what to them will appear like jargon, the language of a foreign nation, by whom they will be carried off into captivity" (Stock).

12. To whom he said, "This is the resting place, let the weary rest"; and, "This is the place of repose"—but they would not listen. In a word, Isaiah informs the Jews that they have a choice: "Do they prefer to be refreshed or to sink under the burden and be overwhelmed?"

13. So then, the word of the LORD to them will become: Do and do, do and do, rule on rule, rule on rule; a little here, a little there—so that they will go and fall backward, be injured and snared and captured. Although the prophet repeats the same words, the meaning is rather different. Having previously spoken about voluntary stupidity, he now warns about a punishment—namely, that God will strike them so they are totally deprived of the benefit of saving teaching and will perceive it as nothing but an empty sound. In short, he concludes from this that the Jews had not profited by the word of God and so will soon be punished for their ingratitude. His word will not be taken from them, but they will be deprived of sound judgment and understanding and will be blind in the clearest light. Thus God blinds and hardens the reprobate more and more because of their disobedience.

14. Therefore hear the word of the LORD, you scoffers who rule this people in Jerusalem. He goes on to show them stronger evidence and at the same time mingles with it a consolation to encourage the godly. There is keen irony when he calls them **scoffers.** It is as if he said, "You think you have enough craftiness to mock God, but you will not succeed in doing so."

15. You boast, "We have entered into a covenant with death, with the grave we have made an agreement. When an overwhelming scourge sweeps by, it cannot touch us, for we have made a lie our refuge and falsehood our hiding place." The prophet now explains why he calls them **scoffers.** It was because they had thrown off all fear of God. He also describes their behavior, saying that they promised themselves they would escape punishment amid all their sins and become even more daring. It is as if they had obtained greater freedom to pursue wicked ways, and they rushed headlong without worrying about where their unruly passions were carrying them.

16. So this is what the Sovereign LORD says: "See, I lay a stone in Zion, a tested stone, a precious cornerstone for a sure foundation; the one who trusts will never be dismayed." Isaiah now comforts the godly and warns the wicked that they will receive the punishment they deserve. He brings forward consolation because the godly were a laughingstock to those crafty men.

He uses the word **cornerstone** because it supports the whole weight of the building; by this name, which is given to it in Psalm 118:22, he commends its strength.

He says it is **in Zion** because Christ must come out of it. It greatly strengthens our faith when we see that he came from the place appointed for this purpose so long before. At the present day **Mount Zion** is everywhere, for the church has spread to the ends of the world.

17. "I will make justice the measuring line and righteousness the plumb line; hail will sweep away your refuge, the lie, and water will overflow your hiding place." It is probable that **the measuring line** and **the plumb line** mean the same thing (see 2 Kings 21:13). Both metaphors are taken from buildings, in which the master builders and masons test everything with a rule, to see that everything is as it should be. Thus it is said that the Lord judges fairly when he restores the church; otherwise, as in a hideous ruin, everything is disordered and confused when the ungodly are exalted and enjoy prosperity, while the godly are despised and sorrowful.

18. "Your covenant with death will be annulled; your agreement with the grave will not stand. When the overwhelming scourge sweeps by, you will be beaten down by it." The state of ease and indifference into which they have sunk arises from a kind of lethargy or drunkenness that hinders them from perceiving the alarming nature of their disease. But the Lord will arouse them from their sleep, no matter how deep it is, and will annul their imaginary alliances.

19. "As often as it comes it will carry you away; morning after morning, by day and by night, it will sweep through." The understanding of this message will bring sheer terror. That is, "It will come to pass that terror alone will enable you to understand true doctrine." In other words, "Until now I have not succeeded in my exhortations to you, but the Lord will find a new way of instructing you—that is, in punishments and calamities by which he will terrify you in such a way that you will know with whom you have to deal."

20. The bed is too short to stretch out on, the blanket too narrow to wrap around you. This metaphor adorns the previous statement. He compares the reprobate, pressed down by God's hand, to those who have concealed themselves in a **bed** that **is too short,** in which they can hardly stretch their limbs or lift their head, and where, in short, instead of rest, they feel sharp pains. He means that the Jews will be shut up in such a way that they will be overwhelmed with the severity of their distresses and that the **bed** that is given for rest will be an instrument of torture.

21. The LORD will rise up as he did at Mount Perazim, he will rouse himself as in the Valley of Gibeon—to do his work, his strange work, and perform his task, his alien task. The prophet contrasts the wicked Israelites with the Philistines and Canaanites. It is as if he said, "The Lord previously performed miracles when he wished to save his people. He will now perform them in order to destroy that people. Because the Israelites have degenerated, they will feel the hand of God for their destruction that their fathers felt for their salvation."

22. Now stop your mocking, or your chains will become heavier; the Lord, the LORD Almighty, has told me of the destruction decreed against the whole land. In other words, "The whole world abounds with shocking impiety; reprobate men have grown wanton in their wickedness, as if there were to be no judgment from God. But throughout the world God will show that he is judge and avenger, and no corner of the earth will be exempt from calamities, because they have despised the word."

23. Listen and hear my voice; pay attention and hear what I say. The purpose of this preface is that men may realize their stupidity in carping at God's judgments and putting an unfavorable construction on them, while even in the ordinary course of nature they have a very bright mirror in which they may see them clearly.

24. When a farmer plows for planting, does he plow continually? Does he keep on breaking up and harrowing the soil? "This apposite simile from the various methods used by the farmer, in preparing his land and in managing the crop after it has been gathered, is addressed to those who might question divine providence, because sentence against the wicked is not executed speedily. God, who teaches the farmer the proper time and way to treat his crops, knows best when and how to punish sinners. He does not reduce them to dust at once, any more than corn is allowed to be beaten until it is inedible, but punishes in mercy, so that he can reclaim them" (Stock).

25. When he has leveled the surface, does he not sow caraway and scatter cummin? Does he not plant wheat in its place, barley in its plot, and spelt in its field? That is, he will not mix various seeds but will allot one part of the field for **wheat,** another for **barley,** and another for **spelt.**

26. His God instructs him and teaches him the right way. From whom did the farmer learn these things but from God? The Lord appointed the universal order of nature; will he not also regulate these things in the right way? Are men so headstrong that they will venture to remonstrate with him or to impugn his wisdom? The general meaning is that we ought not to judge rashly if God does not immediately punish people's wickedness.

27-28. Caraway is not threshed with a sledge, nor is a cartwheel

rolled over cummin; caraway is beaten out with a rod, and cummin with a stick. Grain must be ground to make bread; so one does not go on threshing it forever. Though he drives the wheels of his threshing cart over it, his horses do not grind it. This shows that we ought to restrain people's presumption when, even in the smallest matters, they often make mistakes. If a person who is ignorant about agriculture sees a farmer plowing fields, making furrows, breaking up the earth, and driving oxen up and down the fields, he might laugh at this, thinking it was some childish game. But the farmer would be right to blame him for being ignorant and rash. Everyone who has great modesty will think that those things are not done at random, even if he does not understand what is happening.

29. All this also comes from the LORD Almighty, wonderful in counsel and magnificent in wisdom. Having pointed out the wisdom of God, even in the smallest matters, the prophet tells us, in the same way, to raise our eyes to higher subjects, that we may learn to be reverent when we see his wonderful and hidden judgments.

Isaiah
Chapter 29

1. Woe to you, Ariel, Ariel, the city where David settled! This seems to be another discourse in which Isaiah threatens the city of Jerusalem.

Add year to year and let your cycle of festivals go on. The prophet adds this because the Jews thought they had escaped punishment when any delay was granted to them.

2. Yet I will besiege Ariel; she will mourn and lament, she will be to me like an altar hearth. God now threatens through Isaiah that the Lord will give them mourning and grief instead of the joy of their festivals.

3. I will encamp against you all around; I will encircle you with towers and set up my siege works against you. This war will be carried on under God's direction, and although the Assyrians are spurred on by their lust for power, they will not be able to do anything except by God's command.

4. Brought low, you will speak from the ground; your speech will mumble out of the dust. Your voice will come ghostlike from the earth; out of the dust your speech will whisper. He describes scornfully the arrogance that led the Jews to despise all warnings so long as they enjoyed prosperity, as is the case with all hypocrites. "This pride," says Isaiah in effect, "will be laid low, and this arrogance will cease."

5. But your many enemies will become like fine dust, the ruthless hordes like blown chaff. Suddenly, in an instant . . . I think the prophet is speaking contemptuously of the garrison on which the Jews foolishly relied, for they had in their pay foreign soldiers who were strong men.

6. . . . the LORD Almighty will come with thunder and earthquake and great noise, with windstorm and tempest and flames of a devouring fire. He shows that God's vengeance will be such that all their preparations will be powerless resistance.

7. Then the hordes of all the nations that fight against Ariel, that attack her and her fortress and besiege her, will be as it is with a dream,

with a vision in the night. He censures the Jews for their obstinacy in boldly despising God and all his warnings. The event will be so unexpected that it will appear to be **a dream.** "Although then," he says in effect, "you indulge the hope of uninterrupted repose, the Lord will quickly weigh you and drive away your presumption."

8. . . . . as when a hungry man dreams that he is eating, but he awakens, and his hunger remains; as when a thirsty man dreams that he is drinking, but he awakens faint, with his thirst unquenched. So will it be with the hordes of all the nations that fight against Mount Zion. He compares the Jews to **hungry** people who are indeed asleep but whose empty stomach craves for food. Thus while the Jews watched, they were like **hungry** people. The Lord continually warned them through his prophets and invited them to the divine feasts of the Word. But they despised those feasts and preferred to take refuge wholly in their vices and to fall asleep in them rather than to take a full part in those sacred feasts.

9. Be stunned and amazed, blind yourselves and be sightless; be drunk, but not from wine, stagger, but not from beer. He means that God's judgment will so completely overwhelm their minds that although they torture themselves by thinking and reflecting, they will still be unable to find any outlet or conclusion.

10. The LORD has brought over you a deep sleep: He has sealed your eyes (the prophets); he has covered your heads (the seers). When people are blind, and especially in things so plain and obvious, we perceive God's righteous judgment.

11-12. For you this whole vision is nothing but words sealed in a scroll. And if you give the scroll to someone who can read, and say to him, "Read this, please," he will answer, "I can't; it is sealed." Or if you give the scroll to someone who cannot read, and say, "Read this, please," he will answer, "I don't know how to read." Isaiah means that this stupidity will pervade all classes of people. Both educated and uneducated, he declares, will be so dull that they are completely confounded by the Word of God and see no more in it than a sealed letter.

13. The Lord says: "These people come near to me with their mouth and honor me with their lips, but their hearts are far from me. Their worship of me is made up only of rules taught by men." It is clear that those who learn how to worship God from **rules taught by men** are not only manifestly foolish but wear themselves out with destructive toil; they do nothing but provoke God's anger.

14. "Therefore once more I will astound these people with wonder upon wonder; the wisdom of the wise will perish, the intelligence of the intelligent will vanish." He threatens that he will punish by blinding not only the ignorant but those wise men who were held in high esteem by the people.

15. Woe to those who go to great depths to hide their plans from the

LORD, who do their work in darkness and think, "Who sees us? Who will know?" The prophet was clearly dealing with ungodly people who professed to have some knowledge of God but in reality denied him and were bitter enemies of pure doctrine. Isaiah calls them **those who go to great depths**; they dug themselves hiding places so that they might deceive God.

16. You turn things upside down, as if the potter were thought to be like the clay! Shall what is formed say to him who formed it, "He did not make me"? Can the pot say of the potter, "He knows nothing"? In other words, "You are like clay because I created you with my hand."

17. In a very short time, will not Lebanon be turned into a fertile field and the fertile field seem like a forest? The Lord now declares that he will make those wicked men know who they are. This is like saying, "You are now asleep in your pride, but I shall speedily wake you up." "What is now a **forest** will become a **fertile field,** and a **fertile field** will become a **forest.** Or, to leave this figure, the poor and illiterate will change places with the great and wise of this world, concerning happiness, when the gospel is heralded" (Stock).

18. In that day the deaf will hear the words of the scroll, and out of gloom and darkness the eyes of the blind will see. As long as the punishment lasts, people have no ears or eyes. They do not understand anything. But when the plague and distress has ended, the Lord will open their eyes, that they may see and embrace his goodness and compassion.

19. Once more the humble will rejoice in the LORD; the needy will rejoice in the Holy One of Israel. The prophet speaks of **the humble,** and from this we see that our afflictions prepare us to receive God's grace.

20. The ruthless will vanish, the mockers will disappear, and all who have an eye for evil will be cut down. The restoration of the church consists in the Lord's raising up those who are cast down and having compassion on the poor. But first the church must be purified; so everything that is soiled or corrupted must be trampled underfoot.

21. . . . those who with a word make a man out to be guilty, who ensnare the defender in court and with false testimony deprive the innocent of justice. The prophet describes in more detail the wicked plots in which these ungodly people indulge.

22. Therefore this is what the LORD, who redeemed Abraham, says to the house of Jacob: "No longer will Jacob be ashamed; no longer will their faces grow pale." He comforts the people, so they will not despair in the wretched condition to which they will be reduced. We should recall the time those things must relate to—that is, when the people have been brought into slavery, the temple overturned, and the sacrifices taken away, when it looks as if there is no hope of deliverance. We too should take hold of these promises, even in the most desperate circumstances, and rely on the Lord wholeheartedly.

23. "When they see among them their children, the work of my

hands, they will keep my name holy; they will acknowledge the holiness of the Holy One of Jacob, and will stand in awe of the God of Israel." Hypocrites honor God with their lips, but their hearts are far from him. So the prophet ends this verse by mentioning awe. This means that our praises are valueless unless we honestly and sincerely obey God.

24. "Those who are wayward in spirit will gain understanding; those who complain will accept instruction." The Lord prepares for the restoration of the church, enlightening by his Word his own people who had previously strayed.

Isaiah
Chapter 30

1. **"Woe to the obstinate children,"** declares the LORD, **"to those who carry out plans that are not mine, forming an alliance, but not by my Spirit, heaping sin upon sin."** The prophet exclaims against the Jews because when they were hard-pressed by the Assyrians and other enemies, they fled to Egypt for help.

2. **"Who go down to Egypt without consulting me; who look for help to Pharaoh's protection, to Egypt's shade for refuge."** The prophet condemns them for going **down to Egypt.** As their guilt was aggravated by open obstinacy, he repeats that they did this without **consulting** God, and even in the face of his prohibition.

3. **"But Pharaoh's protection will be to your shame, Egypt's shade will bring you disgrace."** The prophet warns that they will not only be disappointed but will only gain sorrow and **disgrace** for all their labors.

4. **"Though they have officials in Zoan and their envoys have arrived in Hanes . . ."** These wretched people preferred to go to the ends of the earth (for **Zoan** and **Hanes** were the most distant cities of Egypt) rather than receive help from God.

5. **"Everyone will be put to shame because of a people useless to them, who bring neither help nor advantage, but only shame and disgrace."** It is very difficult to convince ungodly people that all they do without the Word of God ends in ruin.

6. **An oracle concerning the animals of the Negev: Through a land of hardship and distress, of lions and lionesses, of adders and darting snakes, the envoys carry their riches on donkeys' backs, their treasures on the humps of camels, to that unprofitable nation.** The prophet now ridicules the enormous cost and prodigious inconveniences they went to in order to ask help from the Egyptians.

7. **To Egypt, whose help is utterly useless. Therefore I call her Rahab the Do-Nothing.** The strength of Egypt will do them no good. But if they had sat still and stayed at home, they would have been kept safe.

8. Go now, write it on a tablet for them, inscribe it on a scroll, that for the days to come it may be an everlasting witness. The prophet wants the unbelief of the Jews to be attested to and sealed by a permanent record, so posterity will know how rebellious that nation was and how right the Lord was to punish them.

9. These are rebellious people, deceitful children, children unwilling to listen to the LORD's instruction. Those who refuse to obey the Word of God are in open rebellion against him as if they could not endure his authority.

10. They say to the seers, "See no more visions!" and to the prophets, "Give us no more visions of what is right! Tell us pleasant things, prophesy illusions." They hate the prophets and think they can root out both the teaching and the teachers. People pay more attention to dreams and wild tales than to sound teaching.

11. "Leave this way, get off this path, and stop confronting us with the Holy One of Israel!" When the prophets are set aside, the Lord too is rejected.

12. Therefore, this is what the Holy One of Israel says: "Because you have rejected this message, relied on oppression and depended on deceit . . ." People contrive to follow some message that suits their way of life, but they refuse to listen to God when he speaks.

13. "This sin will become for you like a high wall, cracked and bulging, that collapses suddenly, in an instant." Isaiah compares them to a **wall** that bulges out and **collapses.** The Lord permits wicked men to swell in their idle boasts but will bring ruin and destruction upon them.

14. "It will break in pieces like pottery, shattered so mercilessly that among its pieces not a fragment will be found for taking coals from a hearth or scooping water out of a cistern." The prophet warns that those who are puffed up with obstinacy against God will perish like a collapsed wall that cannot be restored.

15. This is what the Sovereign LORD, the Holy One of Israel, says: "In repentance and rest is your salvation, in quietness and trust is your strength, but you would have none of it." This verse consists of two clauses, an implied command and a promise. He tells the people to have a quiet disposition and promises that their salvation will be certain.

16. "You said, 'No, we will flee on horses.' Therefore you will flee! You said, 'We will ride off on swift horses.' Therefore your pursuers will be swift!" He shows how they refused to wait calmly for the salvation of the Lord and chose rather to **flee** to the Egyptians.

17. "A thousand will flee at the threat of one; at the threat of five you will all flee away, till you are left like a flagstaff on a mountaintop, like a banner on a hill." The prophet warns them that all the protection they have at home will be of no more use to them than foreign aid, because the Lord will take away their courage. The prophet declares that they will be so few that all that will remain will be an indication of very great ruin. It is as if he said, "This great multitude that you now have dazzles your eyes. But there will be such ruin that you will no longer see any people."

18. Yet the LORD longs to be gracious to you; he rises to show you compassion. For the Lord is a God of justice. Blessed are all who wait for him! They were fearfully harassed by their unbelief. To cure this vice, he tells them to **wait**—that is, to hope. Hope is simply steadfastness of faith, waiting calmly until the Lord fulfills what he has promised.

19. O people of Zion, who live in Jerusalem, you will weep no more. How gracious he will be when you cry for help! As soon as he hears, he will answer you. This means that the Lord will show his kindness and give proof of his aid. The Lord **will answer** not by word but by deed. But we must not think he will instantly comply with our wishes, which are often hasty and unseasonable. He will undoubtedly assist us when the proper time comes, so that we will know he had in view our salvation.

20. Although the Lord gives you the bread of adversity and the water of affliction, your teachers will be hidden no more; with your own eyes you will see them. Isaiah continues to strengthen the believers so that they may not faint. He prepares them to endure future punishment, for God's wrath will press hard on them for a time. By **bread and water** he means extreme want and scarcity of all things.

21. Whether you turn to the right or to the left, your ears will hear a voice behind you, saying, "This is the way; walk in it." Their journey is not to be hampered in any way. The road is straight, and we should not seek to depart from it.

22. Then you will defile your idols overlaid with silver and your images covered with gold; you will throw them away like a menstrual cloth and say to them, "Away with you!" The prophet specifically says that they must show an outward profession of true godliness. They can do this when they proclaim that they have renounced idolatry.

23. He will also send you rain for the seed you sow in the ground, and the food that comes from the land will be rich and plentiful. In that day your cattle will graze in broad meadows. We learn from this that our labors must be watered by the Lord, and he must give the increase, otherwise they will be useless.

24. The oxen and donkeys that work the soil will eat fodder and mash, spread out with fork and shovel. This passage is taken from the law (see Deuteronomy 28:11) and is often quoted by the prophets. So we can discern in the sickness and death of cattle God's indignation and desire for us to be reconciled to him, that our homes may be filled with his goodness.

25. In the day of great slaughter, when the towers fall, streams of water will flow on every high mountain and every lofty hill. Those who obey God and submit to Christ as their king will blessed. God will keep his people safe from violent attacks.

26. **The moon will shine like the sun, and the sunlight will be seven times brighter, like the light of seven full days, when the Lord binds up the bruises of his people and heals the wounds he inflicted.** The prophet was not satisfied with describing an ordinary state of prosperity. So he adds that the Lord will go beyond the course of nature in his kindness and liberality.

27. **See, the Name of the LORD comes from afar, with burning anger and dense clouds of smoke; his lips are full of wrath, and his tongue is a consuming fire.** To show that the celebration of the name of God in Judea is not groundless, the prophet describes the power of God (the power he will use to drive out the enemies of the church) as awesome.

28. **His breath is like a rushing torrent, rising up to the neck. He shakes the nations in the sieve of destruction; he places in the jaws of the peoples a bit that leads them astray.** The prophet says that God's **breath** alone will be like a torrent to overthrow the wicked, who will be overwhelmed suddenly.

29. **And you will sing as on the night you celebrate a holy festival; your hearts will rejoice as when people go up with flutes to the mountain of the LORD, to the Rock of Israel.** Here he declares that all the punishments that he threatened against the Assyrians will benefit the church. He calls God **the Rock of Israel** because it was by his assistance that they were redeemed and preserved.

30. **The LORD will cause men to hear his majestic voice and will make them see his arm coming down with raging anger and consuming fire, with cloudburst, thunderstorm and hail.** The prophet declares that the destruction will be so great that people will be forced to **hear** the **voice** of God—that is, to acknowledge his judgment—and to confess that this calamity came from him, as if he had spoken aloud.

31. **The voice of the LORD will shatter Assyria; with his scepter he will strike them down.** This is added to show that the Assyrians will certainly be defeated (see Matthew 7:2), and because the power of the Assyrian king appeared to be so great that it could not fall.

32. **Every stroke the LORD lays on them with his punishing rod will be to the music of tambourines and harps, as he fights them in battle with the blows of his arm.** He means that the Assyrians will try every method of escaping from the hand of God, but in vain. **Tambourines and harps** express the joy of conquerors when they shout aloud and chant the song of victory.

33. **Topheth has long been prepared; it has been made ready for the king. Its fire pit has been made deep and wide, with an abundance of fire and wood; the breath of the LORD, like a stream of burning sulfur, sets it ablaze. By Topheth** he unquestionably means hell. This denotes their miserable condition and excruciating torments.

Isaiah
Chapter 31

1. Woe to those who go down to Egypt for help, who rely on horses, who trust in the multitude of their chariots and in the great strength of their horsemen, but do not look to the Holy One of Israel, or seek help from the LORD. Isaiah again rebukes the Jews for going to the Egyptians and not to the Lord when they are in danger.

2. Yet he too is wise and can bring disaster; he does not take back his words. He will rise up against the house of the wicked, against those who help evildoers. By calling God **wise** the prophet is not only honoring him for an attribute that always belongs to him but is also censuring the craftiness of those who are too taken up with their own wisdom.

3. But the Egyptians are men and not God; their horses are flesh and not spirit. When the LORD stretches out his hand, he who helps will stumble, he who is helped will fall; both will perish together. Men exalt themselves and claim so much for themselves that you would not think they were mere humans (see Psalm 107:40; Job 18:17). By the word **flesh** the prophet means weakness and frailty.

4. This is what the LORD says to me: "As a lion growls, a great lion over his prey—and though a whole band of shepherds is called together against him, he is not frightened by their shouts or disturbed by their clamor—so the LORD Almighty will come down to do battle on Mount Zion and on its heights." In other words, "The Lord assists you, and will assist you; but he forbids you to ask assistance from the Egyptians." By comparing himself to a **lion,** a very powerful animal, the Lord uses a very appropriate comparison to show that he is in the highest degree both able and willing to defend us.

5. "Like birds hovering overhead, the LORD Almighty will shield Jerusalem; he will shield it and deliver it, he will 'pass over' it and will rescue it." This is the second comparison by which the prophet shows how much care the Lord takes of us, and how earnestly he is bent on making us happy. It is taken from the **birds,** which are prompted by astonishing eagerness to preserve their young. They almost die of hunger themselves and shrink from no danger in order to defend and preserve their young.

6. Return to him you have so greatly revolted against, O Israelites. In calling them **Israelites,** Isaiah does not mean to show them respect; he is reproaching them for their ingratitude. He says God will acknowledge them to be the children of Israel and will fulfill all that he promised to Abraham and the other patriarchs if they return to him with all their heart.

7. For in that day every one of you will reject the idols of silver and gold your sinful hands have made. In other words, "Whenever you look at idols, you see your guilt. Acknowledge the evidence of your treachery and rebellion. And if you are really converted to God, show it in a practical way—that is, by throwing away idols and saying good-bye to superstitions. This is the true fruit of conversion."

8. "Assyria will fall by a sword that is not of man; a sword, not of mortals, will devour them. They will flee before the sword and their young men will be put to forced labor." When the prophet talks about **a sword** here, he means that the deliverance of the church is God's own work. He wants the Jews to know that although no earthly power is visible, God's secret power is sufficient to deliver them.

9. "Their stronghold will fall because of terror; at sight of the battle standard their commanders will panic," declares the LORD, whose fire is in Zion, whose furnace is in Jerusalem. In a word, this means that against wicked men, who have maintained hostility against the church, vengeance is prepared. And the Lord will not only avenge himself but will also avenge his people. Let us therefore enjoy this consolation. Although it may appear as if we are defenseless and exposed to every danger, let us be fully convinced that the Lord will be a **fire** to our adversaries.

Isaiah
Chapter 32

1. See, a king will reign in righteousness and rulers will rule with justice. This prediction undoubtedly relates to Hezekiah and his reign, under which the church was reformed and restored to its former splendor. In a word, Isaiah presents us in this passage with a lifelike picture of the prosperous condition of the church. As this cannot be attained without Christ, this description undoubtedly refers to Christ, of whom Hezekiah was a type, and whose kingdom he foreshadowed.

2. Each man will be like a shelter from the wind and a refuge from the storm, like streams of water in the desert and the shadow of a great rock in a thirsty land. When the prophet calls the **king** (see verse 1) **a shelter from the wind and a refuge from the storm,** he is showing how important a well-regulated government is. If this could properly be said about Hezekiah, how much more can it be said of Christ, in whom we have our best, or rather our only, refuge in those storms by which we must be tossed about as long as we dwell in this world.

3-4. Then the eyes of those who see will no longer be closed, and the ears of those who hear will listen. The mind of the rash will know and understand, and the stammering tongue will be fluent and clear. Here we see more clearly that though the prophet is describing the reign of Hezekiah, he also intends to lead us further. Here he talks about the restoration of the church, which was indeed foreshadowed by Hezekiah but has been actually fulfilled in Christ.

5. No longer will the fool be called noble nor the scoundrel be highly respected. The prophet means that everything will be restored to good order, so that vices will not, as formerly, be reckoned virtues. When the public government is wicked, covetous people are in power and are honored and esteemed, because people judge others by their wealth and power. A poor man is despised by everyone, although he may be truly upright and generous. Such a state of things brings nothing but disorder and confusion.

6. **For the fool speaks folly, his mind is busy with evil: He practices ungodliness and spreads error concerning the LORD; the hungry he leaves empty and from the thirsty he withholds water.** When men are so brutalized that they are not affected by the misery of others and lay aside every feeling of humanity, they must be worse than the beasts themselves, who have some sort of pity for the wants of their own kind.

7. **The scoundrel's methods are wicked, he makes up evil schemes to destroy the poor with lies, even when the plea of the needy is just.** The prophet brings forward various circumstances to present in a more striking light the shamefulness of their wickedness. They **destroy the poor with lies,** those who cannot take care of themselves. Instead of deceiving **the poor,** they should have been relieving their needs.

8. **But the noble man makes noble plans, and by noble deeds he stands.** Many people are so greedy that they are like leeches that suck the blood of others. But let us remember what Isaiah says and listen to Paul's exhortation: "Let us not become weary in doing good" (Galatians 6:9).

9. **You women who are so complacent, rise up and listen to me; you daughters who feel secure, hear what I have to say!** He addresses **women** rather than men in order to show the extent of the calamity. In ordinary circumstances women and children are spared, because they are unfit for war and have no power to defend themselves.

10. **Many days and years shall ye be troubled, ye careless women: for the vintage shall fail, the gathering shall not come** (KJV). When he says, **Many days and years shall ye be troubled,** he is saying that the calamity will last for a long time. When there appears to be no end to our sorrows, we are left with nothing but despair. He warns not only that they will endure these calamities for a year, but that afterwards they must look for new afflictions.

11. **Tremble, you complacent women; shudder, you daughters who feel secure! Strip off your clothes, put sackcloth around your waists.** The prophet describes how mourners dress and behave. Whenever they are in deep mourning, they put on sackcloth and bare other parts of their body, thus showing their grief by dress and attitude. He wants women to wear sackcloth instead of indulging in the luxuries in which they delighted.

12. **Beat your breasts for [lament for, KJV] the pleasant fields, for the fruitful vines.** The word **breasts** should be taken figuratively, denoting fields and vineyards, as the prophet himself declares. It is fair to compare them to the breasts of mothers because by deriving nourishment from them, we suck the milk or blood of the earth. He therefore means that there will be lack of food and nourishment, because the Lord will curse the earth so that it yields no fruits.

13. . . . . **and for the land of my people, a land overgrown with thorns and briers—yes, mourn for all houses of merriment and for this city of**

revelry. It was incredible that this land, which had been set apart for the children of God, would be covered with **thorns and briers.** Thus the prophet rebukes the Jews sharply because they not only nullified God's blessing by their wickedness but drew down his wrath and thus spoiled and defaced the beauty of the land.

14. The fortress will be abandoned, the noisy city deserted; citadel and watchtower will become a wasteland forever, the delight of donkeys, a pasture for flocks. We see that men are dazzled by their own splendor, until they lift their eyes up to heaven. They are lulled to sleep in the midst of their wealth and dread nothing. The prophet therefore declares that all that was splendid, magnificent, and lofty in Judea—cities, palaces, fortresses—would all be brought to nothing.

15. Till the Spirit is poured upon us from on high, and the desert becomes a fertile field, and the fertile field seems like a forest. Isaiah has good reason to say that **the Spirit** will come **from on high** to refresh and fertilize the earth, evidence of reconciliation with God. The restoration of the church comes only from the grace of God, who can remove its barrenness as soon as he has imparted strength from heaven.

16. Justice will dwell in the desert and righteousness live in the fertile field. The prophet shows the actual condition of the church—that is, when **justice** and **righteousness** prevail. People should not be like cattle, just seeking plenty of food and an abundance of outward things.

17. The fruit of righteousness will be peace; the effect of righteousness will be quietness and confidence forever. When **peace** is linked to **righteousness** like this, we see that though wars come from God's wrath provoked by our wickedness, peace springs from God's blessing. When, therefore, we see enemies locked in battle and venting their fury on us, let us seek no other remedy than repentance, for the Lord will easily allay commotions when we have returned to him.

18. My people will live in peaceful dwelling places, in secure homes, in undisturbed places of rest. Wicked men must therefore be uneasy and distressed by a variety of terrors. Where righteousness is banished, peace cannot be found; and where Christ reigns, there alone do we find true peace. Assured peace, therefore, is enjoyed only by believers who appeal to the heavenly tribunal not only by their piety but by their reliance on the mercy of God.

19-20. Though hail flattens the forest and the city is leveled completely, how blessed you will be, sowing your seed by every stream, and letting your cattle and donkeys range free. The prophets often used metaphors to describe Christ's reign. Here the meaning is, "The Lord will remove distress and annoyances from his people and will make them fall on others." He says that God, by his wonderful providence, will prevent all disasters from harming believers, because he will drive their violence in another direction.

Isaiah shows how great the change will be when Christ begins to reign. Previously he had said their desolation would be so great that thorns and briers would spread all over the holy land, expensive houses would be thrown down, and cities and palaces would be razed to the ground. This would happen when the incessant attacks of enemies made their country desolate. But now he says they will be **blessed** because God will give them the abundant produce of all kinds of fruits. When he talks about **sowing your seed by every stream,** it is like saying, "Places that were overrun with water will be fit for **sowing,** and there will be no reason to fear that the water will spoil our fields."

Isaiah
Chapter 33

1. **Woe to you, O destroyer, you who have not been destroyed! Woe to you, O traitor, you who have not been betrayed! When you stop destroying, you will be destroyed; when you stop betraying, you will be betrayed.** In order to give the maximum impact to this discourse, Isaiah addresses the Assyrians themselves: "**Woe to you, O destroyer.** You may now ravage with impunity. No one has power to resist you. But there will one day be those who in their turn will plunder you, just as you have plundered others." He speaks to them collectively, as was often done.

2. **O LORD, be gracious to us; we long for you. Be our strength every morning, our salvation in time of distress.** This sentiment was added by the prophet to remind the godly what they should do in the middle of such distresses. They should engage in prayer and ask God to fulfill his promises.

3. **At the thunder of your voice, the peoples flee; when you rise up, the nations scatter.** He now returns to the previous teaching. He has already shown that the Assyrians will be defeated, although they appear to be out of all danger. He now tells the Jews to look on this as if it had already taken place, though the Assyrians' power was vast, and everyone dreaded them and thought they were invincible.

4. **Your plunder, O nations, is harvested as by young locusts; like a swarm of locusts men pounce on it.** Here he again addresses the Assyrians. But it is unlikely that he is referring to the final ruin of the nation or the defeat of King Sennacherib when his army was destroyed by an angel before the walls of Jerusalem (see 2 Kings 19:35). The latter opinion has been adopted by almost all commentators, but it seems to me to be too limited. I think that the prophet, from the beginning of this chapter, meant to express something more when he spoke of the destruction of that nation. The prophecy might even be extended further and include the Babylonians, who were the latest enemies of the church. But this aside, it is clear that his pen is directed against the monarchy of Nineveh.

5. The LORD is exalted, for he dwells on high; he will fill Zion with justice and righteousness. This lesson is most useful. God does not spare reprobate and irreligious people. By opposing their unlawful desires, his object is to testify how much he loves his elect. It is no ordinary consolation that the glory of God shines most brightly in the salvation of the church.

6. He will be the sure foundation for your times. The prophet promises that the state of the kingdom under the reign of Hezekiah will yet be happy and prosperous, especially when contrasted with its wretched, destructive, and ruinous aspect under the reign of Ahaz. For although the enemy had been driven out, hardly anyone would have expected that the Jews, who had been so heavily oppressed, would be restored to their former order.

A rich store of salvation and wisdom and knowledge; the fear of the LORD is the key to this treasure. This is a remarkable passage. It teaches us that our ingratitude shuts the door against God's blessings, when we disregard their Author and sink into earthly desires. All the benefits that we desire or imagine, even if we actually obtained them, would be of no avail for our salvation if they were not seasoned with the salt of faith and knowledge. Hence it follows that the church is not in a healthy condition unless all its privileges have been preceded by the light of the knowledge of God and that it flourishes only when all the gifts God has bestowed on it are ascribed to him as their author.

7. Look, their brave men cry aloud in the streets; the envoys of peace weep bitterly. It is a token of despair that the ambassadors who had been sent to appease the tyrant were unsuccessful. Hezekiah tried to obtain peace by every method, but **the envoys** returned sad and disconsolate. Isaiah undoubtedly means that Sennacherib haughtily refused to make peace.

8. The highways are deserted, no travelers are on the roads. No one could go in or out. This often happens when war has been declared.

The treaty is broken, its witnesses are despised, no one is respected. This describes the treacherous way in which Sennacherib broke **the treaty** he had previously made with Hezekiah. Although he had promised to maintain peace, as soon as the opportunity arose to invade Judea, he violated his promise and made preparations for war.

9. The land mourns and wastes away. He now describes more fully the wretched plight of the Jews.

Lebanon is ashamed and withers; Sharon is like the Arabah, and Bashan and Carmel drop their leaves. The places he specifies are far away from each other and form almost the boundaries of the Holy Land; thus he shows that no part of it will remain safe. To **Lebanon** he assigns shame, because it is elsewhere said to be covered with high and valuable trees but now **withers**. He declares that **Sharon,** which is a level and fertile district, will be a wilderness, **the Arabah,** and that **Bashan and Carmel,** which abounded in fruits, will **drop their leaves.** Thus he alludes to the natural character of each place and describes the misery and distress in such a way as to illustrate the kindness of God, by whom they would be delivered, even though they appeared to be ruined.

10. "Now will I arise," says the LORD. "Now will I be exalted; now will I be lifted up." In other words, "The Lord will allow you to be brought very low, but when your affairs are at their worst, and after you have tried every remedy without success, the Lord will arise and succor you." Thus even when we are afflicted and brought very low, we ought to acknowledge that our safety comes from God alone.

11. "You conceive chaff, you give birth to straw; your breath is a fire that consumes you." He now addresses the enemies of the church, whose insolence, he says, is foolish and to no purpose.

12. "The peoples will be burned as if to lime." He compares them to the burning of **lime** because their hardness will be bruised, just as fire softens stones, so that they are easily reduced to dust. Uundoubtedly, the more powerfully wicked men are inflamed with a desire to commit injury, the more do they bruise themselves by their own insolence.

"Like cut thornbushes they will be set ablaze." This metaphor is no less appropriate, for although they hinder people from touching them by the painful wounds they inflict on the hands, yet there is no kind of wood that burns more violently or is more quickly consumed.

13. You who are far away, hear what I have done; you who are near, acknowledge my power! Isaiah here makes a preface, as if he were about to speak on a very weighty subject. He bids his hearers to be attentive, which is commonly done when dealing with any important and remarkable subject.

14. The sinners in Zion are terrified; trembling grips the godless: "Who of us can dwell with the consuming fire? Who of us can dwell with everlasting burning?" God is often called a devouring fire, as we learn from Moses (Deuteronomy 4:24 and 9:3), from whom the prophets, as we have frequently remarked, derive their doctrines, as did the apostle (see Hebrews 12:29). This exposition is confirmed by the prophet himself. This mournful complaint is a manifestation of that terror that had recently seized them when, being convinced of their frailty, they cried out in sorrow, "Who shall endure the presence of God?"

15. He who walks righteously and speaks what is right, who rejects gain from extortion and keeps his hand from accepting bribes, who stops his ears against plots of murder and shuts his eyes against contemplating evil— Isaiah explains more fully what we briefly remarked on a little earlier: Those who provoke God's anger and thus drive away from them his forbearance have no right to complain that God is excessively severe. This discourse is directed chiefly against hypocrites, who throw a false veil of piety over their hidden pollutions and crimes and make improper use of the name of God, so that they may indulge more freely in wickedness.

When he says **bribes,** he includes everything that corrupts judges.

Who stops his ears against plots of murder means that we should detest wicked devices by which unprincipled men contrive the ruin of the innocent; we must not even lend our **ears** to their discourses or allow ourselves to be solicited in any way to do what is evil.

Shuts his eyes against contemplating evil. We ought to restrain all our senses, that we may not give wicked men any token of our approval, if we wish to escape the wrath of God and that terrible burning that the prophet spoke about earlier.

16. This is the man who will dwell on the heights, whose refuge will be the mountain fortress. His bread will be supplied, and water will not fail him. So that the Jews may know that the chastisements God had inflicted on them were righteous and might endeavor to be restored to his favor, the prophet says that God's blessing is ready to be bestowed on good and upright men, such as he described in the former verse, and that they are not subject to any danger and have no reason to dread the burning that he had mentioned, because they shall be made to dwell in a place of greatest safety.

17. Your eyes will see the king in his beauty and view a land that stretches afar. Although the prophet changes the person, this verse must be connected with the preceding one, for he addresses the sincere worshipers of God, to whom he promises this additional blessing: **Your eyes will see the king in his beauty.** This promise was very necessary for supporting the hearts of believers when the state of affairs in Judea was so lamentable and so desperate. When Jerusalem was besieged, the king shut up within the city and surrounded by treacherous counselors, the people unsteady and seditious, and everything hastening to ruin, there appeared to be no hope left. Still the royal authority in the family of David was a remarkable pledge of the love of God. Isaiah, therefore, meets this danger by saying that even though they see their king covered with filthy garments, he will be restored to his former rank and splendor.

18. In your thoughts you will ponder the former terror: "Where is that chief officer? Where is the one who took the revenue? Where is the officer in charge of the towers?" Believers are again informed what calamities are at hand, so that they may not sink when they are suddenly overtaken with such heavy afflictions. The prophet describes a very wretched condition in which a free people are oppressed by such cruel tyranny as to have all their property valued and an inventory taken of their houses, possessions, families, and servants.

19. You will see those arrogant people no more, those people of an obscure speech, with their strange, incomprehensible tongue. The prophet dwells at length on the wretched condition of the people, in order to show God's great kindness in delivering them from such extreme terror.

20. Look upon Zion, the city of our festivals; your eyes will see

Jerusalem, a peaceful abode, a tent that will not be moved; its stakes will never be pulled up, nor any of its ropes broken. He says that believers, who had long been agitated in the middle of numerous alarms, will have a safe and **peaceful abode** in the church of God.

21. There the LORD will be our Mighty One. It will be like a place of broad rivers and streams. No galley with oars will ride them, no mighty ship will sail them. When God dwells with us, he confirms and supports what in itself was feeble and takes the place of a very strong fortress for us, with walls and **rivers** surrounding the city on every side. Isaiah is alluding to the situation of the city of Jerusalem, which had only a small rivulet, and no large and rapid rivers like those of Babylon and other cities. He urges them to rest satisfied with the power of God alone and not to covet those broad rivers. It is as if he said, "Our strength will be invincible if God rules over us, for under his guidance and direction we will be abundantly fortified."

22. For the LORD is our judge; the LORD is our lawgiver; the LORD is our king, it is he who will save us. The prophet now explains how God dwells in the church. He is worshiped there and is acknowledged as judge, lawgiver, and king. Those who obey God and yield to him as their king will know by experience that he is the guardian of their salvation; but those who falsely glory in his name will hope in vain that he will assist them. Let us only yield to his authority, hear his voice, and obey him; he will then show that he is our protector and most faithful guardian.

23. Your rigging hangs loose: The mast is not held secure, the sail is not spread. Then an abundance of spoils will be divided and even the lame will carry off plunder. Isaiah here addresses the Assyrians, and in them all the enemies of the church. He has promised the church stability, and now he rebukes the foolish confidence with which ungodly people are puffed up. The Lord will sink their ships, will take away their ropes and masts, and will involve them in universal shipwreck. Let us not therefore be afraid of their fury and insolence, but let us look for the day of the Lord, when he will make their rage and violence fall on their own heads.

24. No one living in Zion will say, "I am ill." The prophet again returns to the church, for the destruction he threatened against the Assyrians tended also to the consolation of the godly, since the safety of the church could not be maintained unless the Lord granted his protection against all the adversaries who attack and molest her on every hand.

And the sins of those who dwell there will be forgiven. This latter clause explains the former. It shows that nothing can prevent the blessings of God from being largely enjoyed by us once our sins have been pardoned. Hence also we conclude that all the miseries that press upon us spring simply from our sins.

Isaiah
Chapter 34

1. Come near, you nations, and listen; pay attention, you peoples! Let the earth hear, and all that is in it, the world, and all that comes out of it! Hitherto the prophet, intending to comfort the children of God, preached, as it were, in their midst. But now, directing his discourse to the Gentiles, he pursues the same subject but in a different manner. He has already shown (in Isaiah 33:6, 20) that the Lord takes care of his people, finding the best means of preserving them. Now he adds something we have often seen in earlier parts of this book: Having permitted wicked men to harass his people for a time, the Lord will at last be their avenger. The prophet therefore pursues the same subject but with a different kind of consolation, for he describes what terrible vengeance the Lord will take on wicked men who had injured his people.

2. The LORD is angry with all nations; his wrath is upon all their armies. He will totally destroy them, he will give them over to slaughter. These predictions were made not on account of the Edomites, who paid no attention to this doctrine, but for the sake of the godly, whom Isaiah wished to comfort, because they were wretchedly harassed by their enemies.

3. Their slain will be thrown out, their dead bodies will send up a stench. By this detail he shows that it will be a great calamity, for if a few people are **slain** they are committed to the earth; but when so many people are killed at once that there are not enough people left to bury them, there is no thought of interment, and therefore the air is polluted by the **stench of their dead bodies.** Hence it is evident that God is sufficiently powerful to lay low innumerable armies. Perhaps, also, the prophet intended to heighten the picture of God's judgment, because to the slaughter of the nations there will be added shame and disgrace, so that they are deprived of the honor and duty of burial.

The mountains will be soaked with their blood. Another figure of speech is used to show more fully the extent of the slaughter, for **their blood** will flow from **the mountains** as if they themselves had melted, just as when the waters run down violently after heavy showers and sweep away the soil along with them. Thus, also, he shows that there will be no means of escape, because the sword will rage as cruelly on the very mountains as on the field of battle.

4. All the stars of the heavens will be dissolved and the sky rolled up like a scroll; all the starry host will fall like withered leaves from the vine, like shriveled figs from the fig tree. Isaiah employs an exaggerated style, as other prophets are also accustomed to do, in order to represent vividly the dreadful nature of God's judgment and to make an impression on people who had dull and sluggish hearts. Otherwise his discourse would have had little influence on people who did not care. He therefore adds that **the stars** themselves, amid such slaughter, will gather blackness as if they were ready to vanish, and he does so in order to show more fully that the event will be a mournful calamity.

5. My sword has drunk its fill in the heavens; see, it descends in judgment on Edom, the people I have totally destroyed. He expressly mentions the Edomites, who were hostile to the people of God, though related to them, and were distinguished by the same mark of religion, for they were descended from Esau (Genesis 36:8) and were the posterity of Abraham. Isaiah shows that this is a just judgment, for God does nothing through cruelty or excessive severity.

6. The sword of the LORD is bathed in blood, it is covered with fat— the blood of lambs and goats, fat from the kidneys of rams. For the LORD has a sacrifice in Bozrah and a great slaughter in Edom. The prophet more or less repeats the same statement but uses a different description, placing the matter in a much stronger light in order to shake off the drowsiness of wicked people who laugh and scoff at all doctrine, as we have said before. It is therefore necessary for God's judgments to be shown in a lifelike picture, that it might not only make a deep impression on dull minds but might encourage believers with holy confidence when they learn that the pride and rebellion of their enemies will not keep them from being dragged like cattle to the slaughter that God brings. Isaiah compares this to sacrifices, for animals are slain in sacrifice for the worship and honor of God, and the destruction of this people will similarly glorify God.

7. And the wild oxen will fall with them, the bull calves and the great bulls. Their land will be drenched with blood, and the dust will be soaked with fat. This verse is closely connected with verse 6, for he adds nothing new but continues the same figure, amplifying what he had said about **rams** and **goats**, to which he adds **bull calves and the great bulls.**

8. For the LORD has a day of vengeance, a year of retribution, to uphold Zion's cause. This verse must be seen as closely connected with the preceding verses, for it points out the object that the Lord has in view in punishing the Edomites with such severity. That object is that he wishes to avenge his people and defend their cause. If the prophet had not given this reason, the previous statements might have seemed obscure or inappropriate; it would have been an uncertain kind of knowledge if we did not consider that God, in punishing wicked men, testifies to his unceasing affection and his determination to preserve his own people.

9. Edom's streams will be turned into pitch, her dust into burning sulfur; her land will become blazing pitch! What the prophet now adds contains nothing new but describes this desolation more fully.

10. It will not be quenched night and day; its smoke will rise forever. From generation to generation it will lie desolate; no one will ever pass through it again. The prophet's language is undoubtedly exaggerated, but the Lord is compelled to act toward us in this manner, for plain words would produce no impression on us.

11. The desert owl and screech owl will possess it; the great owl and the raven will nest there. God will stretch out over Edom the measuring line of chaos and the plumb line of desolation. We ought to learn this very useful lesson: When cities are in some measure restored after having been thrown down, this arises from the distinguished kindness of God; for the efforts of builders or workmen will be unavailing if he does not put his hand both to laying the foundation and to carrying the work forward. In this passage Isaiah threatens the Edomites.

12. Her nobles will have nothing there to be called a kingdom, all her princes will vanish away. This is the utmost curse of God because if men have no political government, they will hardly differ at all from beasts.

13. Thorns will overrun her citadels, nettles and brambles her strongholds. She will become a haunt for jackals, a home for owls. He pursues the same subject, describing a frightful desolation by which splendid houses and palaces are leveled to the ground or reduced to a state so wild that they are of no use to men but produce only briers, thorns, and nettles, which is more disgraceful than if they had been turned into fields and meadows.

14-15. Desert creatures will meet with hyenas, and wild goats will bleat to each other; there the night creatures will also repose and find for themselves places of rest. The owl will nest there and lay eggs, she will hatch them, and care for her young under the shadow of her wings; there also the falcons will gather, each with its mate. Let us not wonder at the dreadful changes when ambition lays hold of plunder and wicked extortions; rather let us contemplate the righteous judgments of God.

16. Look in the scroll of the LORD and read: None of these will be missing, not one will lack her mate. For it is his mouth that has given the order, and his Spirit will gather them together. Isaiah confirms what he said before. God's works are plain enough; yet by his **mouth** (that is, by the Word) he makes them plainer to us, that we may see them more clearly. It is the true contemplation of the works of God when we keep our eye fixed on the mirror of the Word. Our boldness is carried to excess, and we take greater liberty than is proper if heavenly doctrine does not guide us like a lamp.

17. He allots their portions; his hand distributes them by measure. They will possess it forever and dwell there from generation to generation. It is vain for human beings ever to promise themselves a permanent abode, except insofar as every person has been allotted his place, and on the express condition that he will instantly leave it whenever God calls.

Isaiah
Chapter 35

1-2a. The desert and the parched land will be glad; the wilderness will rejoice and blossom. Like the crocus, it will burst into bloom; it will rejoice greatly and shout for joy. Here the prophet describes a wonderful change. In chapter 34 he has described the destruction of Edom, saying that it would be changed into a wilderness. Now he promises fertility to the wilderness; barren wastelands will become highly productive. This is God's own work; as he blesses the whole earth, so he waters some parts of it more lightly and other parts more bountifully by his blessing and afterwards withdraws and removes it altogether because of people's ingratitude.

2b. The glory of Lebanon will be given to it, the splendor of Carmel and Sharon. These metaphors display more fully the fertility already described. Not satisfied with saying that smiling fields will be seen and that dry places will be clothed with the beauty of flowers, where formerly there had been a gloomy wilderness, the prophet adds that there will be the luxuriant beauty that **Lebanon** and **Carmel and Sharon** were famous for.

They will see the glory of the LORD, the splendor of our God. What he had expressed metaphorically, he now explains clearly and directly. Until people learn to know God, they are barren and destitute of everything good; consequently the beginning of our fertility occurs when we are quickened by the presence of God, which cannot come without the inward perception of faith.

3. Strengthen the feeble hands, steady the knees that give way. We might explain this passage generally, as if he said, "Let those who have feeble hands strengthen them; let those whose knees tremble and totter compose and invigorate their hearts." But the following verse shows that the whole of this passage relates to the ministers of the Word. He addresses the teachers of the church and tells them to exhort, arouse, and encourage weak people whose hearts are broken or cast down, that they may become more firm and cheerful.

4. Say to those with fearful hearts, "Be strong, do not fear; your God will come, he will come with vengeance; with divine retribution he will come to save you." First, notice that God does not want his grace to remain concealed and unknown; he wants it to be proclaimed and imparted, that those who totter and tremble may compose and invigorate their hearts. Second, when this warning is deeply fixed in our minds, it banishes sloth. As soon as people realize that God is near them, they either cease to fear or at least rise above fear (see Philippians 4:5-7).

5. Then will the eyes of the blind be opened and the ears of the deaf unstopped. He continues the promise about the restoration of the church, in order to encourage the hearts of the godly, who must have been grievously dismayed by the frightful calamities that he foretold. Since true restoration is accomplished only by Christ, we must therefore come to him if we wish to know the meaning of the words that Isaiah employs in this passage; indeed, it is only by his kindness that we rise again to the hope of a heavenly life.

This renewal comes only from the grace of Christ, and sound strength is therefore regained by those who are converted to Christ, who were previously useless in every respect, like the dead. While we are separated from Christ, either we are destitute of everything that is good, or it is so greatly corrupted in us that it cannot be applied to its proper use but on the contrary is polluted by being abused. Christ gave abundant proofs and examples of this when he restored speech to the mute, eyes to the blind, and perfect strength to the feeble and lame; but what he bestowed on their bodies was only a token of the far more abundant and excellent blessings that he imparts to our souls.

6. Then will the lame leap like a deer, and the tongue of the dumb shout for joy. Water will gush forth in the wilderness and streams in the desert. Next he adds other blessings with which believers will be copiously supplied as soon as the kingdom of Christ is set up. This is like saying there will be no reason to dread scarcity or want once we have been reconciled to God through Christ, because perfect happiness flows to us from him. But the prophet pictures this happiness by using metaphorical expressions.

7. The burning sand will become a pool, the thirsty ground bubbling springs. In the haunts where jackals once lay, grass and reeds and papyrus will grow. He confirms his previous statement that Christ will come in order to enrich his people with an abundance of blessings. The prophet draws what may be called a picture of a happy life. Although this change was not openly visible at the coming of Christ, the prophet has good reason to tell us that during his reign the whole earth will be fruitful; for he had previously said that without Christ all things are cursed to us.

8. And a highway will be there; it will be called the Way of Holiness. The unclean will not journey on it; it will be for those who walk in that Way; wicked fools will not go about on it. Here the Jews are promised that they will be allowed to return to their native country lest, when they were carried into Babylon, they should think they were led into perpetual banishment. Yet this statement is, in my opinion, extended much farther by the prophet. A little earlier he had promised that there would be plenty and an abundance of provisions where there had previously been barrenness; now he says that those places where no one lived before will be occupied with the journeys and habitations of a vast multitude. In short, the whole of Judea will enjoy such harmony and peace with other countries that people will pass from the one country to the other without fear.

9. No lion will be there, nor will any ferocious beast get up on it; they will not be found there. But only the redeemed will walk there. He adds another favor of God: The people, even if they travel through a wilderness, will be protected against every hostile attack.

10. And the ransomed of the LORD will return. They will enter Zion with singing; everlasting joy will crown their heads. Gladness and joy will overtake them, and sorrow and sighing will flee away. The prophet reiterates his teaching that God has decided to redeem his people, and nothing can resist his decree. He calls them **the ransomed of the LORD** so they will think about his power and not judge by human standards the promise he has made about their return. He also says **they will enter Zion** because God wants to bring them out of Babylon and will not leave them when they commence their journey. Notice, too, that the only way we can enter the church is if God redeems us; the example of the ancient people is given us as a general picture showing that no one is rescued from the devil's tyranny (to which we are all subject) until the grace of God goes before—no one will redeem himself. Since this redemption is a gift peculiar to the kingdom of Christ, it follows that he is our only deliverer, as is also attested by the declaration.

Isaiah
Chapter 36

In chapters 36 and 37 the prophet tells a remarkable story, which may be regarded as the seal of his doctrine. He predicts the calamities that will befall his nation and at the same time promises that God will be merciful to them and will drive back the Assyrians and will defend Jerusalem and the Holy Land.

1. In the fourteenth year of King Hezekiah's reign, Sennacherib king of Assyria attacked all the fortified cities of Judah and captured them. The prophet has good reason to specify the time when these things happened, for at that time **Hezekiah** had restored the worship of God throughout the whole of his dominions (2 Kings 18:4). Not satisfied with this, he sent messengers in various directions to invite the Israelites to come quickly from every place to Jerusalem to offer sacrifices and, after long disunion, again to unite in a holy harmony of faith and to worship God according to the injunctions of the law.

2. Then the king of Assyria sent his field commander with a large army from Lachish to King Hezekiah at Jerusalem. When the commander stopped at the aqueduct of the Upper Pool, on the road to the Washerman's Field . . . This story is told at greater length in the books of Kings, where it is shown how eager for peace Hezekiah was—he labored to obtain it on any terms. He had delivered up 300 talents of silver and thirty talents of gold, which that tyrant had demanded; and he found it necessary to seize the vessels of the temple and the golden plates that had been attached to its doors to make up that sum, because his treasury was exhausted (2 Kings 18:14-16).

3. Eliakim son of Hilkiah the palace administrator, Shebna the secretary, and Joah son of Asaph the recorder went out to him. The Lord had promised **Eliakim** that he would give him the chief power in the kingdom after the banishment of Shebna. It now seems as if that promise has failed, for he is sent to the enemy as a suppliant and as one who is about to surrender himself and his companions and to undergo cruel tyranny. Such a situation might fill the hearts of believers with anxiety and lead them to doubt God's promises. Besides, the godly king had such a scarcity of good men that, along with Eliakim, he was compelled to send **Shebna,** whom he well knew to be deceitful and treacherous.

4. The field commander said to them, "Tell Hezekiah, 'This is what the great king, the king of Assyria, says: On what are you basing this confidence of yours?'" The three ambassadors were attended by all the magnificence that yet remained in the kingdom; yet they were not only repulsed but were treated with disdain by the tyrant's delegate and loaded down with disgraceful reproaches. Hezekiah is asked how he had dared to rebel—as if he had been convicted of some wicked revolt!

5. "'You say you have strategy and military strength—but you speak only empty words. On whom are you depending, that you rebel against me?'" In other words, "Hezekiah uses fine words, but it is not by these that war can be started or carried on." The field commander therefore means that he perfectly understands what Hezekiah is doing and what it is that he is chiefly relying on—namely, words and eloquence. But these are of no use for war—wisdom and courage are needed.

6. "'Look now, you are depending on Egypt, that splintered reed of a staff, which pierces a man's hand and wounds him if he leans on it! Such is Pharaoh king of Egypt to all who depend on him.'" The Assyrian field commander employs every method he can to shake the hearts of the people, so that they may all be stunned and surrender absolutely. So, having suggested that Hezekiah's internal resources are contemptible, he goes on to add that his external resources are idle and useless, and that the people of Judah are greatly mistaken if they expect the Egyptians to help at all.

7. "'And if you say to me, "We are depending on the LORD our God"—isn't he the one whose high places and altars Hezekiah removed, saying to Judah and Jerusalem, "You must worship before this altar"?'" By this slander Satan through the Assyrian military leader tried to wound the king's heart so he would sink under the weight of affliction; he wanted to impress the frivolous and fickle multitude. Until now many people retained some attachment to superstition, and there was a strong tendency to fall back into this imposture because the old religion, which they were used to, had been changed; they thought Hezekiah was about to be chastised for his rashness.

8. "'Come now, make a bargain with my master, the king of Assyria: I will give you two thousand horses, if you can put riders on them!'" The Assyrian field commander concludes that Hezekiah cannot do anything better than give up any intention of carrying on war, surrender himself, and promise constant obedience to the king of Assyria. Then Hezekiah's poverty is derided: "If I give you 2,000 horses, you will not find among all your people enough men to ride on them. What then is your strength, or what gives you the confidence to oppose my king?"

9. "How then can you repulse one officer of the least of my master's officials, even though you are depending on Egypt for chariots and horsemen?" He confirms the preceding statement, showing that, so far from being able to endure the presence of the Assyrian king, Hezekiah should not be compared to the least of his captains.

10. "Furthermore, have I come to attack and destroy this land without the LORD? The LORD himself told me to march against this country and destroy it." The field commander now attacks Hezekiah in another way, telling him there will be no point in his assembling his forces and making other warlike preparations. Hezekiah, he says, is not dealing with a mortal man but with God himself, at whose suggestion, and not at his own, Sennacherib came to destroy the country. Those who oppose him will be fighting against God, and consequently all their efforts will be fruitless.

From this we learn that however earnestly we may be devoted to godliness, and however faithfully we may labor to advance the kingdom of Christ, we must not expect to be free from every annoyance. Rather, we should be prepared to endure very heavy afflictions.

11. Then Eliakim, Shebna and Joah said to the field commander, "Please speak to your servants in Aramaic, since we understand it. Don't speak to us in Hebrew in the hearing of the people on the wall." This detail again shows how deeply Hezekiah was depressed. Through his ambassador, he entreats his enemy's servant most humbly, asking him not to speak in this manner in the presence of the people. It is difficult to restrain a people who are naturally giddy and fickle, for they are easily moved and tremble at the smallest alarm.

12. But the commander replied, "Was it only to your master and you that my master sent me to say these things, and not to the men sitting on the wall—who, like you, will have to eat their own filth and drink their own urine?" From this we see how fierce and insolent the enemy was. It is also clear that Hezekiah's kingdom was on the brink of ruin.

13. Then the commander stood and called out in Hebrew, "Hear the words of the great king, the king of Assyria!" When the prophet says **the commander stood**, he expresses the fierceness and insolence of the wicked man; his very attitude shows how haughtily he conducted himself.

14. "This is what the king says: Do not let Hezekiah deceive you. He cannot deliver you!" It was true that they could not be delivered by the hand of Hezekiah, unless God assisted them; and Hezekiah did not lay claim to this or rob God of the honor due to him but, on the contrary, testified that his own safety and that of the people were in the hand of God. But the enemy found it necessary to employ some pretext, as wicked men commonly do at the present day when they slander our doctrine; they employ pretexts that give high plausibility to what they say and that actually deceive people when they are not closely examined.

15. "Do not let Hezekiah persuade you to trust in the LORD when he says, 'The LORD will surely deliver us; this city will not be given into the hand of the king of Assyria.'" He quotes Hezekiah's exhortation to the people and speaks lightly of it as an idle and unfounded speech. Even when wicked people assert the power of God, they treat it with contempt, as we see here. The commander does not openly deny that God can assist, if he chooses to; but he saps the foundations of their faith, doing all he can to minimize God's power. His intention is to discourage the people so that they may despair and be led to submit and receive laws from a victorious tyrant.

16. "Do not listen to Hezekiah. This is what the king of Assyria says: Make peace with me and come out to me. Then every one of you will eat from his own vine and fig tree and drink water from his own cistern." In other words, "Do not believe God, but rather believe my king." This is how Satan deals with us; he veils God's goodness by his clouds, offering us masks of false hope, and secretly and indirectly creeps into the place of God or employs creatures to entangle us in his nets.

17. "Until I come and take you to a land like your own—a land of grain and new wine, a land of bread and vineyards." He now adds another condition far harder than the first, declaring that peace can be made with Sennacherib only by going into banishment. This was nothing else than to abandon the worship of God, degenerate into superstition, and voluntarily relinquish the inheritance God had given them.

18. "Do not let Hezekiah mislead you when he says, 'The LORD will deliver us.' Has the god of any nation ever delivered his land from the hand of the king of Assyria?" This is a different argument: The commander now tries to lead the people away from Hezekiah and from confidence in God. Previously he boasted that he was God's servant and that God had sent him to destroy Judea, and thus he assured himself of certain victory; but now he openly insults God himself. Wicked people do not usually betray their scorn and impiety to start with, but in the end the Lord makes their dispositions known and leads them to reveal the venom of their own heart. Now the wicked field commander bursts out with great violence, boasting that he will gain the victory over God himself.

19. "Where are the gods of Hamath and Arpad? Where are the gods of Sepharvaim? Have they rescued Samaria from my hand?" He mentions chiefly the neighboring cities, whose destruction might affect them more deeply on account of their being better known to the Jews. I have no doubt that these places belonged both to Syria and Israel, as if the commander said, "Look at these two subdued kingdoms, which were presided over by their gods as their guardians. Will your God resist me?"

20. "Who of all the gods of these countries has been able to save his

land from me? How then can the LORD deliver Jerusalem from my hand?" In other words, "Did the gods of these other nations deliver them? And will your God deliver you?" Yet the words appear also to contain irony, as if he said in mockery, "Just as the gods of those nations delivered their worshipers, so will your God assist you." Such insolence of ungodly men arises from their not understanding that God punishes people's sins when they suffer adversity.

21. But the people remained silent and said nothing in reply, because the king had commanded, "Do not answer him." This is added so that we may understand more fully what a deep affliction prevailed in the whole of Judea. The good king had hardly any strength or means of defense and so was speechless even when an enemy insulted him. Hence we are also reminded that we ought not always to argue with wicked people when they reproach God and tear his name to shreds, for in the middle of bitter strife and confused noise the truth will not be heard.

22. Then Eliakim son of Hilkiah the palace administrator, Shebna the secretary, and Joah son of Asaph the recorder went to Hezekiah, with their clothes torn, and told him what the field commander had said. We now see that Eliakim and the other ambassadors were not silent because they approved of the field commander's impiety, nor did they connive at such blasphemies out of dread of danger. They tore their garments, thus showing visibly how offended they were at those wicked slanders. It was the custom of the Jews and other eastern nations to tear their garments when they viewed anything with strong abhorrence.

Notice here, also, that those who hear reproaches uttered against their God tear their garments but take no notice of the insults offered to them as private individuals. People who are ready to take offense at an insult offered to them in their private capacity, where patience is needed, and who are unmoved when they learn that the name of God is dishonored, show that they have no godly zeal or piety.

Isaiah
Chapter 37

1. When King Hezekiah heard this, he tore his clothes and put on sackcloth and went into the temple of the LORD. The prophet declares that the only hope of safety left to the pious king was to bring his complaints before God as a righteous judge. It is wonderful modesty in the holy king, when he has performed so many illustrious works and has been adorned by the excellence of so many virtues, that he does not hesitate to prostrate himself humbly before God. On the other hand, it is wonderful courage and steadfastness of faith when he is not hindered by the weight of so heavy a temptation from freely seeking God by whom he was so severely smitten.

2. He sent Eliakim the palace administrator, Shebna the secretary, and the leading priests, all wearing sackcloth, to the prophet Isaiah son of Amoz. This message was not intended merely to invite Isaiah to join with him in lamentation but to request some consolation. Indeed there is no point pouring prayers into the air if they do not rest on the Word of God. Thus we see that unbelievers are exceedingly noisy in their prayers, and yet they flee from God by despising or disregarding his promises. It therefore showed Hezekiah's sincere piety when, while he prayed earnestly, he also sought a confirmation of his hope, that he might not yield to temptation.

3-4. They told him, "This is what Hezekiah says: This day is a day of distress and rebuke and disgrace, as when children come to the point of birth and there is no strength to deliver them. It may be that the LORD your God will hear the words of the field commander, whom his master, the king of Assyria, has sent to ridicule the living God, and that he will rebuke him for the words the LORD your God has heard." Hezekiah appears to doubt whether or not the Lord is willing to hear him. But note that even when believers know with certainty that the Lord will assist them, they will often speak in this way because they are perplexed by the difficulty of the case.

"**Therefore pray for the remnant that still survives.**" This is the second reason Hezekiah sent messengers to Isaiah—namely, so he would pray along with others. Hence we learn that it is the duty of a prophet not only to comfort the afflicted by the Word of the Lord but also to offer prayers for their salvation. Let not pastors and ministers of the Word, therefore, think they have fully discharged their duty when they have exhorted and taught, if they do not also add prayer.

5. When King Hezekiah's officials came to Isaiah ... The prophet previously said that the pious king's only refuge was to consult the mouth of the Lord; now he shows that he did not consult in vain, for he would receive the consolation he desired.

6. Isaiah said to them, "Tell your master, 'This is what the LORD says: Do not be afraid of what you have heard—those words with which the underlings of the king of Assyria have blasphemed me.'" Isaiah begins by saying that he gives the reply in the name of God, and he expressly declares that the oracle comes from God, both because prophets ought always to beware of bringing forward anything of their own, and because in so difficult a matter the authority of God was necessary. In this manner also the prophet showed that he was giving God's response to the prayers of the pious king. Even false prophets boast of the name of God, but falsely. Isaiah was truly the organ of the Holy Spirit, and therefore he had a right to mention the holy name of him who sent him.

When he tells the king not to be afraid, he exhorts Hezekiah to be of a courageous or at least a calm disposition. Whenever we hear this word, let us be reminded that we are enjoined to cultivate the peace that faith produces in our hearts; for all who trust in God and expect from him deliverance from their distresses rise above all fears by the exercise of patience, so that even in the midst of affliction they have peace.

7. "'Listen! I am going to put a spirit in him so that when he hears a certain report, he will return to his own country, and there I will have him cut down with the sword.'" This means, "Now the Assyrian king is annoying and harassing others and is endeavoring to extend the limits of his empire; but I will raise up enemies against him, in the very heart of his own land, who will defeat him."

8. When the field commander heard that the king of Assyria had left Lachish, he withdrew and found the king fighting against Libnah. The prophet now declares how the field commander, without doing anything, returned to his king, but not to the same place where he had left him, for he understood that the Assyrian king had ceased the siege of **Lachish** and had departed into Egypt for the purpose of attacking **Libnah**.

9. Now Sennacherib received a report that Tirhakah, the Cushite king of Egypt, was marching out to fight against him. When he heard it, he sent messengers to Hezekiah with this word ... From what follows we may conjecture the reason why the king of Assyria suddenly departed from Judea. The kings of Egypt and Ethiopia had formed a league with each other against Sennacherib because they saw that his power was becoming excessive and that his invasion of other countries had no limit. Therefore they readily concluded that if they did not oppose his violence at an early juncture, they also would be in imminent danger from him.

10. **"Say to Hezekiah king of Judah: Do not let the god you depend on deceive you when he says, 'Jerusalem will not be handed over to the king of Assyria.'"** How shocking is this blasphemy—to speak of God the Author of truth and accuse him of falsehood and deceit, as if he actually imposed on his people! What is left to God when his truth is taken away? Nothing is more absolutely his own! God wrung this word from this wicked man who formerly pretended to revere some deity. As we said earlier, the time comes when God does not permit such impiety to remain concealed any longer.

11. **"Surely you have heard what the kings of Assyria have done to all the countries, destroying them completely. And will you be delivered?"** Notice the twofold comparison here.

Sennacherib compares Hezekiah to the kings of Judah who had preceded him because he was inferior to them and yet they were vanquished by the kings of Assyria. And Sennacherib, having obtained greater power than all the rest, is more daring and insolent. It followed that Hezekiah could not resist him.

The other comparison is that of the kings of Assyria, and Sennacherib himself, with the idols of the nations; if the idols could not protect the nations that adored them, neither can the God of Israel defend the nation by which he is adored.

12-13. **"Did the gods of the nations that were destroyed by my forefathers deliver them—the gods of Gozan, Haran, Rezeph and the people of Eden who were in Tel Assar? Where is the king of Hamath, the king of Arpad, the king of the city of Sepharvaim, or of Hena or Ivvah?"**

Gozan is mentioned in 2 Kings 17:6 and 18:11. We may infer that it was a town in Media, though some think it was situated elsewhere; it is enough to know that, with regard to Jerusalem, it lay in an easterly direction. **Haran** is often mentioned in Scripture. Pliny places this town in Arabia; but it is more generally believed to have been in Mesopotamia, and this is confirmed by the journeys of Abraham, who came to it with his father after leaving his native country of Chaldaea (Acts 7:4; Genesis 11:31).

14. **Hezekiah received the letter from the messengers and read it. Then he went up to the temple of the LORD and spread it out before the LORD.** It is not as though the Lord did not know what was contained in the letters, but God allows us to act in this manner toward him in accommodation to our weakness. Neither prayers, nor tears, nor complaints make known to God what we need (see Matthew 6:8). But here we

ought rather to consider what is necessary for us—that is, that God should show that he knows the blasphemies of adversaries, and that those who have uttered them will not remain unpunished. The reason Hezekiah spread the letters of the wicked tyrant before the Lord, then, was so that he might excite his own earnestness and inflame his own ardor in prayer.

15-16. And Hezekiah prayed to the LORD: "O LORD Almighty, God of Israel, enthroned between the cherubim, you alone are God over all the kingdoms of the earth." Not only does he assert God's almighty power, but he also maintains the authority that the Lord exercises over the whole world. These statements are made by the pious king for the purpose of strengthening himself in his faith in God's providence, by which he governs the world and every part of it. All believers ought above all to believe this, that they might not think they pray in vain.

"You have made heaven and earth." Hezekiah draws the same inference from creation itself; it is impossible that God, who is the Creator of **heaven and earth,** should forsake his work. On the contrary, he governs by his providence the human race, which is the chief part of the world. It would be absurd to confine creation within such narrow boundaries as if it were a proof of a sudden and transitory exercise of the power of God; we must extend it to perpetual government. Hence it is evident that tyrants who wish to rule at their pleasure rob God of his honor and therefore are justly punished for their insolence.

17. "Give ear, O LORD, and hear; open your eyes, O LORD, and see; listen to all the words Sennacherib has sent to insult the living God." From these words we conclude how great was the perplexity of Hezekiah; the earnestness that pervades his prayer breathes an amazing power of anguish. So it is clear that he had a struggle attended by uncommon difficulty to escape from the temptation. Though his warmth in prayer shows the strength and eminence of his faith, at the same time it reflects his stormy passions. Whenever we are called to sustain such contests, let us learn by the example of the pious king to combat our passions by everything that is fitted to strengthen our faith, so that the very disturbance may lead us to safety and peace, and so that we may not be terrified by a conviction of our weakness if at any time we are powerfully assailed by fear and perplexity. It is, indeed, the will of the Lord that we toil hard; we must not expect to gain the victory while we rest in indolence, but after diversified contests he promises us a prosperous result, which he will undoubtedly grant.

Since, therefore, God in his infinite goodness chooses to connect our salvation with his glory, we ought to seize on those promises to strengthen our hearts. The wicked may reproach God and vomit up the venom of their heart, hardening themselves in the vain hope that they will not be punished; but there will not be a syllable that the Lord does not hear and that he does not call to account in the end.

18-19. "It is true, O LORD, that the Assyrian kings have laid waste all these peoples and their lands. They have thrown their gods into the fire and destroyed them, for they were not gods but only wood and stone, fashioned by human hands." Hezekiah uses two arguments to show that their gods were *not* gods. First, because they consisted of matter; and second, because they were formed by human hands. Nothing can be more absurd than for a man to assume the right to create a god, not only because that man had a beginning, while God is eternal, but also because not even for a single moment does he subsist by his own power. Let the whole world collect all its strength into a single man—he will not even be able to create a fig.

20. "Now, O LORD our God, deliver us from his hand, so that all kingdoms on earth may know that you alone, O LORD, are God." At the end of his prayer, the pious king rises above the fear he had struggled with; the aids by which he had hitherto fortified himself undoubtedly encouraged him boldly to add this short clause. Although God does not always deliver his people from temporal evils, he had promised he would be the protector of the city. So Hezekiah could firmly believe that all the efforts of that wicked tyrant to destroy the city would be fruitless.

21. Then Isaiah son of Amoz sent a message to Hezekiah: "This is what the LORD, the God of Israel, says: Because you have prayed to me concerning Sennacherib king of Assyria..." This shows the result of the prayer. As soon as matters reach an extreme, God suddenly holds out his hand to assist the pious king by the prophet Isaiah (cf. 2 Kings 19:20). Not that God immediately stretches out his arm to drive away the enemies, but he promises deliverance by the mouth of the prophet and thus calls into exercise the faith of his servant.

22. "This is the word the LORD has spoken against him: The Virgin Daughter of Zion despises and mocks you. The Daughter of Jerusalem tosses her head as you flee." Here the prophet intended to express the weakness of the city of Jerusalem, because she was like an orphan and destitute virgin who was insulted by this base ruffian and infamous robber. God, as the Father to whom this insult is offered, declares that he knows well what are the schemes of that wicked man and what is the condition of the whole of Judea.

23. "Who is it you have insulted and blasphemed? Against whom have you raised your voice and lifted your eyes in pride? Against the Holy One of Israel!" The prophet employs a variety of terms in describing the disdain and insolence of this haughty man, one who in speech, in face, in gesture, in his eyes, and in the whole attitude of his body was absolutely intolerable. Tyrants have such an opinion of themselves that they assume airs and look down on everyone else as if they had descended from heaven.

24. "By your messengers you have heaped insults on the Lord. And you have said, 'With my many chariots I have ascended the heights of the mountains, the utmost heights of Lebanon. I have cut down its tallest cedars, the choicest of its pines. I have reached its remotest heights, the finest of its forests.'" This also makes the insult more base and cruel, for it is harder to bear reproaches from a servant than from his master, the insult being worse when it comes from a lesser person.

25. "'I have dug wells in foreign lands and drunk the water there. With the soles of my feet I have dried up all the streams of Egypt.'" In short, he means that Jerusalem will be unable to resist the siege; it will not be able to hold out any longer but will have to surrender immediately. But while wicked people boast like this, God sits in heaven, from where he will judge them in the end. This narrative of the prophet is intended to lead us to consider the stupendous judgment of God against that tyrant.

26. "Have you not heard? Long ago I ordained it. In days of old I planned it; now I have brought it to pass, that you have turned fortified cities into piles of stone." Most commentators explain this verse as the Lord declaring that this tyrant was not doing anything now or formerly that had not been foretold by the prophet; and thus God was the author of those things. But I explain it in a different manner: Jerusalem will nevertheless be preserved by the assistance of God because he is its protector.

27. "Their people, drained of power, are dismayed and put to shame. They are like plants in the field, like tender green shoots, like grass sprouting on the roof, scorched before it grows up." Here the prophet expresses more fully what he has glanced at briefly before: We should not judge the condition of the church from the stability of this world. Fortified cities may be taken, and the strongest men lose courage and fall into the hands of their enemies, but the church will stand and flourish because it does not rest on its own strength and has its foundation not on the earth but in heaven. There is thus an implied contrast between fortified cities, which alarmed inhabitants are unable to defend, and the church of God, which rests on his grace alone and therefore resists every attack, so that it never fails. The church refers everything to God alone and receives from him the beginnings of life, uninterrupted strength, perseverance, every part of salvation, and every blessing.

Hence we learn that no fortress is of any help if the Lord's hand does not assist. All human strength will be broken and decay if it is not supported by his power; castles, bulwarks, and the most powerful armies will be of no use without him. This is expressed more fully by the metaphors that follow in this verse.

28. "But I know where you stay and when you come and go and how you rage against me." God through Isaiah returns to the insufferable pride of that tyrant, who claimed everything for himself, as if he were subject to no one and dared to despise God as compared to himself and to assault him with reproaches. He rebukes that man's pride and insolence and says, **"But I know where you stay."**

29. "Because you rage against me and because your insolence has reached my ears, I will put my hook in your nose and my bit in your mouth, and I will make you return by the way you came." This is mockery of stupidity and wantonness, as if he said, "I see that by treating you gently, I would gain nothing; for your rage is insatiable. Since you cannot be tamed, I will curb you like a wild animal."

30. This will be the sign for you, O Hezekiah: "This year you will eat what grows by itself, and the second year what springs from that. But in the third year sow and reap, plant vineyards and eat their fruit." God through the prophet now addresses Hezekiah and the whole nation. He does not address Sennacherib as if he expected him to listen but mocks the absent tyrant contemptuously, so he can give believers more confidence. If he had simply said, "Take courage, Hezekiah; though Sennacherib is insolent, in due time I will restrain him," that would have made less impression than thundering against the tyrant and so encouraging believers to despise his presumption. Accordingly, the speech directed to the tyrant is now followed by a timely address to Hezekiah and the nation and a promise of their deliverance—not only that God will rescue them from the jaws of a wild animal, but also that Hezekiah will enjoy a peaceful reign, and the rest of the people will have everything necessary for leading a prosperous and happy life.

31. "Once more a remnant of the house of Judah will take root below and bear fruit above." This is added because the church does not only flourish like grass but brings forth abundant fruit. Thus the Lord completes in her what he has begun.

32. "For out of Jerusalem will come a remnant, and out of Mount Zion a band of survivors. The zeal of the LORD Almighty will accomplish this." He has already foretold the deliverance of the church, using the metaphor of **root** and **fruit**; now he says the same thing directly. He alludes to the siege by which a small number of people who had been left in the city were shut up as in a prison and reduced to very great straits; he says they shall now go out, and the whole country will be open to them, and they shall be at liberty to move wherever they please without fear. The going out is thus contrasted with the narrow limits within which the trembling Jews had been forced to confine themselves for fear of their enemies.

33. "Therefore this is what the LORD says concerning the king of Assyria: He will not enter this city or shoot an arrow here. He will not come before it with shield or build a siege ramp against it." God threatens that he will be like a fortress keeping that king from entering into the city, and he will even meet him, to stop him from coming nearer or fighting against it—that king will not **shoot an arrow.**

34. "By the way that he came he will return; he will not enter this city,"

declares the LORD. To **return by the way that he came** is to depart without achieving anything.

35. "I will defend this city and save it, for my sake and for the sake of David my servant!" This gives the reason for the preceding statement: Sennacherib will not enter the city because the Lord will protect it. When God says he will do this for his own sake, he calls on Hezekiah and all believers to remember his gracious covenant. The Jews had often been severely chastised, yet had obstinately provoked God's wrath against them, and they therefore deserved not only that he should deprive them of all assistance, but that he should execute dreadful vengeance against them. In order to prevent them from despairing, therefore, the prophet shows that God will be their defender, not because he finds any merit in them, but rather because he looks to himself first, that he may adhere firmly to his intention not to cast away Abraham's posterity. He did not adopt them in order to abolish religious worship or to blot out the remembrance of his name on the earth by destroying his sanctuary or to expose his name to the jeers and blasphemies of the nations.

36. Then the angel of the LORD went out and put to death a hundred and eighty-five thousand men in the Assyrian camp. When the people got up the next morning—there were all the dead bodies! The prophet now tells what happened to the Assyrians, so that we will not think the Lord spoke in vain. Isaiah shows, therefore, that his prediction was proved by the event, that it might clearly appear that God had sent him and that he had not uttered anything rashly. Yet we ought not to limit so remarkable a work of God to a single prediction. The authority of the prophet was sustained and his calling sanctioned as to the whole course of his doctrine. He relates a singular and well-known event that had recently happened in order to prove by means of it, to the end of the world, that God had spoken by his mouth.

So that no one should ascribe the miracle to natural causes, it is expressly added that this great multitude was slain by the hand of **the angel of the LORD.** It is nothing new for the Lord to use the ministrations of angels to promote the safety of believers, for whose advantage he has appointed all the armies of heaven; and it tends greatly to confirm our faith when we learn that an incredible number of guardians keep watch over us (Psalm 91:11). The Lord is of himself able, and indeed he alone preserves us, for the angels may be regarded as his hand. That is why they are called principalities and powers (see Romans 8:38; Ephesians 1:21).

37. So Sennacherib king of Assyria broke camp and withdrew. He returned to Nineveh and stayed there. Isaiah now shows how disgraceful was the retreat of this haughty tyrant, who in the wishes of his heart had already devoured the whole of Judea and formerly dared to claim to be more powerful than God himself.

38. One day, while he was worshiping in the temple of his god

Nisroch, his sons Adrammelech and Sharezer cut him down with the sword, and they escaped to the land of Ararat. And Esarhaddon his son succeeded him as king. It is most important to look at this picture of the unhappy death of tyrants, whom the Lord destroys when it looks as though everything is going to be overthrown by their violence. He exposes them and all their power to everybody's scorn. Sennacherib, who had come into Judea with a vast army, returns home with few soldiers; it is as though God were a conqueror leading him in triumph. But the matter does not end here, for he is slain in the very heart of his empire, in the metropolis, in the temple itself (where the most insignificant people were safe from the mob because of reverence for the temple). And he is not slain by a foreign enemy, not by a people in a state of sedition, not by traitors, and not by servants, but by his own **sons,** making the murder even more disgraceful.

Isaiah
Chapter 38

1. In those days Hezekiah became ill and was at the point of death. The prophet Isaiah son of Amoz went to him and said, "This is what the LORD says: Put your house in order, because you are going to die; you will not recover." The prophet now tells us how the pious king was violently assailed by a different kind of temptation; namely, he was seized with a mortal disease and despaired of life. Not only that—he also suffered dreadful agony, a consequence of having received from God a warning of his death, as if God had thundered on his head from heaven in a hostile manner.

The severity of the disease might be very distressing to the good man. First, mortal disease brings with it sharp pains. But most distressing of all was the fact that he might think God opposed and hated him, because as soon as he had been rescued from a great calamity he was confronted with death, as if he had been unworthy of reigning. Besides, at that time he had no children; and there was reason to believe that his death would be followed by great disorder in public affairs.

Every person, when he must depart from this life, ought to testify that he pays regard to his duty and that he provides for the future interests of his family. But his chief concern ought not to be for his will and heirs, but for promoting the salvation of those whom the Lord has committed to his charge.

2. Hezekiah turned his face to the wall and prayed to the LORD... Isaiah now relates how Hezekiah was affected when he received this message, so we can see his piety and faith. He does not break out into rage or indignation like unbelievers but bears the trial patiently. He does not argue with God, as if he had already endured enough distress from his enemies and ought not to be chastised again so severely by a new kind of affliction.

The king attached to the prophet's words more meaning than they actually conveyed. Indeed it would have been a foolish message if God had not supported him by secret influence when the king appeared to have been slain by the external voice of God's servant. But since Hezekiah would never have aimed at repentance if he had been seized with despair, the slaying came first and was then followed by that secret energy that directed the dead man to God.

3. "Remember, O LORD, how I have walked before you faithfully and with wholehearted devotion and have done what is good in your eyes." And Hezekiah wept bitterly. Here he seems to be expostulating with God and remonstrating with him about his own past life, as if he were undeservedly distressed. But actually it is not like that at all; on the contrary, he is fortifying himself against a great and dangerous temptation that might otherwise have been suggested. The great severity of the Lord's chastisement might lead him to think that the Lord had cast him off, forsaken him, and disapproved of him, rejecting all that he had done before. That is why he strengthens and encourages himself, declaring that whatever he did was done by him with a good conscience. In short, he concludes that although he must die, his service has not been displeasing to God, that he may thus open up for himself a path to prayer and good hopes.

4. Then the word of the LORD came to Isaiah . . . Isaiah had departed (cf. verse 5), leaving the sting in the wound, as the saying goes. He had pronounced sentence in the name of God himself and then left him.

It may be thought strange that God, having uttered a sentence, should soon afterwards be moved, as it were, by repentance to reverse it (cf. verse 5), for nothing is more at variance with his nature than a change of purpose. The answer is that while death was threatened against Hezekiah, God had not decreed it but had decided to test Hezekiah's faith in this way. We must therefore suppose a condition to be implied in that threatening; otherwise Hezekiah's repentance or prayer would not have altered God's irreversible decree. The Lord threatened him in the same manner as he threatened Abimelech for his behavior toward Sarah (Genesis 20:3) and as he threatened the Ninevites (Jonah 1:2 and 3:4).

5. "Go and tell Hezekiah, 'This is what the LORD, the God of your father David, says . . .'" At first, when he brought terror, Isaiah reckoned it enough to mention the mere name of God, to whose heavenly judgment seat he summoned Hezekiah; but now, when he brings consolation, he distinguishes God by a special and honorable title in order to point out the cause and origin of grace, as if he said, with the covenant that God made with David in mind, that the Lord is inclined to mercy and so does not deal rigorously with Hezekiah.

"'I have heard your prayer and seen your tears.'" The Lord mentions **tears** as a sign of repentance and likewise of warmth and earnestness; not because in themselves tears procure favor or have any power to appease God, but because they distinguish sincere prayers from those that are offered in a careless manner.

"'I will add fifteen years to your life.'" This might at first sight seem absurd, for we were created on the condition of not being able to pass, by a single moment, the limit marked out for us. But what is said about an extended period must be understood to mean how Hezekiah saw it. He had been excluded from the hope of life, and so the added period must surely have seemed to him to be a gain, as if he had been raised up from the grave to a second life.

6. **"'And I will deliver you and this city from the hand of the king of Assyria. I will defend this city.'"** This promise is far from being superfluous, because along with life it promises protection from the enemy, from whom the king would not otherwise have been safe. It may be regarded as an enlargement and increase of the blessing that the Lord promised to Hezekiah.

7. **"'This is the LORD's sign to you that the LORD will do what he has promised . . .'"** The sacred history relates in the proper order that Hezekiah asked a sign from the Lord (2 Kings 20:8) and that it was granted to him, which the prophet will likewise mention at the end of this chapter. But it is nothing new for Hebrew writers to reverse the order of the narrative for a special purpose. God gives some signs of his own accord, without being asked; and he grants other signs to his people who ask for them. Signs being generally intended to aid our weakness, God does not for the most part wait until we have prayed for them; but at first he appointed those that he knew to be profitable to his church. If at any time, therefore, believers wish to have their faith confirmed by a sign, this circumstance in Isaiah 38, being rare, ought not to be produced as an example.

8. **"'I will make the shadow cast by the sun go back the ten steps it has gone down on the stairway of Ahaz.'" So the sunlight went back the ten steps it had gone down.** The sign that is here given to Hezekiah is the going back of the shadow on the sundial, along with the sun, which had advanced above the horizon. This sign bears a resemblance to the event itself, as all other signs generally do; it is as if he said, "As it is in my power to change the hours of the day and to make the sun go backwards, so it is in my power to lengthen your life."

9. **A writing of Hezekiah king of Judah after his illness and recovery.** Although sacred history gives no account of this writing, it deserves to be recorded and is highly worthy of observation. By it we see that Hezekiah was unwilling to pass in silence or to bury in forgetfulness so remarkable a blessing that he had received from God. By his example he shows what all believers ought to do when God miraculously and in an unusual manner exerts his power on their behalf. They ought to make known their gratitude not only to their contemporaries but also to posterity, as we see that Hezekiah did by this song, which may be regarded as a public record.

10. **I said, "In the prime of my life must I go through the gates of death and be robbed of the rest of my years?"** This is a very melancholy

song, containing complaints rather than prayers. Hence it is evident that he was oppressed by so great perplexity that he was weary with groaning and sunk in lamentations and did not venture to rise up freely to form a prayer. Grumbling to himself like this, he expresses the cause and intensity of his grief.

11. I said, "I will not again see the LORD, the LORD, in the land of the living; no longer will I look on mankind, or be with those who now dwell in this world." In the middle of such earnest longing for an earthly life, Hezekiah would have gone beyond bounds if his grief had not been aggravated by the conviction of God's wrath. Since, therefore, he is violently dragged away by his own fault, as if he were unworthy to enjoy the ordinary light of the sun, he exclaims that he is miserable because he will never again see either God or man. Among believers the statement would have been regarded as liable to this exception, that so long as we dwell on the earth we wander and are distant from God, but when the entanglements of the flesh have been laid aside, we shall see God more closely.

12. "Like a shepherd's tent my house has been pulled down and taken from me. Like a weaver I have rolled up my life, and he has cut me off from the loom; day and night you made an end of me." It is noteworthy that he indiscriminately ascribes the cause of his death sometimes to himself and sometimes to God but at the same time explains the grounds; for when he speaks of himself as the author (**I have rolled up my life**), he does not complain about God or remonstrate that God has robbed him of his life but accuses himself and acknowledges deep blame. His words are equivalent to the proverbial saying, "I have cut this thread for myself, so that I alone am the cause of my death." And yet he has good reason for ascribing to God immediately afterwards (**he has cut me off . . . you made an end of me**) what he had admitted came from himself. Although we give God grounds for dealing severely with us, yet he is the judge who inflicts punishment. In our afflictions, therefore, we ought always to praise his judgment, because he performs his office when he chastises us as we deserve.

13. "I waited patiently till dawn, but like a lion he broke all my bones; day and night you made an end of me." Comparing God with a **lion** should not be thought strange, though God is naturally gracious, merciful, and kind (see Exodus 34:6). Nothing certainly can more truly belong to God than these attributes; but we cannot be aware of that gentleness when we have provoked him by our rebellions and urged him to severity by our wickedness. The godly must sometimes be terrified by God's judgment if they are to be moved more strongly to desire his favor.

14. "I cried like a swift or thrush, I moaned like a mourning dove. My eyes grew weak as I looked to the heavens. I am troubled; O Lord, come to my aid!" Let us learn from the example of Hezekiah to lift up our eyes to heaven when our hearts are afflicted and troubled; and let us know that God does not demand great eloquence from us.

15. But what can I say? He has spoken to me, and he himself has done this. I will walk humbly all my years because of this anguish of my soul. We may infer that God now shows him his dreadful power in order to make him truly humble. I have no doubt that to **walk humbly** denotes a trembling and feeble step, for Hezekiah had been reduced to such great weakness that he despaired of ever afterwards recovering his former strength.

16. Lord, by such things men live; and my spirit finds life in them too. You restored me to health and let me live. He magnifies the greatness of God's favor because it will also be well-known to a future age and will continue to be engraved on the remembrance of all, even when Hezekiah himself is dead; not only so, but it will be reckoned to be a kind of resurrection.

17. Surely it was for my benefit that I suffered such anguish. In your love you kept me from the pit of destruction; you have put all my sins behind your back. By giving the reason, the king now leads us to the fountain itself and points out the method of that cure. Otherwise it might have been thought that hitherto he had spoken only about the cure of the body, but now he shows that he looks at something higher—namely, that he had been guilty before God but by his grace had been forgiven. He affirms, indeed, that life has been restored to him but regards his reconciliation to God as of greater value than a hundred or a thousand lives.

We ought carefully to observe the expression that Isaiah uses here— **you have put all my sins behind your back.** It means that the memory of them is altogether effaced. See Micah 7:19 and Psalm 103:12. By this expression God assures us that he will not impute to us the sins that he has pardoned; and if, notwithstanding this, he chastises us, he does it not as a judge but as a father, to train his children and keep them doing their duty.

18. For the grave cannot praise you, death cannot sing your praise; those who go down to the pit cannot hope for your faithfulness. When he says that he would not have celebrated the praises of God if his life had been taken away, he promises that he will be thankful and will keep it in remembrance and at the same time declares that the highest and most desirable advantage life can yield to him is that he will praise God.

19. The living, the living—they praise you, as I am doing today; fathers tell their children about your faithfulness. We ought to learn a useful lesson from this: Children are given to men on the express condition that every man, by instructing his children, should endeavor, to the utmost of his power, to transmit the name of God to posterity. Therefore, the fathers of families are chiefly enjoined to be careful to talk about the benefits that God has bestowed on them.

20. The LORD will save me, and we will sing with stringed instru-

ments all the days of our lives in the temple of the LORD. Hezekiah acknowledges that he was delivered not by human aid or work but solely by the kindness of God. For the reason stated, he not only prepares himself for singing in gratitude but also calls on others to join him in this duty, and on this account he mentions the **temple,** in which religious people met. Had he been a private individual and one of the common people, it would still have been his duty to offer a public sacrifice to God, that he might encourage others by his example.

21. Then Isaiah said, "Prepare a poultice of figs and apply it to the boil, and he will recover." Isaiah now tells us what the remedy was that he prescribed to Hezekiah. The value of the promise is not lessened by this medicine, which without the word would have been vain and useless, because he had received another supernatural sign by which he had plainly learned that he had received from God alone the life of which he despaired.

22. Hezekiah had asked, "What will be the sign that I will go up to the temple of the LORD?" He means that it will be his chief object throughout his whole life to celebrate the name of God; he did not desire life for the sake of living at ease and enjoying pleasure, but in order to defend the honor of God and the purity of his worship. Let us therefore remember that God prolongs our life not so we may follow the bent of our natural disposition or give ourselves up to luxury, but so we may cultivate piety, perform kind offices to each other, and frequently take part in the assembly of the godly and the public exercises of religion, that we may proclaim the truth and goodness of God.

Isaiah
Chapter 39

1. At that time Merodach-Baladan son of Baladan king of Babylon sent Hezekiah letters and a gift, because he had heard of his illness and recovery. The prophet simply tells us that messengers were sent, but it is important to note that this was done craftily by the Babylonian, in order to flatter and cajole Hezekiah. He was at this time threatening the Assyrians, whom he knew to be justly disliked by the Jews on account of their continual wars. Therefore, in order to obtain Hezekiah as an ally and partisan in the war that was waging against him, he endeavors to obtain Hezekiah's friendship by indirect methods. The mind of the good king was corrupted by ambition, and so he accepted the false blandishments of the tyrant too eagerly and swallowed the bait.

2. Hezekiah received the envoys gladly and showed them what was in his storehouses—the silver, the gold, the spices, the fine oil, his entire armory and everything found among his treasures. There was nothing in his palace or in all his kingdom that Hezekiah did not show them. The prophet plays the part of the historian, merely relating what Hezekiah did. He will afterwards explain why he did it—that is, that Hezekiah, blinded by ambition, made an ostentatious display to the messengers. The prophet censures an improper kind of joy in the king, which afterwards gave rise to an eager desire to treat the Babylonian envoys in a friendly manner. Anyone who merely reads this story will conclude that Hezekiah did nothing wrong. Was it not an act of humanity to give a cheerful and hospitable reception to the messengers and to show them goodwill? It would have been the act of a barbarian to disdain those who had come to the king on a friendly visit and to spurn the friendship of so powerful a foreign ruler. But there lurked in Hezekiah's heart a desire for vain ostentation; he wished to make a favorable display of himself, so the Babylonian ruler might be led to understand that this alliance would not be without advantage to him, ascertaining this from Hezekiah's wealth, forces, and weapons of war. The king deserved to be reproved on yet another ground as well: He directed his mind to foreign and unlawful aid and to that extent denied honor to God, whom he had recently known to be his deliverer on two occasions; otherwise the prophet would not have censured this act so severely.

3. Then Isaiah the prophet went to King Hezekiah and asked, "What did those men say, and where did they come from?" "From a distant land," Hezekiah replied. "They came to me from Babylon." Isaiah continues the same narrative but also adds some teaching. Although he does not say that God had sent him, it is certain that he did this by the influence of the Holy Spirit and by the command of God; he calls himself **the prophet,** indicating that he did not come as a private individual but to perform an office that God had enjoined on him, so that Hezekiah might clearly see he was not dealing with a mortal man.

4. The prophet asked, "What did they see in your palace?" "They saw everything in my palace," Hezekiah said. "There is nothing among my treasures that I did not show them." Isaiah proceeds with his indirect warning, to see if Hezekiah is moved by it and is displeased with himself. But still he does not succeed, though it can hardly be believed that the king was so stupid as not to feel the pricking of the spur, for he knew the prophet had not come, as curious people do, merely to discover news. He knew also that the prophet had not come to jest with him but to state something of importance.

5. Then Isaiah said to Hezekiah, "Hear the word of the LORD Almighty." From this judgment of God we see that Hezekiah's sin was not small, though common sense judges differently. Since God always observes the greatest moderation in chastising people, we may infer from the severity of the punishment that Hezekiah's was no ordinary fault but was a most serious transgression.

6. "The time will surely come when everything in your palace, and all that your fathers have stored up until this day, will be carried off to Babylon. Nothing will be left, says the LORD." It is proper to observe the kind of punishment that the Lord inflicts on Hezekiah: He takes from his successors the things the king boasted about so much, in order that they may have no ground for boasting of them. Thus the Lord punishes the ambition and pride of men, so that their name or kingdom, which they hoped would last forever, is blotted out, and they are treated with contempt, and their memory is accursed. In a word, the Lord overthrows their foolish thoughts, so that they find by experience the very opposite of those inventions by which they deceive themselves.

7. "And some of your descendants, your own flesh and blood who will be born to you, will be taken away, and they will become eunuchs in the palace of the king of Babylon." When Hezekiah understood that his sons would be made captives and slaves, this must have appeared to him to be exceedingly severe. Here again we may learn how much God was displeased with Hezekiah for seeking help from earthly wealth and boasting of it in the presence of wicked men, for God punishes as an unpardonable crime Hezekiah's making an ambitious display of his wealth in the presence of unbelievers.

8. "The word of the LORD you have spoken is good," Hezekiah replied. For he thought, "There will be peace and security in my lifetime." From this reply we learn that Hezekiah was not a stubborn or obstinately haughty man, since he listened patiently to the prophet's reproof, though to begin with he was little moved by it. When he is informed that the Lord is angry, he unhesitatingly acknowledges his guilt and confesses that his punishment is just. Having heard the judgment of God, he does not argue with the prophet but conducts himself with gentleness and modesty and thus gives us an example of genuine submissiveness and obedience. Let us therefore learn from this pious king's example to listen to the Lord calmly, not only when he exhorts or admonishes, but even when he condemns and frightens us by threatening just punishment.

Isaiah
Chapter 40

1. Comfort, comfort my people, says your God. The prophet introduces a new subject. Leaving the people on whom neither threats nor warnings made any favorable impression on account of their desperate wickedness, he turns to posterity, to declare that the people who will be humbled under the cross will experience no lack of consolation under the severest distress. He probably wrote this prophecy when the time of the captivity was at hand, so he would not die leaving the church of God overwhelmed by grievous calamities, without the hope of restoration.

2. Speak tenderly to Jerusalem, and proclaim to her that her hard service has been completed, that her sin has been paid for, that she has received from the LORD's hand double for all her sins. Here God commands his servants the prophets and lays down the message he wants them to deliver publicly: Believers are called to change their song from mourning to joy. But he does not exhort them to be cheerful and courageous in discharging their office but to convey to the minds of believers an assured hope so they may patiently endure the irksome delay until the prophets appear with this delightful message.

God is so gracious to them that he is unwilling to treat them with the utmost severity. These words give a reason for this: When doctors cure diseases, they first remove the causes from which diseases arise, and the Lord does the same with us. The scourges by which he chastises us proceed from our sins; so if he is to stop attacking us, he must first pardon us. Consequently, he says there will be no more punishments because he no longer imputes sin to us.

3. A voice of one calling: "In the desert prepare the way for the LORD; make straight in the wilderness a highway for our God." Isaiah follows the subject he had begun and declares more explicitly that although the people are apparently ruined, he will send them ministers of consolation. At the same time he anticipates an objection that might have been brought forward: "You do indeed promise consolation, but where are the prophets? For we shall be **in a wilderness,** and where shall we get this consolation from?" He therefore testifies that **the wilderness** will not stop them from enjoying that consolation.

4. "Every valley shall be raised up, every mountain and hill made low; the rough ground shall become level, the rugged places a plain." He confirms and asserts the preceding statement, showing that no difficulties can prevent the Lord from delivering and restoring his church whenever he thinks fit. These words might properly be rendered in the imperative mood ("Let every valley be exalted"), so as to be placed in immediate connection with the command that God gives by his prophets to prepare and level the way for himself; but it makes hardly any difference in the meaning.

5. "And the glory of the LORD will be revealed, and all mankind together will see it. For the mouth of the LORD has spoken." He means that this work of redemption will be most splendid, for the Lord will show that he is the Author of it and will illustriously display his majesty and power. This, indeed, is very clearly shown in all places and in all events, but he promises that he will do this especially in protecting and delivering his church, and not without good reason: The deliverance of the church, from its commencement down to the coming of Christ, would be called a renewal of the world.

6. A voice says, "Cry out." And I said, "What shall I cry?" "All men are like grass, and all their glory is like the flowers of the field." He now describes a different **voice** from the one he spoke about before. Hitherto he had spoken about the voice of the prophets, but now he means the **voice** of God himself commanding the prophets to cry. Although the voice of the prophets is the voice of God, whose instruments they are, this distinction is necessary if we are to know when the Lord commands and when the prophets and ministers execute his commandments.

7. "The grass withers and the flowers fall, because the breath of the LORD blows on them. Surely the people are grass." The prophet explains what object he has in view by saying that men, with all their glory, are nothing but **grass**; that is, the Spirit of God will quickly carry them away by a single breath. The meaning may be explained thus: "However illustrious the gifts with which men are endowed, yet as soon as God's Spirit blows on them, they will feel that they are nothing." The false confidence with which they intoxicate themselves springs from this source: They do not come before God but creep into hiding in order to indulge freely in flattering themselves.

8. "The grass withers and the flowers fall, but the word of our God stands forever." This repetition is added in order to bring to naught the glory of the flesh. It also contains a highly valuable consolation: God, when he has cast down his people, immediately raises them up and restores them.

9. You who bring good tidings to Zion, go up on a high mountain. You who bring good tidings to Jerusalem, lift up your voice with a shout, lift it up, do not be afraid; say to the towns of Judah, "Here is your God!" The Lord has already promised that he will give the people prophets who will soothe their grief and fear by promises, and now he commands that this consolation be more widely spread, because it is his pleasure to diffuse his grace throughout the whole of **Judah.**

10. See, the Sovereign LORD comes with power, and his arm rules for him. See, his reward is with him, and his recompense accompanies him. By using the words **reward** and **recompense** he states more clearly what has already been expressed; it is very common for Hebrew writers to express the same thing in two different ways. **Reward** does not here denote something due to merits but the justice of God, by which he testifies that he rewards all who truly and sincerely call upon him.

11. He tends his flock like a shepherd: He gathers the lambs in his arms and carries them close to his heart. In this verse the prophet declares the nature of the work of the Lord; for since he works in various and, indeed, in innumerable ways, the hearer might have been kept in suspense as to the work that God intended to accomplish. Thus the general doctrine would have been less effective in exciting hope. He does not describe every part, but he states in a few words that God has determined to protect and guard his church. This is why he compares him to **a shepherd.** The Lord expresses his infinite love toward us in that he does not refuse to stoop so low as to perform toward us the office of a **shepherd.**

He gently leads those that have young. These words describe God's wonderful condescension; not only is he actuated by a general feeling of regard toward his whole flock, but in proportion to the weakness of any one sheep, he shows his care in watching it, his gentleness in handling it, and his patience in leading it. Here Isaiah leaves out nothing that belongs to the office of a good shepherd; for the shepherd ought to observe every sheep so as to treat it according to its capacity; and sheep ought to be especially supported if they are very weak. In a word, God will be mild, kind, gentle, and compassionate, and thus he will not drive the weak harder than they are able to bear.

12. Who has measured the waters in the hollow of his hand, or with the breadth of his hand marked off the heavens? Who has held the dust of the earth in a basket, or weighed the mountains on the scales and the hills in a balance? After speaking of God's friendly care in defending his people, the prophet now proclaims his power and bestows upon it all possible commendations. This would make less impression on us, however, if we did not attend to the prophet's design. At first sight, ignorant readers would think the prophet crowds together unfinished sentences, which would be absurd. But if we look at his object, he adorns the power of God by a timely and elegant discourse that is a true support of our faith, so that we will not hesitate to believe that he will do what he has promised.

13. Who has understood the Spirit of the LORD, or instructed him as his counselor? What the prophet had already taught concerning the Lord's goodness and power he now adds concerning his wisdom. Notice the connection: Carnal sense wickedly limits the power of God to human means, and it quite wrongly subjects his inscrutable counsel to human reasoning. Until God is exalted above all creatures, many difficulties interrupt the course of his works. Therefore, if we form a judgment according to our own opinion, various scruples will immediately arise. Thus, whenever we do not see how God will do this or that, we doubt if it will take place, because what surpasses our reason appears to be impossible. Consequently, as we ought to contrast God's power with our weakness, so our insolence ought to be repressed by his incomparable wisdom.

14. Whom did the LORD consult to enlighten him, and who taught him the right way? Who was it that taught him knowledge or showed him the path of understanding? The prophet expresses the same thing in many ways, so we may know that nothing is more foolish than man when he ventures to lift himself up into heaven to examine or judge God's works by his own ability. In these words, therefore, Isaiah intended to repress human insolence and rashness more and more.

15. Surely the nations are like a drop in a bucket; they are regarded as dust on the scales; he weighs the islands as though they were fine dust. If we wish to understand the prophet's meaning and to read these words with advantage, we must understand his design. He does not celebrate the greatness of God in a detached manner but extols it, adapting it as much as possible to the present subject, so Israelites might know that this shield alone is sufficient to protect them, and so they will have no reason to dread the efforts or rage or violence of the world, if God be reconciled to them. Thus they may learn to seek God's protection; for if they were not fully convinced of this, every moment would bring cause to despair. Isaiah thus continues the subject, saying that all nations and peoples are nothing when compared with God; by simply breathing on them, he will scatter all the inhabitants of the earth like fine **dust.** In consequence of our being excessively prone and foolishly ingenious in devising reasons for distrust, we imagine that everything Satan does for the purpose of hindering our salvation blocks God's path. To correct this error, the prophet declares that all creatures are nothing before God and that all **the nations** are like insignificant little drops of water.

16. Lebanon is not sufficient for altar fires, nor its animals enough for burnt offerings. That is, "If we must sacrifice to God according to what he deserves, neither the whole of Lebanon, nor the beasts that graze upon it, would be sufficient for a sacrifice."

17. Before him all the nations are as nothing; they are regarded by him as worthless and less than nothing. He repeats what he said before: It is in the power and at the disposal of God to destroy **all the nations** whenever he thinks proper; and even while they remain in their present condition, they are reckoned as nothing before him.

18. To whom, then, will you compare God? What image will you compare him to? The Jews were in great danger from another temptation. Some might have naturally concluded, "What good is it to us to have a special manner of worshiping God that differs from other nations? Our enemies, the Assyrians and Babylonians, fight under the favor and protection of heaven, while we get no benefit from the help of our God whom we worship." God rises up, so that true religion may not be ruined among the Jews on account of their calamity. God proclaims that a grievous injury is done to him if believers, discouraged by adversity, turn aside to the idols and superstitions of the Gentiles. Thus he confirms them in the faith of the promises, that they might not sink under the weight of the punishments that they endure.

19. As for an idol, a craftsman casts it, and a goldsmith overlays it with gold and fashions silver chains for it. These words convey an anticipation, so the Jews might not be frightened when they see the Gentiles laboring with all their might to make idols, for in this way they deceive and ensnare each other. But he attacks the madness of the whole world, saying that everyone is impelled by outrageous zeal to practice superstition, and each person teaches himself to make idols.

20. A man too poor to present such an offering selects wood that will not rot. He looks for a skilled craftsman to set up an idol that will not topple. The prophet concludes that no class of men is free from this crime. The rich and poor alike are guilty and condemned, for the rich make their gods of gold or silver, and the poor use wood they have selected. Hence Isaiah shows that all men are carried away, and that even though they have not the means, still they desire to have something excellent for the worship of their gods. People want to enjoy God's presence. But this can be the beginning and source of idolatry; for God is not present with us in an idol but in his Word and in the power of his Spirit. In the sacraments he offers us an image both of his grace and of spiritual blessings; but this is done with no other intention than to lead us upward to himself.

21. Do you not know? Have you not heard? Has it not been told you from the beginning? Have you not understood since the earth was founded? Having ridiculed the stupidity and madness of the Gentiles, the prophet turns to the Jews; for we are all prone to superstition, and thus we easily fall into it when any example is placed before our eyes.

22. He sits enthroned above the circle of the earth, and its people are like grasshoppers. He stretches out the heavens like a canopy, and spreads them out like a tent to live in. Isaiah pursues the same subject, though in a different manner, extolling God's glory and power. He does this because we are so prone to distrust, and the smallest occasion makes us waver; therefore the prophet is constrained to repeat the same thing in many ways, that he may keep our weak and inconstant hearts trusting in God. He has spoken of the creation of the world, but now he comes to the continual government of it. God not only exerted his power for a single moment in creating the world: He manifests his power no less effectively in preserving it.

23. He brings princes to naught and reduces the rulers of this world to nothing. He continues extolling God's providence, by which he governs the whole world but especially mankind.

24. No sooner are they planted, no sooner are they sown, no sooner do they take root in the ground, than he blows on them and they wither, and a whirlwind sweeps them away like chaff. He shows how light and trivial before God are those things that commonly dazzle our eyes and fill us with amazement, for we cannot think of any great king without being alarmed and stupefied. But he shows that kings and princes are like stubble before God, by whose breath they are driven, as by a whirlwind, at any instant that he pleases. We are therefore taught that we ought never to be overwhelmed by the sight of any creature and so fail to give God the honor and glory that are due to him.

25. "To whom will you compare me? Or who is my equal?" says the Holy One. A grievous injury is done to God, and he is basely degraded from his rank, when idols are brought into collision with him, and when it becomes a subject of debate whether they can do more than God himself.

26. Lift your eyes and look to the heavens: Who created all these? He who brings out the starry host one by one, and calls them each by name. Because of his great power and mighty strength, not one of them is missing. The prophet seems to linger too long on this subject, more especially because it presents no obscurity; he repeats by many statements what is acknowledged by all: God's wonderful power and wisdom can be known from the beautiful order of the world. But we ought to observe what I have already said: We are such wicked and ungrateful judges of the divine power that we often imagine God to be inferior to some feeble man.

27. Why do you say, O Jacob, and complain, O Israel, "My way is hidden from the LORD; my cause is disregarded by my God"? If God delays his assistance for a short time, we think his care does not extend to us.

28. Do you not know? Have you not heard? The LORD is the everlasting God, the Creator of the ends of the earth. He will not grow tired or weary, and his understanding no one can fathom. He repeats the same thing he had said before: The people who had been carefully taught in the school of God were inexcusable for their slothfulness. He chides them sharply for not having profited more by the doctrine of the law and by the other means that God had bestowed in addition to the knowledge that they possessed in common with the Gentiles.

29. He gives strength to the weary and increases the power of the weak. The prophet now applies his general statements to the present subject. We have said that his intention was to give greater encouragement to the people and to lead them to have more hope. Because the Jews were at that time weakened and destitute of strength, he shows that God will help those who were thus exhausted and weakened. He magnifies God's power so that they may conclude that they should not doubt their salvation so long as they enjoy his favor. It was indeed to the people who were held captive in Babylon that the prophet looked; but we ought also to apply this doctrine to ourselves. Whenever our strength fails, and we are almost laid low, we may remind ourselves that the Lord stretches out his hand **to the weary** who are sinking through lack of help.

30. Even youths grow tired and weary, and young men stumble and fall. By this comparison the prophet illustrates more powerfully what he had said before: The strength that God imparts to his elect is invincible and unwearied; human strength fails easily, but God's strength never fails. It is indeed certain that all the vigor that naturally dwells in us proceeds from God. But since men claim as their own what God has bestowed generally on all, the prophet distinguishes between human strength that appears to be innate and the strength by which God peculiarly supports his elect; for God's kindness, which is diffused throughout all nature, is not sufficiently perceived.

31. But those who hope in the LORD will renew their strength. They will soar on wings like eagles; they will run and not grow weary, they will walk and not be faint. The prophet shows that godly people who **hope** in God will not lack **strength.** We must therefore be fully convinced of our weakness if we are to yield to God's power. The Jews, who were oppressed by that cruel captivity, had great need of this doctrine; but for us also, during this wretchedly ruinous condition of the church, it is extremely necessary.

Isaiah
Chapter 41

1. **"Be silent before me, you islands! Let the nations renew their strength! Let them come forward and speak; let us meet together at the place of judgment."** Although the prophet seems to be talking about something new, he is actually continuing the same subject: To shame the Jews, he says he would have been successful if he had been called to plead with unbelievers and blind people. Thus he reproves not only their sluggishness but their stupidity. Yet we need not wonder that the people were overtaken by many terrors and trembled so that they scarcely received solid consolation, for we have abundant experience of how much we are alarmed by adversity. Amidst the depravity and corruption of our nature, we all suffer from two diseases. In prosperity we exalt ourselves extravagantly and shake off the restraint of humility and moderation; but in adversity we either rage or lie in a lifeless condition and have scarcely the least perception of God's goodness. We need not wonder, therefore, that the prophet concentrates on this subject so much, pursuing it in many ways.

He gives the name **islands** to the countries beyond the sea, for the Jews, having no links with them, gave to all that lay beyond the sea that name. So he addresses not only the nations that were at hand but also those that were more distant; he requires them to **be silent** before God.

2. **"Who has stirred up one from the east, calling him in righteousness to his service?"** This shows plainly the prophet's plan: He intends to assure the Jews that they will be in no danger of going astray if they choose to follow the path that he points out to them. And this is why he mentions **Abraham** (compare verse 8). He might have listed other works of God, but he selected an example appropriate to his subject. Being descended from Abraham, whom God had brought out of Chaldea amidst so many dangers, they ought to have hoped that he would equally assist them, since his power was no less than in the previous age and he is not wearied by acts of kindness.

"He hands nations over to him [Abraham] and subdues kings before him. He turns them to dust with his sword, to windblown chaff with his bow." This means that although the good man might be afflicted and tormented every moment by many anxieties, God removes every obstruction that can annoy him. In the book of Genesis Moses does not enumerate all the difficulties that Abraham encountered at his departure, but any person might conclude that this journey could not be free from very great annoyances; it was impossible for that patriarch, when he set out, not to draw upon himself the hatred of the nation and to be universally condemned as a madman for leaving his native land and relations and friends and wandering to an unknown country. And after coming into the land of Canaan, he had to do with wicked and cruel men, with whom he could not agree because he was entirely opposed to their superstitions.

3. "He pursues them and moves on unscathed, by a path his feet have not traveled before." The prophet again commends the extraordinary kindness of God, shown in the greatness of the victory. It is of the highest importance that Abraham obtained it in a country that was unknown to him, for it is difficult and hazardous to pursue enemies in unknown countries; both history and the daily experience of those at war show the value of a knowledge of places. That was no obstacle to Abraham, which shows still more clearly that he was led and assisted by the hand of God to lead his followers courageously.

4. "Who has done this and carried it through, calling forth the generations from the beginning? I, the LORD—with the first of them and with the last—I am he." Although in this passage Isaiah shows only the example of Abraham, he undoubtedly intends to remind the people of all the benefits that the fathers received in ancient times; as if God through him said, "Recall your origin, whence I raised up your father Abraham, by what path I led him; and yet this was not the end of my favors, for since that time I have never ceased to enrich you with every kind of blessings." So when he asks who this one is, he does not speak merely of a single performance but adds other benefits, which followed at various times and which the people ought also to remember.

5. The islands have seen it and fear; the ends of the earth tremble. They approach and come forward. He now shows the excessive ingratitude of the world. Having seen God's works, the people of the world still continued in the same blindness to which it had been abandoned before. In consequence, they are altogether inexcusable because the majesty of God was abundantly revealed, if they had not chosen to shut their eyes of their own accord.

6. . . . each helps the other and says to his brother, "Be strong!" What now follows agrees well with what goes before, if you connect this verse with the last clause of verse 5. So the meaning is, "Although the islands saw and knew my works, so that they trembled at them, yet they

assembled in crowds to make a league among themselves." Why? That they might encourage each other to frame new gods and might confirm each other more and more in their blindness. He therefore aggravates the guilt of the Gentiles by saying that **each helps the other.** Indeed, whoever makes careful inquiry will find that the source of all superstitions is that people by mutual consent darken the light brought to them from heaven.

7. The craftsman encourages the goldsmith, and he who smooths with the hammer spurs on him who strikes the anvil. He says of the welding, "It is good." He nails down the idol so it will not topple. There is nothing that they do not attempt in order to prop up a wavering superstition and tottering idols. In a word, they join hands and render mutual aid in order to resist God. And if anyone wants to throw the blame on his brother, he will gain nothing, for all are devoted to falsehood and devise ways to lie. They trust to their great numbers and elevate themselves and others above God. They encourage each other to worship idols and burn with such desire that nearly the whole world is kindled by it.

8. "But you, O Israel, my servant, Jacob, whom I have chosen, you descendants of Abraham my friend . . ." He now shows how unreasonable it is to confound the people of Israel with the heathen nations, even though all agree in error, even if the whole world is given up to lying. God's free grace had called them and set them apart; so they ought not to give themselves up to the same rage. This is a remarkable passage, and it teaches us that we ought to be satisfied with our calling, so as to be restrained from the pollution of this world.

9. "I took you from the ends of the earth, from its farthest corners I called you. I said, 'You are my servant.'" Isaiah continues the same topic. We know by experience how necessary it is for encouragement to be repeated when adversity presses upon us. So it is no wonder that the prophet dwells at such length on this subject. But from one person, Abraham, he passes to the whole nation, mentioning the benefits that all of them had received from God.

"I have chosen you and have not rejected you." The last expression might be thought superfluous and even untimely if Jewish writers had not frequently employed this form of speech, which is very emphatic. It denotes the firmness of election, as if God said, "Having once adopted you, I did not desert or forsake you, though I had various occasions for casting you off." So great had been the ingratitude of the Jews that he might well have rejected them if he had not resolved to continue to be like himself.

10. "So do not fear, for I am with you; do not be dismayed, for I am your God. I will strengthen you and help you; I will uphold you with my righteous right hand." The previous doctrine aimed to get the people to rely on God. Now the prophet concludes from the numerous blessings by which the Lord manifested his love that the people ought not to be afraid. And we ought carefully to observe the reason that he cites: **"I am with you."** This is a solid foundation of confidence, and if it is fixed in our minds, we will be able to stand firm and unshaken against temptations of every kind.

11. **"All who rage against you will surely be ashamed and disgraced; those who oppose you will be as nothing and perish."** Here the prophet expressly promises assistance to the Jews against their enemies, for if he had merely promised safety, without making any mention of enemies, various thoughts and anxieties might have arisen in their minds. God indeed promises that we will be saved; yet our adversaries still prevail and treat us with the utmost scorn and cruelty. Where then is the salvation that was so freely and abundantly promised? To the general promise, therefore, he also adds this detail: "Though the enemies flourish, they will at length be driven back, covered with shame and disgrace." Salvation is therefore promised on the condition that we will encounter enemies and maintain various contests with them in the meantime. We must not promise ourselves external peace, for we must carry on war unceasingly.

12. **"Though you search for your enemies, you will not find them. Those who wage war against you will be as nothing at all."** Here it ought to be observed that he describes two kinds of enemies: one, those who attack us by open violence; the other, those who attack us by words—that is, who tear us by slander, curses, and reproaches and who carry on various controversies with us as if they were defending a righteous cause, summoning us to courts of justice and often accusing us of crimes of which they have been guilty. These are the stratagems of Satan, and we need not wonder that those who are his servants imitate their dark lord and master. The prophet therefore mentions armed enemies who violently fight against the church and next brings forward troublemakers who annoy the church by deceit and slander and by a false pretense of justice.

13. **"For I am the LORD, your God, who takes hold of your right hand and says to you, Do not fear; I will help you."** If we desire to have composure of mind and to conquer the vexations that come upon us from various quarters, we must pay close attention to our Lord's voice, so as never to withdraw our mind from it. Those who refuse to hear this voice of God or do not listen to it attentively must be miserably tormented by continual doubt and uncertainty.

14. **"Do not be afraid, O worm Jacob, O little Israel, for I myself will help you,"** declares the LORD, your Redeemer, the Holy One of Israel. God appears to speak of the Jews very disrespectfully when he calls them a **worm.** But this comparison agrees better with the distresses of the people and is more adapted to console them than if he had called them an elect nation, a royal priesthood, or a holy tree from a holy root or had adorned

them with other titles of that kind. It would have been absurd to call them by those high-sounding names while they were oppressed by the deepest wretchedness.

15. "See, I will make you into a threshing sledge, new and sharp, with many teeth. You will thresh the mountains and crush them, and reduce the hills to chaff." God through the prophet still speaks of the restoration of the church and promises that she will be victorious over her enemies, so that she crushes them and reduces them to dust; and he declares this by a highly appropriate metaphor. The Jews whom he addresses were nearly crushed, but he declares that, on the contrary, they shall crush their enemies, so that, having been delivered, they will render to them what had been done to themselves. It was necessary for this to be added, for if they had not regained new strength, they would always have been exposed to the unlawful passions of their enemies.

16. "You will winnow them, the wind will pick them up, and a gale will blow them away. But you will rejoice in the LORD and glory in the Holy One of Israel." The meaning is the same as in verse 15, but using a different metaphor. He compares the church to a sieve, and wicked people to the chaff that is scattered in every direction. In other words, "Though the Gentiles bruise and winnow you for a time, a more severe judgment awaits them; for by their destruction they will be bruised and driven away like chaff." But we ought to notice the difference, because here believers are bruised for their good, for they allow themselves to be subdued and placed under the authority of God. In contrast, others who obstinately resist and do not allow themselves to be brought into subjection are scattered by the wind like chaff or stubble.

17. "The poor and needy search for water, but there is none; their tongues are parched with thirst. But I the LORD will answer them; I, the God of Israel, will not forsake them." Here he follows up the subject he had begun to handle at the beginning of chapter 40; he describes the wretched and afflicted condition in which the Jews would be in Babylon, until at length God had compassion on them and helped them. He prepares them for enduring extreme poverty by saying they will be thirsty, for this figure of speech is more appropriate for expressing the severity of the affliction. We know that nothing causes people greater distress than lack of water when they are thirsty.

18-19. "I will make rivers flow on barren heights, and springs within the valleys. I will turn the desert into pools of water, and the parched ground into springs. I will put in the desert the cedar and the acacia, the myrtle and the olive. I will set pines in the wasteland, the fir and the cypress together." He illustrates the former doctrine in a different manner, saying that God has no need of outward and natural means for aiding his church but has at his command secret and wonderful methods by which he can relieve their necessities, contrary to all hope and outward appearance. When no means of relief are seen, we quickly fall into despair and scarcely venture to entertain any hope except insofar as outward aids are presented to our eyes. Deprived of these, we cannot rest on the Lord. But the prophet states that at that time especially they ought to trust, because the Lord has more abundant opportunities of displaying his power when people perceive no ways or methods and everything appears to be utterly desperate. Contrary to everyone's hope and belief, the Lord will assist his people, that we may not let ourselves be driven hither and thither by doubt and hesitation.

20. ". . . so that people may see and know, may consider and understand, that the hand of the LORD has done this, that the Holy One of Israel has created it." While God leads us by all his works to adore him, yet when the restoration of his church is in question, his wonderful power is manifested so as to constrain all to admire him. As we have seen elsewhere and as he will afterwards repeat frequently, when he brought his people back from banishment, he gave a proof fit to be remembered in all ages, as he declares in this passage that he would do. But because we are either sluggish or careless in considering his works, and because they quickly pass away from our view in consequence of our giving so little attention to them, he repeats the same statement in many forms.

21. "Present your case," says the LORD. "Set forth your arguments," says Jacob's King. It was necessary that this be added to the previous teaching, for when we associate with wicked people, they pour ridicule on our hope and charge us with folly, as if we were too simpleminded and credulous. Our faith is attacked and frequently shaken by jeers such as the following: "These people hang on the clouds and believe things that are impossible and contrary to all reason." Since, therefore, the Jews in their captivity would hear such mockeries, it was important for the prophet to fortify them by these warnings. Here he, speaking for God, challenges the Gentiles to bring forward everything that could support their cause, as is usually done in courts of justice.

22-23. "Bring in your idols to tell us what is going to happen. Tell us what the former things were, so that we may consider them and know their final outcome. Or declare to us the things to come, tell us what the future holds, so we may know that you are gods. Do something, whether good or bad, so that we will be dismayed and filled with fear." Not only does the Lord attack idolaters, but he bids them bring forward the gods themselves along with them, as if he said, "Whatever may be their ingenuity, they will not be advocates able to defend so bad a cause." Here we see God sustaining the character of an advocate and speaking in the name of the whole nation; he does not wish to be separated from his church, which he therefore confirms and fortifies against the mockeries of wicked people and other contrivances by which they attack our faith. We ought therefore to cheer up when God undertakes our cause and comes forth publicly against idolaters and, armed with his invincible truth, rises up against the idols and silences their vanity.

24. **"But you are less than nothing and your works are utterly worthless; he who chooses you is detestable."** God now mocks idols in order to confirm the godly in the belief and worship of one God, when by the comparison they see that those who worship idols are miserably deceived and blind.

25. **"I have stirred up one from the north, and he comes—one from the rising sun who calls on my name. He treads on rulers as if they were mortar, as if he were a potter treading the clay."** God through Isaiah goes back to the argument he had used briefly respecting his foreknowledge and power and shows that the name of God belongs only to him in whom these are found; therefore those that neither know nor can do anything are empty idols.

26. **"Who told of this from the beginning, so we could know, or beforehand, so we could say, 'He was right'? No one told of this, no one foretold it, no one heard any words from you."** Again the Lord attacks idols, having maintained his divinity. He asks if idolaters can produce anything of a similar nature to support their worship—that is, if they can bring forward any such instance of foreknowledge or power. Because beyond all controversy God could claim this prerogative for himself alone, he tauntingly says in essence, "We will acknowledge that he by whom such things shall be done is the true God."

27. **"I was the first to tell Zion, 'Look, here they are!'"** In this verse God states more clearly that he predicts future events to the Jews in order to encourage them to believe; if prophecies had no end or purpose, it would not be of much advantage to know future events. God therefore testifies that prophecies are intended by him to promote the faith and edification of the church.

"I gave to Jerusalem a messenger of good tidings." God now describes the manner in which he informs believers about future events—that is, by the agency and ministry of the prophets. This tends greatly to commend preaching, for the Lord does not descend from heaven to instruct us but employs the ministry of his servants and declares that he speaks to us by their mouth; this distinguished blessing of God ought to be embraced with our whole heart.

28. **"I look but there is no one—no one among them to give counsel, no one to give answer when I ask them."** Having spoken about himself, the Lord returns to idols, a continuing contrast between himself and idols. It is as if he said, "I do these things, but idols cannot do them; they have no counsel or wisdom or understanding; they cannot give an answer to those that ask them and cannot give any help to the wretched." In this comparison we ought to observe that he plainly shows himself to be God—first,

by the prophets and their doctrine, and, second, by his works in a similar manner. Nothing of this kind is found in idols. From this it follows that they are not gods and that we ought to rely on him alone.

29. "See, they are all false! Their deeds amount to nothing; their images are but wind and confusion." He pronounces all of **their deeds** to be a failure—that is, of no value. He declares this still more plainly when he says that they are **but wind and confusion.**

Isaiah
Chapter 42

1. "Here is my servant, whom I uphold, my chosen one in whom I delight; I will put my Spirit on him and he will bring justice to the nations." The prophet, speaking for God, appears to break off abruptly to speak of Christ. But we ought to remember that the prophets, when they promise anything hard to believe, often mention Christ immediately afterwards; for in him are ratified all the promises that would otherwise have been doubtful and uncertain (see 2 Corinthians 1:20).

He calls Christ God's **servant** by way of eminence. This name belongs to all the godly because God has adopted them on condition that they direct themselves and their whole life to obedience to him. Godly teachers and those who hold public office in the church are specially called servants of God. But there is something still more extraordinary on account of which this name belongs especially to Christ: He is called a **servant** because God the Father not only enjoined him to teach or to do some particular thing but called him to a singular and incomparable work that has nothing in common with other works.

2. "He will not shout or cry out, or raise his voice in the streets." The prophet shows the nature of Christ's coming: It would be without the pomp or splendor that commonly attends earthly kings, at whose arrival there are uttered various noises and loud cries, as if heaven and earth were about to mingle. In contrast, Isaiah says that Christ will come without any noise or cry—not only for the sake of applauding his modesty but, first, that we may not form any earthly conception of him; second, that, having known his kindness by which he draws us to him, we may cheerfully hasten to meet him; and, lastly, that our faith may not languish, even though his condition is mean and despicable.

3. "A bruised reed he will not break, and a smoldering wick he will not snuff out. In faithfulness he will bring forth justice." After declaring in general that Christ will be unlike earthly princes, he next mentions his mildness in this respect: He will support the weak and feeble. By the metaphor of **a bruised reed,** he means that Christ does not wish to break off and altogether crush those who are half-broken but, on the contrary, to lift them up and support them, so as to maintain and strengthen all that is good in them.

"A smoldering wick he will not snuff out." This metaphor means the same as the previous one and is borrowed from the wicks of lamps, which may displease us by not burning clearly or by giving out smoke, and yet we do not extinguish them but trim and brighten them.

4. **"He will not falter or be discouraged till he establishes justice on earth. In his law the islands will put their hope."** The prophet alludes to the preceding verse and confirms what he said before: Christ will indeed be mild and gentle toward the weak, but he will have no softness or effeminacy, for he will manfully execute the commission he had received from the Father. Many people wish to profit by the name of gentleness, so as to gain the applause and esteem of the world, but at the same time betray truth in a base and shameful manner. I remember that there were in a populous city two preachers, one of whom boldly and loudly reproved vices, while the other endeavored to gain the favor of the people by flatteries. This fawning preacher, who was expounding the prophet Jeremiah, lighted on a passage full of the mildest consolation and having found, as he imagined, a fit opportunity, he began to declaim against those harsh and severe reprovers who frighten people by thunderbolts of words. But on the following day, when the prophet changed his subject and sharply rebuked wicked men with his peculiar vehemence of style, the wretched flatterer was constrained to encounter bitter scorn by retracting the words that were fresh in the recollection of all his hearers. The temporary favor he had gained speedily vanished when he revealed his own disposition and made himself abhorred by the good and the bad.

5. **This is what God the LORD says—he who created the heavens and stretched them out, who spread out the earth and all that comes out of it, who gives breath to its people, and life to those who walk on it.** He confirms what he said at the beginning of the chapter about the reign of Christ: He will renew and restore all things. As this might be thought incredible, he adds here a magnificent description of the power of God, by which our faith ought to be confirmed, especially when the outward aspect of things is directly contrary.

6. **"I, the LORD, have called you in righteousness; I will take hold of your hand."** He means the immediate assistance of God. In other words, "I will direct and establish you in the calling to which I have appointed you. In a word, as your calling is righteous, so I will defend and uphold you, as if by taking hold of your hand I were your leader."

"I will keep you and will make you to be a covenant for the people and a light for the Gentiles." We have here another clear proof of the calling of the Gentiles since God through the prophet expressly states that Christ was appointed to be **a light** to them. He calls him **a light** because the Gentiles were plunged into the deepest and thickest darkness at the time when the Lord illuminated none but the Jews. The blame lies solely with ourselves if we do not become partakers of this salvation, for he calls everyone to himself without a single exception and gives Christ to all, that we may be illuminated by him. If only we open our eyes, he alone will dispel the darkness and illuminate our minds by the light of truth.

7. **". . . to open eyes that are blind, to free captives from prison and to release from the dungeon those who sit in darkness."** Here he explains more fully for what end Christ will be sent by the Father, that we may see more clearly what advantage he yields us, and how much we need his assistance. He reminds all people of their blindness, that they may acknowledge it if they wish to be illuminated by Christ. In short, by these metaphors he says what condition people are in until Christ shines upon them as their Redeemer; that is, they are most wretched, empty, and destitute of all blessings and are surrounded and overwhelmed by innumerable distresses until they are delivered by Christ.

8. **"I am the LORD; that is my name!"** We can infer the nature and extent of the disease of unbelief since the Lord can hardly satisfy himself with any words to express the cure of it. By nature we are prone to distrust and do not believe God when he speaks, until he entirely subdues our stubbornness. Besides, we are so superficial that we keep falling back into the same fault if he does not use many bridles to restrain us. Again, therefore, he returns to the confirmation we mentioned before, so that his promises may remain unshaken.

"I will not give my glory to another or my praise to idols." That is, "I will not let **my glory** be diminished, which it would be if I were found to be false or fickle in my promises." He declares that he will abide by his promises because he wishes to vindicate his **glory** and preserve it entire, that it may not be diminished in any respect.

This is a remarkable passage, by which we are taught that the **glory** of God is chiefly visible in his fulfillment of what he has promised. We obtain a singular confirmation of our faith from the fact that the Lord never deceives and never swerves from his promises and the fact that nothing can hinder what he has determined. Satan tries by amazing arts to obscure this **glory** of God and to bestow it on men and on false gods; therefore the Lord testifies that he will not permit himself to be regarded as fickle or deceitful in his promises.

9. **"See, the former things have taken place, and new things I declare; before they spring into being I announce them to you."** God now recalls the earlier predictions, by whose fulfillment he shows that confidence ought to be placed in him for the future; what we have known by actual experience ought to tend greatly to confirm our belief. It is as if he

said, "I have spoken so frequently to your fathers, and you have found me to be true in all things; and yet you cannot place confidence in me about future events. The experiences of past transactions produce no effect upon you and do not excite you to do better."

10. Sing to the LORD a new song, his praise from the ends of the earth, you who go down to the sea, and all that is in it, you islands, and all who live in them. Isaiah now exhorts the people to have gratitude. Remembering God's favors should always excite us to give thanks and to celebrate his praises. Besides, by this exhortation he calls believers to look on the prophecy as actually accomplished and confirms the promises of which God spoke. Note what the prophet aims to tell us: There is no reason for believers to give way to sorrow, even though they are severely oppressed. Good hope ought to encourage them to engage in gladness as they prepare to give thanks.

11. Let the desert and its towns raise their voices; let the settlements where Kedar lives rejoice. Let the people of Sela sing for joy; let them shout from the mountaintops. The prophet includes all the parts of the world but particularly mentions those that were better known to the Jews; on the west Judea had the sea, and on the east the desert and Arabia. When he speaks of **the desert . . . the settlements where Kedar lives,** he means Arabia; but this includes the whole of the East. It is like saying that these praises shall be heard from the rising to the setting of the sun; for God shall be worshiped everywhere, though formerly he was worshiped only in Judea. Thus the state of affairs will be changed, and that praise will be heard in the most distant parts of the earth.

12. Let them give glory to the LORD and proclaim his praise in the islands. He explains what the nature of that shouting will be—that is, to celebrate the praises of God, for his goodness and mercy will be seen everywhere. The prophet enjoins them to celebrate this redemption with a cheerful voice because the blessed consequences of it will be shared by all the nations.

13. The LORD will march out like a mighty man, like a warrior he will stir up his zeal; with a shout he will raise the battle cry and will triumph over his enemies. What Isaiah now adds is intended to prepare believers to conquer temptations. He ascribes to God strength and power, that they might know they will find in him a sure defense. In adversity we are perplexed because we doubt if God will be able to help us, especially when by delaying he appears in some measure to reject our prayers. The prophet extols God's power loudly, so that all may learn to rely on him.

14. "For a long time I have kept silent, I have been quiet and held myself back. But now, like a woman in childbirth, I cry out, I gasp and pant." The prophet has in mind the temptations that commonly give us great uneasiness when God delays his aid. We are tempted by impatience and fear that his promises are false. We reckon it unreasonable that God should be silent and fall asleep, so to speak, while the wicked go forth with boasting; that he should hold back while they burn with eagerness to do mischief; that he should wink at their crimes while they keenly pursue every kind of cruelty. When the people's minds were distressed and almost overwhelmed, the prophet wished to comfort them, so that they might not think God had forsaken them, though everything appeared to be desperate.

15. "I will lay waste the mountains and hills and dry up all their vegetation; I will turn rivers into islands and dry up the pools." The prophet means that all the defenses and military forces on which the wicked pride themselves will not prevent God from setting his people free. It was necessary to add this to what he had said before, for when we see enemies exceedingly powerful and almost invincible, we tremble and do not look for God's assistance, which would be necessary to keep our faith strong. The prophet therefore dwells on this point in order to show that no power or army whatsoever can resist the Lord when he wishes to deliver his people. In short, he shows that there will be such a revolution that those who formerly were most powerful will be crushed and will gain nothing by all their attempts against the Lord.

16. "I will lead the blind by ways they have not known, along unfamiliar paths I will guide them; I will turn the darkness into light before them and make the rough places smooth. These are the things I will do; I will not forsake them." Having shown that the strength of the enemies cannot keep God from delivering his people, he goes on with the consolation he had hinted at before. By the word **blind** he describes those whose affairs are so difficult, intricate, and disordered that they know not which way to turn or in what direction to flee and, in short, see no means of escape but only deep gulfs on every hand.

17. "But those who trust in idols, who say to images, 'You are our gods,' will be turned back in utter shame." This enables us to see more clearly who the former doctrine relates to, for this verse distinguishes between the worshipers of God and the worshipers of idols. The Lord will be a leader to his own people, in marked contrast with **those who trust in idols.** The Lord gives us a choice, either to be saved by his grace or to perish miserably; all those who place their hope of salvation in idols will perish, but those who trust in the Word of God are certain of salvation. They are often heavily afflicted, but he will not allow their hope to be put to shame in the end; the end result will prove that the prophet was not wrong to make this distinction.

18. "Hear, you deaf; look, you blind, and see!" He here uses the word **blind** in a different sense from verse 16, when he metaphorically described those who had no understanding and were overwhelmed by such a mass of afflictions that they were blinded by their sorrow. Here the **blind** are those who shut their eyes in the midst of light and do not behold the works of God. The **deaf** are those who refuse to hear him and sink down into stupidity and slothfulness amidst the dregs of their ignorance. He therefore condemns the Jews for blindness; in fact, in my own opinion, he condemns everyone.

19. "Who is blind but my servant, and deaf like the messenger I send? Who is blind like the one committed to me, blind like the servant of the LORD?" Isaiah had accused all people of blindness, but especially the Jews, because they ought to have seen more clearly than all the rest. They not only had ordinary light and understanding but enjoyed the Word, by which the Lord abundantly revealed himself to them. All the rest were also **blind**; but the Jews ought to have seen and known God since they were illuminated by his law and doctrine, as by a very bright lamp. Because the Jews shut their eyes when they had such clear light, he addresses to them this special reproof. It is as if God said to them, "In vain do I debate with those who are alienated from me, and it is not wonderful that they are **blind**; but it is monstrous that this should have happened to my servants (before whose eyes light has been placed), for them to be deaf to the doctrine that sounds continually in their ears."

20. "You have seen many things, but have paid no attention; your ears are open, but you hear nothing." The prophet explains the double nature of this blindness/deafness. This shows clearly that he is speaking of the Jews, who had quenched God's light by their wicked contempt. Our guilt will be double when we come to the judgment seat of God if we shut our eyes when he exhibits the light and shut our ears when he teaches by his Word.

21. "It pleased the LORD for the sake of his righteousness to make his law great and glorious." In order to aggravate still more the guilt of the Jews, Isaiah now shows that it was not God who prevented them from leading a prosperous and happy life. He had already said that the distresses and afflictions they endured were punishment for their blindness, which they had brought upon themselves by disobeying his **law.** In their obstinacy they were rejecting all relief.

22. "But this is a people plundered and looted, all of them trapped in pits or hidden away in prisons. They have become plunder, with no one to rescue them; they have been made loot, with no one to say, 'Send them back.'" Isaiah now declares that it is their own fault that they are miserable and appointed to destruction, because they rejected God who would otherwise have been inclined to do good to them, and because they deliberately set aside all remedies and wished for death, as is commonly the case with people who are past hope. Thus he excuses God and brings a heavy accusation against the people. They rejected God by their ingratitude and abused his fatherly kindness.

23. Which of you will listen to this or pay close attention in time to come? Isaiah continues the same subject. He means that the Jews are and will be so stupid that they will not see, even when they are warned. He addresses them directly because they ought to have been better educated and taught than others, and yet they understood nothing and did not observe the judgments of God, even though they were perfectly clear.

24. Who handed Jacob over to become loot, and Israel to the plunderers? Was it not the LORD, against whom we have sinned? For they would not follow his ways; they did not obey his law. Here the prophet aggravates the guilt of the Jews. Previously he had included himself as a member of that body and confessed his guilt—not that he resembled the great body of the people or approved of their crimes, but with such a huge mass of vices he could not be free from some degree of infection, like other parts of the body. But also, because he was very different from the great body of the people, he changes the person and adds, **they would not follow.** Such deep-rooted obduracy is offensive to him, so there is no way he can conceal it or express approval of it; for the subject now in hand is not ordinary vices but contempt and rejection of God, manifested by fiercely and haughtily shaking off his yoke. This is why Isaiah excludes himself from their number.

25. So he poured out on them his burning anger, the violence of war. It enveloped them in flames, yet they did not understand; it consumed them, but they did not take it to heart. The Lord had begun and would continue to punish the Jews very severely; so the prophet uses metaphorical language to express this. He says that the Lord **poured out on them his burning anger** as if a thunderbolt were discharged with violence, or as if waters burst forth to spread devastation far and wide on the surrounding countryside.

To **take** something **to heart** is to consider it attentively and diligently. If the thought came into our minds and was deeply engraved on our hearts that God is Judge and has punished us justly, we would immediately repent. At present the world is oppressed by so many calamities that there is scarcely a spot that is free from the wrath of God; yet no one takes any notice. Because people argue with him fiercely and rebelliously, we need not wonder that he inflicts such dreadful punishment on them and pours out his wrath on all sides, for the world opposes him with inveterate rebellion.

Isaiah
Chapter 43

1. But now, this is what the LORD says—he who created you, O Jacob, he who formed you, O Israel: "Fear not, for I have redeemed you; I have summoned you by name; you are mine." It is hard to say whether this is a different discourse or the same one as before. The prophets whose writings have come down to us did not separate their discourses into distinct chapters, so as to enable us to know what they spoke each day. For my own part, I think it is probable that this doctrine is connected with the preceding one; he had spoken severely against the Jews and threatened destruction to them, and now he wished to moderate that severity. The Lord always cares for the godly; and wickedness never abounds to such an extent that he does not at the same time preserve his people and provide for their safety, that they may not be involved in similar destruction.

This passage ought to be carefully noted. It might seem that everyone is in league to destroy us and that the Lord's anger is burning fiercely and that we are very near destruction. But if just two or three godly people are left, we should not despair, for Jehovah tells them, **"Fear not."** God does not cease to comfort his people and to gently soothe their sorrows, so that amidst the utmost despair they may preserve their hope firm and unshaken.

"I have summoned you by name." The verb here means to admit into close relationship, as when we are adopted by God to be his children.

2. **"When you pass through the waters, I will be with you; and when you pass through the rivers, they will not sweep over you. When you walk through the fire, you will not be burned; the flames will not set you ablaze."** This is an anticipation by which the Lord declares that those who rely on his immediate assistance have no reason to sink under adversity. It is stated more fully here than in the preceding verse, because while he shows that the church will not be exempt from calamities and afflictions but must maintain a constant warfare, he encourages patience and courage. In other words, "The Lord has not redeemed you so that you might enjoy pleasures

and luxuries or so that you might abandon yourself to ease and indolence, but rather so you should be prepared to endure all sorts of evils."

By **fire** and **waters** he means every kind of miseries to which we are liable in this life. We must contend not with just one kind but with infinitely diversified calamities.

3. "For I am the LORD, your God, the Holy One of Israel, your Savior; I give Egypt for your ransom, Cush and Seba in your stead." He confirms the preceding statement by the experience of the past: The Lord had formerly assisted his people in such a manner that it was reasonable and proper for believers to rely on his grace now.

4. "Since you are precious and honored in my sight, and because I love you, I will give men in exchange for you, and people in exchange for your life." By these words God through Isaiah excludes all personal worth on the part of the people, so they would not boast of having obtained anything by their own merit. Indeed, the cause of salvation, and of all the blessings that we receive, is the undeserved love of God. It is also the cause of all our excellence, for if he judged us according to our own qualifications, he would not value us even as straw. We must therefore set aside every idea of merit or of personal worth, of which we have none, and must ascribe everything to the grace of God alone.

5. "Do not be afraid, for I am with you; I will bring your children from the east and gather you from the west." Isaiah frequently repeats the exhortation **"Do not be afraid,"** but we ought not to look upon it as superfluous, for we know and feel how prone we are by nature to fear and distrust. Scarcely any words can express the church's great alarm at that time. As soon as we begin to call God's promises into question, our minds are distracted by various thoughts; we are alarmed and continually tormented by the greatness and diversity of the dangers, until at length we are stupefied and have no perception of the grace of God.

6. "I will say to the north, 'Give them up!' and to the south, 'Do not hold them back.' Bring my sons from afar and my daughters from the ends of the earth." These four parts [**east** and **west** in verse 5, **north** and **south** in this verse] include the whole world, as is usual in all languages. But Isaiah speaks in somewhat loftier language than Moses and others, because he wished the people to view the event as if it had actually occurred. This purpose is admirably served by the lifelike descriptions that bring it before our eyes. He might, indeed, have said it in fewer words, but this manner of address is far more forcible. He represents God as commanding, with supreme authority, all creatures and every part of the world to set his people free.

By **my sons** he means that not all Israel will be gathered, but only that which is the true Israel. Not all who are the physical descendants of Abraham are true Israelites—many of them are illegitimate (see Romans 9:6-7).

7. ". . . everyone who is called by my name, whom I created for my

glory ..." The Lord testifies that the salvation of his people concerns himself, and he can no more throw away the care of his people than he can expose his name to reproach and disgrace, which he will never do. In a word, his **glory,** of which he is the continual defender, is intimately connected with the salvation of his people.

"... **whom I formed and made.**" God repeats the same thing in many different ways, to amplify it so they may be more fully convinced that he wishes to carry through to the end the work he has begun.

This passage, therefore, recommends to us the extraordinary grace of God, by which we not only have our human birth but also are renewed in his image.

8. Lead out those who have eyes but are blind, who have ears but are deaf. In other words, "I will bring out the blind, so as to restore sight to them. I will bring out the deaf, so that they recover their hearing." First the people are delivered, and then **eyes** and **ears** are restored to them. The Lord did this when he brought his people out of Babylon; but undoubtedly the prophet looks farther—that is, to the kingdom of Christ. That is when believers were gathered not only out of Babylon, but out of all places of the earth.

9. All the nations gather together and the peoples assemble. Which of them foretold this and proclaimed to us the former things? Let them bring in their witnesses to prove they were right, so that others may hear and say, "It is true." The prophet speaks in the person of God, as he has done before, and bids defiance to all idols. It is very necessary, and was at that time especially necessary, to distinguish between the true God and false gods. It is easy indeed to ascribe to God the glory of divinity, but it is very difficult to claim it for him so exclusively that all false gods are reduced to nothing. At that time the error regarding them had received greater confirmation, for at the ruin of the nation unbelievers applauded the gods as if they had vanquished the true God. The prophet therefore suggests to believers the reply that they should make to the jeers of their enemies. Those men might sally forth in crowds to defend their errors, but he enjoins the small number to stand firm against all their forces.

10. "You are my witnesses," declares the LORD, "and my servant whom I have chosen, so that you may know and believe me and understand that I am he. Before me no god was formed, nor will there be one after me." Having summoned the Gentiles to a contest and having proven that the stories they circulated concerning their idols were false and unfounded, God now separates himself from them and produces his **witnesses,** that he might not be thought to be of the same class with them. He justly boasts, therefore, that his people are his true **witnesses,** for the Jews had been instructed by heavenly oracles as far as was necessary for attaining perfect certainty.

11. "I, even I, am the LORD, and apart from me there is no savior."

Not only is God's eternal essence demonstrated here but also his power and goodness, which he constantly exercises toward us, and by which he is fully revealed. To make us realize this, he adds an epithet as a distinguishing mark: He is the only Savior. The world falls into the mistake of giving an empty name to God and at the same time giving his authority to another.

12. **"I have revealed and saved and proclaimed—I, and not some foreign god among you. You are my witnesses," declares the LORD, "that I am God."** This verse is a sort of recapitulation of the previous one, for Jehovah says again that he foretold future events and that he had actually accomplished what he foretold. The word **saved** speaks of his power and goodness. In a word, he means that only he who both knows and does all things is God.

13. **"Yes, and from ancient days I am he. No one can deliver out of my hand. When I act, who can reverse it?"** His supreme and infinite power is proved from his eternity. If he were not eternal, he could neither exercise authority over all things, nor be the defender of his people, nor dispose of creatures according to his pleasure. But since he is eternal, all things must be subject to his authority. It means the same thing when he says that no obstacle can prevent what he has decreed. The Jews did not need to be alarmed or dispirited by the forces or number of their enemies.

14. **This is what the LORD says—your Redeemer, the Holy One of Israel: "For your sake I will send to Babylon and bring down as fugitives all the Babylonians, in the ships in which they took pride."** Cyrus would be but a hired soldier rendering his services to the Lord for delivering his people. It is true that Isaiah does not name Cyrus, but he speaks of the army he has under his command for subduing the Babylonians. We know this was accomplished by Cyrus and Darius, and that it was under the direction of God who had foretold it long before. Not only does God speak to those who saw these things happen, but to all others whom he wished to comfort by this hope of deliverance, of which they could not have formed the smallest conception. He addresses captives who had been oppressed by the cruel tyranny of the Babylonians and appeared to be beyond all hope of obtaining deliverance. They might be apt to regard those promises as absurd, because to human eyes there was no visible hope of redemption.

15. **"I am the LORD, your Holy One, Israel's Creator, your King."** He is called **Holy One** because he has chosen and separated a people, that he might consecrate them to himself. The title reminds them of the adoption by which he united them to himself in a special way, so that they might understand that he will be their Father and Savior. For the same reason we ought now to acknowledge him as our **Holy One** because he has set us apart to be members of the church, of which we are assured by our calling.

The name **Creator** must not be viewed as referring to universal creation, by which unbelievers also are created, but to the new creation, on account of which we are also called his "workmanship" (see Ephesians 2:10).

The title **King** might indeed be thought absurd; for not even the semblance of a kingdom was visible, and nothing was to be seen among the Jews but what was covered with shame and disgrace, in consequence of their having been deprived of all aid and relief. Yet there was room for the exercise of faith, that they might hope for the restoration of the kingdom, though apparently ruined and almost extinguished, and might acknowledge God to be their **King.**

16. This is what the LORD says—he who made a way through the sea, a path through the mighty waters. Again the prophet repeats and confirms what was otherwise incredible; and in order that this confirmation might have greater weight, he speaks what God himself would say. The prophet therefore represents God as actually present and declares that he is the same God who surmounted every obstacle by his power, that he might be the Redeemer of his people. At that former time he opened up a way through the sea (Exodus 14:21) and afterwards through the mighty waters of the Jordan, which the Lord dried up, though it was running very rapidly (see Joshua 3:16). He expressly describes these portentous miracles because the people might think that their return to Judea was impossible and that all that was promised concerning it was fiction.

17. . . . who drew out the chariots and horses, the army and reinforcements together, and they lay there, never to rise again, extinguished, snuffed out like a wick. Isaiah shows that no power will hinder God from delivering his people whenever he thinks it proper. The sea that lay between them could not prevent God from bringing out his people; he divided its waters and drowned the pursuing enemies, with their horses and chariots (Exodus 14:28). This is therefore an amplification, as if he said, "Even if the whole world joins together for your destruction and attempts to hinder the deliverance of my church, it will gain nothing; not only will the Lord find a way through whirlpools when he chooses, but he will overthrow and scatter all opposing efforts and will crush the enemies so that they will never again raise their head."

18. "Forget the former things; do not dwell on the past." Until now the prophet has shown God's great power in delivering the people. He now declares that all the miracles that God wrought in that first redemption were of little importance compared with the more remarkable miracle that would soon be done; that is, that the glory of this second deliverance will be so great as to throw the first one into the shade.

19. "See, I am doing a new thing! Now it springs up; do you not perceive it? I am making a way in the desert and streams in the wasteland." This shows more clearly what the prophet meant in the previous verse, for he declares that God will do **a new thing**—that is, a work unheard of and uncommon, which on account of its greatness and excellence will overshadow all other works—just as the brightness of the sun, when it fills heaven and earth, causes the stars to disappear.

20. **"The wild animals honor me, the jackals and the owls, because I provide water in the desert and streams in the wasteland."** He adorns the preceding statement; for when things are in such a desperate state, it is right that magnificent language should be employed in extolling God's power, that words might supply what seems to be lacking in the reality. The meaning is that God's power will be so visible and manifest that the very beasts will be impressed with it and will acknowledge and worship God.

". . . to give drink to my people, my chosen." That these wretched exiles may not be driven from the hope of heavenly grace and assistance, God through Isaiah reminds them of their adoption. In effect, he says that in this sad and ruinous state they still continued to be the people of God, because he who once chose them does not change his purpose.

21. **". . . the people I formed for myself that they may proclaim my praise."** The prophet means that the Lord will necessarily do what he had said, because his glory is concerned in the preservation of the people he has chosen for himself. These words are therefore meant to console the people. "Do you think I will let my glory fall to the ground? It is connected with your salvation, and therefore your salvation will be the object of my care. In a word, know that you will be saved, because you cannot perish unless my glory perishes too. You will therefore survive because I want you to proclaim my glory continually."

22. **"Yet you have not called upon me, O Jacob, you have not wearied yourselves for me, O Israel."** God through Isaiah confirms by an indirect reproof what he said in the preceding verse: It was not by any merits of his people that he was induced to act so kindly toward them. This deliverance, therefore, ought to be ascribed purely to God's goodness. In order to prove this, he says, **"Yet you have not called upon me."** Calling on the name of God includes the whole of the worship of God, the chief part of which is calling upon him.

23. **"You have not brought me sheep for burnt offerings, nor honored me with your sacrifices. I have not burdened you with grain offerings nor wearied you with demands for incense."** At the very time when the people were sacrificing, they could not boast of their merits or personal worth, as if they had laid God under obligation in this manner; for they were lacking in the sacrifices that God chiefly approves—that is, faith and obedience, without which nothing can be acceptable to God. There was no integrity of heart. Although, therefore, they brought beasts to the temple every day and sacrificed them, yet he rightly says that they offered him nothing. Sacrifices could not be accepted by God when they were separated from truth and were offered to another rather than to the true

God; for he did not demand them in themselves but only so far as the people treated them as exercises of faith and obedience. Hence we infer that the prophet says nothing new but continues to exhibit the same doctrine—namely, that God rejects all services that are rendered in a slavish spirit or in any other respect are defective.

24. "You have not bought any fragrant calamus for me, or lavished on me the fat of your sacrifices. But you have burdened me with your sins and wearied me with your offenses." God speaking through his prophet refers to **calamus,** a cane plant from which precious ointment was composed, as we are informed in Exodus 30:23. The high priests, the tabernacle of the congregation, and the ark of the testimony, together with its vessels, were anointed with it. So here he says, "Even though you buy cane for me with money, you should not think that is an expense bestowed on me, as if I approved of it." They did not benefit from those ceremonies because they did not exercise faith or worship God with a pure conscience.

25. "I, even I, am he who blots out your transgressions, for my own sake, and remembers your sins no more." He concludes the previous statement by this exclamation, as if he said that he may boast of his right (he blots out the iniquities of his people and restores them to freedom). They have no merits by which they could obtain this, since they deserve the severest punishment, and even destruction. The same word is repeated by him (**"I, even I"**), so as to criticize people more sharply for their ingratitude in robbing him of the honor that belongs to him alone or in some way casting it into the shade.

The meaning of **blots out your transgressions** may be summed up by saying that the people ought to hope for their return simply because God will freely pardon their sins. He will of his own accord be appeased by his mercy and will stretch out his fatherly hand.

26. "Review the past for me, let us argue the matter together; state the case for your innocence." Because human pride cannot be easily corrected, the Lord pursues this argument and dwells much upon it. In order to lead the Jews to throw away all confidence in their works, and to make them more humble, he gives them liberty to say and argue whatever they please in support of their cause if they do not acknowledge that they are vanquished. He shows that it is exceedingly foolish of humans to claim anything for themselves; for though he gives them liberty to boast, they will be found utterly unable to plead and will have nothing to say in defense of their cause.

27. "Your first father sinned; your spokesmen rebelled against me." He adds **spokesmen** in order to show that the blame did not lie with the people alone; those who ought to have been the guides of others—that is, the priests and the prophets—were the first to stumble and led others into error. In a word he shows that no class was free from vices and corruptions. "Let them now go and boast of their virtues, and let them produce the slightest reason (other than my own goodness) why I ought to protect them."

28. "So I will disgrace the dignitaries of your temple, and I will consign Jacob to destruction and Israel to scorn." The Lord is said to **disgrace** his church when he despises it and throws it aside as a thing of no value. The same Hebrew word is used in this sense in Psalm 89:39 and many other passages. Having been set apart and sanctified by God, we dwell under his protection and guardianship, so long as we are holy. Similarly, when we are deprived of it, we are said to be **disgraced** because we cease to be sacred and are rendered unworthy of his protection.

Isaiah
Chapter 44

1. "But now listen, O Jacob, my servant, Israel, whom I have chosen."
A little earlier God through Isaiah had rebuked the transgressions of the
people and declared that they all deserved eternal perdition because both
the princes and the people had polluted everything by their crimes. Now
he mitigates that severity of punishment and comforts the people. In other
words, "Though grievous afflictions are about to overtake you, listen to
what I will do for your sake." The verse must be viewed in connection
with the previous argument: The Lord declares that he will never permit
his people to perish altogether, even when they are grievously afflicted. We
may infer from this that God is never so angry with his church as not to
leave some room for mercy, as we have already seen on many occasions.
The consequence is that whenever the prophets threaten, they always add
some consolation.

But lest we should imagine that people have earned this by their good
conduct, he adds, **whom I have chosen.** We do not serve God because we
are entitled to it or deserve it, but because he renders us fit by a free
election.

**2. "This is what the LORD says—he who made you, who formed you
in the womb, and who will help you: Do not be afraid, O Jacob, my servant, Jeshurun, whom I have chosen."** Although he treated the Jews
harshly, that they might be stripped of all false confidence and might
humbly take themselves to the grace of God, he now caresses them pleas-
antly by a mild and gentle discourse, so that they might know they will
not sustain any loss by self-denial. We must therefore supply here the following contrasts: "You, Jacob, are indeed nothing in yourself, but God
your Maker will not despise his work. No nobleness of birth would keep
you from being lost, but the adoption that the heavenly Father has chosen
to give you will be more than enough to redeem you."

3. "For I will pour water on the thirsty land, and streams on the dry

ground." God continues the same subject and also explains the nature of the assistance that he has promised. But we ought always to remember that these prophecies relate to the sorrowful and afflicted period that he has already spoken about—that is, when the people, in the extremity to which they were reduced, thought that they were altogether forsaken and that all God's promises were empty. Isaiah, speaking for God, meets this doubt and compares the people to a dry and thirsty land that has no moisture at all.

They were worn-out, then, by affliction, and the water of life was decayed; yet, if they were not to throw away courage in their deepest distress, they would have to set before their minds this declaration of the prophet. We, too, when we are brought into the greatest dangers and see nothing before us but immediate death ought similarly to betake ourselves to these promises, so they may give us support against all temptations. Yet we must feel our drought and poverty, that our thirsty souls may partake of this refreshing influence of the waters.

"I will pour out my Spirit on your offspring, and my blessing on your descendants." Jehovah himself explains what he means by waters and rivers—that is, his Spirit. The Spirit is compared to **water** because without him everything decays and perishes through drought, and because by the secret watering of his power he brings life to the whole world, and because the barrenness occasioned by drought and heat is cured so that the earth puts on a new face.

4. "They will spring up like grass in a meadow, like poplar trees by flowing streams." When the Spirit of God has been sent forth, the whole face of the earth is renewed, and those fields that formerly were burnt up with thirst are green and flourish, just as the plants grow when they are watered by the rains. By these metaphors he extends the view of this subject and more fully shows that it is quite as easy for God to enlarge by additional offspring the church, which was desolate and which had been reduced to ruinous and frightful solitude, as to impart to the earth the power of bringing forth.

5. "One will say, 'I belong to the LORD'; another will call himself by the name of Jacob; still another will write on his hand, 'The LORD's,' and will take the name Israel." The general meaning is that there will be a vast assembly of people united in faith and in obedience to the one true God. But the prophet thinks about the custom in a census when every person either pronounces or writes his own name; so he uses the following modes of expression: "One will write with his hand, 'I am God's' and will take the surname of Israel; another will acknowledge that he is God's and will be called by the name of Jacob." He describes something new and uncommon, for he who formerly had nothing to do with God will boast that God has adopted him.

6. "This is what the LORD says—Israel's King and Redeemer, the

LORD Almighty." Having used the unutterable name of God, the prophet also calls him **King** and **Redeemer**. It is not enough that we perceive the power of God, if we are not convinced of his goodwill toward us.

"I am the first and I am the last; apart from me there is no God." God is not asserting his eternity but is showing that he is always like himself. Thus they can hope that he will be to them in the future what they have found him to be in the past.

7. **"Who then is like me? Let him proclaim it. Let him declare and lay out before me what has happened since I established my ancient people, and what is yet to come—yes, let him foretell what will come."** Here the Lord compares himself with idols, as we have already seen in another passage. In the present instance the object is that when the Jews were fiercely insulted by the Babylonian conquerors, they did not need to be discouraged or think their hopes were disappointed, for the taunts that were hurled at them by wicked men were exceedingly harsh and insolent.

8. **"Do not tremble, do not be afraid. Did I not proclaim this and foretell it long ago? You are my witnesses. Is there any God besides me? No, there is no other Rock; I know not one."** Isaiah now explains why he had spoken about God's power: It was in order to confirm the people's faith. From the preceding statements he draws this conclusion: "Since the Lord is so powerful and governs all things at his pleasure, the people he has taken under his protection ought not to fear."

9. **All who make idols are nothing, and the things they treasure are worthless. Those who would speak up for them are blind; they are ignorant, to their own shame.** The Lord now shows, on the contrary, how wretched idolaters are who wander amidst their **worthless** treasures and do not build upon the eternal truth of God; they have no knowledge or sound understanding.

10. **Who shapes a god and casts an idol, which can profit him nothing?** He pours ridicule on the madness of people who dare to make gods; it is a shocking and detestable thing that people should take so much upon them as to try to create God.

11. **He and his kind will be put to shame; craftsmen are nothing but men. Let them all come together and take their stand; they will be brought down to terror and infamy.** Not only does he attack the workers and makers of idols—he also attacks generally all their worshipers, because they are so dull and stupid that as soon as the trunk of a tree has received some new shape, they look upon it as containing the power of God. He means that not only will the makers of idols be punished for their effrontery, but so too will all who have entangled themselves in the same superstitions; it is right that those who share the same guilt should be subjected to the same punishment.

12. **The blacksmith takes a tool and works with it in the coals; he shapes an idol with hammers, he forges it with the might of his arm.**

He gets hungry and loses his strength; he drinks no water and grows faint. The prophet has good reason for drawing up this long description. He has to shake off the stupidity and madness of superstitious people, if they can at all be awakened, or at least to prevent the Jews from indulging in similar folly when they were surrounded on all sides by innumerable worshipers of false gods.

13. **The carpenter measures with a line and makes an outline with a marker; he roughs it out with chisels and marks it with compasses. He shapes it in the form of man, of man in all his glory, that it may dwell in a shrine.** The prophet shows the folly of such intense labor; for their toil brings no other reward than to see their idols resting without motion in the position that has been assigned to them, just as if a sluggard were reclining on a couch.

14. **He cut down cedars, or perhaps took a cypress or oak. He let it grow among the trees of the forest, or planted a pine, and the rain made it grow.** The prophet expresses not only the zeal and furious eagerness of idolaters but also their rebellion and obstinacy; for when he says they **cut down cedars,** and **planted a pine,** he shows that they persevere a long time in their madness and are not just prompted by a sudden impulse to manufacture gods. "Not only," says he, "do they choose trees that are already grown, but they even plant and water and cultivate them, then wait until they have come to their full size, so as to be fit material for making an idol."

15-17. **It is man's fuel for burning; some of it he takes and warms himself, he kindles a fire and bakes bread. But he also fashions a god and worships it; he makes an idol and bows down to it. Half of the wood he burns in the fire; over it he prepares his meal, he roasts his meat and eats his fill. He also warms himself and says, "Ah! I am warm; I see the fire." From the rest he makes a god, his idol; he bows down to it and worships. He prays to it and says, "Save me; you are my god."** Nothing is so inconsistent with the majesty of God as such images; and he who worships them endeavors to shut God up in them and to treat him as fancy takes him. The prophet is right, then, to attack such corruptions and to sharply censure the mad zeal of superstitious people, since nothing more detestable can be uttered or imagined.

18. **They know nothing, they understand nothing; their eyes are plastered over so they cannot see, and their minds closed so they cannot understand.** He concludes that it would have been impossible for people endued with reason to have fallen into this mistake if they had not been altogether blind and mad; if any spark of reason had remained in them, they would have seen how absurd and ridiculous it was to adore a part of the wood that they had burned and that they had seen with their own eyes consumed and reduced to ashes.

19. **No one stops to think, no one has the knowledge or understand-**

ing to say, "Half of it I used for fuel; I even baked bread over its coals, I roasted meat and I ate. Shall I make a detestable thing from what is left? Shall I bow down to a block of wood?" He confirms the preceding statement and takes away every ground of excuse, because unbelievers of their own accord cherish their ignorance. Though people are naturally careful and prudent in worldly matters, they are altogether blind in the worship of God. This is simply because they pay great attention to their individual interests but are not moved by any anxiety about the heavenly kingdom. The prophet reproves them for disregarding godliness because, on a long and winding road, unbelievers do not reflect whether they are keeping the right way or, on the contrary, are uselessly tiring themselves with wicked errors.

20. He feeds on ashes, a deluded heart misleads him; he cannot save himself, or say, "Is not this thing in my right hand a lie?" This verse also confirms the preceding statement. He means that men are haughty and puffed up but also that they are empty and worthless because they are full of deceptions that have nothing solid or lasting. With such pride men will rather burst than be satisfied.

21. "Remember these things, O Jacob, for you are my servant, O Israel. I have made you, you are my servant; O Israel, I will not forget you." God now applies to the use of the people what he had so often said about the superstitions and falsehoods of the Gentiles, by which people who are not well instructed are deceived in the worship of God.

22. "I have swept away your offenses like a cloud, your sins like the morning mist. Return to me, for I have redeemed you." The Lord promises his people future deliverance, for our hearts cannot be actually raised toward God if we do not perceive that he is reconciled to us. In order, therefore, that he might keep the people whom he has bound to himself, he adds a promise by which he comforts them, that they may be fully convinced that the banishment will not be perpetual. God, being a most indulgent Father, moderates his chastisements in such a manner that he always forgives his children.

23. "Sing for joy, O heavens, for the LORD has done this; shout aloud, O earth beneath. Burst into song, you mountains, you forests and all your trees, for the LORD has redeemed Jacob, he displays his glory in Israel." He now urges the Jews to render thanksgiving, not only so they can testify in this way, but so their own expectation of deliverance will be strengthened. He enjoins believers to look upon this as an event already accomplished, as if the Lord had already delivered them.

24. "This is what the LORD says—your Redeemer, who formed you in the womb: I am the LORD, who has made all things, who alone stretched out the heavens, who spread out the earth by myself." The prophet, speaking for the Lord, describes in his own manner the strength and power of God; mere promises would have little authority and

weight if God's power were not brought forward to remove all doubt from our hearts.

25. "Who foils the signs of false prophets and makes fools of diviners, who overthrows the learning of the wise and turns it into nonsense." The prophet expressly added this because Babylon surpassed other nations not only in force of arms and in troops and resources but likewise in remarkable sagacity, by which she appeared to penetrate even to heaven. What injury could befall those who foresaw at a distance future events and could easily, as was commonly supposed, ward off imminent dangers?

26. "Who carries out the words of his servants and fulfills the predictions of his messengers, who says of Jerusalem, 'It shall be inhabited,' of the towns of Judah, 'They shall be built,' and of their ruins, 'I will restore them.'" The prophet now applies to his purpose what he said earlier. Although he spoke in general terms, he still had a specific object in view—to adapt to the circumstances of the present occasion all that he said, that the people might not be alarmed at the wisdom claimed by the Chaldeans or doubt that God would one day deliver them. With their unfounded predictions, therefore, he contrasts the promises of God, that they might not imagine that monarchy to be free from all danger.

27. "Who says to the watery deep, 'Be dry, and I will dry up your streams.'" He seems to be alluding to the former redemption (Exodus 14:29), when the Lord brought the people out of Egypt through the Red Sea; as if he said, "I did this for your fathers, and therefore you ought to hope for the same thing from me, and not to imagine that a return to your native land will be closed against you."

28. "Who says of Cyrus, 'He is my shepherd and will accomplish all that I please.'" This is a remarkable passage, in which we see not only God's wonderful providence but also a striking proof of the truth and certainty of the prophecies. **Cyrus** was named here long before he was born.

"'He will say of Jerusalem, "Let it be rebuilt," and of the temple, "Let its foundations be laid."'" This is the conclusion, by which the previous statements are confirmed. Thus they can rest assured that **Jerusalem** will infallibly be built and can learn from this how dear and precious they are to God. They will see the monarchy of all the East transferred to the Persians. At the same time the prophet points out the end for which Jerusalem was to be rebuilt—namely, that the pure worship of God might be restored. He does not promise this restoration so people may seek their own ease, but so the Lord's people may purely and sincerely call upon him without any disturbance.

Isaiah
Chapter 45

1. "This is what the LORD says to his anointed, to Cyrus, whose right hand I take hold of to subdue nations before him and to strip kings of their armor, to open doors before him so that gates will not be shut." Isaiah continues the subject that he had begun to handle. He shows that it was not in vain that God promised deliverance to his people, since the manner of it was altogether decreed and appointed by him. God frequently chooses to hold us in suspense and thus conceals from us the method he has ready at hand, but in this instance he indulges the weakness of his people and explains the method by which he will deliver them.

He names the person—**Cyrus**—by whose hand he will bring them back. Since their faith would be sharply tried by other temptations, he wished in this respect to provide against doubt, so the difficulty of the event would not shake them. In order to impart greater efficacy to this discourse, he also intends these words for Cyrus himself: "I have chosen you to be a king to me. I will take hold of your hand and will subject the nations to your authority, so that they will open up a passage for you and voluntarily surrender."

2-3. "I will go before you and will level the mountains; I will break down gates of bronze and cut through bars of iron. I will give you the treasures of darkness, riches stored in secret places, so that you may know that I am the LORD, the God of Israel, who calls you by name." These two verses contain nothing new; but in general God says that Cyrus will gain an easy and rapid victory because he will have the Lord for the leader of his expedition.

4. "For the sake of Jacob my servant, of Israel my chosen, I call you by name and bestow on you a title of honor, though you do not acknowledge me." God shows why he would grant such great success to this prince. It is in order that God may preserve his people, as if he said, "You will indeed obtain a signal victory, but I will have regard to my own people rather than to you; it is for their sake that I subject kings and nations to your power." By these predictions the Lord intended to encourage the hearts of believers, that they might not despair amidst their distresses. But undoubtedly he intended likewise to excite Cyrus to acknowledge that he owed to that nation all that he was to accomplish, that he might be more disposed to treat them with all kindness.

5. "I am the LORD, and there is no other; apart from me there is no God. I will strengthen you, though you have not acknowledged me." He confirms the preceding statement, and the repetition is not superfluous. It was proper to repeat often to Cyrus that there is one God, by whose hands all rulers and nations are governed, that he might be drawn aside from all delusions and be converted to the God of Israel. Besides, it is clearly stated that we ought not to try to find divinity in any other. "Beware of ascribing this victory to idols or forming any confused idea of a god such as people imagine; know that the God of Israel is the only author of this victory."

6. "So that from the rising of the sun to the place of its setting men may know there is none besides me. I am the LORD, and there is no other." He means that this favor will be so remarkable that it will be acknowledged and admired by all nations. This was not immediately fulfilled, for although the fame of that victory spread far and wide, few people understood that the God of Israel was the author of it. But it was immediately made known to neighboring lands and was communicated by one nation to another, until the report of it eventually spread throughout the whole world.

7. "I form the light and create darkness, I bring prosperity and create disaster; I, the LORD, do all these things." It is as if he said that those who formerly ascribed everything either to fortune or to idols will acknowledge the true God, so as to ascribe power and the government and glory of all things to him alone.

8. "You heavens above, rain down righteousness; let the clouds shower it down. Let the earth open wide, let salvation spring up, let righteousness grow with it; I, the LORD, have created it." The prophet continues to speak in the name of God, who in the exercise of his authority calls on heaven and earth to lend their services to the restoration of the church. This verse is meant to confirm very powerfully the godly in the hope of future redemption, for the people, wherever they looked, saw nothing but despair. If they turned their eyes toward heaven, there they beheld the wrath of God; if toward the earth, there they beheld afflictions and chastisements. Therefore nothing meant to lead them to entertain favorable hope was visible. On this account God through the prophet confirms them and enjoins heaven and earth, which held out nothing but threats and terrors, to bring forth **salvation** and **righteousness**.

9-10. "Woe to him who quarrels with his Maker, to him who is but a

potsherd among the potsherds on the ground. Does the clay say to the potter, 'What are you making?' Does your work say, 'He has no hands'? Woe to him who says to his father, 'What have you begotten?' or to his mother, 'What have you brought to birth?'" The prophet restrains the complaints of people who in times of adversity grumble and fight against God. This was a timely warning, so that the Jews, by patiently and calmly bearing their cross, might receive the consolation that was offered to them. For whenever God holds us in suspense, the flesh prompts us to grumble, "Why does he not do more quickly what he intends to do? Of what benefit is it to him to torture us by his delay?" The prophet, therefore, in order to chastise this insolence, says in effect, "Does the **potsherd** dispute with **the potter**? Do sons debate with their fathers? Has not God a right to treat us as he thinks fit? What remains but that we shall bear patiently the punishments that he inflicts on us? We must therefore allow God to do what belongs to him and must not take anything from his power and authority."

11. "This is what the LORD says—the Holy One of Israel, and its Maker: Concerning things to come, do you question me about my children, or give me orders about the work of my hands?" It does not belong to us to command God, and it will not be possible for anyone to profit by the Word of God if they do not have a humble heart. Also, remember that God is robbed of a father's right if he does not retain the absolute and uncontrolled government of his church.

12. "It is I who made the earth and created mankind upon it. My own hands stretched out the heavens; I marshaled their starry hosts." There is an indirect contrast here between God and the idols worshiped by superstitious people. I understand this verse in the following way: "Shall I, whose vast and inconceivable wisdom and power shine brightly in heaven and earth, not only be bound by human laws but be degraded below the ordinary lot of men? And if there be any doubts of my justice, shall not I, who rule and govern all things by my hand, be careful of those whom I have adopted into my family? Shall I not watch over their salvation?" Thus it is an argument from the less to the greater, and this meaning is agreeable to Scripture as a whole. We know that we have been adopted by God in such a manner that, having been brought under his protection, we are guarded by his hand; so none can hurt us but by his permission.

13. "I will raise up Cyrus in my righteousness: I will make all his ways straight. He will rebuild my city and set my exiles free, but not for a price or reward, says the LORD Almighty." The prophet now continues the subject on which he had entered at the beginning of the chapter. Having undertaken to soothe their affliction, which was very sharp and severe, God through Isaiah holds out the hope of deliverance and stretches out his hand to them, that they may look for an absolutely certain redemption. "Though you think you are ruined, the Lord will protect you against

destruction." (**In my righteousness** means "justly and truly" and must be understood relatively; it assigns the reason why God determined to raise up Cyrus—that is, because God is a faithful guardian of his church and does not disappoint his worshipers.)

14. This is what the LORD says: "The products of Egypt and the merchandise of Cush, and those tall Sabeans—they will come over to you and will be yours; they will trudge behind you, coming over to you in chains. They will bow down before you and plead with you, saying, 'Surely God is with you, and there is no other; there is no other god.'" He is still speaking of the restoration that was afterwards effected under Cyrus; but we must remember what we noticed before—those promises must be extended farther, for this passage includes the whole time that followed, down to the coming of Christ. Whoever shall duly consider and weigh this prophet's ordinary style will find in his words nothing extravagant and will not look upon his language as exaggerated.

The products of Egypt and the merchandise of Cush. The prophet alludes to the expenses that Cyrus contributed for building and adorning the temple.

15. Truly you are a God who hides himself, O God and Savior of Israel. Isaiah now exclaims that we need to be very patient if we are to enjoy God's promises; for the people might have been prompted to despair when the wicked had everything they wished, but everything adverse befell themselves.

16-17. All the makers of idols will be put to shame and disgraced; they will go off into disgrace together. But Israel will be saved by the LORD with an everlasting salvation; you will never be put to shame or disgraced, to ages everlasting. Here the prophet compares the Jews with the Gentiles in order to address a grievous and dangerous temptation that might come to them when they saw the Gentiles enjoying prosperity; for amidst such great troubles they might have suspected that God was favorable to the Gentiles or that he had cast away the care of his people or that everything was governed by the blind impulse of fortune. The prophet, therefore, assures them that although for a time the Gentiles would flourish and appear to be exalted, in the end they will perish and Israel will be saved.

18. For this is what the LORD says—he who created the heavens, he is God; he who fashioned and made the earth, he founded it; he did not create it to be empty, but formed it to be inhabited—he says: "I am the LORD, and there is no other." This verse tends to confirm the previous one; the prophet means that the Jews are fully convinced that the Lord will at length deliver them, though they are now oppressed by wretched bondage. In a word, as long as the earth endures, the church of God will exist; as long as the sun and moon last, it will not fail.

19. "I have not spoken in secret, from somewhere in a land of dark-

ness; I have not said to Jacob's descendants, 'Seek me in vain.' I, the LORD, speak the truth; I declare what is right." He now recalls the people to the doctrine of the law, because God cannot be comprehended by human faculties. Though he is concealed from carnal reason, he abundantly reveals himself and affords the remedy by his Word, which supplies what was wanting, that we may not desire anything more. If this had not been granted, we would have no hope and would have lost all courage.

20. "Gather together and come; assemble, you fugitives from the nations. Ignorant are those who carry about idols of wood, who pray to gods that cannot save." He challenges all superstitious people and, as it were, appoints a day for them to submit to a righteous judgment, as we have seen in expounding other passages, in order to show that they can plead nothing that will not be speedily overturned.

21. "Declare what is to be, present it—let them take counsel together. Who foretold this long ago, who declared it from the distant past? Was it not I, the LORD? And there is no God apart from me, a righteous God and a Savior; there is none but me." He again challenges all those who might have annoyed the Jews and shaken their faith by their taunts. God always keeps this object in view—to fortify the faith of the people against all the assaults of the Gentiles. Amidst temptations so numerous and so severe, the Jews might sink under their terrible afflictions if there were no powerful arguments on the other side to induce them to worship and trust the true God. Therefore he permits heathens to produce and bring forward everything they can find in support of their cause.

22. "Turn to me and be saved, all you ends of the earth; for I am God, and there is no other." Hitherto the Lord through his prophet addressed the Jews alone, as if to them alone salvation belonged; but now he extends his discourse farther. He invites the whole world to the hope of salvation and at the same time brings a charge of ingratitude against all the nations who, being devoted to their errors, purposely avoided, as it were, the light of life; what could be more base than to reject their own salvation deliberately? He therefore commands all to look to him and to the precept adds a promise, which gives it greater weight and confirms it more than if he had used a bald command.

23. "By myself I have sworn, my mouth has uttered in all integrity a word that will not be revoked: Before me every knee will bow; by me every tongue will swear." The Lord adds a clearer confirmation of the preceding statement; in consequence of this calling being unusual and marvelous, he adds an oath, as is usually done when something is new and hard to believe. The Jews might have objected that they alone were called by the name of the elect people; but when God confirms it by an oath, this removes all debate. The Lord through the prophet still aims at the same object—namely, that the glory of God will be so visible in the restoration of the church as to arouse the whole world to the admiration of it from the

rising to the setting of the sun—or to express it more briefly, that this demonstration of the power of God shall be so splendid and illustrious as to strike all nations with fear.

24. "They will say of me, 'In the LORD alone are righteousness and strength.'" All who have raged against him will come to him and be put to shame. He shows the nature of true faith and of the true worship of God—that is, when we not only acknowledge or perceive by the understanding that there is a God but also feel what he wishes to be toward us. Whoever is satisfied with a bare knowledge departs very widely from faith, which must invite us to God in such a manner that we shall feel him to be in us.

25. But in the LORD all the descendants of Israel will be found righteous and will exult. Isaiah now makes a brief reply to an objection that might be urged: It seemed absurd to say that the Lord called the Gentiles, who had always been alienated from him. In order to remove this doubt, the prophet declares that the Lord will nevertheless stand by his promises; that even if he chooses the Gentiles, the covenant that he made with the fathers will not fall to the ground, because the elect people will enjoy the privileges of their rank.

Isaiah
Chapter 46

1. Bel bows down, Nebo stoops low; their idols are borne by beasts of burden. The images that are carried about are burdensome, a burden for the weary. Isaiah continues the same subject. We need not trouble ourselves about the chapter divisions, which have not always been done accurately.

Bel and **Nebo** were idols worshiped by the Babylonians and probably were their chief patrons; idolaters always have some particular gods under whose protection, above all others, they consider themselves to be placed. Under their names the prophet includes also the rest of the idols and declares that all the superstitions and false worship of the Gentiles will be overthrown when God shall triumph over their worshipers and lay them low; it shall then be manifest that he is the righteous avenger of his church.

2. They stoop and bow down together; unable to rescue the burden, they themselves go off into captivity. He ridicules the vanity of such gods as these, which have neither strength nor motion, cannot defend or support themselves, and need the aid of beasts of burden to carry them. There is, therefore, here an implied contrast between idols and the true God, who has no need of anything whatever.

3. "Listen to me, O house of Jacob, all you who remain of the house of Israel, you whom I have upheld since you were conceived, and have carried since your birth." Here the prophet beautifully points out the vast difference between the true God and idols. He has already said that the Babylonian gods must be drawn on carts because they consist of dead matter. Now he ascribes a widely different office to the God of Israel—namely, that he carries his people like a mother who carries the child in her womb and afterwards carries it on her bosom. He therefore uses a highly appropriate contrast and concludes in effect from the preceding statements, "Acknowledge that I am the true God and that I differ widely from idols, which are useless and dead weights; for you have known and experienced my power by constant benefits, which I have not ceased to confer upon you from the womb. I have begotten and brought you forth. Even when you were little children, I carried you in my arms, and I will be the guardian of your life until the end."

4. "Even to your old age and gray hairs I am he, I am he who will sustain you. I have made you and I will carry you; I will sustain you and I will rescue you." He uses the same argument again. God does not regard what we deserve but continues his grace toward us, and we ought to draw confidence from this. "You created us not only so that we might be human beings, but so we might be your children; and you will continue until the end to care for us continually like a father and mother."

5. "To whom will you compare me or count me equal? To whom will you liken me that we may be compared?" Here the prophet introduces the Lord as remonstrating with the Jews because they distrusted and doubted his power and, in a word, because they put him on a level with idols and even placed idols above him.

6. "Some pour out gold from their bags and weigh out silver on the scales; they hire a goldsmith to make it into a god, and they bow down and worship it." The prophet has said this before, and now he repeats it in order to fix this doctrine more and more deeply in people's hearts. Superstition has struck its roots so deeply that it cannot be torn out unless the Lord entirely changes our nature.

7. "They lift it to their shoulders and carry it; they set it up in its place, and there it stands. From that spot it cannot move. Though one cries out to it, it does not answer; it cannot save him from his troubles." The picture is still more heightened by the description contained in this verse: Since the idols have no feeling of any kind, those who fly to them to ask assistance must be not only stupid but very obstinate.

8. "Remember this, fix it in mind, take it to heart, you rebels." He means that they are not of sound understanding.

9. "Remember the former things, those of long ago; I am God, and there is no other; I am God, and there is none like me." This is an explanation of the preceding statement; he expresses more fully what he meant—that is, that God has testified of himself by sufficiently numerous proofs and has shown his nature and greatness, and that not merely for two or three days or for a few years but at all times. He had continued his benefits and had incessantly bestowed his grace upon them. Hence the Lord infers that as his divinity is shown so clearly, it ought to prevent them from giving their hearts to anyone else.

10. "I make known the end from the beginning, from ancient times, what is still to come. I say: My purpose will stand, and I will do all that I please." He now explains more fully how he wants the Jews to remember the past; namely, they were taught by constant predictions, as far as

was necessary for their advantage. But from this preface he immediately makes a transition to the hope of deliverance.

11. "From the east I summon a bird of prey; from a far-off land, a man to fulfill my purpose. What I have said, that will I bring about; what I have planned, that will I do." After speaking of God's fore-knowledge and power, God through the prophet applies to his own purpose the general statement he had made. He intended to comfort the Jews and to show that they were not led into captivity in such a manner as to leave no hope of deliverance; therefore he adds a specific instance and promises that Cyrus will come, though it seemed incredible.

The metaphor of **a bird of prey** is beautiful, for the approach of Cyrus was so sudden and unexpected that he seemed to fly like a **bird.** He suddenly invaded Babylon and took it by storm, even when the Babylonians imagined that every entrance was closed against him.

12. "Listen to me, you stubborn-hearted, you who are far from righteousness." Again God rebukes the Israelites because they could not place confidence in him or receive any consolation in adversity. That rebuke is indeed sharp and severe, but it was well deserved by those whose hearts were not soothed by any promise or by any invitation, however gracious, that God addressed to them.

Notice the two epithets that the Lord employs here—**stubborn-hearted** and **far from righteousness.** By these expressions he means that poor, distressed persons shut the door against his assistance on account of their obstinacy because by murmuring or fretting they shake off the fear of God and thus throw themselves into despair, so that they openly rage against God. He addresses the Jews who, though they were almost over-whelmed, yet were swelled with pride and insolence and, having thrown off the fear of God, rose to more and more outrageous madness, as frequently happens to many persons at the present day who are made more rebellious by distress and afflictions.

13. "I am bringing my righteousness near; it is not far away; and my salvation will not be delayed. I will grant salvation to Zion, my splendor to Israel." He means the same thing by **salvation** and **righteousness,** for the most remarkable instance of the **righteousness** of God is when he preserves, guards, and delivers his people. It is not superfluous to say that this is not **delayed,** for he describes the greatness of his mercy by saying that the Lord opens up a course for his justice, notwithstanding the reluctance and opposition of the people.

My splendor to Israel. He connects his **splendor** or glory with the **salvation** of believers (see Ephesians 1:6 and 3:16). The glory of God is most illustriously displayed when he rescues his people from destruction and restores them to liberty, for he wanted an indissoluble bond to connect the salvation of the church with his righteousness.

Isaiah
Chapter 47

1. **"Go down, sit in the dust, Virgin Daughter of Babylon; sit on the ground without a throne, Daughter of the Babylonians. No more will you be called tender or delicate."** Isaiah speaking for the Lord now explains more fully what he had briefly noticed concerning the counsel of God and its execution. He openly describes the destruction of Babylon, because no hope whatever of the return of the people could be entertained so long as the Babylonian monarchy flourished. Accordingly, he has connected two things—namely, the overthrow of that monarchy, and the deliverance of the people that followed it. For the elevated rank of that city was like a deep grave in which the Jews were buried, and when it had been opened, the Lord brought his people back to their former life.

2. **"Take millstones and grind flour; take off your veil. Lift up your skirts, bare your legs, and wade through the streams."** The whole of this description tends to show that there will be a great change among the Babylonians, so that their city, which was formerly held in the highest honor, will be sunk in the lowest disgrace and subjected to outrages of every kind, and thus it will exhibit a striking display of the wrath of God. These are marks of the most degrading slavery, for the lowest slaves were shut up in a mill. The condition of the captives who were reduced to this must therefore have been very miserable, for in other cases captives were sometimes treated mildly and gently by their conquerors. But here he describes a very wretched condition, so believers may not doubt that they will be freely permitted to depart when the Babylonians, who had held them prisoners, are themselves imprisoned.

3. **"Your nakedness will be exposed and your shame uncovered. I will take vengeance; I will spare no one."** This is the conclusion of the previous statement. So long as Babylon was in a flourishing condition, she preserved her reputation and was highly honored, for wealth and power, like

veils, often conceal a great number of sores that, when the veils have been removed, become visible and look quite disgraceful.

4. Our Redeemer—the LORD Almighty is his name—is the Holy One of Israel. The prophet shows what the Lord's purpose is in inflicting punishment on the Babylonians. It is for the salvation of his people.

The Holy One of Israel. This is like saying that it is not for nothing that he has chosen this people and separated it from other nations.

5. "Sit in silence, go into darkness, Daughter of the Babylonians; no more will you be called queen of kingdoms." He continues the same subject, showing that the end of the Babylonian monarchy is at hand. As this seemed incredible, he therefore repeats the same thing by a variety of expressions and repeats what might have been said in a few words; he brings forward lifelike descriptions in order to place the event, as it were, before their eyes. Bidding her to **sit in silence** is an indication of shame or disgrace.

6. "I was angry with my people and desecrated my inheritance; I gave them into your hand." With these words God through his prophet forewarns the Jews, as he has often done before, that the distressing condition of captivity was a scourge that he had inflicted; if it had proceeded from any other source, there would be no remedy from the hand of God.

"And you showed no mercy. Even on the aged you laid a very heavy yoke." In the previous clause God indirectly called the Jews to repentance because by their own crimes they drew down upon themselves so many calamities. Now he accuses the Babylonians of having seized this occasion for exercising cruelty, just as if one were to become the executioner of a child whom a father had put into his hands to be chastised. Hence it follows that the Babylonians have no right to be proud, as if they had subdued the Jews and carried them into captivity by their own power. On the contrary, because they have wickedly abused the victory and treated the captives cruelly, God will be right to punish them.

7. "You said, 'I will continue forever—the eternal queen!' But you did not consider these things or reflect on what might happen." Here the Lord censures the haughtiness of the Babylonians in promising themselves perpetual dominion and in thinking that they could not fall from their great height through any adverse event. The children of this world are intoxicated by prosperity and despise everyone as compared with themselves; but Isaiah mocks this confidence and shows that God regards it with the greatest abhorrence.

8. "Now then, listen, you wanton creature, lounging in your security and saying to yourself, 'I am, and there is none besides me. I will never be a widow or suffer the loss of children.'" God through the prophet again threatens the destruction of Babylon and employs appropriate words for strengthening the hearts of believers, that the prosperity of the Babylonians might not stupefy them or lead them to despondency. He does not address Babylon in order to impress her but to comfort believers.

9. **"Both of these will overtake you in a moment, on a single day: loss of children and widowhood. They will come upon you in full measure, in spite of your many sorceries and all your potent spells."** Because Babylon supposed she was beyond the reach of all danger, the prophet speaking for God threatens her with sore distress—**loss of children and widowhood.** He declares that both calamities will come upon her so that her miserable destitution will expose her to the utmost contempt.

10. **"You have trusted in your wickedness and have said, 'No one sees me.' Your wisdom and knowledge mislead you when you say to yourself, 'I am, and there is none besides me.'"** He explains what he said in verse 9, though it may be extended further, so as to be a censure of the fraud, oppression, violence, and unjust practices by which the Babylonians raised themselves to such great power. Almost all large kingdoms are great robberies, as a distinguished robber admitted; the only way they enlarge their dominions is by extorting from others by violence and oppression and by driving out lawful owners from their dwellings, so they alone may reign at large.

11. **"Disaster will come upon you, and you will not know how to conjure it away. A calamity will fall upon you that you cannot ward off with a ransom; a catastrophe you cannot foresee will suddenly come upon you."** Continuing the subject he had introduced before, God through the prophet ridicules the foolish confidence of the Babylonians, who thought they could foresee every event by the position of the stars. He says they will soon be overtaken by what Scripture threatens generally against everyone who despises God.

12. **"Keep on, then, with your magic spells and with your many sorceries, which you have labored at since childhood. Perhaps you will succeed, perhaps you will cause terror."** The prophet speaks as we are accustomed to speak to desperate men, on whom no warnings produce any good effect: "Do what you usually do. In the end you will know what good the diviners and soothsayers do you."

13. **"All the counsel you have received has only worn you out! Let your astrologers come forward, those stargazers who make predictions month by month, let them save you from what is coming upon you."** He now declares more plainly what he had formerly expressed in somewhat obscure language. All the schemes that Babylon had previously adopted would lead to her ruin, for she nourished within herself a vain confidence arising from a belief in her power and wisdom, as if nothing could harm her.

14. **"Surely they are like stubble; the fire will burn them up. They cannot even save themselves from the power of the flame. Here are no coals to warm anyone; here is no fire to sit by."** With still greater eager-

ness the Lord attacks those astrologers who strengthened the pride of Babylon by their empty boasting; for impostors of this sort usually take all fear of God away from people's hearts by ascribing everything to the stars, so that nothing is left to the providence of God. For this reason he kindles indignation against the Babylonians and says they will be **like stubble** that is quickly consumed. He does not compare them to wood, which is of some use for giving heat, but to **stubble.**

15. **"That is all they can do for you—these you have labored with and trafficked with since childhood. Each of them goes on in his error; there is not one that can save you."** Having threatened destruction to those astronomers, he again returns to the Babylonians and threatens that they must not look for assistance from the quarter from which they expected it, and that they ought not to rely on the vain counsels they had worried about in vain for so long and so eagerly.

Isaiah
Chapter 48

1. **"Listen to this, O house of Jacob, you who are called by the name of Israel and come from the line of Judah, you who take oaths in the name of the LORD and invoke the God of Israel—but not in truth or righteousness—.** . . . God through Isaiah now addresses the Jews (who were also the people he had chiefly in his eye in the whole of chapter 47). The prophet was not sent to the Babylonians but addresses them in the hope that the Jews, to whom he had been specially appointed, should hear him. He foretold the destruction of the Babylonians so that the Jews might calmly wait for deliverance and at the same time might not be afraid of the greatness and power of their enemies, and so that, relying on these promises, they might stand unmoved against all temptations. But the Jews were obstinate and did not believe those promises, and Isaiah foresaw how very hard-hearted and obstinate they would be during their captivity; so he reproves them with greater severity.

2. **". . . you who call yourselves citizens of the holy city and rely on the God of Israel—the LORD Almighty is his name."** He continues the same subject and by different words exposes their false boasting; for they falsely boasted that they were **citizens of the holy city,** which they defiled by their vices and crimes.

3. **"I foretold the former things long ago, my mouth announced them and I made them known; then suddenly I acted, and they came to pass."** God through Isaiah accuses the Jews of ingratitude because they distrust God, who has given every possible proof of his goodness in order to establish them in sincere confidence; he removes their every excuse, saying that he **foretold the former things long ago.**

I understand the predictions of which the prophet speaks to include the ancient prophecies by which God foretold to Abraham (Genesis 15:13-14) that his seed would be held captive and would afterwards be freed again; but afterwards, in their due order, other predictions were added at different times. These were fulfilled partly at one time and partly at another. He shows, therefore, that all that the Lord predicted was justified by events.

4. "For I knew how stubborn you were; the sinews of your neck were iron, your forehead was bronze." Here the Lord solemnly declares through the prophet that it was because the people were so hard-hearted that he spoke of future events—as if he said that he acted more liberally toward them than he ought to have done. Not that this was his only aim, for we know that the chief use of doctrine belongs to believers, who gently submit themselves and cheerfully obey. But Isaiah had to deal with obstinate people, and he rightly says that if their depravity had not been incurable, God's use of many successive predictions to ratify his law would have been effective.

5. "Therefore I told you these things long ago; before they happened I announced them to you so that you could not say, 'My idols did them; my wooden image and metal god ordained them.'" He repeats the same statement (see verse 3) so that when the people have been delivered from Babylon, they might acknowledge God's kindness and not ascribe this deliverance to idols or to fortune. Why does the prophet mention **idols,** seeing that the Jews professed the worship of one God? The answer is that they had been corrupted by associating with the Gentiles and had degenerated into superstitions to such an extent that they had entirely forgotten God.

6. "You have heard these things; look at them all. Will you not admit them? From now on I will tell you of new things, of hidden things unknown to you." This makes it still more clear that the prophet as God's spokesman is speaking of a future captivity and of the redemption that will follow it. He intends to provide for the advantage both of the people of his own time and of posterity. If those who were then alive received no benefit, at least posterity might take warning and repent.

7. "They are created now, and not long ago; you have not heard of them before today. So you cannot say, 'Yes, I knew of them.'" The prophet shows that he is not reasoning about things that are known or that have been learned by actual experience. His object is not merely to correct the haughtiness that is natural to everyone (for they claim for themselves what belongs only to God) but also to show that no part of this event may be ascribed to fortune or to any other cause.

8. "You have neither heard nor understood; from of old your ear has not been open. Well do I know how treacherous you are; you were called a rebel from birth." By these words the Lord means that he has good reason for earnestly persuading and entreating the people to acknowledge that it was by him that they were chastised and afterward delivered from such great distress. The people's rebelliousness might have prompted them to complain that it was useless to repeat this so often.

9. "For my own name's sake I delay my wrath; for the sake of my

praise I hold it back from you, so as not to cut you off." Having reproached the people for the malice that was natural to their fathers from the beginning and that had passed down to children and grandchildren, God now reminds them that it is because of his mercy that they survive. Otherwise they would have deserved to perish a thousand times over. This warning served two purposes. First, believers needed to be supported, so during their captivity they might not lose courage. Second, when they had received permission to return, it was no less important for them to be humbled, that they might acknowledge that they owed their deliverance only to God's undeserved goodness.

10. "See, I have refined you, though not as silver; I have tested you in the furnace of affliction." The Lord shows that he exercises such moderation in chastising his people that he provides for their salvation. Formerly he had said he had spared or would spare them because he had regard to his glory. He now declares that he does indeed wound them, but these wounds are of service to them; it is for the purpose of refining and testing that he chastises them, and we too refine what we do not wish to be lost.

11. "For my own sake, for my own sake, I do this. How can I let myself be defamed? I will not yield my glory to another." Isaiah speaking for the Lord repeats the statement he had already made but adds a question, in the way Hebrew writers often do when they speak of what is absurd: "Is it possible that my name should be profaned?"

12. "Listen to me, O Jacob, Israel, whom I have called: I am he; I am the first and I am the last." We have already explained why the Lord declares his eternity. It is so we may know that he is always like himself, and so we may not measure him by our capacity. He bids us **listen** because we are easily led into errors and are carried away by false opinions, a consequence of refusing to lend our ears to him.

13. "My own hand laid the foundations of the earth, and my right hand spread out the heavens; when I summon them, they all stand up together." Here the prophet explains more clearly what he meant in the preceding verse. After speaking of God's constant and unvarying will toward us, he also praises God's power as evidenced by the works that we see every day. In these works the Lord may be said to present himself to our view; and coming out of his sanctuary, he approaches us by means of them.

14. "Come together, all of you, and listen: Which of the idols has foretold these things? The LORD's chosen ally will carry out his purpose against Babylon; his arm will be against the Babylonians." There can be no doubt that the prophet is addressing the Jews, though here he utters nothing that ought not to be acknowledged by everyone. But because unbelieving and irreligious people have no ears, he does not invite *them* to **listen.** We know that the Jews enjoyed this privilege above other

nations, for God revealed himself to them (Psalm 147:19-20; Romans 3:2). Therefore, much less excusable was either their slothfulness or their obstinacy in paying scarcely any regard to their own prosperity.

15. "I, even I, have spoken; yes, I have called him. I will bring him, and he will succeed in his mission." Once again he reminds the Jews of the predictions and claims for God this honor; by foretelling the event in due time, he has removed all doubt. Next he adds that all that had been foretold will be accomplished. Accordingly, in the repetition of the pronoun—**"I, even I, have spoken"**—there is a double emphasis. First, none but the God of Israel has spoken about future and hidden events. And second, because he is faithful and never deceives, all the events he has foretold will certainly take place.

16. "Come near me and listen to this: From the first announcement I have not spoken in secret; at the time it happens, I am there." And now the Sovereign LORD has sent me, with his Spirit. Again he addresses the Jews. Bidding them draw near, it is as if he goes out to meet them and to receive them kindly. Yet at the same time he indirectly glances at their revolt, showing that they will not be capable of receiving sound doctrine if they do not withdraw from error. It was no small crime that they were so far removed from God, to whom they ought to have been united in friendship. They were at a great distance from him, not in regard to space, but as to the agreement of the heart.

17. This is what the LORD says—your Redeemer, the Holy One of Israel: "I am the LORD your God, who teaches you what is best for you, who directs you in the way you should go." I connect this verse with the four following verses because they relate to the same subject and because in them the Lord promises deliverance to his people, but in such a manner as first to show that it was their own fault that they were reduced to slavery. He did not want the people to grumble and object that if the Lord wished to assist them, it would have been better to be kept in their native country than to be carried away and brought back, for physicians who cure a disease that they might have prevented are held to be less entitled to thanks.

18. "If only you had paid attention to my commands, your peace would have been like a river, your righteousness like the waves of the sea." The people might complain of being carried into captivity, and the prophet tries to counter this grumbling by pointing out the reason, which was that they did not submit to the doctrine of salvation and did not allow themselves to benefit from it.

19. "Your descendants would have been like the sand, your children like its numberless grains; their name would never be cut off nor destroyed from before me." Having many offspring to help the older people contributes to a happy life. When he mentions **sand,** he seems to be alluding to the promise that was made to Abraham (Genesis 22:17). He repeats the same sentiment in slightly different words (as Hebrew writers used to do), substituting **children** for **descendants,** and **grains** for **sand.** In a word, he shows that the people prevented God from causing them to enjoy the fruit of that promise.

20. **"Leave Babylon, flee from the Babylonians! Announce this with shouts of joy and proclaim it. Send it out to the ends of the earth; say, 'The LORD has redeemed his servant Jacob.'"** This is the second clause of this remonstrance, in which the Lord solemnly declares that he will be the Redeemer of his people, though they have been unworthy and ungrateful. He says that he acted like a good teacher, but the people refused to listen to him; and so it was their own fault that they drew down on themselves the punishment of captivity. He now declares his unwearied forbearance, adding that he will still assist them in order to bring them out of slavery. He therefore commands them to go out of the land of Babylon, in which they were captives. Hence we see that God has good cause to remonstrate with us, and yet in his unutterable goodness he relieves our afflictions and assists those who had been unworthy, even those who had insolently rejected his grace.

21. **"They did not thirst when he led them through the deserts; he made water flow for them from the rock; he split the rock and water gushed out."** The Jews did not see the way open for their return, and there were great and dangerous wildernesses in the way; but the prophet asserts the power of God and gives examples of it, that they might not be afraid of any difficulty. He therefore bids them consider whether or not he had sufficient power to rescue their fathers from the slavery of Egypt and to lead them through desolate wildernesses, in which he supplied them with food and **water** and everything that was necessary for them.

22. **"There is no peace,"** says the LORD, **"for the wicked."** The Lord denies **wicked** people that **peace** of which they are unworthy. This is expressly added, so that hypocrites might not, as they usually do, cherish false confidence in these promises. He declares that the promises do not belong to them, in order to shut them out altogether from the hope of salvation. But Isaiah also seems to have had his eye on something else: Since most people, under the influence of impiety, rejected this blessing, many weak and feeble people might hesitate and might be afraid of the majority opinion, just as in our own day we see feeble consciences disturbed when they see the majority of people despise the doctrine of salvation.

Isaiah
Chapter 49

1. Listen to me, you islands; hear this, you distant nations: Before I was born the LORD called me; from my birth he has made mention of my name. After dealing with the future deliverance of the people, Isaiah comes now to Christ, under whose guidance the people were brought out of Babylon, as they had earlier been brought out of Egypt. The earlier prophecy must have been confirmed by this doctrine because they would scarcely have hoped that the Lord would deliver them if they had not looked to Christ, by whom alone desponding souls can be comforted and strengthened; from him they ought not only to expect eternal salvation but ought equally to expect temporal deliverance. Besides, when the prophets are talking about the restoration of the church they commonly bring Christ into view, not only because he wants to be the minister of the church, but because on him was founded the adoption of the people.

2. He made my mouth like a sharpened sword, in the shadow of his hand he hid me; he made me into a polished arrow and concealed me in his quiver. He makes a double comparison here—a **sword** and a **quiver**—in order to denote the power and energy of the doctrine. He also shows why he was called and why he was honored by such a great name—namely, that he might teach, for this is what he means by the word **mouth.** The Father has therefore not appointed Christ to rule as heads of state do, by force of arms and by surrounding himself with other external defenses, making himself an object of terror to his people. His whole authority consists in doctrine. He wants to be sought and acknowledged in the preaching of this doctrine, for he will not be found anywhere else.

3. He said to me, "You are my servant, Israel, in whom I will display my splendor." It is very important to connect this verse with what precedes it, because this shows that the prophet now speaks not only of a single man but of the whole nation; this has not been duly considered by commentators. This passage must not be limited to the person of Christ and ought not to be referred to Israel alone. Here we should pay attention to the customary language of Scripture. When the whole body of the church is spoken of, Christ is brought forward conspicuously so as to include all the children of God. In Christ, who is the Head, are contained the rest of the members; all the seed are indissolubly bound in him. Similarly, under the name **Israel,** by which he means Christ, Isaiah includes the whole body of the people, as members under the Head.

4. But I said, "I have labored to no purpose; I have spent my strength in vain and for nothing. Yet what is due me is in the LORD's hand, and my reward is with my God." The prophet here brings forward a grievous complaint in the name of the church, but he does so in such a manner that we must begin with the Head. Christ complains along with his members, then, that it seems as if his labor were thrown away. He had pronounced a striking commendation on the power and efficacy of the word that proceeds out of his mouth, though it scarcely does any good, and the glory that God demands from its service is not apparent. Therefore he introduces the church as complaining that her labors are fruitless because people do not repent at the preaching of heavenly doctrine. It was very necessary that the prophet should add this. First, we have to understand that the fruit that he mentions is not always visible to human eyes; otherwise we might question the truth of the Word and might doubt if what is so obstinately rejected by many was indeed the Word of God. Second, this was necessary in order that we may advance with unshaken firmness and may commit our labor to the Lord, who will not let it be unproductive in the end. The prophet therefore intended to guard against a dangerous temptation, so that we might not, on account of human obstinacy, lose courage in the middle of our course.

5. And now the LORD says—he who formed me in the womb to be his servant to bring Jacob back to him and gather Israel to himself, for I am honored in the eyes of the LORD and my God has been my strength—. . . In this verse he confirms his previous statement and yields more abundant consolation by repeating his calling and the testimony of conscience, which ought to be regarded by us as a fortress; for nothing gives us greater distress and anxiety than to doubt the authority or direction by which we undertake everything. For this reason Isaiah reminds us of the certainty of our calling.

6. . . . he says: "It is too small a thing for you to be my servant to restore the tribes of Jacob and bring back those of Israel I have kept. I will also make you a light for the Gentiles, that you may bring my salvation to the ends of the earth." Isaiah proceeds still farther and shows that the labor of Christ, and of the whole church, will be glorious not only before God but also before men. Although at first it seems useless, the Lord will cause some fruit to spring from it, contrary to human expectation. It was already enough that our labor should be approved by God;

but when he adds that it will not be unprofitable even in human eyes, this ought still more abundantly to comfort and more vehemently to excite us. Hence it follows that we ought to have good hope of success, but that we ought to leave it to the disposal of God himself, so that the blessing that he promises may be revealed at the proper time, to whatever extent and in whatever manner he shall think proper.

7. This is what the LORD says—the Redeemer and Holy One of Israel—to him who was despised and abhorred by the nation, to the servant of rulers: "Kings will see you and arise, princes will see and bow down, because of the LORD, who is faithful, the Holy One of Israel, who has chosen you." Isaiah pursues the same subject, so that when the people suffered that terrible calamity, they might cherish the hope of a better condition. To make it more certain, he calls God, who promised these things, **the Redeemer and Holy One of Israel.**

Princes will give God great admiration and honor because they will perceive that he is **faithful** to his promises. The Lord wishes to be acknowledged to be true not by mere imagination but by actual experience—that is, by preserving the people whom he has adopted. Let us therefore learn from this that we ought not to judge God's promises by our condition but by his truth, so that when we see nothing before us but destruction and death, we may remember this sentiment, by which the Lord calls to himself the contemptible and abominable.

8. This is what the LORD says: "In the time of my favor I will answer you, and in the day of salvation I will help you." From this verse again we learn more clearly that the prophet, while addressing the whole body of the church, begins with Christ, who is the head.

"I will keep you and will make you to be a covenant for the people, to restore the land and to reassign its desolate inheritances . . ." This makes it clearer still that all that had formerly been said was promised to Christ, not for the sake of his personal advantage but on our behalf. He has been appointed to be the mediator of the covenant because the Jews by their sins had revolted against God, who had made an everlasting covenant with them. It is Christ who renewed the covenant that had been broken or dissolved.

9. ". . . to say to the captives, 'Come out,' and to those in darkness, 'Be free!' They will feed beside the roads and find pasture on every barren hill." These words describe the change that took place when Christ came. And yet the prophet unquestionably intends to administer consolation to the Jews in their extremity. They see that they are almost given up to destruction, and yet he does not want them to think it incredible that they will be restored to a better condition. God through the prophet shows the general nature of Christ's office and explains what is meant by restoring desolate heritages. Before the coming of Christ, we were **captives** under a miserable yoke and kept in **darkness.** These metaphors mean that so long as we are without Christ, we are overwhelmed by a load of all evils (**darkness** excludes everything that relates to the kingdom of Christ—faith, righteousness, truth, innocence, and everything of that nature). We are therefore **in darkness** until Christ says, **"Be free."** We are **captives** until he says, **"Come out."**

10. "They will neither hunger nor thirst, nor will the desert heat or the sun beat upon them. He who has compassion on them will guide them and lead them beside springs of water." He confirms what was said in the former verse: Because there is food in the hand of God, the Jews will not lack provisions for their journey. No doubt he reminds them that when their fathers were threatened with death in the wilderness through a scarcity of bread and of every kind of food, God gave them manna from heaven every day for forty years (Exodus 16:35).

11. "I will turn all my mountains into roads, and my highways will be raised up." Here he directly and expressly discusses the return of the people, for there would have been no point in his promising such great happiness to the church if the people were not to be restored to their former liberty. This means he will remove every obstacle that might prevent the return of the people; the **mountains** seem impassable, but he will make them passable. In short, he will level both the **mountains** and the valleys in order to make it easy for the people to return to Judea. Thus when the church is about to be completely restored, no obstructions, however great and formidable, can hinder God from being finally victorious.

12. "See, they will come from afar—some from the north, some from the west, some from the region of Sinim." While Isaiah promises a return from Babylon, he also extends this prediction to the time of Christ, as may be easily learned from what goes before. We must remember what we said previously: The second birth of the church is described here. He promises not only that the Jews will return to Jerusalem to build the temple, but also that those who had formerly been aliens from the church will be collected from every corner of the world.

13. Shout for joy, O heavens; rejoice, O earth; burst into song, O mountains! For the LORD comforts his people and will have compassion on his afflicted ones. Though Isaiah exhorts and encourages all the godly to engage in thanksgiving, he also aims to confirm the promise that might have been regarded as doubtful; for afflictions trouble our consciences and cause them to waver, so that it is not so easy to rely firmly on the promises of God. In short, people either remain in suspense or tremble or utterly fall and even faint. So long as they are oppressed by fear or anxiety or grief, they scarcely accept any consolation; therefore they need to be confirmed in various ways. The reason Isaiah describes the advantages of this deliverance in such lofty terms is so that believers, though they behold nothing around them but death and ruin, can sustain their heart by the hope of something better.

14. But Zion said, "The LORD has forsaken me, the Lord has forgotten me." In order to magnify his grace the more, God complains that the hearts of the Jews were so narrow and closed that the road was almost shut against him; but he had overcome their wicked thoughts by his great goodness. Yet at the same time he endeavors to correct this fault, so that the deliverance that is offered and, as it were, set before them may be received by them with open hearts, and so that, as he is willing to assist them, they, on the other hand, might be prepared to cherish favorable hopes.

15. "Can a mother forget the baby at her breast and have no compassion on the child she has borne? Though she may forget, I will not forget you!" To put right their lack of trust, he adds an exhortation full of the sweetest consolation. He shows how strong is his anxiety about his people, appropriately comparing himself to a mother whose love toward her offspring is so strong and ardent as to leave far behind it a father's love. Thus he did not satisfy himself with proposing the example of a father (which on other occasions he very frequently employs), but in order to express his very strong affection, he chose to liken himself to a **mother**.

16. "See, I have engraved you on the palms of my hands; your walls are ever before me." This comparison describes the Lord's inconceivable care for us. It is as if he said, "I cannot look at my hands without seeing you in them. I carry you engraved on my heart, so that no forgetfulness can efface you; in a word, I cannot forget you without forgetting myself."

17-18. "Your sons hasten back, and those who laid you waste depart from you. Lift up your eyes and look around; all your sons gather and come to you. As surely as I live," declares the LORD, "you will wear them all as ornaments; you will put them on, like a bride." He arouses the church to look at this magnificent work of restoration as if it were actually before her eyes and to see the crowds of people who will flock into it from every quarter.

When he says the elect of the church **gather,** he means she will be one body under Christ and, as it were, "one fold [under] one shepherd" (see John 10:16).

19. "Though you were ruined and made desolate and your land laid waste, now you will be too small for your people, and those who devoured you will be far away." The prophet uses the metaphor of a ruinous city whose walls and houses are rebuilt, to which the citizens return in such vast numbers that its circumference must be enlarged because its former extent cannot contain them all. Thus he means not only the return of the people from Babylon but the restoration that was effected through Christ—that is, when the church was spread far and wide not only throughout Judea but throughout the whole world.

20. "The children born during your bereavement will yet say in your hearing, 'This place is too small for us; give us more space to live in.'"

Isaiah continues the same subject and, using a different metaphor, promises the restoration of the church. He compares her to a widowed or rather a barren mother, in order to describe her wretched and distressful condition; she was overwhelmed by so many distresses that the memory of the nation appeared to have wholly perished.

21. "Then you will say in your heart, 'Who bore me these? I was bereaved and barren; I was exiled and rejected. Who brought these up? I was left all alone, but these—where have they come from?'" By these words he declares that the restoration of the church, of which he now speaks, will be wonderful; he represents her as amazed at having been restored in a strange and unexpected way.

22. This is what the Sovereign LORD says: "See, I will beckon to the Gentiles, I will lift up my banner to the peoples; they will bring your sons in their arms and carry your daughters on their shoulders." Isaiah confirms what he said a little earlier: Although the church had been **barren** and **bereaved** for a long time, the Lord would cause her to have many off-spring and to be amazed at her own fruitfulness. He does this in order to remove all doubt that might have found its way into their hearts.

He declares that he will give children to the church not only from among the Jews, as formerly, but also from among **the Gentiles.**

23. "Kings will be your foster fathers, and their queens your nursing mothers. They will bow down before you with their faces to the ground; they will lick the dust at your feet. Then you will know that I am the LORD; those who hope in me will not be disappointed." Having spoken of the obedience of **the Gentiles,** he shows that this relates not just to the common people but to **kings** also. He compares **kings** to **foster fathers** who bring up other people's children, and **queens** to **nursing mothers** who give out their labor for hire. Why so? Because **kings** and **queens** will supply everything necessary for nourishing the offspring of the church. Having driven out Christ from their dominions, they will now acknowledge him to be the supreme King and will give him all honor, obe-dience, and worship.

24. Can plunder be taken from warriors, or captives rescued from the fierce? It might have been thought incredible that the Jews should be rescued out of the hands of so powerful an enemy, by whom they had been taken in fair battle and reduced to slavery. Isaiah therefore adds this question as uttered by the whole of the common people (among whom it was probably the general gossip).

25. But this is what the LORD says: "Yes, captives will be taken from warriors, and plunder retrieved from the fierce." However they may boast of having a right to govern and glory in an empty title, the Lord declares that they are most wicked robbers. He threatens to be an avenger and to snatch their prey from them. God does not overturn just dominion;

hence it follows that the dominion they usurped over the people of God was mere robbery and wicked tyranny.

"**I will contend with those who contend with you, and your children I will save.**" We derive great consolation from knowing that we are united with God by so close a bond that he sets himself in opposition to all who contend with us. In short, he declares that he is the enemy of our enemies. Notice also that when we are not oppressed by enemies, we are restored to liberty and life. When we are saved, it is not some human achievement; so no one may say that he himself has done what God commands us to expect as an extraordinary blessing from himself alone.

26. "I will make your oppressors eat their own flesh; they will be drunk on their own blood, as with wine. Then all mankind will know that I, the LORD, am your Savior, your Redeemer, the Mighty One of Jacob." When the Lord delivers his people from destruction, he will be acknowledged by everyone as the God of Israel and the true and only God. He intended it to be a demonstration of his divinity when he openly manifested himself to be the Redeemer and Savior of his people.

Isaiah
Chapter 50

1. This is what the LORD says: "Where is your mother's certificate of divorce with which I sent her away?" There are various interpretations of this passage. To have a general understanding of it, we must notice that the Lord everywhere tells us that he is like a husband and that his people are united to him like a wife. This is a spiritual marriage that has been consecrated by his eternal doctrine and sealed by the blood of Christ. He takes us under his protection as a dearly loved wife, on condition that we remain faithful to him in chastity. So when we have been false to him, he rejects us; and then he is said to issue a lawful divorce against us, as when a husband sent an adulterous wife away.

Thus when the Jews were suffering so many great calamities and found it easy to conclude that God had rejected and divorced them, the cause of the divorce came to be the subject of inquiry. People are usually eloquent in apologizing for themselves and endeavor to put the blame on God; and the Jews complained about their condition at that time as if the Lord had done wrong in divorcing them. They were far from thinking that the promises had been set aside and the covenant annulled by their crimes. They even laid the blame on their ancestors, as if they were being punished for other people's sins (see Ezekiel 18:2). They all said this; so the Lord asks them to produce the **certificate of divorce** that proves they are blameless and have been rejected without reason.

A **certificate of divorce** was granted to wives who had been divorced unjustly. By it the husband had to testify that his wife had lived chastely and honorably, so that it was evident the only ground for divorce was that she did not please the husband. Thus the woman was at liberty to go away, and the blame rested solely on the husband whose sullenness and bad temper was the reason for the divorce (see Deuteronomy 24:1). Jesus shows that Moses gave the people this divorce law because their hearts were "hard" (Matthew 19:8). It is a highly appropriate metaphor, therefore, by which the Lord here shows that he is not the author of the divorce, but that the people went away by their own fault, following their own desires; they had utterly broken the marriage bond. It is as if he were saying that they threw off the accusation and laid the blame on God as if they had been provided with a defense, whereas in truth they had violated the marriage bond and could produce nothing to make the divorce lawful.

"Or to which of my creditors did I sell you?" He uses another metaphor to demonstrate the same thing. When a person was overwhelmed by debt, he had to give his children in payment. The Lord, therefore, asks in effect, "Have I been constrained to do this? Have I sold your children or given them in payment to another creditor? Am I like a spendthrift or a bad manager who allows himself to be overwhelmed by debt?" In other words, "You cannot bring this reproach against me; so it is clear that you have been sold and reduced to slavery because of your transgressions."

"Because of your sins you were sold; because of your transgressions your mother was sent away." The Lord defends his majesty against all slander, saying that it is the Jews' own fault they have been divorced and **sold.** The same expression is used by Paul when he says that we are sold as slaves to sin (Romans 7:14), but in a different sense—in the same way as Hebrew writers speak of abandoned people whose wickedness is desperate. Here the prophet merely intends to charge the people with guilt because by their own transgressions they have brought upon themselves all the evils they endure.

Did the Lord divorce his heritage? Did he nullify the covenant? Certainly not. Rather the Lord is said to **divorce** his heritage (as in Psalm 89:39 he is said to renounce the covenant) because that is the only conclusion that can be drawn from present appearances. When he did not bestow his usual favor on them, it was a kind of divorce or rejection. In a word, we should note these two contrasts: The wife is divorced either through the husband's fault or because she is unchaste and adulterous; and children are sold either because of their father's poverty or through their own fault.

2. "When I came, why was there no one?" This could be a reason why the people brought a mass of evils on themselves by provoking God's anger and also by their obstinacy cut off the hope of obtaining pardon and salvation. But I think God is going still further. He has explained that he had good reason for divorcing the people because they had of their own accord given themselves up to slavery when they might have been free; now he adds that it is still not he who prevents them from being set free straightaway. In verse 1 he showed that the Jews were wholly to blame; here in verse 2 he says it is their own fault that they grow old and rot in their distresses. The Lord was ready to help them, but they rejected his grace and kindness. Why did the Lord come if not to stretch his hand out to the Jews? So it follows that it was fair for them to be deprived of his grace, for they would not receive it. The Lord is said to come when he gives any token of his presence. He approaches by the preaching of the Word and by various benefits that he bestows on us and by the tokens that he uses to show us his fatherly goodness (see Deuteronomy 4:33). He constantly held out to them the hope of pardon, urging them to repent; so he has good reason to speak of it as monstrous when there was **no one** to meet him.

"When I called, why was there no one to answer?" The same idea is repeated in different words. When God calls, we ought to be ready and submissive. God offered to end their distress, but he was obstinately despised, as if he were speaking to deaf mutes. They are to blame, then, for not having been delivered sooner. Nor can they excuse themselves by saying they had heartily desired salvation but had not obtained it. His power was no less, and he would not have hesitated to stretch out his hand to them in distress if they had not wickedly refused his aid.

"Was my arm too short to ransom you? Do I lack the strength to rescue you? By a mere rebuke I dry up the sea, I turn rivers into a desert; their fish rot for lack of water and die of thirst." He points out his power in rescuing the people from Egypt. They should not imagine that he is less powerful now; they should acknowledge that their sins hinder the manifestation of that power.

3. "I clothe the sky with darkness and make sackcloth its covering." He also mentions the thick darkness that was spread over all Egypt for three days (Exodus 10:22). At that time the heavens were clothed as with a mourning dress; fine weather makes us glad, but darkness makes us sad. (If anyone prefers to see these as general statements, he can; but I think it is probable that he is glancing at the story of the deliverance from Egypt, from which it might easily be inferred that God, who had helped their ancestors so miraculously, was prevented from helping their present distress by their ingratitude.)

4. The Sovereign LORD has given me an instructed tongue, to know the word that sustains the weary. Having twice convicted them of guilt, the prophet adds a consolation in his usual manner; for when the Lord covers us with shame, he intends immediately to free us from it. So although Isaiah has shown that the people have been rejected for the best possible reasons and have perished through their own fault, he promises them help. And because more than usual proof was needed to believe such a thing, he begins by saying that God has sent him. This passage is usually explained as referring to Christ, because later on he says he has been beaten, and nowhere does it say that happened to Isaiah. But there is no great force in this argument, for David complains that his garments were divided (Psalm 22:18), which applies literally to Christ (Matthew 27:35; John 19:24), and yet it does not follow that this did not happen to David himself. For my own part I have no doubt that Isaiah represents all God's servants—not only those from the beginning but those who were to come.

309

He says that the Lord has given him **an instructed tongue,** so that the promises by which he cheers the people might have greater weight. Our faith wavers if we suspect that someone speaks from himself alone; and the condition of that people was so wretched that no human arguments could induce them to hope for deliverance. It amounts to this: The message of approaching salvation is brought to them from heaven; and if people do not receive it, that proves how rebellious and disobedient they are. The prophet means these words literally, in order to make people believe what he says; but we may infer from them generally that no one is fit to teach who has not first been qualified by God. This reminds all godly teachers to ask the Spirit of God for what they could not otherwise possess. They must indeed study diligently, so as not to ascend the pulpit until they have been fully prepared; but they must hold to the principle that everything necessary for discharging their office is a gift of the Holy Spirit. And, indeed, if they were not organs of the Holy Spirit, it would be extremely rash to stand up publicly in the name of God.

The word **weary** is applied to those who are overwhelmed by many afflictions (see Isaiah 40:29; Matthew 11:28). He therefore means that God has been his teacher, that he may be able to soothe wretched people by appropriate consolation. The most important duty of ministers of the Word is to comfort wretched people who are oppressed by afflictions. We are also taught what each of us ought chiefly to seek in the Scriptures—namely, that we may have doctrine appropriate and suitable for relieving our distresses.

He wakens me morning by morning. Here the prophet testifies that the Lord so cares for the wretched and oppressed that he helps them at the appropriate time. I do acknowledge that we are often destitute of consolation; but though God often permits us to languish, he knows every moment what is suitable for meeting our need by his aid. If his assistance is somewhat late, this happens through our own fault, when we withdraw from his grace both by our indolence and by rebellion. However, he always watches carefully and runs to give aid. Even when we resist, he calls us to him, that we may be refreshed by tasting his grace and kindness. The phrase **morning by morning** expresses continuance and earnestness, that we may not think he is liable to sudden impulses as we are; he will not cast off or quickly forget those whom he has undertaken to guard. On the contrary, he continues to make them the objects of his grace until the end and never leaves them without consolation.

. . . . wakens my ear to listen like one being taught. God teaches all whose ministry he intends to employ for the salvation of his church. It would have been nothing much to be instructed in human fashion, if they had not within them the Spirit of God as their instructor. The only people who are good teachers are those who have been good scholars. Those who do not deign to learn because they think they are wise enough are doubly fools, since God judges learned only those who permit themselves to be taught before becoming teachers, so that they may have clear knowledge of the things they communicate to others and may only teach publicly what they can testify has come from God.

5. The Sovereign LORD has opened my ears, and I have not been rebellious; I have not drawn back. He repeats what he has already said and here includes not just doctrine but the whole calling. The Lord opens a person's ears when he powerfully affects that person's heart and moves him to obedience (see Psalm 40:6; John 6:45). The meaning may be rendered, "God's servant undertakes nothing at random; but being fully convinced of God's calling, he discharges the office of a teacher, though it is laborious and difficult, because he is ready to obey."

6. I offered my back to those who beat me, my cheeks to those who pulled out my beard. He contrasts his unshaken courage with the reproaches, jeers, and insolence of wicked people. This is like saying, "Whatever resistance may be attempted by those who despise God, he will baffle all their insults, so that he will never repent of the labors he has undertaken." This passage shows plainly that ministers of the Word cannot perform their office faithfully without being fiercely assailed on all sides. As soon as Isaiah says he has obeyed God's command, he adds that he has **offered** his **back to those who beat** him. When faithful servants of God administer the doctrine of the Word, they must endure fighting, reproach, hatred, slander, and various attacks from adversaries who loathe the warning and reproving those servants have to undertake. Isaiah describes not only persecutions by wicked people but the world's reproach, because wicked people want to be thought to have good cause for opposing the ministers of the Word and persecuting their doctrine, and they wish those ministers to be regarded as criminals and malefactors, universally hated and abhorred. For these reasons they heap slander on them, as we know from people calling us heretics, deceivers, seditious people, and so on, just as Christ and the apostles found (Matthew 27:63; John 7:12; Acts 16:20).

I did not hide my face from mocking and spitting. He says that external foes spat and inflicted blows on him, and he glances at the slanders he is compelled to bear from internal foes. People are always springing up from the very bosom of the church to attack the prophets insolently. Those who wish to serve God must be prepared to endure all these things calmly, walking through "bad report" and through "good report" (2 Corinthians 6:8). This doctrine applies to all believers but especially to teachers of the Word.

7. Because the Sovereign LORD helps me, I will not be disgraced. The prophet tells us the source of the great courage that he and God's other servants need: It comes from God's assistance. So he urges others also to be firm and gives a sort of picture of the condition of all the ministers of the Word. By turning aside form the world, they may turn wholly to God and have their eyes entirely fixed on him. There will never be any contest so arduous that they will not gain the victory by trusting such a leader.

Therefore have I set my face like flint, and I know I will not be put to shame. Whatever happens, he will not be afraid. Terror or alarm, like other passions, is visible in people's faces. The servants of God, being treated so shamefully, would inevitably have sunk under such attacks if they had not withstood them like a stone (see also Jeremiah 1:18 and Ezekiel 3:9). Isaiah boldly declares his conviction that things will turn out well in the end. Special help is promised to godly teachers and ministers of the Word. The fiercer Satan's attacks, and the stronger the world's hostility, the more the Lord defends and guards them by extraordinary protection. Hence we should conclude that all those who, when they come to the contest, tremble and lose courage have never been properly qualified for discharging their office. Anyone who does not know how to strive does not know how to serve God and the church and is not fit to administer the doctrine of the Word.

8. He who vindicates me is near. Who then will bring charges against me? Nothing the prophet describes is unique to himself. He testifies how the Lord will always act toward faithful ministers. Whoever has the testimony that God has sent him and knows that he is discharging his office faithfully will boldly despise all adversaries and will not be moved by their reproaches, for he is vindicated by the Lord.

Let us face each other! Who is my accuser? Let him confront me! Godly teachers ought to have such confidence that they will not hesitate to defy their adversaries boldly. Satan, with his agents, does not always dare attack openly, especially when he fights by lies; he tries to take people by surprise, ambushing them and tunneling underground. But God's servants are not afraid to face the enemy openly and argue with him, if the adversaries are willing. The force of truth is so great that it does not dread the light of day.

Godly ministers should be ready to give a reason for their doctrine. But who is willing to listen patiently to them? Adversaries will approach, of course, but they have their swords drawn to kill them, and they sharpen their tongues to tear them in pieces with all sorts of slander. In short, their whole defense consists in arms or deceitful tricks; they do not dare use scriptural arguments to do battle. We, therefore, can rely on the justice of our cause and freely defy them to fight us. They may condemn us without listening to our vindication; they may have many people to support the sentence they have pronounced. But we have no reason to be afraid. God, whose cause we plead, is our Judge and will acquit us in the end.

9. It is the Sovereign LORD who helps me. Who is he that will condemn me? Isaiah is speaking of the ministry of the Word, which the Lord will defend against the attacks of the wicked. He will not let his people be overwhelmed by their fraud of violence.

They will all wear out like a garment; the moths will eat them up. Though deadly foes attack him, he still maintains his position boldly, because all who fight against the Word of God will fall away through their own frailty. People of this world may shine like dazzling garments but will perish; but believers, who now are covered with filth, will in the end obtain new brightness and will shine brilliantly like the stars.

10. **Who among you fears the LORD and obeys the word of his servant?** Having spoken of God's invincible aid, by which all prophets are protected, Isaiah addresses believers, telling them to let themselves be guided by the Word of God and become obedient. From this we may infer how far a holy boasting raised him above his slanderers. The vast numbers of wicked people had great influence among the Jews at that time, and the danger was that they would extinguish the faith of a small band of believers. Isaiah addresses them separately, that they may detach themselves from the crowd and not take part in anything wicked that God has condemned.

Wherever there is no religion and no fear of God, there can be no way open to teaching. We see how audaciously people reject doctrine, though in other respects they wish to be thought clever and wise. They are swollen with pride; they detest modesty and humility and are stupid regarding the wisdom of God. True fear of God will never be found if people do not listen to his Word.

He speaks **the word of his servant** rather than "of God," for God wishes to be heard through his ministers, whom he uses to teach us. Isaiah speaks first of himself and then of everyone else who has been invested with the same office. There is an implied contrast between the obedience that he demands and the wicked eagerness to despise doctrine that we see in irreligious people (who by their insolence encourage many idle and foolish people to practice similar contempt).

Let him who walks in the dark, who has no light, trust in the name of the LORD and rely on his God. Believers might have objected that the fruit of their piety was not visible, but that they were wretchedly afflicted, as if they had lived a life of abandoned wickedness. The prophet anticipates this complaint by affirming that believers may have been harshly treated so far, but it is not in vain that they obey God and his Word. If they walk **in the dark,** they will at length enjoy the **light** of the Lord. By darkness the prophet here means not the ignorance or blindness of human understanding, but the afflictions that almost always overwhelm the children of God. This is the consolation he mentioned in verse 4.

11. **But now, all you who light fires and provide yourselves with flaming torches, go, walk in the light of your fires and of the torches you have set ablaze.** He criticizes the Jews for choosing to kindle their

own **light** instead of drawing near to the light of God. Note the contrast between the light of God and the **light** of men—that is, between the consolation brought to us by the Word of God and the empty words of comfort uttered by human beings when they struggle to alleviate their distress with idle and useless things. The prophet has promised light to believers who obey the Lord's voice; now he shows that the Jews have rejected this light in order to kindle another **light** for themselves. He warns them that ultimately they will be consumed by this **light,** as by fire. Christ also criticized the Jews for enjoying John's light (John 5:35) because they misused his official character in order to obscure or rather to extinguish the glory of Christ. To bring forward John's official character in order to cover with darkness the glory of Christ was nothing but extinguishing the light of God shining in a mortal man, in order to kindle another light for themselves, not that it might guide them by pointing out the road, but so that by foolishly rejoicing in it they might be driven about in every direction.

When Isaiah speaks about their **torches,** he is hinting at their various thoughts by which they were carried about uncertainly sometimes in one direction and sometimes in another. In this way he makes fun of their folly because they willingly and eagerly ran wherever their foolish pleasures drew them. "You will know by experience how useless and transitory your light is," he says in effect, "when your unwarranted hopes have deceived you." Other commentators interpret this as meaning that wicked people kindle against themselves the fire of God's wrath; but the prophet was looking higher, and that idea does not seem to agree with this passage.

This is what you shall receive from my hand: You will lie down in torment. Wicked people are drunk with false confidence and think they are beyond the reach of all danger; they view the future with reckless disregard and trust to their own light (that is, to the means of defense with which they imagine themselves to be very abundantly provided). But the Lord declares that they will **lie down in torment** and that this will come from his **hand.** In a word, people who have forsaken the light of the Word and who seek consolation from some other quarter will perish miserably.

Isaiah
Chapter 51

1. **"Listen to me, you who pursue righteousness and who seek the LORD: Look to the rock from which you were cut and to the quarry from which you were hewn."** The prophet now exhorts the Jews not to despair because they are few in number; for they had been cut down and diminished to such a degree that they appeared to be on the verge of being reduced to nothing, with little or no hope that anyone would succeed them. He therefore reminds them of their origin, that they might know that though they are a small remnant, God can increase and multiply them. He bids them to contemplate their father Abraham (verse 2) who, though he was a single individual, grew to a vast number and received from God a numerous posterity. Hence they might infer that God, who in so short a period had multiplied their ancestors, would in the future multiply them also, because his power has not been diminished and his will has not been changed.

2. **"Look to Abraham, your father, and to Sarah, who gave you birth. When I called him he was but one, and I blessed him and made him many."** This application plainly shows the point of this exhortation of the prophet. It was to encourage the hearts of believers to cherish the hope of a better condition. God says, **"When I called him he was but one"** not only because Abraham had no one else when he was called out of his country, but because the Lord led him to dwell in the land of Canaan without children up to a worn-out old age, so that he had no hope of having children, especially because Sarah also was barren. And when at length, as a solace for their childless condition, one son was given to them, not long afterwards he seemed to be led to the slaughter. Yet the Lord increased and enriched Abraham with a great number of children.

3. **"The LORD will surely comfort Zion and will look with compassion on all her ruins; he will make her deserts like Eden, her wastelands like the garden of the LORD."** The prophet shows that in the person of

Abraham there was exhibited an example that applies to all ages; as the Lord produced from one man so numerous an offspring, so he will also people his church by wonderful and unknown methods—and not just once, but whenever she is thought to be childless and solitary. The verse may be explained as meaning, "The Lord will comfort his church not only when she is in a flourishing condition, but also when she is desolate and reduced to solitude." She must have been laid desolate, and her frightful ruins must have brought her to the verge of destruction before she felt the aid that is here described.

"Joy and gladness will be found in her, thanksgiving and the sound of singing." He means that the change will be so great that the church will no longer groan or complain; for so long as the church was oppressed by a harsh captivity, nothing could be heard in her but mourning and lamentation. Now restored, she will rejoice and give thanks to God. Thus we are also exhorted to have gratitude, that we may burst out into praise and thanksgiving to God when we experience his goodness.

4. "Listen to me, my people; hear me, my nation: The law will go out from me; my justice will become a light to the nations." There are good reasons why the Lord so frequently demands to be heard. We know by experience how slow we are to hear him, especially in adversity; and even when we have great need of consolation, we reject it by our impatience, and we faint. As sore afflictions press upon us, then, we ought to endeavor more earnestly to enlarge our hearts and to rouse ourselves and shake off our slothfulness, so that we may receive consolation. What is here demanded is that we sustain our hearts by patience until the season of grace comes in full.

5. "My righteousness draws near speedily, my salvation is on the way, and my arm will bring justice to the nations. The islands will look to me and wait in hope for my arm." God through his prophet confirms the former doctrine. The **righteousness** of the Lord relates to those who know by experience that he is righteous. While the people were oppressed by cruel bondage, they knew, indeed, that they were being justly punished for their sins; but they might wonder that they were so much forsaken, because the worship of God ceased, and his name was blasphemed by wicked people who pursued their wicked career without punishment. In order, therefore, to bring them some consolation, the prophet promises that God will speedily assist them, so that everyone acknowledges that he is faithful and just.

6. "Lift up your eyes to the heavens, look at the earth beneath; the heavens will vanish like smoke, the earth will wear out like a garment and its inhabitants die like flies. But my salvation will last forever, my righteousness will never fail." When we see such great changes in the world, we are apt to think that the church comes within the same violent influence. Therefore we need to have our minds raised above the ordinary course of nature; otherwise, the salvation of the church will appear to hang on a thread and to be carried hither and thither by the billows and tempests. Yet we may see both in heaven and on earth how wisely God regulates all things, with what fatherly kindness he upholds and defends his workmanship and the frame of the world, and how fair he is in providing for all his creatures.

7. **"Hear me, you who know what is right, you people who have my law in your hearts: Do not fear the reproach of men or be terrified by their insults."** When wicked people enjoy prosperity, they laugh at our faith and ridicule our distresses and afflictions. The prophet, speaking for God, therefore urges believers to be patient, that they might not dread their reproaches or be dismayed by their slanders. The reason given is that their prosperity will not last long.

8. **"For the moth will eat them up like a garment; the worm will devour them like wool. But my righteousness will last forever, my salvation through all generations."** Because the believing servants of God must endure many reproaches and slanders from the enemies of the Word, the prophet exhorts and encourages them to bear it courageously. It frequently happens that we are more deeply moved by the harsh insults of other people than by fire and sword; but we ought to reckon it praise and glory to be the object of their contempt and abhorrence.

9. **Awake, awake! Clothe yourself with strength, O arm of the LORD; awake, as in days gone by, as in generations of old. Was it not you who cut Rahab to pieces, who pierced that monster through?** Here the prophet teaches us that when God cheers us by his promises, we ought also to pray earnestly that he will do what he has promised. He does not comfort us in order to render us slothful, but that we may be inflamed with a stronger desire to pray and may continually exercise our faith. The prophet speaks according to our feelings; for we think God is asleep as long as he does not come to relieve our needs; and the Lord indulges us so far as to permit us to speak and pray according to the feeling of our weakness.

10. **Was it not you who dried up the sea, the waters of the great deep, who made a road in the depths of the sea so that the redeemed might cross over?** Isaiah does not describe all the miracles that God performed when he brought his people out of the bondage of Egypt, but he intended to include in a few words all that are related by Moses, so that the Jews, having been briefly addressed, might consider the various ways in which the Lord had demonstrated his power. The drying up of the Red Sea is mentioned not only on account of the extraordinary excellence of the miracle, but because the numerous miracles that preceded it aimed to get the people (who had been rescued from unjust violence and tyranny) to pass into the Promised Land.

11. **The ransomed of the LORD will return. They will enter Zion with**

singing; everlasting joy will crown their heads. Gladness and joy will overtake them, and sorrow and sighing will flee away. He now describes more plainly what he had briefly remarked upon. After describing the magnificent works of God by which he had displayed his power in Egypt in order to deliver his people, Isaiah concludes that neither the sea, nor the lofty rocks, nor the whirlpools, nor even hell itself can prevent God from leading forth his people out of Babylon. To confirm this more fully and to apply that example, he calls them ransomed, that they might know that when God calls himself the deliverer of his people, this applies to them, and so they might not doubt that in delivering them he will produce an example such as had already been seen.

12. "I, even I, am he who comforts you. Who are you that you fear mortal men, the sons of men, who are but grass ... ?" Here the Lord not only promises grace and salvation to the Jews but remonstrates with them for refusing to believe him and for valuing his power less than they ought. It is exceedingly base to tremble at human threats to such a degree as to care nothing about God's assistance; for he displays his power for this purpose—that he may at least fortify us against every attack.

13. ". . . that you forget the LORD your Maker, who stretched out the heavens and laid the foundations of the earth, that you live in constant terror every day because of the wrath of the oppressor, who is bent on destruction? For where is the wrath of the oppressor?" It is not enough to imagine that there is some God; rather we ought to acknowledge and embrace him as ours.

Who stretched out the heavens and laid the foundations of the earth. God had shown special kindness to his people; to this the prophet adds his boundless power, which he contrasts with the weakness of the sons of men, who are but grass (verse 12).

14. "The cowering prisoners will soon be set free; they will not die in their dungeon, nor will they lack bread." God hastens to come and deliver his people, so that they come safely out of the dungeon. The Lord does not promise his people some sudden assistance just to bring them out of prison, but also so that, having been delivered, they may be the objects of his kindness. He promises everything necessary for their food and support, that they may be convinced that he will always take care of them; his practice is not only to assist his people for a moment but to remain with them continually.

15. "For I am the LORD your God, who churns up the sea so that its waves roar—the LORD Almighty is his name." Again the Lord declares his power; for so great is people's unbelief and sluggishness that the very smallest temptation shows that they are not fully convinced of it, even though it is frequently declared. They quickly fall back upon themselves when they are hard-pressed by afflictions; and when they hear that *anything* is in God's power, they do not think it applies to them.

16. "I have put my words in your mouth and covered you with the shadow of my hand—I who set the heavens in place, who laid the foundations of the earth, and who say to Zion, 'You are my people.'" Again Isaiah returns to the doctrine he had stated before—namely, that the Lord comforts his church. So he now says that God put into the mouth of the prophets what they should say. Hence we may infer that these words do not proceed from men, who often prove false, but from God who cannot lie (see Titus 1:2). The Lord speaks to all the prophets—first to Isaiah, and then to the rest in turn; but at last we must come to Christ. These things must not be limited either to Isaiah or to Christ but must be extended to all the prophets. The Lord wants believers to hear the consolation from the prophets as if he were present and addressed them, and he even declares that he speaks openly by their mouth.

17. Awake, awake! Rise up, O Jerusalem, you who have drunk from the hand of the LORD the cup of his wrath, you who have drained to its dregs the goblet that makes men stagger. The church was about to endure grievous calamities, and therefore the prophet fortifies her by consolation and meets a doubt that might arise, for the Jews, oppressed by tyrants, saw no fulfillment of these promises. The meaning therefore is that the church, though afflicted and tossed about in various ways, will nevertheless be set up again, so as to regain her full vigor. By the word **awake** he recalls her, as it were, from death and the grave, as if he had said that no ruins will be so dismal, no desolations so horrible, as to be able to stop God from effecting this restoration.

18. Of all the sons she bore there was none to guide her; of all the sons she reared there was none to take her by the hand. He describes the sorest calamity of the church: She receives no sympathy or consolation from her own children. This accumulated misery is described by him in order that, though her condition is desperate, she may still expect consolation from God, who will never disappoint his servants, even if they sink to the depths. Although the church has been forsaken by men, and even by those whom she nourished in her bosom and carried in her arms, yet she will be helped by God.

19. These double calamities have come upon you—who can comfort you?—ruin and destruction, famine and sword—who can console you? Here Isaiah promises the church that things will eventually be different, for the Lord will rescue her from the deepest abyss. God threatens extreme wretchedness, so that believers may prepare to be patient and not cease to send up prayers and supplications from the depth of their distresses. The general meaning is that the church will be burdened with afflictions of every kind, so that she will appear to be on the brink of utter ruin. She will endure very heavy calamities from outside and will not receive any aid or sympathy from her own children.

20. Your sons have fainted; they lie at the head of every street, like

antelope caught in a net. They are filled with the wrath of the LORD and the rebuke of your God. He describes more fully the lamentable and wretched condition of the church, saying that her children are prostrate. A mother cannot experience any grief more bitter than to have her children slain before her eyes, and not one or two of them, but so great a number as to fill the roads with the slaughter.

The metaphor of being **caught in a net** is taken from the capture of wild animals. Even the strongest of them have been caught in snares.

21. Therefore hear this, you afflicted one, made drunk, but not with wine. He now shows more clearly why he spoke of the calamities of the church. It was so believers might be fully persuaded that they would obtain consolation from God, though they were reduced to the extremity of distress. But why does he call the church wretched when nothing is more happy than to be God's people, and that happiness cannot be taken away by any tribulations? The answer is that she seems to be **afflicted,** and the Lord addresses her in that way because, as we have already said, he helps the wretched and succors the destitute.

22. This is what your Sovereign LORD says, your God, who defends his people: "See, I have taken out of your hand the cup that made you stagger; from that cup, the goblet of my wrath, you will never drink again." These are not random epithets that the prophet is adding to the name Jehovah (that he is the Lord or Defender of his church, that he is God, and lastly, that he is her Avenger). We ought always to consider the nature of our relation to God; he addresses us in a familiar manner in consequence of having once chosen us to be his people by uniting himself to us in an everlasting covenant. This preface encouraged the Jews in ancient times not to hesitate to embrace what is here promised; and at the present day the same argument applies to a new people, who have been taken under God's care and protection no less than they.

23. "I will put it into the hands of your tormentors, who said to you, 'Fall prostrate that we may walk over you.' And you made your back like the ground, like a street to be walked over." This is another part of the consolation, in which the Lord promises that he will not only deliver the church from those heavy distresses but will also lay upon her enemies the calamities with which she is afflicted. If therefore we are afflicted, our condition will quickly be changed, and our enemies will be severely punished. The temporary punishments that God inflicts on them are the beginnings of the eternal punishment to which they will finally be condemned.

Isaiah
Chapter 52

1. Awake, awake, O Zion, clothe yourself with strength. Put on your garments of splendor, O Jerusalem, the holy city. The uncircumcised and defiled will not enter you again. Isaiah confirms the previous teaching to arouse still more those who had been weighed down by grief and sorrow. He had to add these things as spurs, so that the doctrine might penetrate their drowsy hearts more easily; for he addresses the church, which appeared to be in a benumbed and drowsy condition. He bids her **awake,** that she may collect her strength and revive her courage. He repeats it a second time, and quite rightly, for it is difficult to arouse and reanimate those whose hearts have been struck and even laid prostrate by a sense of God's anger.

2. Shake off your dust; rise up, sit enthroned, O Jerusalem. Free yourself from the chains on your neck, O captive Daughter of Zion. He explains more fully the deliverance of the church. When he says **shake off your dust,** let us not on that account think that our liberty is in our power, so that we can obtain it whenever we think fit; only God can raise us from the dust or lift us up when we are prostrate and, by breaking or loosing our chains, set us at liberty. Why then does the prophet use the imperative? It is unreasonable to demand what we cannot perform. The answer is that the imperative form of address has a much more powerful tendency to arouse than if he had employed plain narrative; therefore he declares that when God has restored her to her former freedom, she will come out of the mire.

3. For this is what the LORD says: "You were sold for nothing, and without money you will be redeemed." God is not like a spendthrift who is compelled to sell his children or offer them in payment. So in this passage he declares that they were **sold for nothing** and were given up to their enemies for no other reason than because they had provoked him by their sins. There will be no greater difficulty in delivering them than in giving them up to their enemies. Let it suffice to know that when God chooses to deliver his people, it will not be necessary to make a pecuniary bargain with the Babylonians. In spite of their opposition, he will have no difficulty in driving them away from their unjust possession.

4. **For this is what the Sovereign LORD says: "At first my people went down to Egypt to live; lately, Assyria has oppressed them."** By **Assyria** he means the Babylonians, who were under a united monarchy with the Assyrians; but he takes special notice of **Assyria** because that nation was the first to grievously distress the Jews and prepared the way for captivity.

5. **"And now what do I have here?" declares the LORD. "For my people have been taken away for nothing, and those who rule them mock," declares the LORD. "And all day long my name is constantly blasphemed."** He confirms that it is unreasonable that he should silently permit his people to be oppressed any longer. By these words he is somewhat critical of his own delay, as if he said, "Shall I not stretch out my hand? Shall I not avenge my people? If Pharaoh did not hinder me, though he was a lawful master, shall the violence of robbers hinder me?" He next enumerates the reasons that ought to move him to bring back his people.

6. **"Therefore my people will know my name; therefore in that day they will know that it is I who foretold it. Yes, it is I."** In this verse the prophet speaking for God concludes what he had glanced at in the two preceding verses: At length the people must be redeemed by God, who cannot be unlike himself; for if he redeemed the fathers, if he always assisted the church, their posterity, whom he has adopted in the same manner, will never be suffered by him to be overwhelmed. We ought carefully to observe the word **know,** for to **know** the **name** of the Lord is to lay aside every false opinion and to **know** him from his Word, which is his true image, and next from his works. We must not imagine God in terms of human fancy but must comprehend him as he declares himself to us.

7. **How beautiful on the mountains are the feet of those who bring good news, who proclaim peace, who bring good tidings, who proclaim salvation, who say to Zion, "Your God reigns!"** The prophet again confirms the certainty of the Word of God, so that believers may be fully persuaded that they will be restored to their former liberty, and so this sure hope may comfort their hearts during that hard bondage. He pronounces magnificent commendations on this message, so believers may be convinced that God holds out to them in their calamity the hope of future **salvation.** Indeed, when God speaks, they ought to accept the consolation, relying on it so that they wait calmly and patiently for the promise to be fulfilled. Thus, in order that believers may bridle their desires by patience, he splendidly adorns the Word of God. "Will you be so ungrateful as not to rest satisfied with the incomparable treasure of the Word, which contains so many benefits? Will you give way to unruly passions? Will you

complain about God?" People were drawn away by various attractions and did not fully rely on the Word of God. The prophet wishes to guard them against distrust, and therefore he praises the excellence of right doctrine.

8. Listen! Your watchmen lift up their voices; together they shout for joy. When the LORD returns to Zion, they will see it with their own eyes. He continues his argument; he shows there will be such a restoration of the people that the messengers will venture boldly to proclaim it. To **lift up their voices** has the same meaning as the phrase **on the mountains** that he used in verse 7. The matter will not be hidden but will be so clear and evident as to excite universal admiration.

9. Burst into songs of joy together, you ruins of Jerusalem, for the LORD has comforted his people, he has redeemed Jerusalem. He exhorts believers to engage in thanksgiving but chiefly confirms them in the hope and confidence of this salvation, as if the actual enjoyment of it already called them to thank God for it. We are not sufficiently moved when the Lord testifies that he will assist us, and we think that we are deceived if he does not actually show it. On this account the prophets insist much on strengthening the hearts of believers and placing the fact almost before their eyes.

10. The LORD will lay bare his holy arm in the sight of all the nations, and all the ends of the earth will see the salvation of our God. The prophet has borrowed this comparison from soldiers who stretch out their arms when they make ready for battle. To **bare his holy arm** does not here mean to hold out the naked arm but to exert it. When we sit in idleness, we either have our arms folded or conceal them; in the same way we conceive of God according to the grossness of our senses and think that, like a wearied or indolent man, he does not move a finger until he publicly displays his power.

11. Depart, depart, go out from there! Touch no unclean thing! Come out from it and be pure, you who carry the vessels of the LORD. He tells them to keep themselves **pure** and free from the defilements with which the Babylonians polluted themselves. There was a risk of their being corrupted by the pollution of the Gentiles, just as we are all prone to evil and are easily led away by bad examples. Accordingly, he exhorts them, though they are captives, not to do anything for the purpose of pleasing their masters or of having their condition improved, not to allow themselves to be drawn aside from the pure worship of God, not to be polluted by their idolatry, not to pretend that they worship idols or approve of their religion, for this is detestable uncleanness that the prophet tells them to shun.

12. But you will not leave in haste or go in flight; for the LORD will go before you, the God of Israel will be your rear guard. The prophet again magnifies a benefit of redemption, for it seemed incredible when almost all of them were in such despair. He chiefly addresses those who will be led into captivity, that they might not lose courage in that wretched condition. He promises that this deliverance will in one sense not be like their flight from Egypt; there is an implied contrast between the deliverance from Egypt and the deliverance from Babylon.

13. See, my servant will act wisely; he will be raised and lifted up and highly exalted. Having spoken of the restoration of the church, Isaiah passes on to Christ, in whom all things are gathered together. He calls Christ **my servant** on account of the office committed to him. Christ ought not to be regarded merely as a private individual but as holding the office to which the Father has appointed him—to be leader of the people and restorer of all things. So whatever he affirms concerning himself we ought to understand as applying also to us.

14. Just as there were many who were appalled at him—his appearance was so disfigured beyond that of any man and his form marred beyond human likeness—. . . The exalted state of Christ was not visible at first sight, and on this pretense it might be rejected. On this account, the prophet informs them that Christ must first be rejected and humbled and anticipates that doubt that might have arisen from his singularly debased and unseemly condition. In other words, "There is no reason why people should be shocked at that unseemliness and disgrace that will be speedily followed by eternal happiness."

15. . . . so will he sprinkle many nations, and kings will shut their mouths because of him. For what they were not told, they will see, and what they have not heard, they will understand. He means that the Lord will pour out his Word over **many nations.** He next mentions the effect of doctrine: Kings will **shut their mouths**—that is, in astonishment.

By the word **understand** he shows that faith consists in certainty and clear understanding. Wherever, therefore, knowledge of this kind is wanting, faith too is unquestionably wanting.

Isaiah
Chapter 53

1. Who has believed our message and to whom has the arm of the LORD been revealed? This chapter ought to have begun with chapter 52, verse 13, and these words ought to be connected with what goes before. Here the prophet pauses, as it were, in the middle of his discourse. Having previously said that the name of Christ would be proclaimed everywhere and would be revealed to unknown nations and yet would look so ordinary that it might seem as if these things were fables, he breaks off his discourse and exclaims in effect that "nobody will believe those things."

At the same time, he describes his sadness about people being so unbelieving as to reject their salvation. Thus this is a holy complaint made by one who wanted Christ to be known by everyone, and yet who sees that there are few who believe the Gospel and therefore groans and cries out, **Who has believed our message?**

2. He grew up before him like a tender shoot, and like a root out of dry ground. He had no beauty or majesty to attract us to him, nothing in his appearance that we should desire him. This verse refers to what was said earlier: Christ will at first have no magnificence or outward display to human sight; but before God he will nevertheless be highly exalted and will be held in great estimation. Hence we see that we must not judge the glory of Christ by human view but must discern by faith what the Holy Scriptures teach us about him.

3. He was despised and rejected by men, a man of sorrows, and familiar with suffering. Like one from whom men hide their faces he was despised, and we esteemed him not. This verse conveys the same statement as the previous one: Namely, Christ will be **rejected** by men in consequence of their beholding in him nothing but grief and infirmity. These things needed to be repeated often so that the Jews might not form a false conception of Christ and his kingdom. In order to know his glory, we must proceed from his death to his resurrection. Many stumble at his death, as if he had been vanquished and overwhelmed by it; but we ought to contemplate his power and majesty in the resurrection. If anyone chooses to begin with the resurrection, he will not be following the order laid down by the prophet, nor comprehending the Lord's strength and power.

4. Surely he took up our infirmities and carried our sorrows. Matthew quotes this prediction [8:16-17] after saying that Christ cured various diseases, though it is certain that he was appointed not to cure bodies but rather to cure souls; it is spiritual disease that the prophet means. But in the miracles that Christ performed in curing bodies, he gave proof of the salvation that he brings to our souls. That healing had therefore a more extensive reference than to bodies, because he was appointed to be the physician of souls; accordingly Matthew applies to the outward sign what belonged to the truth and reality.

Yet we considered him stricken by God, smitten by him, and afflicted. In this second clause the prophet shows how ungrateful and wicked the people were. They did not know why Christ was so severely afflicted but imagined that God smote him on account of his own sins, though they knew that he was perfectly innocent, an innocence attested even by his earthly judge.

5. But he was pierced for our transgressions, he was crushed for our iniquities; the punishment that brought us peace was upon him, and by his wounds we are healed. He again repeats the cause of Christ's great afflictions, in order to meet the scandal that might have arisen from it. The spectacle of the cross alienates many people from Christ, when they consider what is presented to their eyes and do not notice the object to be accomplished. But all offense is removed when we know that by his death our sins have been expiated, and salvation has been obtained for us.

6. We all, like sheep, have gone astray, each of us has turned to his own way; and the LORD has laid on him the iniquity of us all. In order to impress more deeply on our hearts the benefit of the death of Christ, Isaiah shows how necessary is the healing that he formerly mentioned. If we do not perceive our wretchedness and poverty, we will never know how desirable is that remedy that Christ has brought to us or approach him with proper warmth of affection. As soon as we know that we are ruined, aware of our wretchedness, we eagerly run to avail ourselves of the remedy, which otherwise would be held by us in no estimation. In order, therefore, that Christ may be appreciated by us, let us each consider and examine ourselves, so as to acknowledge that we are ruined until we are redeemed by Christ.

We see here that there are no exceptions, for the prophet includes **all**. The whole human race would have perished if Christ had not brought relief.

7. He was oppressed and afflicted, yet he did not open his mouth; he was led like a lamb to the slaughter, and as a sheep before her shearers

is silent, so he did not open his mouth. Here we are urged to be patient and meek, following the example of Christ, so we may be ready to endure reproaches and cruel assaults, distress and torture. In the word **lamb** there is probably an allusion to the sacrifices under the law; and in this sense he is elsewhere called "the Lamb of God" (John 1:29, 36).

8. By oppression and judgment he was taken away. And who can speak of his descendants? For he was cut off from the land of the living. At first sight it might seem absurd that the death of Christ is the cause and source of our life; but because he bore the punishment of our sins, we ought to apply to ourselves all the shame that appears in the cross. In Christ shines the wonderful love of God, which renders his glory visible to us, so that we ought to be brought to rapturous admiration.

For the transgression of my people he was stricken. He repeats that the wound was inflicted on Christ for the sins of the people; we should diligently consider that it was for our sake, and not for his own, that he suffered. He bore the punishment we would have endured if he had not offered this atonement. We ought to perceive in ourselves the guilt of which he bore the accusation and punishment, having offered himself in our name to the Father, that by his condemnation we may be set free.

9. He was assigned a grave with the wicked, and with the rich in his death, though he had done no violence, nor was any deceit in his mouth. In two ways he describes the perfect innocence of Christ; namely, he never offended either in deed or in word. Everybody acknowledges that this cannot be said of any mortal, and hence it follows that it applies to Christ alone.

10. Yet it was the LORD's will to crush him and cause him to suffer, and though the LORD makes his life a guilt offering, he will see his offspring and prolong his days, and the will of the LORD will prosper in his hand. This illustrates more fully that the prophet, in asserting Christ's innocence, aims at something more than to defend him from all reproach. We should consider the cause in order to experience the effect. God appoints nothing at random; so it follows that the cause of Christ's death is lawful. We must also keep in view the contrast. There was no fault in Christ; why, then, did the Lord choose that he should suffer? Because he stood in our place, and only by his death could God's justice be satisfied.

11. After the suffering of his soul, he will see the light of life and be satisfied; by his knowledge my righteous servant will justify many, and he will bear their iniquities. Isaiah continues the same subject. He declares that after Christ has suffered, he will obtain the fruit of his death in people's salvation.

By the word **justify** he points out the effect of this teaching. Thus people are not only taught righteousness in the school of Christ but are actually justified. This is the difference between the righteousness of faith and the righteousness of the law. Although the law shows what it is to be righteous, Paul affirms that it is impossible to obtain righteousness by it, and experience proves the same thing; the law is a mirror in which we behold our own unrighteousness. (See Romans 3:20, Galatians 2:16, 21, and 3:10-11.)

Now, the doctrine that Christ teaches concerning righteousness is nothing but the knowledge of him; and this is faith—embracing the benefit of his death and fully relying on him.

12. Therefore I will give him a portion among the great, and he will divide the spoils with the strong, because he poured out his life unto death, and was numbered with the transgressors. Isaiah again says what was the result of Christ's death, adding this doctrine of the victory that Christ obtained by his death. He had said earlier that we are reconciled to the Father by his death, but that would not have confirmed our hearts sufficiently. Here he borrows a comparison from the ordinary form of a triumphal procession held by those who have won a remarkable victory and are received and decorated with great pomp and splendor. Christ too, as a valiant and illustrious general, triumphed over the enemies whom he had vanquished.

For he bore the sin of many, and made intercession for the transgressors. By way of correction, the prophet adds that when we hear of the shame of Christ's death, we must not think it was a blot on Christ's character. We must not be prejudiced in that way and thus be prevented from receiving the victory he obtained for us—that is, the fruit of his death. He shows, therefore, that this was done in order that Christ might take our sins upon him. His aim is that whenever his death is mentioned, we should remember the atonement made for us.

Isaiah
Chapter 54

1. **"Sing, O barren woman, you who never bore a child; burst into song, shout for joy, you who were never in labor; because more are the children of the desolate woman than of her who has a husband," says the LORD.** Having spoken of the death of Christ, Isaiah passes on with good reason to the church, that we may feel more deeply the value and efficacy of his death. Christ suffered for the church, and not for himself. This is the order in our Confession of Faith, for, having professed that we believe in Christ who suffered and was crucified for us, we add that we believe in the church, which flowed, as it were, from his side. Accordingly, when the prophet has spoken about Christ's death and resurrection and triumph, he properly comes to the church (which ought never to be separated from her Head), so each individual believer may learn by his own experience that Christ has not suffered in vain.

2. **"Enlarge the place of your tent, stretch your tent curtains wide, do not hold back; lengthen your cords, strengthen your stakes."** He continues his argument using different metaphors, and he promises that the Lord will not only restore his church but will bestow upon her a condition far more excellent.

Tents were extensively used in that country. The church is compared to them because it has no settled home in this world; it appears to be wandering and unsettled, a consequence of being moved from one place to another on account of various changes. But I am fully persuaded that the prophet had in his eye that earlier deliverance when they were led through the wilderness and dwelt in tents for forty years, for which reason they kept a public festival every year by God's command.

3. **"For you will spread out to the right and to the left; your descendants will dispossess nations and settle in their desolate cities."** Now follows the reason why God commanded the **cords** to be lengthened for enlarging the tents. A moderate space would not contain a numerous peo-

ple, whom the Lord will gather into one from every quarter. Because Judea was hideous on account of its ruins and desolation, God says the forsaken cities will be inhabited.

4. "Do not be afraid; you will not suffer shame. Do not fear disgrace; you will not be humiliated. You will forget the shame of your youth and remember no more the reproach of your widowhood." Here, as before, he strengthens the hearts of believers and addresses the whole church; for the calamity was universal, and the church appeared to be totally ruined. He tells her to cheer up and next gives the reason: The outcome of her troubles will be such that she **will not suffer shame.** It is as if he said, "Although for a time you are wretched, your affairs will be prosperous." See Psalm 25:3.

5. "For your Maker is your husband—the LORD Almighty is his name—the Holy One of Israel is your Redeemer; he is called the God of all the earth." God through Isaiah gives the reason why Israel will forget all the distresses and calamities she has endured. It is because God will receive her back into favor. Captivity might be said to be a kind of divorce, as we formerly saw (see Isaiah 50:1). He now says, **"For your Maker is your husband."** God calls himself the **Maker** of his church not only because he created the church as he created other people, but because he condescended to adopt her as his heritage. This privilege may be regarded as a new life.

He calls himself **Redeemer** in order that he might more fully confirm the people in the hope that although the former deliverance appeared to be canceled, because the people were again led into captivity, yet they would be restored in such a manner as to know that the grace of God is not without effect.

6. "The LORD will call you back as if you were a wife deserted and distressed in spirit—a wife who married young, only to be rejected," says your God. He meets a doubt that might arise in the minds of believers amidst so distressing a calamity. It seemed as if the Lord had rejected them, and so they had nothing to look for but destruction. The prophet therefore reminds them that they ought not to despair because of being forsaken like this, for God in his mercy is ready to be reconciled and is even willing to raise them from the dead.

7. "For a brief moment I abandoned you, but with deep compassion I will bring you back." God speaking through the prophet explains the former statement more fully and shows the nature of this divorce—she will soon be restored to her former condition. He magnifies his mercy and extenuates the sorrow by which the hearts of believers might be oppressed. We quickly lose courage and faint if the Lord is not near and if he does not quickly stretch out his hand to us.

8. "In a surge of anger I hid my face from you for a moment, but with everlasting kindness I will have compassion on you," says the

LORD your Redeemer. He repeats and enforces this statement to impress it more deeply on the hearts of believers, that they might not be at all discouraged by adversity. Amidst that frightful darkness, it was not easy for the captives to see God's smiling face.

9. "To me this is like the days of Noah, when I swore that the waters of Noah would never again cover the earth. So now I have sworn not to be angry with you, never to rebuke you again." I think we ought carefully to inquire into the meaning of these words, which commentators pass over lightly. God means that this calamity will resemble the Flood. He was satisfied with a single deluge and would never again send another, and now he is satisfied with this one destruction, so to speak, of the church and will never again permit the face of it to be destroyed. This is how I think we should explain this passage and apply the metaphor: The desolation of Judea will be to God like the deluge that happened in the days of Noah. As he swore at that time that he would never afterward inflict such punishment on the crimes that stripped the earth of its inhabitants, so he will not destroy the church again as he did in the Babylonian captivity. In a word, the Lord promises that from now on he will restrain his wrath and will not punish his people with such great severity.

10. "Though the mountains be shaken and the hills be removed, yet my unfailing love for you will not be shaken nor my covenant of peace be removed," says the LORD, who has compassion on you. He confirms the previous statement, declaring that sooner shall the whole world be turned upside-down than his mercy fail.

He calls it my covenant of peace because the Lord offers all of us what belongs to perfect happiness, just as the Hebrew writers, under the word *peace*, include all posterity. Since therefore this covenant contains solid and perfect happiness, it follows that all who are excluded from it are miserable.

11. "O afflicted city, lashed by storms and not comforted, I will build you with stones of turquoise, your foundations with sapphires." God continues the same subject, promising not only that the church will be restored to her ancient splendor but that he will cause her to be adorned with attire of greater magnificence, as if it had been wholly composed of precious stones.

12. "I will make your battlements of rubies, your gates of sparkling jewels, and all your walls of precious stones." These metaphors show that, as has already been said, the condition of the church would be far better than at any former period. The church is compared to a building, which is customary in every part of Scripture (see Jeremiah 24:6; Matthew 16:18). For this reason he now draws a picture of a costly and magnificent structure. But it should be noted that the prophet represents God as the architect of this building, for this work ought to be entirely ascribed to him alone.

13. "All your sons will be taught by the LORD, and great will be your children's peace." The phrase **taught by the LORD** deserves attention: All that belongs to the church proceeds solely from the grace of God. If we are sparkling jewels as a consequence of being **taught by the Lord,** it follows that this does not proceed from nature. There are two ways in which the Lord teaches us—by external preaching and by the secret revelation of the Holy Spirit.

14. "In righteousness you will be established: Tyranny will be far from you; you will have nothing to fear. Terror will be far removed; it will not come near you." God means that he will be the maker and architect of his church. I am aware that some explain this differently and think that **righteousness** means "good works." He contrasts **righteousness** with the violence and oppression by which the church has been thrown down. It is as if he said that it will not be a frail building or one that might seem imposing for a short time by its deceptive appearance. God will sincerely defend his work and, being righteous, will not only restore it completely but will afterwards preserve it in safety for a long period.

15. "If anyone does attack you, it will not be my doing; whoever attacks you will surrender to you." The general import is that although many rise up for the purpose of overwhelming the church, all their efforts and attacks will fail. Isaiah speaking for the Lord promises God's assistance not only against external foes but against enemies that are domestic and internal.

16. "See, it is I who created the blacksmith who fans the coals into flame and forges a weapon fit for its work. And it is I who have created the destroyer to work havoc." The Lord shows how easily and readily he delivers his church from the base attacks of wicked people; they can do nothing except insofar as the Lord permits them, though he makes use of them as instruments for chastising his people. Moreover, this may be appropriately viewed as referring both to the Babylonians and to other foes who afterwards distressed the elect people.

17. "No weapon forged against you will prevail, and you will refute every tongue that accuses you. This is the heritage of the servants of the LORD, and this is their vindication from me," declares the LORD. He infers again that even if wicked people exert themselves to the utmost, they will gain nothing, for their attacks are guided and restrained by God's secret purpose.

Isaiah
Chapter 55

1. **"Come, all you who are thirsty, come to the waters; and you who have no money, come, buy and eat! Come, buy wine and milk without money and without cost."** Here the prophet highly commends God's goodness. A remarkable commendation of the grace of God is exhibited to us in the kingdom of Christ; for the prophet does not instruct us what has been done once but also what is done every day, while the Lord invites us by his doctrine to the enjoyment of all blessings.

2. **"Why spend money on what is not bread, and your labor on what does not satisfy? Listen, listen to me, and eat what is good, and your soul will delight in the richest of fare."** He complains of people's ingratitude and madness in rejecting or disdaining the kindness of God, who offers all things freely, and yet harassing themselves greatly about various trifles that cannot yield them any advantage. People are so enchanted by the devil that they choose rather to wander through deserts and to vex themselves in vain than to rely on the grace that God offers them.

The word **bread** here means the same as **waters** in verse 1, and he gives the name **labor** to what in verse 1 he called **money**. In other words, "People toil without any advantage; for when they follow their own ideas, however eagerly they may vex and weary themselves, they have no right to expect any reward." Thus he affirms that those who labor in an inconsiderate manner cannot be satisfied; those who forsake God and attempt new methods of salvation can never be content.

This wording makes it still more evident that God leaves nothing undone that could correct and arouse our tardiness. Yet there is an implied reproof: People must be excessively stupid if, when they are so gently called, they do not instantly obey. In this remarkable passage we see that our whole happiness lies in obeying the Word of God. When God speaks in this manner, the object that he has in view is to lead us to life; therefore the blame lies wholly with ourselves because we disregard this saving and life-giving word.

3-4. "Give ear and come to me; hear me, that your soul may live. I will make an everlasting covenant with you, my faithful love promised to David. See, I have made him a witness to the peoples, a leader and commander of the peoples." The prophet explains more fully why he had earlier mentioned David. It was David who had been entrusted with the promise of a future Redeemer, and this discourse might be expressed with a view to his public character, so far as he was the surety of the covenant; he did not act for himself individually but was appointed to be a sort of mediator between God and the people. Yet it is beyond all doubt that the prophet leads them directly to Christ, to whom the transition from David was easy and natural. In other words, "The successor of David will come, by whose hand perfect salvation and happiness has been promised."

5. "Surely you will summon nations you know not, and nations that do not know you will hasten to you, because of the LORD your God, the Holy One of Israel, for he has endowed you with splendor." Isaiah explains at greater length what he had formerly touched on: Christ will be the leader not of a single people but of all the peoples. He says they will be ready to obey, though hitherto they were unknown. This does not mean that the Son of God, by whom they were created, did not know them, but he paid no regard to them until they began to be reckoned as belonging to the church.

6. Seek the LORD while he may be found; call on him while he is near. After speaking about the success of the Gospel among the Gentiles, who were previously strangers to the kingdom of God, he urges the Jews to be ashamed of loitering while others run. They were the first to be called; so it is shameful that they should be last. This exhortation, therefore, relates strictly to the Jews, to whom the example of the Gentiles is held out in order to excite their jealousy.

7. Let the wicked forsake his way and the evil man his thoughts. Let him turn to the LORD, and he will have mercy on him, and to our God, for he will freely pardon. He confirms the previous statement: Having earlier called people to receive God's grace, he now describes at greater length the manner of receiving it. We know how hypocrites loudly call on God whenever they desire relief from their distresses and yet shut up their hearts by wicked obstinacy; therefore, so the Jews may not be hypocritical in seeking God, the prophet exhorts them to sincere piety. Hence we infer that the doctrine of repentance ought always to accompany the promise of salvation; the only way people can experience God's goodness is by abhorring themselves on account of their sins and renouncing themselves and the world.

8. "For my thoughts are not your thoughts, neither are your ways my ways," declares the LORD. He draws a distinction between God's disposition and man's disposition. Men are wont to judge and measure God by themselves. Their hearts are moved by angry passions and are very hard to appease, and therefore they think they cannot be reconciled to God once they have offended him. But the Lord shows that he is far from resembling human beings. It is as if he said, "I am not a mortal man, that I should show myself to be harsh and irreconcilable to you. My thoughts are very different from yours. You are implacable and can with difficulty be brought back to a state of friendship with those from whom you have received an injury; but I am not like you, that I should treat you so cruelly."

9. **"As the heavens are higher than the earth, so are my ways higher than your ways and my thoughts than your thoughts."** In short, God is infinitely compassionate and infinitely ready to forgive; so it is solely due to our unbelief if we do not obtain pardon from him. There is nothing that troubles our consciences more than when we think that God is like ourselves, for the consequence is that we do not dare approach him. We flee from him as an enemy and are never at rest.

10. **"As the rain and the snow come down from heaven, and do not return to it without watering the earth and making it bud and flourish, so that it yields seed for the sower and bread for the eater ..."** After speaking of his tender affection and inconceivable forbearance toward us, God again brings forward the promises, so that, by relying on them, we may banish all doubt of being free from every danger.

11. **". . . so is my word that goes out from my mouth: It will not return to me empty, but will accomplish what I desire and achieve the purpose for which I sent it."** This doctrine must be frequently repeated and inculcated, so we may know that God will do what he has said. For this reason, when we hear the promises of God we ought to consider what is his purpose in them, so that when he promises the free pardon of our sins, we may be fully assured that we are reconciled through Christ.

12. **"You will go out in joy and be led forth in peace; the mountains and hills will burst into song before you, and all the trees of the field will clap their hands."** When the prophet spoke of the mercy of God, his aim was to convince the Jews that the Lord would deliver them. He now applies to his purpose what was contained in his discourse concerning the infinite goodness of God and shows that the Lord's thoughts are very unlike human thoughts. We should apply general statements for present use. Finally, he deals with the restoration of the people, which depended on God's undeserved mercy.

By **the mountains and hills** he means that everything they come across on the journey, though in other respects it may be injurious, will aid those who return to Jerusalem. By these metaphors he shows that all created things bow to the will of God and rejoice and lend their aid to carry on his work.

13. **"Instead of the thornbush will grow the pine tree, and instead of**

briers the myrtle will grow. This will be for the LORD's renown, for an everlasting sign, which will not be destroyed." He further extols the power of God, which would be visible in the restoration of the people; he shows that there will be such a change that their way back will be easy. These things relate to the kingdom of Christ and on that account ought to be understood in a spiritual sense. The prophet begins with the departure from Babylon and includes the whole condition of the church until Christ was manifested to the world.

When he says **this will be for the LORD's renown,** he shows the purpose of the church's restoration—so the name of God may be more illustrious among human beings and so memory of him may flourish and be maintained. On this account he adds that it will be **an everlasting sign**—that is, a monument and a memorial. The church may be tossed and agitated in various ways in various tempests; yet because the Lord wants his name to be remembered forever, he will guard and defend her.

Isaiah
Chapter 56

1. This is what the LORD says: "Maintain justice and do what is right, for my salvation is close at hand and my righteousness will soon be revealed." This is a remarkable passage in which the prophet shows what God demands from us as soon as he holds out tokens of his favor or promises that he will be ready to be reconciled to us, so our reconciliation may be secured. He demands from us such a conversion as will change our minds and hearts, that they may forsake the world and rise toward heaven; he likewise calls for the fruits of repentance.

In the instruction to **maintain justice and do what is right** are included all the duties that people owe to each other—not only abstaining from doing wrong, but also helping our neighbors. This is the sum of the second table of the law, and in keeping it we give proof of our piety, if we have any.

2. "Blessed is the man who does this, the man who holds it fast, who keeps the Sabbath without desecrating it." God calls people **blessed** if they embrace this doctrine and devote themselves to walking uprightly. Thus he indirectly leads us to conclude that many will be deaf or disobedient; but lest their wickedness or indifference should hold the elect back, he urges them to follow this course because of the advantage that it yields. Thus, to make sure that believers do not delay, he exclaims that those who have been favored with such wisdom are **blessed.**

"And keeps his hand from doing any evil." He now adds another synecdoche, describing the duties that people owe to each other. What it amounts to is that the only way to serve God aright is by sincere piety and a blameless life, as he has also included in these two parts the rule of leading a holy life. In a word, this is an exposition of true righteousness that is contained in the law of the Lord, that we may acquiesce in it; in vain do we seek any other road to perfection. Here also are thrown down all false worship and superstitions and, finally, everything that is devised by human beings in opposition to God's Word.

3. Let no foreigner who has bound himself to the LORD say, "The LORD will surely exclude me from his people." And let not any eunuch complain, "I am only a dry tree." The prophet shows that the grace of God will be such that even people who were formerly estranged from him, and against whom the door might be said to have been shut, may obtain a new condition or may be perfectly restored. And he anticipates their objection, so that they may not say they are rejected or unworthy or foreigners or excluded by any mark; for the Lord will remove every obstacle. This may refer both to Jews, who had been brought into a condition similar to that of foreign nations by a temporary rejection, and to the heathen nations themselves.

4. For this is what the LORD says: "To the eunuchs who keep my Sabbaths, who choose what pleases me and hold fast to my covenant— . . ." Now follows a confirmation: The sincere worshipers of God, who keep the **Sabbaths** and follow the righteousness of the law, even if they are **eunuchs** or labor under any other obstruction, shall nevertheless have a place in the church. Thus God speaking through the prophet appears to annihilate all the external marks in which alone the Jews gloried. The high rank of the church is not external but spiritual; although believers have no emblems of distinction in the eyes of the world and are even despised and reproached, yet they rank high in the sight of God.

5. ". . . to them I will give within my temple and its walls a memorial and a name better than sons and daughters; I will give them an everlasting name that will not be cut off." Here we see that everyone, however unworthy, may obtain admission into the kingdom of God. He alludes to Jerusalem and to the temple in which the Lord placed a memorial of his name. No place was given in it to any but to the Jews alone; and they would have reckoned the temple to be polluted if any of the Gentiles had entered into it. But the Lord now admits, without distinction, those whom he previously forbade. Indeed he set aside this distinction when we who were the children of strangers were brought by him into the temple— that is, into his church, which is not confined, as formerly, within those narrow limits of Judea but is extended through the whole world.

6. "And foreigners who bind themselves to the LORD to serve him, to love the name of the LORD, and to worship him, all who keep the Sabbath without desecrating it . . ." He repeats what he said before: God will open the doors of his temple to everyone without distinction, so that there will no longer be a distinction between the Jew and the Greek. He declares that those whom God brings into a state of friendship with himself by the Word, which is the bond of our adoption, are joined to God.

". . . and who hold fast to my covenant." Here he describes the zeal and steadfastness of those who submit themselves to God and cleave to his

Word; therefore, if we are joined to God by a covenant, we ought to hold by it constantly and adhere firmly to sound doctrine, so that it may not be possible to withdraw or separate us from him in any manner.

7. "These I will bring to my holy mountain and give them joy in my house of prayer. Their burnt offerings and sacrifices will be accepted on my altar; for my house will be called a house of prayer for all nations." These expressions describe what he had stated before: Foreigners who were formerly excluded from the church of God are called to it; henceforth the distinction between circumcision and uncircumcision will be abolished.

How strongly the Jews abhor this sentiment is well known, for although they read these words of the prophet, they reckon it to be utterly monstrous that the Gentiles should be called to this distinguished benefit of God that was especially intended for them. Yet the prophet's meaning is so plain that it cannot be questioned without the greatest impudence. He extols this grace from the fruit that it yields; true and perfect happiness is being reconciled to God and enjoying his favor. We know, indeed, that wicked people indulge excessively in mirth; but that mirth is turned into gnashing of teeth because the curse of God rests upon it.

8. The Sovereign LORD declares—he who gathers the exiles of Israel: "I will gather still others to them besides those already gathered." Again Isaiah confirms what he said before about the restoration of the people. Although he extolled in lofty terms the grace of God, by which the Lord would deliver his people, the condition of the church was such that promises of this kind seemed ridiculous. Such repetitions, therefore, are not superfluous but had to be added in order to strengthen feeble minds, that they might be fully convinced of what would otherwise have been incredible.

9. Come, all you beasts of the field, come and devour, all you beasts of the forest! This prediction appears to be at variance with what goes before. What the prophet has hitherto said was full of the most delightful consolation, but now he appears to threaten fiercely and to predict frightful ruin. These statements might indeed appear to be contradictory; but, having comforted believers, it ought not to be thought inconsistent if he forewarns them of a future calamity. He does not want them to lose courage when they see everything near destruction; he wants them to be prompted by necessity to seek God's grace all the more warmly and earnestly.

10. Israel's watchmen are blind, they all lack knowledge; they are all mute dogs, they cannot bark; they lie around and dream, they love to sleep. He now gives the reason why the people must be destroyed. It is because they are governed by wicked princes and pastors—not that he wishes to throw the blame on them alone, thinking that the people are innocent, but this was the beginning of the evil. We are not exempted from blame if we follow blind guides; on the contrary, we are justly punished for our transgressions. The Lord takes away good guides from those whom he intends to punish for their ingratitude.

By calling them **mute dogs,** he charges them with slothfulness and indifference. It is the duty of a good shepherd to be industrious and careful. So when the Lord calls them slothful and indifferent, he shows that they had nothing about them that ought to belong to a shepherd.

11. They are dogs with mighty appetites; they never have enough. They are shepherds who lack understanding. The third vice he condemns in wicked pastors is insatiable avarice. Though they are lazy in all that relates to good government, they have a strong and ravenous appetite for food.

They all turn to their own way, each seeks his own gain. That is, "They attend eagerly to their own affairs; every person thinks of his own advantage." In short, he means there is no one who does not wish to be preferred above others, as if every man had been born for himself.

12. "Come," each one cries, "let me get wine! Let us drink our fill of beer! And tomorrow will be like today, or even far better." Having spoken of the avarice and carelessness of pastors, he points out their desperate wickedness and obstinacy; he brings forward their hard-hearted speeches, from which it is evident that they could not be brought back to the right path by any admonitions but fearlessly despised them all.

He does not reprove them for drinking wine and strong drink, which in itself is not sinful; he criticizes the mental drunkenness and brutality by which people haughtily and insolently despise God's Word. In other passages drunkenness and the abuse of wine are condemned; but here the prophet exclaims against the madness and insolence with which pastors exalted themselves against God and trampled underfoot all threats, warnings, and reproofs—in short, all false religion.

Isaiah
Chapter 57

1. The righteous perish, and no one ponders it in his heart; devout men are taken away, and no one understands that the righteous are taken away to be spared from evil. Isaiah continues his subject. Having shown how fearlessly hypocrites indulge in their luxuries and how impudently they despise God's Word, he now complains that they do not consider God's works in or for his people. We have been placed here, as in a spacious theater, to behold the works of God; and there is no work of God so small that we ought to pass it by lightly—they should all be observed carefully and diligently.

2. Those who walk uprightly enter into peace; they find rest as they lie in death. The prophet describes the condition of believers in death. The wicked, who think there is no life but the present, imagine that good people have perished because in death they see nothing but ruin. For this reason the prophet says that **peace** will come, which is more desirable than a thousand lives full of trouble; this is like comparing them with discharged soldiers who are allowed to enjoy ease and quietness.

3. "But you—come here, you sons of a sorceress, you offspring of adulterers and prostitutes!" Having spoken of the happy and peaceful death of good people, the prophet breaks out with great vehemence against the wicked, who did not cease to lead a base and shameful life and were not moved by the death of believers. He had said that good people enjoy peace, and now he threatens that the wicked will have ceaseless war. He taught that to the holy servants of God death will be like a hiding-place, to shelter them from the whirlwind and storm and other tempests, and thus he threatened the worst of evils against the obstinate despisers of God. Here we ought to observe the contrast between good people who walk before God and the wicked, who never stop rebelling against God. The former will enjoy peace when they die; the latter will have no peace during life and will feel dreadful torments in death.

4. "Whom are you mocking? At whom do you sneer and stick out your tongue? Are you not a brood of rebels, the offspring of liars?" The prophet shows that there is no reason why the Jews should boast so proudly of what they claimed by birth, seeing that they mocked God and the prophets. They thought they were dealing with human beings when they rejected the Word, just as we see that wicked people today, while they fearlessly despise the doctrine of God and laugh at ministers, nevertheless shelter themselves and falsely glory in the name of God. This is why the prophet bears hard witness against them and censures them severely.

5. "You burn with lust among the oaks and under every spreading tree." Idolaters have no moderation and do not permit themselves to be reclaimed from their madness by any arguments. In the sight of God idolatry is a base kind of fornication.

"You sacrifice your children in the ravines and under the overhanging crags." Here he bears still harder on the Jews and shows they are not the true seed of Abraham, seeing that they pollute themselves with superstitions of every kind. In consequence of the delight that the Jews took in such practices, he exposes their vileness. "You shelter yourselves, indeed, under the name of religion, but I declare that you commit fornication with idols." He shows that they are treacherous and have departed from the law of God by abominable idolatry and mentions one kind of shocking and even accursed and monstrous worship—namely, the sacrificing of children, from which it is very evident how powerful is the spirit of error once people have turned aside from God.

6. "The idols among the smooth stones of the ravines are your portion; they, they are your lot. Yes, to them you have poured out drink offerings and offered grain offerings. In the light of these things, should I relent?" He continues the same subject, reproving in various ways the superstitions that abounded in Judea, for no place was altogether free from idolatry. There were no rocks, no rivers, no valleys, no corner whatever in which they had not erected a monument of their superstition. They had their groves and mountains in which they sacrificed after the manner of the Gentiles.

7. "You have made your bed on a high and lofty hill; there you went up to offer your sacrifices." He repeats the metaphor that we touched on earlier. Superstitious people commit fornication with their idols because, by forsaking the simplicity of the Word, they violate the bond of that holy marriage into which God has entered with them and prostitute themselves to Satan. But now God through Isaiah wants to express something more: When he says they made their **bed on a high and lofty hill,** he means that they are not at all ashamed of their shameful conduct. As a harlot who has lost all shame does not dread the sight of men or care about her reputation, so they openly and shamefully commit fornication in a lofty and conspicuous place.

8. "Behind your doors and your doorposts you have put your pagan symbols. Forsaking me, you uncovered your bed, you climbed into it and opened it wide; you made a pact with those whose beds you love, and you looked on their nakedness." He dwells at length on the crime of which we have already spoken, so the people may no longer flatter themselves in their inventions. Isaiah is probably alluding to the words of Moses, by which God commanded them to have the law continually placed before them, to attach it to the posts of their houses, and to keep it written and wrapped around their arms and the fringes of their garments, that they might be constantly reminded of their duty (see Deuteronomy 6:9; 11:20). But the Jews, on the contrary, polluted the doors and posts of their houses by tokens of idolatry and left no corner free or pure from such pollutions. Thus they came to everywhere forget God and the law and put in their place the excitements of their own lust.

9. "You went to Molech with olive oil and increased your perfumes. You sent your ambassadors far away; you descended to the grave itself!" Here the prophet censures another vice closely allied to the former, for ungodliness begets various errors and leads into grievous and intricate distresses those minds that are frivolous and destitute of the fear of God. It is proper that they who refuse to rest on God should be tossed about, or rather driven up and down. Isaiah therefore reproaches the Jews with having labored much and long in seeking the assistance of the wicked—that is, with having attempted to bring the Egyptians against the Assyrians—and next, when they had been disappointed of their hope, with having begun to resort to the Babylonians.

10. "You were wearied by all your ways, but you would not say, 'It is hopeless.' You found renewal of your strength, and so you did not faint." He means that people undertake superfluous and useless labors when they do not follow God. They vex themselves in vain, as has been already said; nothing that is attempted in opposition to God can ever be successful. Besides, he wittily ridicules the wicked practices of those who choose rather to waste themselves by incessant toil than to advance calmly wherever God calls them.

11. "Whom have you so dreaded and feared that you have been false to me, and have neither remembered me nor pondered this in your hearts? Is it not because I have long been silent that you do not fear me?" Here Isaiah speaking for God breaks out more vehemently against the Jews because they were destitute of the fear of God, though they boasted of their holiness and sheltered themselves under an empty title of religion. Not only do hypocrites flatter themselves in their superstitions—they are also regarded by the common people as holy and pious, and therefore they act haughtily and insolently toward God and men. But the prophet declares that true fear of God cannot exist where the worship is not pure and consistent with his Word.

12. "I will expose your righteousness and your works, and they will not benefit you." The prophet affirms that the Lord will no longer endure what he formerly endured, and that henceforth he must follow a different method. By **"your righteousness"** he means all the wickedness and all the errors by which they were stained and corrupted.

13. "When you cry out for help, let your collection of idols save you! The wind will carry all of them off, a mere breath will blow them away. But the man who makes me his refuge will inherit the land and possess my holy mountain." He states more fully what he had touched on in the previous verse: They will be ashamed.

By **the land** I have no doubt that he means Judea, in which the Jews wanted to remain in safety, for he afterwards mentions **my holy mountain**—that is, the mountain on which the temple was built. So the Jews did not ascribe to the Lord that which belonged to him when they fled but called to the Assyrians or Egyptians for help. From this we should draw a universal doctrine—namely, that our affairs will succeed admirably if we hope in the Lord; but if we throw away confidence in him, we certainly need not wonder if we waver and are tossed about in various ways.

14. And it will be said: "Build up, build up, prepare the road! Remove the obstacles out of the way of my people." Because the promise that those who hoped in the Lord would possess the land might be thought ridiculous (for soon afterward they were to be driven out of it), for the sake of the believers who still remained, the prophet adds this second promise, pledging that although they have been driven out of the land of Canaan and banished to a distant country, they will be brought back to it. He anticipates a doubt that might arise, so that good people might not despair during that painful and long-continued banishment or imagine that God's promise had failed.

15. For this is what the high and lofty One says—he who lives forever, whose name is holy: "I live in a high and holy place, but also with him who is contrite and lowly in spirit, to revive the spirit of the lowly and to revive the heart of the contrite." He confirms the earlier statement about the restoration of the people from captivity.

We are fickle and apply our minds sometimes to one subject and sometimes to another; our hearts do not remain fixed on that which we have embraced. Isaiah therefore distinguishes between God **who lives forever** and human beings; for on him no shadow of change falls, but we do not have such steadfastness as to exercise constant care for those who need our help.

With him who is contrite and lowly in spirit. The wicked are oppressed by various calamities but do not cease to be fierce and haughty. It will be vain for them to hope that God will draw near to them, for their hearts must be lowly and utterly cast down if they expect to obtain any assistance from God.

16. "I will not accuse forever, nor will I always be angry, for then the spirit of man would grow faint before me—the breath of man that I have created." The prophet speaking for God continues the same doctrine, for it was difficult to persuade them of this. During that painful captivity they thought that God was their enemy and could scarcely obtain any taste of the grace of God, by which their hearts might be encouraged or relieved. Isaiah therefore meets this doubt, showing that the punishments they endure will be for a short time and that God will not always be angry with them. God has indeed good reason to be angry, but he will relinquish his right and will abate that which he might have demanded. Thus the prophet connects the wrath of God with that moderation by which he soothes believers, that they may not be discouraged. He argues from the nature of God; this promise is especially directed to the church.

17. "I was enraged by his sinful greed; I punished him, and hid my face in anger, yet he kept on in his willful ways." Here the Lord complains of the obstinate wickedness of the people and shows that he had very good reason for punishing the people in this manner; so there can be no complaint of his immoderate cruelty.

We may take **sinful greed** generally to mean every kind of sinful desire. It was on account of the various and numerous vices by which the Jews were polluted that the Lord was angry and inflicted on them severe punishments.

18. "I have seen his ways, but I will heal him; I will guide him and restore comfort to him." Here the Lord, in great contrast, magnifies his kindness because he is gracious to that people, though they are obstinate and rebellious, and he anticipates his grace and mercy to them. In other words, "I labored to bring this people back to repentance by my chastisements because they were pursuing their lusts violently. But they were obstinate and untameable; all that I did was of no avail. I might justly, indeed, have ruined them, but I choose rather to heal and preserve. This cannot be done but by distinguished and incomparable mercy. I will therefore cease to punish them." For these reasons Isaiah gradually magnifies the mercy of God, whom he represents as a physician considering what remedies are best adapted for healing this people. Our diseases are incurable if the Lord does not give us his mercy.

19. ". . . creating praise on the lips of the mourners in Israel. Peace, peace, to those far and near," says the LORD. "And I will heal them." This is an explanation of the previous statement or of the manner in which the Lord will give consolation to this people. He will promise and offer peace to them. By **the lips of the mourners** he means that he will cause them to hear the glad tidings of **peace,** by which they will be filled with joy.

I think he is talking about the proclamation of **peace,** a ministry committed to the prophets and afterward enjoined on the apostles and the other ministers of the Gospel (see 2 Corinthians 5:20). The repetition of the word **peace** is intended to express not only certainty but also uninterrupted continuance. In other words, "You now hear nothing but dreadful threatenings. The doctrine of grace and salvation is silent because you are incapable of receiving it. Such is your obstinacy that I must deal with you by threatenings and terrors. But I will one day restore the doctrine of **peace** and open the lips of the prophets, that they may proclaim it to you."

20. But the wicked are like the tossing sea, which cannot rest, whose waves cast up mire and mud. Having previously spoken of the **peace** that good people will enjoy, the prophet now threatens that **the wicked,** on the contrary, will have continual war and incessant uneasiness and distress of heart. Good people value more highly the excellent blessing of peace, and reprobates know their condition will get no better, a consequence of the peace that is promised only to the children of God. Because the reprobate make false claims on God's name and glory in it vainly, the prophet shows that there is no reason why they should flatter themselves or advance any claim on the ground of this promise, since they can have no share in this peace.

21. "There is no peace," says my God, "for the wicked." The Lord speaking through his prophet confirms the preceding statement—namely, that it will be no good for the reprobate to try to seek **peace,** for everywhere they will meet with war. It is God who threatens war, and therefore there can be no hope of **peace.** Indeed, **wicked** people would indeed wish to enjoy **peace,** and they ardently long for it; there is nothing they desire more eagerly than to be at ease and to lull their consciences, that they may freely enjoy their pleasures and indulge in their vices. They drive away all thoughts of God's judgment and endeavor to stupefy themselves, to repose in indolence, and to think that these are the best ways and methods of obtaining **peace.** But they never will enjoy it; for until men have been reconciled to God, conscience will never cease to annoy and carry on war with them.

Isaiah
Chapter 58

1. **"Shout it aloud, do not hold back. Raise your voice like a trumpet. Declare to my people their rebellion and to the house of Jacob their sins."** This chapter has been badly divided, for these words are connected with what goes before. If we are to understand the prophet's meaning, we must read them as if there had been no separation. The prophet has testified that the people will be punished in such a manner as to leave some hope of peace and next threatened that the wicked, who by indolent pride endeavor to escape from God, will have continual war. He now confirms that doctrine and informs them that God has commanded him to **shout it aloud**—that is, to use a common expression, "proclaim it at the top of your voice."

He has good reason to call them **the house of Jacob,** for the majority of the people were corrupt. We should carefully note this distinction: The prophets sometimes address everybody in general and sometimes just a few believers. He uses clever and bitter mockery when he calls **my people** and **the house of Jacob** those who had degenerated from their family lineage and had basely revolted against the faith of their fathers.

2. **"For day after day they seek me out; they seem eager to know my ways, as if they were a nation that does what is right and has not forsaken the commands of its God. They ask me for just decisions and seem eager for God to come near them."** Here he aims to remove every ground of objection from hypocrites, who had their answers ready, saying: "We fear, serve, and love God; we seek him with our whole heart. Why do you rebuke us as if we were irreligious persons? We wish to regulate our life according to the injunctions of the law." To meet this objection, God through the prophet affirms that nothing they do is pure or sincere, that everything is pretended and hypocritical and consequently is of no value before God, who demands the whole heart (see Genesis 17:1).

3. **"'Why have we fasted,' they say, 'and you have not seen it? Why**

have we humbled ourselves, and you have not noticed?' Yet on the day of your fasting, you do as you please and exploit all your workers." He takes the same subject farther, saying that feigned and perverse worshipers of God are not only blinded by their hypocrisy but also swell with pride so that they dare to grumble at God openly and to complain when he presses hard upon them, as if he had done them a grievous injury. "Are you rejecting our services, fasts, and prayers? Why are they not acceptable to you? Do we vex ourselves in vain?"

He has admitted that hypocrites have some outward show of holiness, by which they deceive people; but now he declares that inwardly they are also puffed up and intoxicated by pride, while they have pretended good works by which they think they satisfy God. And on this pretense they openly oppose the prophets and indulge in the worst vices, such as unbelief, rebellion and obstinacy against God, distrust, cruelty, and fraud. These, they think, are light matters and are easily washed away by external exercises; the former are their preeminent merits, in which they think the worship of God consists, and through which they hope to obtain the pardon of all their sins.

4. "Your fasting ends in quarreling and strife, and in striking each other with wicked fists. You cannot fast as you do today and expect your voice to be heard on high." This verse should be linked with the end of the preceding verse. In the previous clause he introduced hypocrites as complaining of the prophets' violence and harshness; in this clause he gives the reason why the Lord loathes their fasts and their other performances. It is because they do not proceed from pure affection of heart. What the inclination of their heart is, he shows from its fruits; he sends them back to the duties of the second table, from which it is easily seen what we are. Purity of heart is manifested by our living innocently and abstaining from all deceit and injustice. These are the marks of pure affection, in the absence of which the Lord rejects and even abhors all external worship.

5. "Is this the kind of fast I have chosen, only a day for a man to humble himself? Is it only for bowing one's head like a reed and for lying on sackcloth and ashes? Is that what you call a fast, a day acceptable to the LORD?" God confirms the preceding statement and shows that fasting is neither desired nor approved by God in itself but only insofar as it is directed to its true end. He did not want it completely abolished, only its improper use—that is, because they believed the worship of God to consist in it. By neglecting or even despising true godliness, they thought bodily exercise was enough; hypocrites always put forward external ceremonies as if they were able to appease God.

6. "Is not this the kind of fasting I have chosen: to loose the chains of injustice and untie the cords of the yoke, to set the oppressed free and break every yoke?" The prophet speaking for the Lord shows the real duties of piety and what God chiefly recommends to us—namely, to relieve those who are wretched and pressed with a heavy burden. But the prophet appears to abolish fasting universally when, in place of it, he lists those works that are most highly acceptable to God. The answer is that fasting is approved when it is accompanied by the love that we owe to our fellow human beings. The prophet therefore tells us to be tested against the principle that our consciences should be whole and pure, that we should be kind to each other. If this state of affairs prevails, then any fasting that is added to it will be pleasing and acceptable to God. He does not mention purity of heart at all here, but it is described by works, its fruits, from which it is easily seen what kind of heart we have.

7. "Is it not to share your food with the hungry and to provide the poor wanderer with shelter—when you see the naked, to clothe him, and not to turn away from your own flesh and blood?" He goes on to describe the duties of love for our neighbor, which he had described briefly in the preceding verse. Having said that we must abstain from every act of injustice, he now shows that we ought to exercise kindness toward the wretched and those who need our assistance. Uprightness and righteousness are divided into two parts. First, we should injure nobody; and second, we should bestow our wealth and abundance on the poor and needy. These two ought to be combined, for it is not enough to abstain from acts of injustice if you refuse to help the needy.

8. "Then your light will break forth like the dawn, and your healing will quickly appear; then your righteousness will go before you, and the glory of the LORD will be your rear guard." The prophet shows that God is not too rigorous and does not demand from us more than is proper, and that hypocrites have no reason to complain of his excessive severity. When their works are condemned, they grumble and reply that God can never be satisfied, that they do not know what they should do or what course they should follow. The Lord replies that he demands nothing but a pure and honest heart—that is, an upright conscience, and that if they have this, he will receive them graciously, will bear testimony to their holiness, and will bestow every kind of blessing on those whose faults he justly chastises. And lastly, there is no reason why they should grumble at him as excessively stern and harsh, because they will find him to be kind and bountiful when they lay down all hypocrisy and devote themselves sincerely to his service.

9. "Then you will call, and the LORD will answer; you will cry for help, and he will say: Here am I." Isaiah continues what he already said: Everything will go well with the Jews if they are inoffensive and free from doing wrong to anyone, showing their piety and religion.

"If you do away with the yoke of oppression, with the pointing finger and malicious talk . . ." In the latter part of the verse God through Isaiah repeats that he will be reconciled to the Jews if they repent. The word **yoke** includes all the annoyances that are offered to the poor; in other words, "If you cease to annoy your brothers and abstain from all violence and deceit, the Lord will bestow upon you every kind of blessing."

10. "... and if you spend yourselves on behalf of the hungry and satisfy the needs of the oppressed, then your light will rise in the darkness, and your night will become like the noonday." He goes on to recommend the duties of the love that we owe to one another. The sum of the whole discourse is this: It is no good serving God if we only offer him trivial and bare ceremonies. This is not the right and proper worship of God, who commands and enjoins us to lead an upright and innocent life with our neighbors, willingly to give ourselves and our labors to them, and to be prepared to help them readily and cheerfully whenever it is necessary. We should observe the two parts of this duty that God through the prophet has expressly described. In the first place he recommends to us mercy and kindness; and in the second place he exhorts us to the work itself and the effect. It would not be enough to perform acts of kindness toward other people if our disposition toward them were not warm and affectionate (see 1 Corinthians 13:3).

11. "The LORD will guide you always; he will satisfy your needs in a sun-scorched land and will strengthen your frame." He now describes more clearly what he mentioned briefly and figuratively: God will be their guide, so that they shall lack nothing for a full abundance of blessings. God is said to **guide** us when we actually feel that he goes before us, as if he were placed before our eyes.

"You will be like a well-watered garden, like a spring whose waters never fail." Isaiah continues to describe God's kindness, which he displays toward his sincere worshipers, so that we may not seek the causes of barrenness anywhere but in ourselves. God's kindness never dries up but always flows, if we do not stop its course by our own fault.

12. "Your people will rebuild the ancient ruins and will raise up the age-old foundations; you will be called Repairer of Broken Walls, Restorer of Streets with Dwellings." Here the prophet says that the people will be like a ruined building, and next, that they will be perfectly restored. He says that the Jews will be repairers and surveyors; that is, the Lord will make use of their labors. We ought to ascribe everything to the power of God, who is pleased to bestow upon us so high an honor as to permit our hands to be applied to his work. We have here a remarkable promise about gathering and raising up the ruins of the church. Since the Lord chooses to use our labor, let us not hesitate to be entirely devoted to it; even if the world opposes and mocks us, thinking us fools, let us take courage and conquer every difficulty. Our hearts ought to be completely confident when we know that we are doing the Lord's work and that he has commanded us to accomplish it.

13. "If you keep your feet from breaking the Sabbath and from

doing as you please on my holy day, if you call the Sabbath a delight and the LORD's holy day honorable, and if you honor it by not going your own way and not doing as you please or speaking idle words ..." The word **delight** must be viewed as referring to God and not to men because nothing can be more pleasing or acceptable to God than the observance of the Sabbath and sincere worship. The prophet speaking for the Lord carefully tells us that we do wrong if we lay aside God's commandments and esteem highly those things that are of no value. He warns people that they ought to form their judgment by God's will alone. He mentions certain sorts of duties again, showing clearly that the true observance of the Sabbath consists in self-denial and genuine conversion.

14. "... then you will find your joy in the LORD, and I will cause you to ride on the heights of the land and to feast on the inheritance of your father Jacob." By these words he promises a return to their native country and a safe habitation in it. We know that Judea was situated on a lofty place above the neighboring countries, while the situation of Babylon was much lower; so the people trembled as if they were shut up in a cave. He next tells more plainly what he meant by the word **ride,** for he promises the possession of that country that had been promised and given to the fathers, which they at that time enjoyed and of which they were afterward deprived for a time.

The mouth of the LORD has spoken. He added this, so they might know beyond all controversy that all these things were true. This must be viewed as referring not only to those promises but also to the beginning of the chapter. He rebuked hypocrites who thought they were defending themselves in a just cause and showed that they were suffering the just punishment of their sins and that it was pointless to argue with God and bring forward in opposition to him their own works, which were altogether empty and worthless. On that account he brings them back to the true observance of the Sabbath and shows that it would be well with them if they worshiped God in a right manner. At length he concludes that they do not have to deal with a mortal man; rather, he who pronounces these things is God the Judge.

Isaiah
Chapter 59

1. Surely the arm of the LORD is not too short to save, nor his ear too dull to hear. This discourse closely resembles the preceding one: God's prophet has unmasked hypocrites who vainly boasted of themselves, he has shown that the punishment inflicted on them was just, and now he replies to other objections. Hypocrites accuse God either of weakness or of excessive severity; so he shows that God does not lack either the power or the will to save his people but is prevented by their wickedness from exercising his kindness toward them. Therefore, they are wrong to blame God and utter slanders against him; on the contrary, they should be accusing themselves.

2. But your iniquities have separated you from your God; your sins have hidden his face from you, so that he will not hear. What this amounts to is that they cannot say God has changed, as if he had deviated from his natural disposition. The whole blame lies with themselves. By their own sins they to some extent prevent his kindness and refuse his help. Hence we infer that our sins alone deprive us of the grace of God and cause separation between us and him. What the prophet says about the people of his time applies to all ages since he pleads the cause of God against the slanders of the wicked. God is always like himself and is not wearied in doing good; his power is not diminished, but we hinder the entrance of his grace.

3. For your hands are stained with blood, your fingers with guilt. Your lips have spoken lies, and your tongue mutters wicked things. He now brings forward their actions, so they may not practice evasion or call into question those sins that have separated them from God. He removes their every excuse by bringing forward particular instances as if their shameful life were exhibited on an open stage. He speaks in the second person because, like an advocate, he argues and pleads the cause of God and therefore speaks of himself as not belonging to the rank of the wicked, with whom he did not wish to be classed. Though he was not entirely free from sin, he feared and served God and enjoyed liberty of conscience.

4. No one calls for justice; no one pleads his case with integrity. They rely on empty arguments and speak lies; they conceive trouble and give birth to evil. He means that none of them studies what is right or proper or opposes the acts of injustice that are committed by the strong against the weak; and this leads to growing licentiousness because everyone winks at it, and there is no one who cares about the defense of justice. It is not enough that we abstain from violence if we do not, as far as is in our power, hinder it from being committed by others. Indeed, whoever permits what he is able to hinder does in some sense command it; silence is a sort of consent.

5. They hatch the eggs of vipers and spin a spider's web. Whoever eats their eggs will die, and when one is broken, an adder is hatched. The prophet proceeds farther, comparing the Jews not only to women but to venomous beasts, to make it more evident that everything that proceeds from them is destructive and deadly. He says that **they hatch the eggs of vipers;** a viper cannot lay an egg that is not venomous, and they are so inured to wickedness and so full of it that they can throw out nothing but poison.

By **spin a spider's web** he means that they are so barren and destitute of anything good that they even deceive by looking virtuous. By two marks he describes wicked people. First, the works they perform reveal their corrupt nature; second, those works are of no value whatever and contribute nothing toward making them kind, amiable, charitable, and faithful to those with whom they are in contact.

6. Their cobwebs are useless for clothing; they cannot cover themselves with what they make. Their deeds are evil deeds, and acts of violence are in their hands. He repeats and confirms the same statement: Everything they attempt or undertake is always useless to mankind because they purposely shrink from all acts of kindness. They devote themselves to evil deeds; no advantage of any kind can be expected from the life of anyone who desires to be barren and destitute of all justice. Those whose only skill is in mischief, who work hard to avoid doing good, are wild animals and ought not to be called human. He immediately adds, without using imagery, that they are devoted to iniquity.

7. Their feet rush into sin; they are swift to shed innocent blood. Their thoughts are evil thoughts; ruin and destruction mark their ways. In various ways he paints for us the picture of what may be called extreme wickedness—when people shake off and cast away from them the fear of God and then throw themselves into every kind of wickedness and break out into all cruelty, extortion, and outrage. He says they **rush** because they are eager to do evil. Having formerly spoken of **hands** and the **tongue,** he also adds **feet** in order to show that they are proficient in every kind of villainy and that there is no part of their body that is entirely free from iniquity.

8. The way of peace they do not know; there is no justice in their paths. They have turned them into crooked roads; no one who walks in them will know peace. He says that **the way of peace they do not know**

because their cruelty deprives them of the **justice** by which human society is maintained, the foundation of which is mutual **peace** and kindness; **justice** and integrity are nourished by **peace.** If everyone rushes on his neighbors and attacks them with unbridled rage, there is open war; harmony cannot be preserved among us unless equity is observed by every individual.

9. So justice is far from us, and righteousness does not reach us. We look for light, but all is darkness; for brightness, but we walk in deep shadows. After describing the corrupt and depraved state of the people, he shows that the severe chastisements inflicted on them are richly deserved. They cannot complain of being treated with greater harshness and severity than was proper. Thus he has painted, as in a picture, those vices that were publicly known, that they might more fully perceive in how many and in what various ways they were guilty before God. And now he repeats that it is no wonder God treats such obstinate dispositions with greater severity and gives them their just recompense.

10. Like the blind we grope along the wall, feeling our way like men without eyes. At midday we stumble as if it were twilight; among the strong, we are like the dead. He explains the same thing by different forms of expression; in consequence of the grievous complaints that were heard among the people, he determined to omit nothing that was fitted to describe their calamities. It is perhaps by way of concession that he mentions those things, as if he said, "Our affairs are reduced to the deepest misery, but we ought chiefly to consider the cause, for we have deserved all this and far worse."

11. We all growl like bears; we moan mournfully like doves. We look for justice, but find none; for deliverance, but it is far away. He describes two classes of those who cannot silently endure their afflictions without making them known by external signs; some howl fiercely, and others moan like doves. This latter metaphor was employed by him in describing the groans of Hezekiah (see Isaiah 38:14); and this happens when we endeavor to restrain our sorrow and yet cannot prevent the outward signs of grief from breaking out. The meaning is that sometimes the violence of their grief constrained them to utter loud cries and sometimes they complained in low and murmuring sounds, but in both cases without avail because their condition was not changed for the better.

12. For our offenses are many in your sight, and our sins testify against us. Our offenses are ever with us, and we acknowledge our iniquities. He confirms what he said before—namely, that the people act unjustly in accusing God of cruelty and in not understanding that they are being justly punished for their iniquities, the huge mass of which towers up to heaven. In this sense the prophet says that their sins are many.

13. . . . . rebellion and treachery against the LORD, turning our backs on our God, fomenting oppression and revolt, uttering lies our hearts have conceived. Here he names certain sorts of sin in order to arouse the people more keenly to acknowledge their wickedness. It must be regarded as monstrous that people who have been chastised and almost crushed by God's hand are still proud and so obstinate that they cannot bend or be humbled by a conviction of their sin. The Lord tries to soften our obduracy by wounds; but when chastisement does us no good, our case must be given up as hopeless. Isaiah therefore labors to show how wretched is the condition of the people who endured severe hardships, yet complained against God and did not let themselves be brought into a state of obedience. He frequently repeats this warning and reproves them sharply in order to subdue their obstinacy.

14. So justice is driven back, and righteousness stands at a distance; truth has stumbled in the streets, honesty cannot enter. It is a mistake to suppose that the prophet returns to his earlier subject and speaks of the punishments that the people had suffered at the hand of God. He is still carrying on the preceding narrative, explaining the diseases under which the people suffered, that they may see clearly that their punishment is fair.

15. Truth is nowhere to be found, and whoever shuns evil becomes a prey. The LORD looked and was displeased that there was no justice. The prophet means that all uprightness was so greatly abhorred that the true worshipers of God, if any remained, were not permitted to be safe. In other words, "Whoever wishes to live among men must vie with them in wickedness." Or as the proverb goes, "Among wolves we must howl; but he who wishes to live innocently shall be torn in pieces, just as a sheep is torn apart by wolves."

16. He saw that there was no one, and he was appalled that there was no one to intercede. Isaiah continues the same subject but more fully. What he said in the preceding verse, that it displeased the Lord that **there was no justice,** might have been obscure. In this passage he states that the Lord saw **there was no one** to assist the church.

So his own arm worked salvation for him, and his own righteousness sustained him. By these words he means that we ought not to despair, even if we receive no human help. Yet, minimizing every other assistance, he pronounces that the **salvation** of his own nation, and consequently of all mankind, is due, from first to last, to God's undeserved goodness and absolute power. God is quite sufficient for himself; his power and strength are sufficient to redeem the Jews, and he stretches out his hand to the feeble. When the prophet says that people can do nothing to promote their salvation, he brings down all pride, so that, being stripped of confidence in their works, they will approach God.

17. He put on righteousness as his breastplate, and the helmet of salvation on his head; he put on the garments of vengeance and wrapped himself in zeal as in a cloak. Here he equips God with his armor, for the purpose of both confirming more and more the confidence of believers and of stripping everyone of all confidence in their own strength. What this amounts to is that God lacks nothing for discomfiting his enemies and gaining the victory; from his righteousness, power, and grace, and from his ardent love for his people, he will make for himself complete armor. This is again worthy of remark, for although we acknowledge that God is sufficiently powerful, yet we are not satisfied with it but seek other help. Thus our minds are always inclined to unbelief, and so they fasten on inferior means and are greatly entangled by them.

In order to correct this vice, Isaiah presents this lifelike description, as if he said, "Know that God has in his hand all the safeguards of your salvation and will lack nothing to deliver you in spite of enemies and to bring you back to your native country. Therefore there is no reason why you should tremble."

18. According to what they have done, so will he repay wrath to his enemies and retribution to his foes; he will repay the islands their due. The prophet confirms the statement of the preceding verse, showing what will be the nature of the vengeance with which the Lord is clothed; namely, he is prepared to pay his enemies back. We must attend to the reason why the prophet describes the Lord as thus armed, indignant, and ready for vengeance. It is because the salvation of the church is connected with the destruction of the wicked, and therefore God must be armed against the enemies who wish to destroy us.

Hence we see God's infinite love toward us, loving us so warmly that he bears hostility to our enemies and declares that he will pay them back. So strong is his affection to his little flock that he sets a higher value on them than on the whole world. This is why he says that **he will repay the islands [that is, distant overseas lands] their due**; in order to deliver his people, he overthrew monarchies that were powerful and that appeared to be invincible. But although here he mentions only mortal men, we must begin with Satan, who is their head.

19. From the west, men will fear the name of the LORD, and from the rising of the sun, they will revere his glory. For he will come like a pent-up flood that the breath of the LORD drives along. He now testifies that this work of redemption will be so splendid and illustrious that the whole world will wonder, behold, praise, and celebrate and, struck with fear, will give God the glory. It is uncertain whether he means the conversion of the Gentiles or the terror with which God dismays his enemies. For my own part I am more inclined to the former opinion. Even to the utmost boundaries of the earth, the name of God will be revered and honored, so that the Gentiles will not only tremble but will serve and adore him with true repentance.

Like a pent-up flood. The enemy attack will be so fierce that, like a rapid and impetuous torrent, it will seem to sweep away and destroy everything; but the Lord will cause it instantly to subside and disappear. This is therefore intended to heighten the description of the divine power by which the vast strength and dreadful fury of the enemies are repelled, diverted, and fall to pieces.

20. **"The Redeemer will come to Zion, to those in Jacob who repent of their sins," declares the LORD.** He confirms what he said before: The people will be delivered, and God will be the author of this blessing. So he tells the people to cheer up, for their captivity will not last forever. Next, he urges them to place the hope of redemption in God alone, that they may fix their minds solely on his promises.

By the name **Zion** he denotes here, as in other passages, captives and exiles; however far they had been banished from their country, they still carried the temple in their hearts.

21. **"As for me, this is my covenant with them," says the LORD.** Because it was difficult to believe what the prophet has said so far, he endeavors in various ways to strengthen the Jews, that they might rely with unshaken confidence on this promise of salvation and might ascribe to God so much honor as to trust in his Word. We should note carefully the word **covenant,** by which the prophet points out the greatness and excellence of this promise. The promises are more extensive and may be regarded as the stones of the building, while the foundation of it is the **covenant,** which supports the whole mass. He makes use of this word, therefore, so they will not think it contained something ordinary; and he adds that even if the Lord did not do this immediately, they could nevertheless expect it with firm and unshaken hope. A contrast seems to be implied, so that believers would cheerfully look forward to the new covenant that was to be established in the hand of Christ.

"My Spirit, who is on you, and my words that I have put in your mouth will not depart from your mouth, or from the mouths of your children, or from the mouths of their descendants from this time on and forever," says the LORD. It might be thought feeble and trivial when he tells the church to be satisfied with the **words** and the **Spirit**—as if it were great happiness to hang in suspense on nothing but God's promises. Yet although the prophet commends the value and excellence of doctrine, I have no doubt that it is not separated from its effect. God regulates and dispenses his grace in such a way that as long as believers remain in this world, he always trains them to have patience and does not in every instance answer their prayers. He therefore brings them back to doctrine. In other words, "You will indeed find that I am kind to you in various ways; but there is no happiness that will be of greater importance to you or that you ought to desire more earnestly than to feel that I am present by the Word and the Spirit." Hence we infer that it is a most valuable treasure of the church that he has chosen to dwell in the hearts of believers by his Spirit and to preserve among them the doctrine of his Gospel.

Isaiah
Chapter 60

1. "Arise, shine, for your light has come, and the glory of the LORD rises upon you." Isaiah speaking for God now shows the efficacy of the word he spoke about earlier, for the Lord raises up a prostrate and afflicted church and restores her to her brightness. Because the prophet represents the person of God, he now declares his authority. He uses the form of a command, that the word spoken might be more efficacious, as if in the exercise of absolute power he put the church in possession of that happier condition he had promised. This amounts to saying that believers may know he does not scatter his words in the air but speaks with effect.

2. "See, darkness covers the earth and thick darkness is over the peoples, but the LORD rises upon you and his glory appears over you." He now shows more clearly, with a comparison, the grace that he mentioned earlier, so that we might form some idea of how much God loves his elect and how extraordinary is the privilege he bestows on them. What he says amounts to this: Though we are weighed down by innumerable afflictions, and while the whole world, as it were, sinks under them, God will take care of his people in order to enrich them with various benefits. He shows, therefore, that the light of grace and favor that he mentioned will not be indiscriminately enjoyed by everybody but will be peculiar to the people of God.

3. "Nations will come to your light, and kings to the brightness of your dawn." He confirms what we have already said: The only **light** for men and women is when the Lord shines on them by his Word. All indeed acknowledge this, but they do not set as high a value as they ought on this benefit; they imagine it to be something ordinary that belongs naturally to everyone. But the prophet speaking for God shows that this grace is supernatural and therefore should be distinguished from nature. This is clearly shown by the repetition of the words **upon you . . . over you** in the preceding verse.

4. "Lift up your eyes and look about you: All assemble and come to you; your sons come from afar, and your daughters are carried on the arm." By a variety of expressions he confirms the promise of the church's restoration, which seemed altogether incredible. Nor was it easy to convince the Jews of this while the state of their affairs was so wretched and confused. At that time the kingdom of Judah alone remained, growing less every day until it was utterly devastated; and when the people were led into captivity amidst that frightful dispersion and melancholy oppression, everything was so desperate that the church seemed to be entirely ruined. It was therefore proper to confirm this doctrine by a variety of expressions, so that hearts naturally prone to distrust might no longer doubt. For this reason he leads the Jews to look at the event as actually at hand, though it was at a great distance, so they might not hesitate any more than if they could already see it.

5. "Then you will look and be radiant, your heart will throb and swell with joy; the wealth on the seas will be brought to you, to you the riches of the nations will come." At first sight these things appear to be somewhat inconsistent with each other: Before, he spoke of the fact as present, and now he presents it as future. But he was speaking before about faith, which sees things that are not visible to human sense, whereas now he is talking about the actual event; or at least he is limiting the statement so believers will continue to be patient.

6. "Herds of camels will cover your land, young camels of Midian and Ephah. And all from Sheba will come, bearing gold and incense and proclaiming the praise of the LORD." The prophet describes figuratively the glory of the church and accommodates his discourse to the time and to the people he is dealing with. The Jews must be instructed first, and then the Gentiles, to whom the truth of those things has come. It is as if he said that nations far distant will come with their wealth into the power of God, for when he foretells that the church will be enriched, this must not be understood as referring to human individuals. On account of the unity of the Head and the members, what belongs to God and to Christ is transferred to the church.

7. "All Kedar's flocks will be gathered to you, the rams of Nebaioth will serve you; they will be accepted as offerings on my altar." He mentions those countries that lay toward the East, and chiefly Arabia and neighboring places, which he calls **Kedar** and **Nebaioth.**

"And I will adorn my glorious temple." He promises the true restoration of the people, for the chief part of their happiness lay in the continuation of the **temple,** where men called on God in a right manner. We must begin with this: God reigns among us, by which we are made truly happy. For this reason when the Lord declares that the church will be restored, he mentions the **temple,** the glory of which he will restore, as if he said, "My house is now exposed to the mockery of the Gentiles, but I will at length restore to it the glory of which it has been deprived."

8. "Who are these that fly along like clouds, like doves to their nests?" Not satisfied with describing this gift of God, the prophet breaks out into admiration and exclaims, **"Who are these?"** This is far more forceful than if he had simply referred to an inconceivable multitude or had even made use of the same metaphors. He intended, therefore, to describe how splendid this multiplication would be when he could not find words sufficient to express it.

The metaphor of **doves** is highly appropriate to this subject, for when they are dispersed through the fields, they appear no different from untamed birds; and yet they are domesticated and have their dovecotes to go to and to build their nests in. Thus believers, enlightened by faith, begin to perceive their assembly, to which they fly from frightful dispersion. How necessary this warning was will be readily perceived by all who take into account men's wretched and alarming condition at that time. The prophets had carefully instructed the Jews for many years with hardly any success. So what was to be expected from the Gentiles, who were altogether alienated from God?

9. "Surely the islands look to me; in the lead are the ships of Tarshish, bringing your sons from afar, with their silver and gold, to the honor of the LORD your God, the Holy One of Israel, for he has endowed you with splendor." The general meaning is that God intends to elevate his church to the highest honor and adorn her with necessary ornaments. So that believers may not doubt this promise or ascribe anything to their own merits, God himself promises that he will be the author of this event—**for he has endowed you with splendor.** In addition, the prophet declares that the riches of the Gentiles, which a little earlier he seemed to represent as the prey of the church or the prize of victory, will be a sacred offering to God. Thus he states more clearly what I have already said: There is nothing that we ought to desire more earnestly than that the whole world should bow to God's authority.

10. "Foreigners will rebuild your walls, and their kings will serve you. Though in anger I struck you, in favor I will show you compassion." God through the prophet continues the same subject. Formerly he said that foreigners would submit to his authority in order to build the temple; now he says that **foreigners** will **rebuild** the **walls.** He uses various comparisons in promising the restoration of the church. It is customary in Scripture, when the church is spoken of, to exhibit sometimes the temple and sometimes Jerusalem. He promises that **foreigners** and strangers will assist in raising this building, so the Jews will not be worried by their poverty or their small number and consequently lose heart. During the captivity they might be tempted to distrust, so that they might think they could not achieve the return to their native country that they hoped for.

But Cyrus enabled this when he supplied them with a large amount of gold and silver. But in him these things were merely foreshadowed. They were actually fulfilled in Christ, to whose reign they must entirely relate.

11. "Your gates will always stand open, they will never be shut, day or night, so that men may bring you the wealth of the nations—their kings led in triumphal procession." When he says **the wealth of the nations** will belong to the church, let us not view this as referring to carnal luxury but to obedience, which the whole world will render to God in the church.

12. "For the nation or kingdom that will not serve you will perish; it will be utterly ruined." The prophet speaking for God is encouraging believers, so they will not doubt that the restoration will be as he has described. Those events were altogether incredible; and though we have obtained abundant confirmation of them from the actual event (for they have been made manifest to the eyes of all), yet, unless we are guided by the Spirit of the Lord, we could hardly conceive of them in our mind. He shows, therefore, that there is no reason why the Jews should doubt the restoration of the temple, because the Gentiles would aid them to the utmost of their power. But here Isaiah is thinking of something higher than the building of the visible temple; he means the obedience that kings and nobles and the common people render to the church when they promote, as far as they are able, pure doctrine.

13. "The glory of Lebanon will come to you, the pine, the fir and the cypress together, to adorn the place of my sanctuary; and I will glorify the place of my feet." Isaiah again uses the metaphor that he used before when he compared the church of God to a building or a city. He mentions things that were necessary for building—**the pine, the fir and the cypress** that grew in **Lebanon,** a forest abounding in excellent trees.

To adorn the place of my sanctuary. All that is excellent and beautiful in Lebanon will be carried into the church. These figures contain an emblematic reference to the spiritual worship of God; the Lord adorns his church with the title of a **sanctuary** because he dwells in the midst of it. Yet he always alludes to the temple, so as to accommodate himself to the time and to ordinary custom. Thus he holds out to us the pattern of the temple that stood at Jerusalem, so that under the image of it we may contemplate the "holy temple" (Ephesians 2:21) of which we are the "living stones" and living substance (1 Peter 2:5).

14. "The sons of your oppressors will come bowing before you; all who despise you will bow down at your feet and will call you the City of the LORD, Zion of the Holy One of Israel." He continues the same subject, showing how splendid this work of redemption will be, for those who persecuted or despised the church **will come,** will bow down humbly before her, and will submit to her with their whole heart. By **the sons of your oppressors** he means the persecutors and enemies who oppressed her. This was indeed partly fulfilled when the Jews returned to their native country; but that return was nothing more than a shadow of the deliverance that we have obtained through Christ.

15. **"Although you have been forsaken and hated, with no one traveling through, I will make you the everlasting pride and the joy of all generations."** The prophet has in his eye the intermediate period that was already at hand, for soon after his death the people were deprived of their heritage and led into captivity, so that everyone thought there was no remaining hope of their safety. Believers might be reduced to despair, thinking, "We are undone. There can be no remedy for affairs so desperate, and we ought not to hope for a better condition." So he shows that those grievous calamities cannot prevent God from restoring them. They seemed for a time to be forsaken when the Lord chastised them; yet it was easy for him to raise them again to prosperity and to a better condition than before.

16. **"You will drink the milk of nations and be nursed at royal breasts. Then you will know that I, the LORD, am your Savior, your Redeemer, the Mighty One of Jacob."** He speaks of the extension of the church that he had mentioned before; but it was important for the same things to be repeated frequently because it seemed incredible that the church, which had been reduced to such great and numerous calamities, would be restored and spread throughout the whole world. Her condition was desperate; but at length, out of that slender remnant that had been, as it were, snatched from the burning, to the great astonishment of all, she was restored, and her seed was spread far and wide through every part of the world.

17. **"Instead of bronze I will bring you gold, and silver in place of iron. Instead of wood I will bring you bronze, and iron in place of stones. I will make peace your governor and righteousness your ruler."** God through Isaiah alludes to the building of the ancient temple and compares it with the heavenly and spiritual temple, as if he said, "When you are led into captivity, you will deplore the ruin of the temple. But I will cause you to build one far more excellent." Everything will be full of magnificence and splendor in the temple that replaces the previous one.

18. **"No longer will violence be heard in your land, nor ruin or destruction within your borders, but you will call your walls Salvation and your gates Praise."** Here he states more clearly what we have already said: Namely, while the prophet is talking about the prosperous condition of the church, he indirectly contrasts the miseries and calamities by which they had been afflicted in various ways. He promises, therefore, that they will never afterward be subjected to such afflictions. Various afflictions did afterwards befall them, but the people were never scattered in such a manner as not to have some remaining form of the church and thus enjoy peace and feel that they were protected and kept by the hand of God.

19-20. "The sun will no more be your light by day, nor will the brightness of the moon shine on you, for the LORD will be your everlasting light, and your God will be your glory. Your sun will never set again, and your moon will wane no more; the LORD will be your everlasting light, and your days of sorrow will end." He teaches that the prosperity of the church will not be temporary but permanent. He distinguishes it from the ordinary human condition, where nothing is steadfast or permanent; there is nothing under the sun, however well regulated, that is not subject to various changes. But we ought not to judge the church in light of the dangers of the present life, for she is preserved in the midst of the billows. In other words, "Do not judge from present appearances. God will be your sun, so that you have no need of light from the sun or the moon. So do not dread any change or revolution of affairs; for you will have a perpetual and unchangeable light."

21. "Then will all your people be righteous and they will possess the land forever. They are the shoot I have planted, the work of my hands, for the display of my splendor." Here God shows the true establishment of the church—namely, when she is purged of the ungodly, and none but righteous people have a place in her. Yet we know that in the church hypocrites have always mingled with the true children of God. This verse is a description of the whole reign of Christ—not such as it shall be at any one moment, but in its perfection.

22. "The least of you will become a thousand, the smallest a mighty nation. I am the LORD; in its time I will do this swiftly." He confirms what he said before: Though they were few in number, the church of God would be populous. When the prophet foretold these things, there was still a vast multitude of people; but afterwards it was so greatly diminished that not more than a feeble remnant was left, as we saw earlier.

Isaiah
Chapter 61

1. The Spirit of the Sovereign LORD is on me, because the LORD has anointed me to preach good news to the poor. He has sent me to bind up the brokenhearted, to proclaim freedom for the captives and release for the prisoners. This chapter is added as a seal to the previous one, to confirm what has hitherto been said about restoring the church of Christ. For this purpose Christ testifies that he has been anointed by God, in consequence of which he was later right to apply this prophecy to himself; he has exhibited clearly and openly what others have laid down in an obscure manner.

This passage ought to be carefully observed, for no one can claim the right or authority to teach unless he can show that he has been prompted to it by the Spirit of God. The prophet does not claim for himself the right and authority to teach before he has shown that the Lord has **sent** him **to bind up the brokenhearted.** He uses numerous metaphors to explain the same thing more clearly. By binding up, he means nothing else than healing; but he expresses something more than in the preceding clause, for he shows that the preaching of the Word is not an empty sound but a powerful medicine whose effect is felt not by obdurate and hard-hearted people but by wounded consciences.

2. . . . to proclaim the year of the LORD's favor and the day of vengeance of our God, to comfort all who mourn. Here he expressly mentions the time of bestowing such distinguished grace, in order to remove the doubts that might arise. We know by daily experience how numerous and diversified are the anxious cares that distract the heart. Christ affirms that he is the herald of future grace, the time of which he fixes as the time of the **favor** of God; as he was to be the Redeemer of the church by free grace, so it was in his power, and justly so, to select the time.

The punishment that was to be inflicted on the people would leave room for forgiveness. In order to convince them of this more fully, Isaiah says that the Lord has charged him with this office, that he may proclaim deliverance (not just himself but also others) until the arrival of the chief messenger—namely, Christ. It is Christ who actually bestows and exhibits what God at that time commanded to be made known for a future period.

3-4. . . . and provide for those who grieve in Zion—to bestow on them a crown of beauty instead of ashes, the oil of gladness instead of mourning, and a garment of praise instead of a spirit of despair. They will be called oaks of righteousness, a planting of the LORD for the display of his splendor. They will rebuild the ancient ruins and restore the places long devastated; they will renew the ruined cities that have been devastated for generations. He goes on to describe at greater length the restoration of the church—chiefly so that the Jews might hope confidently for deliverance, because those promises seemed altogether incredible.

5. Aliens will shepherd your flocks; foreigners will work your fields and vineyards. He means that **foreigners** and strangers will be ready to yield obedience to them, for in consequence of their being at that time separated from the rest of the nations, no one was willing to assist them.

6. And you will be called priests of the LORD, you will be named ministers of our God. You will feed on the wealth of nations, and in their riches you will boast. This verse sheds somewhat more light on verse 5, for in the second part the prophet foretells that believers will enjoy the riches of the Gentiles and will be raised to glory as their successors.

Two main things should be noticed in these words, if we are to understand them fully. First, when the prophets wish to describe the glory and happiness of the kingdom of Christ, they compare them with human affairs. Second, when they speak of the church, they connect the Head with the members in such a manner that sometimes they look more at the Head than at the members.

7. Instead of their shame my people will receive a double portion, and instead of disgrace they will rejoice in their inheritance; and so they will inherit a double portion in their land, and everlasting joy will be theirs. He confirms a former statement (verse 3), where he said that believers who were **mourning** in sackcloth and covered with **ashes** would be sprinkled with **the oil of gladness**. This change of **mourning** into **joy** is promised again.

8. "For I, the LORD, love justice; I hate robbery and iniquity. In my faithfulness I will reward them and make an everlasting covenant with them." He not only confirms what he promised in the name of the Lord but also urges the Jews to repent and shows where they should expect salvation to come from and how great is the Judge with whom we are dealing. He reasons from the nature of God about by what manner they ought to regulate their life, that they may not by their wickedness reject the grace that is offered to them.

9. "Their descendants will be known among the nations and their offspring among the peoples. All who see them will acknowledge that they are a people the LORD has blessed." Here the prophet deals more clearly with the extension of the church, which at that time might be said to be confined within a narrow corner of the earth and afterward, as we have already seen, was exceedingly diminished and impaired (Isaiah 1:9; 10:22). The church, says Isaiah, will be spread throughout the whole world, so as to be visible to all the nations. And yet this did not happen even in the reign of Solomon, when the Jews flourished most in wealth and splendor (1 Kings 10:21, 27). Now this seemed quite incredible, and that is why the prophets take such pains to convince people of it and repeat it very frequently. The Jews were not to measure this restoration by their own understanding or by present appearances.

10. I delight greatly in the LORD; my soul rejoices in my God. Isaiah represents the church as giving thanks to God, in order to convince them more fully of the truth of what he said before.

For he has clothed me with garments of salvation and arrayed me in a robe of righteousness, as a bridegroom adorns his head like a priest, and as a bride adorns herself with her jewels. These things were still indeed at a great distance but must have been seen and understood by the eyes of faith; the eyes should be raised to heaven when the prophet talks of salvation and righteousness. Nothing is visible here, and much less could so great happiness have been perceived by the senses while everything tended toward destruction. But because even now we do not see any such beauty of the church, which is even contemptible in the eyes of the world under the revolting dress of the cross, we need faith, which comprehends heavenly and invisible things.

11. For as the soil makes the sprout come up and a garden causes seeds to grow, so the Sovereign LORD will make righteousness and praise spring up before all nations. Using a beautiful comparison, the prophet confirms the former promises, reminding the Jews of the ordinary power of God, which shines brightly in the creatures themselves. The earth every year puts forth her bud, the gardens grow green after the sowing time, and, in short, herbs and plants, which appear to be dead during the winter, revive in the spring and resume their vigor. These are proofs and very clear illustrations of the divine power and kindness toward us. Since this is so, should people doubt it? Will not he who gave this power and strength to the earth display it even more in delivering his people? And will he not cause the elect seed to bud, since he promised that it would remain in the world forever?

Isaiah
Chapter 62

1. For Zion's sake I will not keep silent, for Jerusalem's sake I will not remain quiet, till her righteousness shines out like the dawn, her salvation like a blazing torch. The sad captivity that was almost to blot out the name of the whole nation was at hand. It was necessary to confirm and encourage believers by many words, so that with strong and assured confidence they might rely on these promises under the burden of the cross. Here, therefore, the prophet, discharging the office that had been entrusted to him, openly declares that he will not be slack in the performance of his duty and will not stop speaking until he encourages believers with the hope of future salvation, that they may know and be fully convinced that God will deliver his church.

It is necessary for these things to be repeated frequently because our minds are so depraved that we speedily forget God's promises. When the prophet says he **will not remain quiet,** he is also reminding others of their duty, so they may take courage and look for their restoration with assured confidence even though it may be long delayed. God's voice addresses them constantly, and they must answer it with unwearied attention.

2. The nations will see your righteousness, and all kings your glory; you will be called by a new name that the mouth of the LORD will bestow. He now states more plainly the reason why he formerly said he would not be **silent**—namely, so believers may be fully convinced that salvation is not promised to them in vain. He uses the word **glory** to mean "salvation." We see here the argument by which prophets must gain strength to persevere—namely, the Lord is faithful and will in the end fulfill what he has promised, even if he delays for a time.

Isaiah proceeds with the same subject, and we need not wonder at this, for no one, judging by the flesh, could have formed such vast conceptions and expectations. Besides, he intended to fix the hearts of believers on the kingdom of Christ. It was necessary to adorn and magnify this by such illustrious titles because hitherto it was not only obscure but at a great distance. When the Jews saw they were still very far from their former honor, a double danger had to be avoided—despising the grace of God and, on the other hand, resting satisfied with the mere beginnings, disregarding Christ and devoting their whole attention to earthly advantages. The prophet therefore reminds them that the return to their native country was only the forerunner of the exalted rank that was to be expected at the manifestation of Christ.

3-4. You will be a crown of splendor in the LORD's hand, a royal diadem in the hand of your God. No longer will they call you Deserted, or name your land Desolate. But you will be called Hephzibah, and your land Beulah; for the LORD will take delight in you, and your land will be married. This metaphor of marriage, by which he denotes the restoration of the people, is very beautiful and conveys twofold instruction. He shows that the state of variance between God and the church will be terminated—first, because she will be received as a wife by her appeased husband; and second, because the multitude of people will take away the reproach of widowhood.

5. As a young man marries a maiden, so will your sons marry you; as a bridegroom rejoices over his bride, so will your God rejoice over you. This verse is an explanation and confirmation of the preceding verse.

6. I have posted watchmen on your walls, O Jerusalem; they will never be silent day or night. You who call on the LORD, give yourselves no rest. The prophet intended to describe the perfect happiness of the kingdom of Christ; so he collects all that belongs to the prosperous condition of any country or city. To other advantages he adds guards and a garrison. The greatest abundance of all good things would be of little avail if we were not safe from enemies; therefore he declares that the Lord will not only supply the church with all that is necessary, but he will also appoint faithful guards to ward off enemies and robbers, that he may thus be recognized, both within and without, as the author of a happy life.

7. . . . and give him no rest till he establishes Jerusalem. Here are two distinct benefits. First, faithful pastors watch over the safety of the church; second, the church is upheld and preserved in her condition by their agency. But God, who speaks here, claims these benefits as his own.

. . . and makes her the praise of the earth. This means to render the church glorious, that the ground of joy may shine out from it. When we feel nothing but God's severity, we become silent and are overwhelmed with shame; but when he frees us from our afflictions and causes us to recover, he at the same time opens our mouth, for he supplies us with the ground of praise and thanksgiving.

8. The LORD has sworn by his right hand and by his mighty arm: "Never again will I give your grain as food for your enemies, and never again will foreigners drink the new wine for which you have toiled."

He proceeds with the metaphors that he used before. Owing to the corruption of our nature, the kingdom of Christ cannot be described in terms we can understand. So it was necessary to represent it by imagery. He had promised, first, an abundance of all things, and next, faithful guardianship, that the condition of believers might be safe. Here he promises tranquillity and rest, so that they may peacefully enjoy their blessings and may not in the future be defrauded of them. In other words, "Whatever you had in your hands before was exposed to plunder and robbery; but now you will have everything well secured and will freely partake of your corn and wine. In a word, you will enjoy your prosperity in peace."

9. "But those who harvest it will eat it and praise the LORD, and those who gather the grapes will drink it in the courts of my sanctuary." This is an explanation and confirmation of the preceding statement; having testified that he will no longer permit that which the church possesses to be laid open as a prey, the Lord adds that she will enjoy her possessions.

10. Pass through, pass through the gates! Prepare the way for the people. Build up, build up the highway! Remove the stones. Raise a banner for the nations. From the preceding statement Isaiah draws the conclusion that there will be free passage through the gates of the city, which formerly were shut or in a ruinous state—shut when it was besieged by enemies, and in a ruinous state when the city was thrown down and leveled to the ground. He means there will be such a restoration of the city that its inhabitants will be numerous, and there shall be frequent passing to and from it.

11. The LORD has made proclamation to the ends of the earth: "Say to the Daughter of Zion, 'See, your Savior comes! See, his reward is with him, and his recompense accompanies him.'" The Lord, by acting miraculously and beyond human judgment or expectation, will cause all the nations to know that this is done by his command.

Undoubtedly Say to the Daughter of Zion refers literally to the ministers of the Word and to the prophets, whom the Lord invests with this office of promising deliverance and salvation to the church. Hence we conclude that these promises are not merely limited to a single age but must be extended to the end of the world; beginning at the return from Babylon into Judea, we must advance as far as the coming of Christ, by which this prophecy was at length accomplished and redemption brought to a conclusion, for the Savior came when the grace of God was proclaimed by the Gospel. In a word, the prophet foretells that the voice of God will one day resound from the rising to the setting of the sun and will be heard not just by a single nation but by all nations.

12. They will be called The Holy People, the Redeemed of the LORD; and you will be called Sought After, The City No Longer Deserted. He describes the benefit of the coming of the Lord. By showing that God

takes care of his elect as his heritage, the Lord will make it evident to the whole world that the covenant of adoption that he made with Abraham was not deceptive. He calls them **The Holy People** because the Lord has separated and consecrated them to himself. Although he governs all nations, he has deigned to choose the seed of Abraham and to make them the object of his special care (Exodus 19:5).

In this sense God declares that they will be a holy people when he appears as their Savior and Redeemer; as the people are said to be profaned when they lie amidst filth, being afflicted and distressed by the reproaches of the wicked, so they are said to be sanctified when the Lord actually shows that he presides over their salvation. This was accomplished by a wonderful redemption. At that time God also testified that he remembered his heritage, which to human sight he appeared to have forsaken and disregarded. The words **Sought After . . . No Longer Deserted** denote a contrast between the time when God divorced his people and the time when he again reconciled to himself those whom he had cast off.

Isaiah
Chapter 63

1. Who is this coming from Edom, from Bozrah, with his garments stained crimson? Who is this, robed in splendor, striding forward in the greatness of his strength? "It is I, speaking in righteousness, mighty to save." This chapter has been violently distorted by Christians, as if what is said here related to Christ, whereas the prophet speaks simply of God himself. They have imagined that here Christ is **red** (verse 2; **crimson,** verse 1) because he was wet with his own blood that he shed on the cross. But the prophet meant nothing of that sort. The obvious meaning is that the Lord emerges with red garments in the view of his people, so all may know that he is their protector and avenger; for when the people were weighed down by innumerable evils, and at the same time the Edomites and other enemies, as if they had been placed beyond the reach of all danger, freely indulged in wickedness but remained unpunished, a dangerous temptation could arise, as if these things happened by chance or as if God did not care for his people or chastised them too severely. If the Jews were punished for despising God, much more should the Edomites and other avowed enemies of the name of God have been punished.

2. Why are your garments red, like those of one treading the winepress? The prophet proceeds with the same subject; but since it would have impaired the force of the narrative, he does not immediately explain whence came the **red** color of God's garments but continues to put forth questions, that he might arouse their minds to consider what is strange and uncommon. He means that this sprinkling of blood is something remarkable and extraordinary. The comparison drawn from a **winepress** is highly appropriate, for the town **Bozrah,** which he mentioned a little before, lay in a vine-bearing district. In other words, "There will be other vintages than those that are customary, for blood shall be shed instead of the juice of the grapes."

3. "I have trodden the winepress alone; from the nations no one was

with me. **I trampled them in my anger and trod them down in my wrath; their blood spattered my garments, and I stained all my clothing.**" The prophet now explains the vision and the reason why the Lord was stained with blood. It is because he will take vengeance on the Edomites and other enemies who treated his people cruelly. It would be absurd to say that these things relate to Christ because he alone and without human aid redeemed us. Rather, here we see that God will punish the Edomites in such a manner that he will have no need of human assistance; he will be sufficiently able to destroy them.

4. "For the day of vengeance was in my heart, and the year of my redemption has come." In the former clause of this verse Isaiah intimates that God does not cease to discharge his office, though he does not instantly execute his judgments, but on the contrary delays until the best time, which he knows well. It is not up to us to tell him when or how he ought to do this or that; rather we ought to bow submissively to his decree, that he may administer all things according to his pleasure. Let us not, therefore, imagine that he is asleep or that he is idle when he delays.

5. "I looked, but there was no one to help, I was appalled that no one gave support; so my own arm worked salvation for me, and my own wrath sustained me." Although the Jews were destitute of all assistance, and no one aided them by word or deed, yet Isaiah shows that the arm of the Lord is sufficient by itself to punish enemies and to set his people free. He shows, therefore, that from God alone they ought to expect salvation, that they might not gaze around in every direction but might have their eyes wholly fixed on God, who has no need of the assistance of others.

The prophet represents God as **appalled**—amazed—that there is no one to stretch out a hand to him when he wishes to execute his judgments, that he might impress more deeply on the minds of believers the doctrine that God has no need of human aid but is sufficient in himself for procuring salvation to his people.

6. "I trampled the nations in my anger; in my wrath I made them drunk and poured their blood on the ground." From the preceding statement he draws the conclusion that God's wrath is sufficiently powerful to destroy the wicked, without calling for the assistance of others; he does this in order that the Jews might not be deterred from cherishing favorable hopes by the strength that is arrayed against them.

The expression **made them drunk** must here be taken in a different sense from what it has had in some passages. Here it simply means "filled them to their heart's content," a metaphor that the prophets frequently use.

7. I will tell of the kindnesses of the LORD, the deeds for which he is to be praised, according to all the LORD has done for us—yes, the many good things he has done for the house of Israel, according to his compassion and many kindnesses. Isaiah brings consolation to his people in distressed and calamitous circumstances and by his example bids the Jews, when they were oppressed by afflictions, to recall God's benefits in the past and to devote themselves to prayer, that they might not be like hypocrites who only in prosperity feel the goodness of God and are so much cast down by adversity as to remember no benefit. When the Lord chastises us, we ought to mention and celebrate his benefits and to cherish better hopes for the future. The Lord is always the same and does not change his purpose or his inclination; therefore if we leave room for his compassion, we will never be left destitute.

8. He said, "Surely they are my people, sons who will not be false to me"; and so he became their Savior. Isaiah mentions the election of the people and represents God as speaking of it, that we may keep in view the end of our calling. The Lord wished to have a special people who would call upon him. And yet he accuses the people of ingratitude. Not that the Lord can be deceived, for he clearly foresaw what they would become and also declared it by Moses (Deuteronomy 32:15); but Scripture speaks like this when it is altogether owing to people's ingratitude that they disappoint God.

9. In all their distress he too was distressed, and the angel of his presence saved them. In his love and mercy he redeemed them; he lifted them up and carried them all the days of old. Isaiah enlarges on the goodness of God toward his people and shows that he was kind to the fathers so long as they permitted themselves to be governed by him. He so cared for them that he himself bore their **distresses** and afflictions. By speaking like this he declares the incomparable **love** that God bears toward his people. In order to move us more powerfully and draw us to himself, the Lord accommodates himself to human understanding by attributing to himself all the affection, **love,** and compassion that a father can have. And yet in human affairs it is impossible to conceive of any sort of kindness or benevolence that God does not immeasurably surpass.

10. Yet they rebelled and grieved his Holy Spirit. So he turned and became their enemy and he himself fought against them. The prophet now states that the Lord ceased to show kindness to his people because they revolted against and turned aside from him. The question turns on this point: "God exercised his kindness toward our fathers for a long time; why do not we experience the same kindness? Is he unlike himself?" By no means. But we ourselves, by our rebellion, refuse and even drive away his goodness. The prophet not only accuses the people of his own age but also condemns previous ages. We see how, even when they had Moses for their leader, they grumbled against God and rebelled (Exodus 17:2; Numbers 11:1; 20:3-5).

We are said to irritate the **Holy Spirit** by our wickedness. This human form of expression is intended to produce in us stronger abhorrence for sin, which provokes God's wrath and hatred.

11. Then his people recalled the days of old, the days of Moses and his people—where is he who brought them through the sea, with the shepherd of his flock? Where is he who set his Holy Spirit among them . . . ? The purpose of the chastisement is that the people may be roused from their lethargy and recall the things they had formerly forgotten. We are so intoxicated by prosperity that we altogether forget God.

12. . . . who sent his glorious arm of power to be at Moses' right hand, who divided the waters before them, to gain for himself everlasting renown. Here he goes on to describe the miraculous deliverance of the people, who were led out of Egypt under the guidance of Moses; and he goes on to relate the complaints that might occur to the minds of the afflicted Jews. Here we see two things connected—namely, the **right hand** of **Moses** and the **arm** of God's majesty. The Lord employs human labors and ministry in such a manner that his praise and glory must not in any degree be diminished or obscured; while these things are transacted under Moses as the leader, everything is ascribed to God. The ministers of the Gospel are said to "forgive sins" (John 20:23), a task that belongs to God alone, but does this detract from his authority and majesty? Not at all; for they are only his instruments and lend their labor to God, to whom the undivided praise ought to be rendered.

13. . . . who led them through the depths? Like a horse in open country, they did not stumble. These things are added for the purpose of setting God's benefit in a stronger light. He brings forward comparisons in order to describe the extraordinary power of God.

14. Like cattle that go down to the plain, they were given rest by the Spirit of the LORD. This is how you guided your people to make for yourself a glorious name. In a word, he informs them that the Red Sea was no obstacle to the people, who marched through as if walking on level ground.

A little earlier (verse 12) he spoke of **an everlasting name** (KJV); now, with the same sense, he speaks of **a glorious name.** The people argue with God that if he wished to obtain **a glorious name,** he must not now throw away all care for it; otherwise the memory of the benefits he had bestowed on the fathers would be entirely blotted out.

15. Look down from heaven and see from your lofty throne, holy and glorious. Where are your zeal and your might? Your tenderness and compassion are withheld from us. In the name of the whole people, he has related the benefits of former times; now he applies this to the present subject, entreating the Lord to pay regard to his people.

16. But you are our Father, though Abraham does not know us or Israel acknowledge us; you, O LORD, are our Father, our Redeemer from of old is your name. God permits us to reveal our hearts familiarly before him. Prayer is nothing else than the opening up of our heart before

God; the greatest alleviation is to pour our cares, distresses, and anxieties into his heart.

17. Why, O LORD, do you make us wander from your ways and harden our hearts so we do not revere you? Return for the sake of your servants, the tribes that are your inheritance. Because these modes of expression appear to be rough and harsh, some think that unbelievers are here introduced as complaining against God and uttering blasphemies, with the rage and obstinacy of people who are in a state of despair. But the context in which these words occur does not allow that interpretation at all. The prophet points out the fruit that would result from the calamities and afflictions of the Jews because, having been subdued and tamed, they no longer are fierce or indulge in their vices. They are therefore ashamed that in times past they departed so far from the right way, and they now acknowledge their own fault.

18. For a little while your people possessed your holy place, but now our enemies have trampled down your sanctuary. It is wonderful that the people should call it a little while, for 1,400 years had elapsed since the people began to possess that land. But we must take into account the promise by which he said the seed of Abraham would have it as an everlasting inheritance; this was a short time when compared with eternity.

19. We are yours from of old; but you have not ruled over them, they have not been called by your name. This means the same as what goes before: The calling of God must not be made void. Indeed the Lord does not wish that we should call upon him in vain; prayers would be unprofitable and useless if the Lord took no care of us. The church is distinguished by this mark: His name is placed upon her. Unbelievers cannot call upon him; there is no access to him but through the Word, of which they have no knowledge. Therefore, wherever there is faith, there is also a calling on him; and if there is no faith, it is certain that there is no hope or confidence.

Isaiah
Chapter 64

1. Oh, that you would rend the heavens and come down, that the mountains would tremble before you! God is said to **rend the heavens** when he unexpectedly gives some uncommon and striking proof of his power. When people are hard-pressed, they commonly look up to heaven, from which they expect assistance; miracles, interrupting the order of nature, open up for themselves an unusual path. When God renders no assistance, he appears to be shut up in heaven, disregarding what is taking place on earth. For this reason he is said to open and **rend the heavens** when he holds out to us some testimony of his presence; otherwise we think that he is at a great distance from us.

2. As when fire sets twigs ablaze and causes water to boil, come down to make your name known to your enemies and cause the nations to quake before you! He says that **fire . . . causes water to boil** because, contrary to custom, fire and lightning were mingled with violent showers. It is as if he said that the fire of God melted the hardest bodies and that the waters were consumed by its heat. To the same purpose he adds, **that the mountains would tremble before you!** God opened a passage for his people through the most dreadful obstacles.

3. For when you did awesome things that we did not expect, you came down, and the mountains trembled before you. He says that the Israelites saw what they did not at all expect. God had forewarned them and had given them the experience of his power in many ways; yet the alarming spectacle of which he speaks goes far beyond our senses and the capacity of the human mind.

4. Since ancient times no one has heard, no ear has perceived, no eye has seen any God besides you, who acts on behalf of those who wait for him. This verse confirms what has been already said: Believers do not here ask for anything unusual, but only that God may show himself to be to them what he formerly showed himself to be to the fathers, and that he may continue to exercise his kindness, and that, since his practice has been to assist his people and to give them undoubted tokens of his presence, he may not cease in the future to cause his strength and power to shine forth more and more brightly. The prophet represents believers as praying to God in such a manner that they strengthen themselves by remembering the past and seek God's help with greater courage.

5. You come to the help of those who gladly do right, who remember your ways. But when we continued to sin against them, you were angry. How then can we be saved? He proceeds with the same subject. The people deplore their hard lot, feeling no alleviation in their adversity, although in the past God used to stretch out his hand to the fathers. When they find that God is so unlike what he had been, they do not grumble against him but throw all the blame on themselves. Let us learn from this never to think of the chastisements that the Lord inflicts without at the same time calling to mind our sins, that we may confess that we are justly punished and may acknowledge our guilt.

6. All of us have become like one who is unclean, and all our righteous acts are like filthy rags. The believers go on in their complaint; they deplore their condition because God appears to take no account of them.

We all shrivel up like a leaf, and like the wind our sins sweep us away. This very beautiful comparison shows that people utterly fade and decay when they feel God is angry with them; as is admirably described in Psalm 90:6 and 103:16. Justly, therefore, are we compared to leaves, for **like the wind, our sins sweep us away.**

7. No one calls on your name or strives to lay hold of you; for you have hidden your face from us and made us waste away because of our sins. He confirms what was formerly said; he exhorts believers, even though God's punishment of them appears to be severe, still to believe that they deserve such a punishment. Heinous sins are mentioned by him; and though it would be tedious to go over all of them in detail, he points out the source itself and says that the worship of God is neglected. The words **calls on your name** include, as is customary in Scripture, the whole worship of God; the most important part of God's worship is to call upon him and to testify to our confidence in him. Prayers and supplications undoubtedly were always practiced among them; but because the heart was far removed from God, he reckons all pretended ceremonies as of no value.

8. Yet, O LORD, you are our Father. We are the clay, you are the potter; we are all the work of your hand. After complaining of their miseries, by which they were almost overwhelmed, they now more openly ask pardon from God and a mitigation of their distresses and with greater boldness plead with God that they are still his children. Adoption alone could encourage them to cherish favorable hopes, so they might not cease to rely on their Father, though overwhelmed by the load of afflictions. This order should be carefully observed, for in order that we may be truly humbled in our hearts, we need to be cast down, laid low, and almost crushed. But when despair seizes us, we must lay hold on this altar of consolation. He is saying in effect, "Since God has been pleased to elect us to be his children, we ought to expect salvation from him, even when matters are at their worst." Thus, with a view to the gracious covenant, the Israelites affirm that they are the children of God, in order that they may experience his fatherly kindness and that his promise may not be made void.

9. Do not be angry beyond measure, O LORD; do not remember our sins forever. Oh, look upon us, we pray, for we are all your people. The people pray that the severity of punishment and the fierceness of the wrath of God may be abated—not because God ever goes beyond measure, but because they would be altogether overwhelmed if he chose to act toward them with strict justice. They therefore ask a mitigation of punishment.

10. Your sacred cities have become a desert; even Zion is a desert, Jerusalem a desolation. The church again recounts her miseries, that she may move God to mercy and obtain pardon. She says that the **cities** have been reduced to **a desert** and, for the sake of amplification, adds that **Zion is a desert,** referring to the royal residence in which God wished that people would call upon him.

11. Our holy and glorious temple, where our fathers praised you, has been burned with fire, and all that we treasured lies in ruins. Because the worship of God was at that time corrupted and adulterated, and almost all had rebelled with superstition and ungodliness, he mentions not the present but the former age. In other words, "We have not offered you the worship we ought, but this is the temple in which **our fathers** worshiped you in purity. Will you permit it to be profaned and destroyed? Will not this disgrace recoil on yourself since it relates to the worship of your name?"

12. After all this, O LORD, will you hold yourself back? Will you keep silent and punish us beyond measure? The people strengthen themselves by assured confidence that God will not permit his glory to be trampled underfoot, though people provoke him by innumerable transgressions. This can yield no consolation of any kind to hypocrites but relates solely to those who are moved by a true sense of the mercy of God. Such persons believe and are fully persuaded, though death threatens them, that God will nevertheless have regard to his own glory and will at least be gracious to the remnant, that the seed may not perish.

Let us use this prayer whenever we are attacked by our enemies—not in the manner of hypocrites (who haughtily boast of the glory of God, of which they have no experience whatever), but with repentance and faith, so we may obtain the fruit of that glory.

Isaiah
Chapter 65

1. **"I revealed myself to those who did not ask for me; I was found by those who did not seek me. To a nation that did not call on my name, I said, 'Here am I, here am I.'"** The prophet now passes on to another doctrine, showing that God has good reason for rejecting and casting off the Jews. Neither threats nor warnings have brought them back from their errors into the right way. But in order that they might not think the Lord's covenant would on that account be made void, God adds that he will have another people that formerly was no people, and that where he was formerly unknown, his name will be well-known and highly celebrated. The Jews looked on this as monstrous and reckoned it altogether inconsistent with the covenant that the Lord had made with Abraham (Genesis 17:7) if such a benefit were extended to any others than his posterity. But God speaking through the prophet intended to strip them of the foolish confidence of imagining that he was bound to the posterity of Abraham; he had only restricted himself to them on an absolute condition, and if this were violated by them, they would be deprived, as covenant-breakers and traitors, of all the advantage derived from the covenant. Nor was this promise made to Abraham alone and to those who were descended from him, but rather to all who might be ingrafted by faith into his family. It is helpful to consider the second verse, in which he explains the cause of the rejection, that we may more fully understand the prophet's design.

2. **"All day long I have held out my hands to an obstinate people, who walk in ways not good, pursuing their own imaginations."** The Lord accuses the Jews and complains of their ingratitude and rebellion; thus he proves that there is no reason why they should say that he does them wrong if he bestows his grace on others. The Jews conducted themselves proudly and insolently toward God, as if they had been chosen because of their own merit. On account of their ingratitude and insolence

the Lord rejects them as unworthy and complains that it was in vain that he **held out** his **hands** to draw and bring them back to him.

3. ". . . a people who continually provoke me to my very face, offering sacrifices in gardens and burning incense on altars of brick." Here he describes and illustrates more largely in what respects the Jews were rebellious against God. It was because they had forsaken the command of God and had polluted themselves by various superstitions. He had said a little earlier (63:17) that the Jews had estranged themselves from God because they wandered after their own inventions. Now he points out the fruit of that licentiousness: They had given free rein to their thoughts and so had overturned the pure worship of God. Undoubtedly the origin of all superstitions is that people are delighted with their own inventions and choose to be wise in their own eyes rather than restrain their senses in obedience to God. In vain do people offer their so-called devotions and good intentions; God so abhors and detests them that people who have followed them are guilty of breaking the covenant and deserting their allegiance. There is nothing that we ought to undertake of our own accord; rather we ought to obey God when he commands. In a word, the beginning and perfection of lawful worship is a readiness to obey.

4. ". . . who sit among the graves and spend their nights keeping secret vigil." He names other kinds of superstitions also; although the description is obscure because it is so brief, we may easily learn from other passages what their nature was. Necromancy was generally practiced among heathen nations, and the Jews also consulted demons **among the graves** instead of consulting God alone, as they ought to have done. As if seeking answers from the dead, they took pleasure in being deceived by the illusions of demons. How solemnly the Lord had forbidden it appears very clearly from Deuteronomy 18:10-11.

. **". . . who eat the flesh of pigs, and whose pots hold broth of unclean meat."** Previously he complained that the worship of God was polluted by strange inventions; now he adds that they set aside every distinction, so that they do not distinguish between the clean and the unclean. He brings forward a single instance: They do not abstain from **the flesh of pigs.** Was this a small matter? Very far from it, for we ought not to judge from our own opinion, but from that of the legislator, how heinous a sin it is. Nothing that the Lord has forbidden ought to be reckoned trivial. (See Leviticus 11:7; Deuteronomy 14:8.)

5. ". . . who say, 'Keep away; don't come near me, for I am too sacred for you!' Such people are smoke in my nostrils, a fire that keeps burning all day." He points out extreme impiety in the Jews, who obstinately and rebelliously opposed God's worshipers and refused to listen to any warnings. There is some hope of repentance so long as we lend an ear to warnings and reproofs; but if we reject them, our case is undoubtedly hopeless. Though these words are obscure, their meaning amounts to this:

Hypocrites disdainfully and fiercely repel faithful advisers because they either make false claims to holiness or, on account of pride, do not allow themselves to be reproved; hypocrisy is never free from supercilious disdain and haughtiness.

6-7. "See, it stands written before me: I will not keep silent but will pay back in full; I will pay it back into their laps—both your sins and the sins of your fathers," says the LORD. "Because they burned sacrifices on the mountains and defied me on the hills, I will measure into their laps the full payment for their former deeds." This alludes to the normal custom of judges, who keep before them in writing the processes of investigation regarding any matter, together with the testimonies, acts, and everything of that nature, so that when it becomes necessary to make use of them, the guilt of the culprit may be easily proved. We write down those things that we wish to be remembered by posterity. The Lord therefore testifies that these things can never fade into oblivion because they have been **written**; although he may pass them over in silence for a time, the wicked will not escape unpunished but in the end will know that he is a righteous judge.

8. This is what the LORD says: "As when juice is still found in a cluster of grapes and men say, 'Don't destroy it, there is yet some good in it,' so will I do in behalf of my servants; I will not destroy them all." Here God speaking through the prophet softens the preceding statement. To say that the Lord would destroy the fathers and the children along with them could strike believers with such horror as to lead them to think their salvation was past all hope. We must therefore take care to be on our guard and notice why the Lord is angry with us: He wants to frighten us so as to lead us to himself, and not to throw us into despair. He holds out hope to believers, that they might not lose courage; by showing consolation, he encourages them to repent. He confirms this by a comparison.

9. "I will bring forth descendants from Jacob, and from Judah those who will possess my mountains; my chosen people will inherit them, and there will my servants live." The Lord through Isaiah explains the preceding verse in other words and shows that he wishes to reserve for himself some **descendants** who will call upon him; the Lord chastises his people in such a manner as to guarantee the existence of the church, in which his truth and the pure religion can be preserved. We should take care to remember that we must not be terrified by any calamities or ruins or by any hideous desolation of the church.

My chosen people will inherit them. He means that the Jews will return to their original condition, so they can enjoy that country as their own inheritance from which they had been driven out.

10. "Sharon will become a pasture for flocks, and the Valley of Achor a resting place for herds, for my people who seek me." By these images he simply means that the land, which was a desert, will be inhabited again.

A comparison is implied: "Because her inhabitants were banished to a distant country, she will be forsaken and desolate; and yet she will eventually be inhabited, so as to abound in **flocks** and **herds** and have lands that are fertile and fit for **pasture** and supply abundantly everything that is necessary to feed and support human beings." **Sharon** was a place suitable for **pasture,** and so was **Achor**; but the former was suitable for **flocks,** and the latter to **herds.** Here we see that the promises of God contain blessings not only for the future but also for our present life, that we may taste his bounty and kindness more and more.

11. **"But as for you who forsake the LORD and forget my holy mountain, who spread a table for Fortune and fill bowls of mixed wine for Destiny . . ."** By **my holy mountain** he denotes figuratively the rule of a holy life that had been laid down in the Word of the Lord. The temple had been built by the command of the Lord, that men might call upon him; so was the altar on which the Lord wanted sacrifices offered. Thus any sacrifices and oblations offered in other places or to other gods or in any way different from the strict observance of the ceremonies of the law were impure. It is not lawful for people to do anything they have thought up themselves. The Lord demands nothing but obedience (1 Samuel 15:22), and there is no obedience without faith, and there is no faith without the Word (Romans 10:17), by which alone we are at liberty to inquire or think concerning God.

12. **"I will destine you for the sword, and you will all bend down for the slaughter; for I called but you did not answer, I spoke but you did not listen. You did evil in my sight and chose what displeases me."** He heightens the extent and heinousness of their treason, saying that the Jews sinned through deliberate malice and on purpose rather than through ignorance. They had been often instructed and warned but had disdainfully rejected all warnings and consequently were far less excusable than others to whom no prophets were sent. Although no one can plead ignorance as an excuse, much less can it be pleaded by the Jews and those to whom the Word of God is proclaimed and who on that account will be condemned and punished more severely than others.

13-14. **Therefore this is what the Sovereign LORD says: "My servants will eat, but you will go hungry; my servants will drink, but you will go thirsty; my servants will rejoice, but you will be put to shame. My servants will sing out of the joy of their hearts, but you will cry out from anguish of heart and wail in brokenness of spirit."** Here also the prophet more clearly distinguishes between hypocrites, who held a place in the church, and the true and lawful children.

The Lord, therefore, is not here promising what he does not actually bestow; further, this happiness must not be estimated by the outward condition of things. This is still more evident from what follows, where he speaks of **joy** and thanksgiving. The prophet undoubtedly intends to state in a few words that contentment lies not in an abundance of earthly enjoyments but in calm peace of mind and spiritual **joy,** for unbelievers have no relish for such things, but to believers a persuasion of God's fatherly love is more delightful than all earthly enjoyments. We ought to look for all prosperity from God alone, who will not permit his people to lack anything that belongs to a happy life.

15. **"You will leave your name to my chosen ones as a curse; the Sovereign LORD will put you to death, but to his servants he will give another name."** God through the prophet continues the same doctrine, teaching that he will in the end separate hypocrites from true **servants.** And indeed we need not wonder that the prophet dwells so much on this point, for there is nothing of which it is harder to convince hypocrites, who are puffed up with pride and who deceive and blind themselves. He affirms that their **name** will be **as a curse** because they thought they were the holy seed and that nothing else under heaven was worthy of being remembered.

16. **"Whoever invokes a blessing in the land will do so by the God of truth; he who takes an oath in the land will swear by the God of truth. For the past troubles will be forgotten and hidden from my eyes."** Here the whole world is contrasted with a corner of Judea, which might be said to contain the worship of God. Since the time when God began to be manifested everywhere, he is not worshiped in one particular district but in all places without distinction. (See John 4:21.)

Blessing and **takes an oath** denote the whole of the worship of God. Taking **an oath** is a kind of worship of God, for by it we declare that all judgment belongs to him, and we acknowledge that he is perfectly acquainted with all that we do. We bless when we wish to obtain from him all prosperity and render thanksgiving to him alone—in short, when we acknowledge that our prosperity comes from no other source than from his undeserved kindness.

17. **"Behold, I will create new heavens and a new earth. The former things will not be remembered, nor will they come to mind."** By these metaphors he promises a remarkable change of affairs, as if God said that he has both the inclination and the power not only to restore his church but to restore it so that it appears to gain new life and to dwell in a new world. These are exaggerated modes of expression; but the greatness of such a blessing, which was to be manifested at the coming of Christ, could not be described in any other way. Nor does he mean only the first coming but the whole reign, which must be extended as far as the last coming, as we have already said in expounding other passages.

18. **"But be glad and rejoice forever in what I will create, for I will create Jerusalem to be a delight and its people a joy."** God through his prophet exhorts believers to rejoice in a manner befitting the benefit they have received from him. He added this for the sake of amplification

because people do not adequately consider God's benefits, especially the highest and most excellent of all. Either they disregard them altogether, or they value them less than they ought. Believers must therefore be stirred and exhorted like this so that they may not show themselves unthankful or unmindful or think that it is inconsequential that Christ has redeemed them and that they carry in their hearts the pledge of eternal and heavenly life. That is why Isaiah shows that the only way for believers to give due praise for redemption is by remaining joyful throughout their lives and celebrating God's praises.

19. "I will rejoice over Jerusalem and take delight in my people; the sound of weeping and of crying will be heard in it no more." The Lord expresses more here than in the previous verse, for by these words he means that he will not only give people ground for rejoicing but will even share with them in that joy. So great is his love toward us that he delights in our prosperity. It greatly strengthens our faith when we learn that God is moved, and so powerfully moved, by such affection toward us. If we are in painful and distressed circumstances, he says that he is affected by grief and sorrow; on the other hand, if our condition is pleasant and comfortable, he says that he takes great pleasure in our prosperity.

20. "Never again will there be in it an infant that lives but a few days, or an old man who does not live out his years; he who dies at a hundred will be thought a mere youth; he who fails to reach a hundred will be considered accursed." Notice here that blessings either of soul or body are found only in the kingdom of Christ—that is, in the church, apart from which there is nothing but cursing. Hence it follows that all who have no share in that kingdom are wretched and unhappy; however fresh and vigorous they may appear to be, they are nevertheless, in the sight of God, rotten and stinking corpses.

21-22. "They will build houses and dwell in them; they will plant vineyards and eat their fruit. No longer will they build houses and others live in them, or plant and others eat." In these verses the Lord mentions what is written in the law. The blessings of the law are that those who have obeyed God will dwell in the houses they have built and will gather fruit from the trees they have planted (Leviticus 26:10). On the other hand, the disobedient will be expelled from the houses they built, will give place to foreigners, and will be deprived of the fruits of the trees they planted.

"For as the days of a tree, so will be the days of my people; my chosen ones will long enjoy the works of their hands." In other words, "You will plant vineyards and will eat the fruit of them; and you will not be removed from this life before receiving the fruit, which will be enjoyed not only by yourselves but by your children and posterity." He uses the metaphor of a tree because he had previously spoken about planting vineyards; accordingly he promises that the people will enjoy both their houses and their vineyards in peace and will not be molested by enemies or robbers, and this peaceful condition will last as long as the life of **a tree.**

23. "They will not toil in vain or bear children doomed to misfortune; for they will be a people blessed by the LORD, they and their descendants with them." God names other kinds of blessings that he promises to the kingdom of Christ. God always blessed his people, but the blessings were in some measure suspended until the coming of Christ, in whom was displayed full and complete happiness. In a word, both Jews and Gentiles will be happy, in all respects, under the reign of Christ. As it is a token of God's wrath and curse when we obtain no advantage from our labor, so, on the other hand, it is a token of blessing when we clearly see the fruit of our labor. For this reason he says that those who return from captivity, in order that they may obtain a true and complete deliverance, will not labor in vain.

24. "Before they call I will answer; while they are still speaking I will hear." This is a remarkable promise, for nothing is more desirable than to have God reconciled to us and to have it in our power to draw near to him with freedom and boldness. We are surrounded by innumerable distresses and calamities; yet we cannot be miserable while we are at liberty to approach the Lord. Here therefore the Lord promises that we shall not pray in vain. This was also promised to the fathers under the law. It is certain that since the beginning of the world God has listened to the fathers, to all who called upon him; this is the most valuable fruit of faith.

25. "The wolf and the lamb will feed together, and the lion will eat straw like the ox, but dust will be the serpent's food. They will neither harm nor destroy on all my holy mountain," says the LORD. The Lord means that everything will be fully restored when Christ reigns. There seems to be an implied comparison here between Adam and Christ. We know that all the afflictions of the present life flowed from the sin of the first man; at that time we were deprived of the dominion and sovereignty that God had given to man (Genesis 1:28), over animals of every kind, all of which at first undoubtedly bowed cheerfully to the dominion of man and were obedient to his will. But now most of them rise up against man and even fight against each other. Thus when wolves, bears, lions, and other savage animals are hurtful to man and to other beasts from which we obtain some advantage, and when even animals that ought to have been useful to man are hostile to him, we should attribute this to human sin, because disobedience overthrew the order of things. But it is the office of Christ to bring back everything to its condition and order, and so the Lord declares that the confusion or ruin that now exists in human affairs will be removed by the coming of Christ. At that time, corruptions having been taken away, the world will return to its original state.

Isaiah
Chapter 66

1. This is what the LORD says: "Heaven is my throne and the earth is my footstool. Where is the house you will build for me? Where will my resting place be?" This discourse is different from the preceding one; here God through the prophet exclaims against the Jews, who were puffed up with vain confidence in the sacrifices and the temple, indulged freely in their pleasures, and flattered themselves in their sins under this pretense. He shows that this confidence is not only foolish and groundless but diabolical and accursed; it is mocking God grossly to try to serve and appease him by outward ceremonies. Accordingly, the Lord reproaches them with endeavoring to frame an idol in place of him when they shut him up in the temple. Next, he speaks of the renewal of the church and of its extension throughout the whole world.

The prophet aims to shake off the complacency of hypocritical worshipers of God; so he begins with his nature. By assigning **heaven** for the Lord's habitation, the prophet means that the majesty of God fills all things and is diffused everywhere, and that, so far from being shut up in the temple, he is not shut up or confined within any place whatever. The Scripture often teaches that God is in heaven—not that he is shut up in it, but in order that we may raise our minds above the world and may not entertain any low, carnal, or earthly conceptions of him. The mere sight of heaven ought to carry us higher and transport us to wonder.

2. "Has not my hand made all these things, and so they came into being?" declares the LORD. God through the prophet refutes people's false idea of the worship of God when they think that sacrifices and outward ceremonies are of great value in themselves. In fact, God cares nothing about ceremonies; they are empty and useless masks when people think they satisfy God by means of them. When God says he **made all these things,** this must not be understood as referring solely to the temple, but to all that was there offered to God. He says he **made all these things**

in order that we may know he has no need of this external worship. All the animals were created by him and are his own (Psalm 50:10), though the Jews hoped to obtain his favor by sacrificing them.

"**This is the one I esteem: he who is humble and contrite in spirit.**" A definition of lawful worship is added, for I have no doubt that the Lord implies a contrast between people who are **humble and contrite in spirit** and the splendor and elegance of ceremonies, by which people's eyes are commonly dazzled, so as to be carried away in admiration. On the contrary, God testifies that he demands **humble** and downcast minds, those that tremble at his commandments. By these words he describes inward purity of heart and a sincere desire for godliness and at the same time shows the way in which we should be prepared to please God.

"**And trembles at my word.**" It might be thought strange at first sight that God demands trembling in believers, since nothing is more sweet or gentle than the Word of the Lord, and nothing is more opposite to it than to excite terror. The answer is that there are two kinds of trembling: People are terrified when they hate God and flee from him; but the other sort of terror affects the heart and promotes the obedience of those who reverence and fear God.

We ought carefully to note the expression that he uses—**trembles at my word.** Many people boast that they reverence and fear God; but by disregarding his Word, they at the same time show that they despise God. All the reverence that we owe to God must be paid to his Word, in which he wishes to be fully recognized. What this amounts to is that the sacrifice that God prefers above all others is when believers, by true self-denial, lie low in such abasement as to have no lofty opinion about themselves but permit themselves to be reduced to nothing.

3. "But whoever sacrifices a bull is like one who kills a man, and whoever offers a lamb, like one who breaks a dog's neck; whoever makes a grain offering is like one who presents pig's blood, and whoever burns memorial incense, like one who worships an idol. They have chosen their own ways, and their souls delight in their abominations." There are two clauses in this verse. In the first Isaiah plainly declares that all the sacrifices of his nation are of no value in the sight of God but are held by him in abomination. In the latter he describes the dreadful corruption by which they mingled the ceremonies of the Gentiles with the sacrifices of the law and in this way corrupted and perverted everything.

4. "So I also will choose harsh treatment for them and will bring upon them what they dread. For when I called, no one answered, when I spoke, no one listened. They did evil in my sight and chose what displeases me." The prophet means that the Jews gain nothing by giving various excuses, because God does not care for human cunning or fine words. Indeed, it is not right to measure God by our own capacity, and we ought not to depend on human judgment; it is our duty to judge God's works by his Word.

He says in effect, "I will scatter the clouds that they endeavor to spread over themselves, so that their delusions are obvious to everyone. They appear to be hidden now, but one day they will be dragged into public view." The meaning may be summed up thus: "Because the Jews have indulged so freely in sinning that everything they chose was preferred by them to the commandments of God, so also, in his turn, God will lay open their delusions at his pleasure."

5. Hear the word of the LORD, you who tremble at his word: "Your brothers who hate you, and exclude you because of my name, have said, 'Let the LORD be glorified, that we may see your joy!' Yet they will be put to shame." Isaiah directs his discourse to the true worshipers of God and promises them what they could scarcely have expected during those terrible calamities. He expressly addresses them because at that time there were many who falsely boasted of the name of God.

It is as if he said, "God, by his coming, will cause believers to know that they have not hoped in vain; he will appear for the advantage of believers and for the destruction of those who maintain that he will appear as the defender of wickedness, of which he will actually be the severe avenger. The former will enjoy gladness and consolation, while the latter will be ashamed, for they will quickly feel that God's judgment, which they now laugh at, is at hand."

6. "Hear that uproar from the city, hear that noise from the temple! It is the sound of the LORD repaying his enemies all they deserve." He confirms the preceding statement—namely, that God has not threatened in vain but will speedily come to take vengeance on hypocrites, in order that what has been promised concerning gladness may be more eagerly expected by believers.

It is uncertain who the **enemies** are that he describes. The passage may be explained as relating to the Babylonians, whose destruction was the deliverance of his church; or it may refer to other enemies, who were nourished in the heart of the church. I favor the latter opinion, though I do not deny that it may be seen as referring to any kind of enemies.

7. "Before she goes into labor, she gives birth; before the pains come upon her, she delivers a son." He comforted believers beforehand, so they would not be discouraged by the insolence and contempt of brothers whom God would at length punish. Having thus commanded them to wait for the coming of the Lord with a steady and resolute heart, the prophet speaking for God adds that God will punish them in such a manner that by their destruction he will provide for the safety of believers. He does not speak of one or two people but of the whole church, which he compares to a woman. The prophet has used the same metaphor before. God chiefly aims at gathering us into one body, that we may have in it a testimony of our adoption and may acknowledge him to be our father and may be nourished in the womb of the church as our mother. This metaphor of a mother is therefore highly appropriate. It means that the church will be restored in such a manner that she will have many children, though she may appear for a time to be childless and barren.

8. "Who has ever heard of such a thing? Who has ever seen such things? Can a country be born in a day or a nation be brought forth in a moment? Yet no sooner is Zion in labor than she gives birth to her children." The Lord through Isaiah says what a great thing it is that he has spoken of. There will be a wonderful and unheard-of restoration of the church, so much so that believers will not judge it by the order of nature but by the grace of God.

He illustrates the glory of the miracle by a metaphor. No **country** ever came into the world in an instant, for people assemble gradually and grow in number and spread their nation. But the case is very different with the church, which all at once and in more than one place brings forth a vast number of **children.** It amounts to this: God, in a wonderful manner, will cause innumerable **children** of the church, in an extraordinary manner, to be born all at once and suddenly.

9. "Do I bring to the moment of birth and not give delivery?" says the LORD. "Do I close up the womb when I bring to delivery?" says your God. The preceding verse extolled God's work in lofty terms, and now the Lord shows that this should not be thought incredible and that we ought not to doubt his power, which surpasses all the order of nature. If we consider who it is that speaks, and how easy it is for him to do what he has promised, we shall not remain in such uncertainty as not instantly to recollect that the renewal of the world is in the hand of him who would have no difficulty in creating a hundred worlds in a moment.

10. "Rejoice with Jerusalem and be glad for her, all you who love her; rejoice greatly with her, all you who mourn over her." God promises that those who formerly were sad and melancholy will be joyful. Isaiah speaking for the Lord has in view not his own age but the time of the captivity, during which believers continually groaned and, overwhelmed with grief, almost despaired. Therefore he exhorts and stimulates to joy all believers who are moved by strong affection toward the church and reckon nothing more desirable than her prosperity. Thus he teaches them that the only people who will have a share in this valuable blessing are those who are prompted by a godly love of the church and desire to seek her deliverance, even when she is contemptible in the eyes of the world.

11. "For you will nurse and be satisfied at her comforting breasts; you will drink deeply and delight in her overflowing abundance." This verse ought to be linked with the preceding verse. The prophet explains the reason for the promised joy—namely, because the wretched and miserable condition of the church will be changed into a happy and prosperous condition. By the words **at her comforting breasts,** he alludes to young infants, as if he said, "that you may enjoy your mother with every advantage and may hang on her breasts." Here all believers, whatever their age, are compared by him to children, that they may remember their infirmity and be strengthened with the Lord's strength.

12. For this is what the LORD says: "I will extend peace to her like a river, and the wealth of nations like a flooding stream; you will nurse and be carried on her arm and dandled on her knees." God continues his metaphor, comparing the children of God to infants who are carried in the arms and warmed in the bosom of their mothers, who even play with them. In order that he may express more strongly his affection toward us, he compares himself to a mother, whose love exceeds every other by a wide margin (compare Isaiah 49:15). The Lord wishes to be like a mother to us, so that instead of the annoyances, reproaches, distresses, and anxieties that we have endured, he may treat us gently and, as it were, fondle us in his bosom. By the word **peace** he means prosperity.

13. "As a mother comforts her child, so will I comfort you." It is wonderful that the prophet, who appeared to have already spoken enough about this renewal, dwells on it so grandly. As he can neither express the greatness and warmth of the love that God bears toward us, nor satisfy himself with speaking about it, he mentions and repeats it frequently.

"And you will be comforted over Jerusalem." There are two ways in which this may be explained. It may be said that believers will have joyful hearts when they see the church restored, or that the church, after being restored, will discharge her duty by gladdening her children. I prefer the latter interpretation, though either of them is admissible. The former appears to be a richer interpretation; but we must consider what the prophet meant, and not merely what we think the most beautiful. In the first place, indeed, he makes God the author of the joy, and rightly so; but in the second place he adds that Jerusalem is God's handmaid (see verse 12). This is not addressed to irreligious scorners who are not moved by any solicitude about the church, but to those who with holy zeal declare that they are her children.

14. When you see this, your heart will rejoice and you will flourish like grass; the hand of the LORD will be made known to his servants, but his fury will be shown to his foes. By the word **see,** he expresses undoubted experience, so that believers may not doubt the result but may embrace this prediction with full belief and patiently endure the barrenness of the church for a time.

He illustrates his statement by a metaphor, saying that their bones will regain their former vigor just as faded **grass** becomes fresh and green again.

15. See, the LORD is coming with fire, and his chariots are like a whirlwind; he will bring down his anger with fury, and his rebuke with

flames of fire. The object of this lifelike description is that believers, when they see worthless people laughing at their distresses and growing more and more insolent, might not on that account turn aside from the right path or lose courage. He intended not only to attack wicked people who are unmoved by threats and who scorn all instruction but to comfort good people, that they might feel they are happy because they are under God's protection and might not attach themselves to the wicked on account of the prosperity of all their undertakings.

16. **For with fire and with his sword the LORD will execute judgment upon all men, and many will be those slain by the LORD.** Here the prophet brings forward nothing new but merely confirms the former statement and shows that this judgment will be dreadful, so that none may think it is a matter of small importance. Accordingly, he describes that horror in strong language, so that the wicked may fear, and so that believers, on the other hand, may keep themselves holy and chaste and may withdraw from the society of the wicked.

17. **"Those who consecrate and purify themselves to go into the gardens, following the one in the midst of those who eat the flesh of pigs and rats and other abominable things—they will meet their end together," declares the LORD.** God through Isaiah now describes those enemies against whom he had said that his anger would be kindled; for it might have been doubted whether he spoke of foreign and avowed enemies or directed his discourse to those who despised God, although they had been mixed with those who were elect and holy. Therefore he plainly addresses the false and degenerate Jews.

They polluted themselves with various superstitions, although they imagined that by means of those superstitions they were making themselves pure in the sight of God. Others, without any reserve, despised God and all religion. This is therefore a general statement, in which God includes all the ungodly, of whatever sort—both those who openly display their wickedness and those who hide and cover it by various disguises.

18. **"And I, because of their actions and their imaginations, am about to come and gather all nations and tongues, and they will come and see my glory."** He confirms what he said in the preceding verse—namely, that all the ungodly will be punished. The Lord may permit them for a time to sin with impunity; but believers, being convinced they will be punished one day, should guard against following their example. The Lord here testifies that he sees and observes their works and that one day he will actually show that nothing can be concealed from his eyes.

To **see** the **glory** of the Lord is nothing else than to enjoy the grace he had bestowed on the Jews; for the special privilege of that nation was that they saw God's glory and had tokens of his presence. He says that now the Gentiles, who had not enjoyed these benefits, will **see** that **glory,** for the Lord will reveal himself to everyone without exception.

19. **"I will set a sign among them, and I will send some of those who survive to the nations."** The prophet speaking for God heightens the description of what has already been said about the terrible vengeance that the Lord will bring on the ungodly; all would have perished without distinction if the Lord had not marked some of them with his seal. From the general destruction of the whole nation, therefore, he says he will reserve a small number. (See also Isaiah 1:9 and 10:22.) Some of this reserved group, he says, will be his heralds to celebrate his name among the Gentiles.

"To Tarshish, to the Libyans and Lydians (famous as archers), to Tubal and Greece, and to the distant islands that have not heard of my fame or seen my glory." By **Tarshish** he denotes Cilicia, including the whole coast of the Mediterranean opposite Judea. (Others think it means Africa and Cappadocia.) **Tubal** is Italy, and **the distant islands** means all unknown countries—all that lay beyond the sea.

"They will proclaim my glory among the nations." He means that the knowledge of God will spread throughout the world. Greece, Italy, and other nations had heard nothing of the pure religion and true worship of God; God is therefore promising that his glory will be known in every part of the world.

20. **"And they will bring all your brothers, from all the nations, to my holy mountain in Jerusalem as an offering to the LORD—on horses, in chariots and wagons, and on mules and camels,"** says the LORD. **"They will bring them, as the Israelites bring their grain offerings, to the temple of the LORD in ceremonially clean vessels."** All who escape and survive, though few in number now, will be priests who will bring sacrifices to God from all places. He alludes to the ceremonies of the law but points out the difference between those oblations and the sacrifices of the old law, for God appoints a new kind of punishment and new sacrifices. He had said he would gather all the nations, and now he shows that the priests he had appointed will not labor in vain, for he will grant prosperity to what they undertake.

People who were previously strangers are called **brothers** because he is thinking of the new relationship that arises from faith. We know that foreign nations were grafted by faith into the family of Abraham. Other commentators bring out a different meaning, which I do not absolutely reject: "When God gathers a new people to himself out of foreign nations, the Jews, who had been scattered in all directions, will be brought into one place." This was also accomplished; but it seems more appropriate to refer this to the calling of the Gentiles, because at that time a brotherly relationship began to be established among all whom God wished to adopt as his children. The time when Abraham became "a father of many nations" (Genesis 17:5; Romans 4:17) was when God adopted the Gentiles and joined them to himself by a covenant, that they might follow the faith of

Abraham. We were aliens from the church of God, but the prophet, speaking for God, calls us the **brothers** of the Jews because he had previously cast false brothers out of their place.

It is our duty to observe the fruit that is produced by the godly labors of those who serve the Lord faithfully: They **bring** their **brothers** from deadly errors to God, the source of life. This should cheer and support them amidst tribulations. The Lord does not allow any of his own people to perish. Thus we enjoy a great privilege when he wishes to use our labors to deliver our **brothers.**

He says **from all the nations** because there will no longer be any difference between Jews and Gentiles. God will form a church out of all nations (see Ephesians 2:14; Psalm 2:8).

When God speaks of **my holy mountain** he accommodates himself to the custom of that period, for he was worshiped in the temple at Jerusalem. But now the temple is diffused everywhere, for we are free to "lift up holy hands in prayer . . . everywhere" (1 Timothy 2:8). Similarly, he mentions **offerings** that were offered in the temple, although the sacrifices that are now to be offered differ greatly from the old sacrifices. The apostles and other priests of Christ offered people as living sacrifices to God by the Gospel (Romans 15:16). Whoever we gain to Christ, we offer in sacrifice, that they may be wholly consecrated to God. Moreover, we all sacrifice when we devote and dedicate ourselves to God and offer him unreserved obedience (Romans 12:1).

Many people might think, "How can people come to us from such distant countries?" He replies: "There will be no lack of horses, chariots, and wagons, for the Lord has at his command all that can help his people and lead them to the end he has in view." Nothing will stop God from gathering his church; he will have at his command all the necessary means, so that none of those he has called may fail on the way.

21. "And I will select some of them also to be priests and Levites," says the LORD. The prophet speaking for God had made known that the church of God would be collected from all nations, so that in spite of every difficulty and obstruction, even distant nations would come near to him. But now he goes further, telling them that the Gentiles will not only be adopted by God but will also be elevated by him to the highest honor. Already it was a great honor that unclean and polluted nations were reckoned a holy people; but now here is something far more wonderful—they are elevated to the highest rank.

From this we see that the priesthood under Christ is very different from what it was under the law. Under the law one tribe exclusively was admitted to the priesthood, and the Gentiles, as unclean, were even forbidden to enter the temple. But now all are admitted without distinction. Some people expound this passage in a general way, saying that the Gentiles will be priests; that is, they will offer themselves to God, for

Scripture often calls believers "a royal priesthood" (1 Peter 2:9; Revelation 1:6; 5:10). But he appears specially to describe ministers and teachers whom the Lord also chose from among the Gentiles and appointed to the distinguished office of preaching the Gospel—men such as Luke, Timothy, and others who offered spiritual sacrifices to God by the Gospel.

22. "As the new heavens and the new earth that I make will endure before me," declares the LORD, "so will your name and descendants endure." He promises that the restoration of the church will be of such a nature that it will last forever. Many might be afraid it would be ruined a second time, and he therefore declares that henceforth, having been restored by him, its condition will be permanent. When God speaks of **the new heavens and the new earth,** he is looking to the reign of Christ, by whom all things have been renewed (Hebrews 8:13). The purpose of this newness is that the condition of the church may always be prosperous and happy. What is old tends to decay; what is restored and renewed must last longer.

God had promised that the sun and the moon, while they remained in heaven, would witness the eternal succession, that David's posterity might not be cut off. But because the people's treachery and ingratitude had caused an interruption, the restoration effected by Christ actually confirmed that prediction. In a word, he explains what he said about renewing the world, so that people would not think he meant trees or animals or the stars; it refers to people's inner renewal. People in ancient times were mistaken when they thought these things related absolutely to the last judgment; they had not given enough weight to the context or to the authority of the writer of the letter to the Hebrews. I do not deny that they extend to that judgment, because we must not hope for a perfect restoration before Christ, the life of the world, appears. But we must begin higher, with the deliverance by which Christ regenerates his people (2 Corinthians 7:1).

23. "From one New Moon to another and from one Sabbath to another, all mankind will come and bow down before me," says the LORD. The prophet speaking for God again points out the difference between the spiritual worship of God that will occur under Christ's reign and the carnal worship under the law. Sacrifices were offered every month at the new moon. Sabbaths and festivals were carefully observed. But under the reign of Christ there are no fixed days of sacrifice; our festivals and rejoicings continue from day to day in unbroken succession. The Lord wants "pure sacrifices" offered to him daily (1 Peter 2:5), not like those under the law or like those offered by men who foolishly rely on their ceremonies as if they were expiations of crime or who dare to boast that they sacrifice Jesus Christ. Rather, they are spiritual sacrifices, so that we may reverence and adore God with pure and sincere worship (John 4:24). Some people think this passage proves the abrogation of the law and of ancient ceremonies, but I do not think there are grounds enough for this. Certainly those legal ceremonies have been set aside, as may be gathered from this passage; but I would rather use other passages that contain stronger evidence to prove the point. Here there is only a contrast between the Sabbath and festivals that were celebrated under the law and the perpetual Sabbath that we have today (Hebrews 4:9-10).

24. "And they will go out and look upon the dead bodies of those who rebelled against me; their worm will not die, nor will their fire be quenched." Those who are adopted into the church will see all around them the dreadful vengeance of God. Yet there is an implied contrast: "Out of the dark prison in which they had been confined they will come into the light again."

God does not mean that the slaughter will take place in the assembly of believers, for this would greatly diminish the happiness of the church, in which he displays all testimonies of joy and gladness. He has spoken already of the perpetual glory with which he will dignify his people; now he threatens the punishment that he will inflict on reprobates, that the godly may be more careful to keep themselves in the fear of God.

When he says they will be tormented by **fire,** this is metaphorical. The plain meaning is that the wicked will have a bad conscience as their executioner, to torment them without end, and the torment that awaits them is greater than all other torments; and finally, they will tremble and be agitated in a dreadful and shocking manner.

"And they will be loathsome to all mankind." Wicked people are now held in the highest honor and from their lofty position look down with contempt on good people. So the prophet threatens a shocking change. Along with unutterable torments, they will also endure the deepest disgrace. It is just and right that those who despised and reproached God's glory will be loaded with every reproach and will be objects of abhorrence to angels and the whole world.